Learning a Living

First Results of the Adult Literacy and Life Skills Survey

Ottawa and Paris

Statistics Canada

Organisation for Economic Co-operation and Development

ORGANISATION FOR ECONOMIC CO-OPERATION AND DEVELOPMENT

The OECD is a unique forum where the governments of 30 democracies work together to address the economic, social and environmental challenges of globalisation. The OECD is also at the forefront of efforts to understand and to help governments respond to new developments and concerns, such as corporate governance, the information economy and the challenges of an ageing population. The Organisation provides a setting where governments can compare policy experiences, seek answers to common problems, identify good practice and work to co-ordinate domestic and international policies.

The OECD member countries are: Australia, Austria, Belgium, Canada, the Czech Republic, Denmark, Finland, France, Germany, Greece, Hungary, Iceland, Ireland, Italy, Japan, Korea, Luxembourg, Mexico, the Netherlands, New Zealand, Norway, Poland, Portugal, the Slovak Republic, Spain, Sweden, Switzerland, Turkey, the United Kingdom and the United States. The Commission of the European Communities takes part in the work of the OECD.

OECD Publishing disseminates widely the results of the Organisation's statistics gathering and research on economic, social and environmental issues, as well as the conventions, guidelines and standards agreed by its members.

Also available in French under the title:

Apprentissage et réussite : Premiers résultats de l'enquête sur la littératie et les compétences des adultes

STATISTICS CANADA

Statistics Canada, Canada's central statistical agency, has the mandate to "collect, compile, analyse, and publish statistical information relating to the commercial, industrial, financial, social, economic and general activities and condition of the people of Canada." The organization, a federal government agency, is headed by the Chief Statistician of Canada and reports to Parliament through the Minister of Industry Canada.

Statistics Canada provides information to governments at every level and is the source of statistical information for business, labour, academic and social institutions, professional associations, the international statistical community, and the general public. This information is produced at the national and provincial levels and, in some cases, for major population centres and other sub-provincial or "small" areas.

The Agency fosters relations not only within Canada but also throughout the world, by participating in a number of international meetings and professional exchanges. Statistics Canada was responsible for managing the design and implementation of the International Adult Literacy Survey in co-operation with the Educational Testing Service of Princeton, New Jersey, and national survey teams.

Note of Appreciation

Canada owes the success of its statistical system to a long standing co-operative effort involving Statistics Canada, the citizens of Canada, its businesses, governments and other institutions. Accurate and timely statistical information could not be produced without their continued co-operation and good will.

> In the age of electricity and automation, the globe becomes a community of continuous learning, a single campus in which everybody irrespective of age, is involved in learning a living.
>
> *Marshall McLuhan, 1964*

Foreword

Change is a defining feature of modern life. Technologies change, the organization of work changes, terms of trade change, communities evolve and social roles change as individuals negotiate the life course. Hence change is unavoidable. It obliges individuals, families, schools, firms and nations to adapt. People and institutions that have the ability to adapt are resilient; they survive and have a chance to flourish. In contrast, those lacking the ability to adapt become vulnerable and dependent. The ability to adapt to change depends, to a large extent, on the pool of skills upon which individuals, institutions and nations can call.

The fundamental goal of the Adult Literacy and Life Skills Survey (ALL) is to shed new light on the twin processes of skill gain and loss. This is achieved through measurement of prose and document literacy of adults for a second time in some countries. Further, the study has extended the range of skills measured by adding problem solving, numeracy and information and communication technology (ICT) skill. This allows one to examine the profiles of important foundation skills. Thus the study makes it possible, for the first time, to explore the interrelationships among skill domains as well as their links to major antecedents and outcomes, such as the quantity and quality of initial education and skill's impact on employability, wages, and health.

This report is meant to assist individuals, educators, employers and other decision makers in four areas:

- Removing skill deficits that act as barriers to innovation, productivity and high rates of economic growth;
- Limiting and reversing social exclusion and income inequality;
- Reducing the unit cost of delivering public health care and education services;
- Improving quality in a broad range of contexts from public services to quality of life.

The footprint of good policy is evident in all countries surveyed. Bermuda is highly skilled and its population reports the highest level of health. Canada has succeeded in building equitably distributed ICT skills that have boosted productivity and growth. Italy has realized the most rapid improvement in skills benefiting the entire population. Norway has achieved uniformly high levels of skill, an inclusive society and is the closest to realizing lifelong learning for all. Nuevo Leon in Mexico has managed the most marked improvement in the quality of recent education output. Switzerland has lifted the performance of the least skilled the most. Proportionally to population size, the United States has built the largest pool of highly skilled adults in the world.

T. Scott Murray
Director-General
Center for Education Statistics
Social and Institutional Statistics
Statistics Canada

Eugene Owen
Senior Advisor
International Programs
National Center for
Education Statistics
United States Department
of Education

Barry McGaw
Director for Education
Organisation for Economic
Social Co-operation
and Development
(OECD)

Table of Contents

Table of Contents

Table of Contents

Table of Contents

List of Figures

Table of Contents

Table of Contents

List of Tables

Table of Contents

Chapter 6

Chapter 7

Chapter 8

Table of Contents

Table of Contents

Introduction

Overview of the study

The Adult Literacy and Life Skills Survey (ALL) is a large-scale co-operative effort undertaken by governments, national statistics agencies, research institutions and multi-lateral agencies. The development and management of the study were co-ordinated by Statistics Canada and the Educational Testing Service (ETS) in collaboration with the National Center for Education Statistics (NCES) of the United States Department of Education, the Organisation for Economic Co-operation and Development (OECD), the Regional Office for Latin America and the Caribbean (OREALC) and the Institute for Statistics (UIS) of the United Nations Educational, Scientific and Cultural Organisation (UNESCO).

The survey instruments were developed by international teams of experts with financing provided by the Governments of Canada and the United States. A highly diverse group of countries and experts drawn from around the world participated in the validation of the instruments. Participating governments absorbed the costs of national data collection and a share of the international overheads associated with implementation.

The ALL study builds on the International Adult Literacy Survey (IALS), the world's first internationally comparative survey of adult skills undertaken in three rounds of data collection between 1994 and 1998. The foundation skills measured in the ALL survey include prose literacy, document literacy, numeracy, and problem solving. Additional skills assessed indirectly include familiarity with and use of information and communication technologies.

This volume presents an initial set of findings for a group of seven countries or regions that collected data in 2003. They include Bermuda, Canada, Italy, Norway, Switzerland, the United States and the Mexican State of Nuevo Leon. As this report goes to press a second group of countries is in the field preparing for their ALL data collection in 2005.

Definitions of skill

Like IALS the ALL defines skills along a continuum of proficiency. There is no arbitrary standard distinguishing adults who have or do not have skills. For example, many previous studies have distinguished between adults who are either "literate" or "illiterate". Instead, the ALL study conceptualizes proficiency along a continuum and this is used to denote how well adults use information to function in society and the economy.

Four skill domains are conceptualized in ALL. Two of them, namely prose and document literacy are defined and measured in the same manner as in IALS. Numeracy and problem solving are new domains. The conceptualization and definitions of the four skill domains as well as examples of test items used for the assessment are described in detail in Annex A and in *The Adult Literacy and Life Skills Survey: New Frameworks for Assessment* (Statistics Canada). The operational definition for each skill domain is summarized here in Box A.

Box A

Four skill assessment domains in ALL

- *Prose literacy* – the knowledge and skills needed to understand and use information from texts including editorials, news stories, brochures and instruction manuals.
- *Document literacy* – the knowledge and skills required to locate and use information contained in various formats, including job applications, payroll forms, transportation schedules, maps, tables and charts.
- *Numeracy* – the knowledge and skills required to effectively manage the mathematical demands of diverse situations.
- *Problem solving* – Problem solving involves goal-directed thinking and action in situations for which no routine solution procedure is available. The problem solver has a more or less well defined goal, but does not immediately know how to reach it. The incongruence of goals and admissible operators constitutes a problem. The understanding of the problem situation and its step-by-step transformation, based on planning and reasoning, constitute the process of problem solving.

Measurement of skills

The ALL employed the same methodology as in IALS to measure skill proficiency. For each domain, proficiency is denoted on a scale ranging from 0 to 500 points. Each score denotes a point at which a person has an 80 per cent chance of successfully completing tasks that are associated with a similar level of difficulty. For the prose and document literacy domains as well as the numeracy domain, experts have defined five broad levels of difficulty, each corresponding to a range of scores. For the problem solving domain, experts have defined four broad levels of difficulty. See Tables I.1 and I.2 for a description of the levels. Also see Annex A for a more in depth presentation of each domain.

TABLE I.1

Five levels of difficulty for the prose, document and numeracy domains

	Prose	Document	Numeracy
Level 1 (0-225)	Most of the tasks in this level require the respondent to read relatively short text to locate a single piece of information which is identical to or synonymous with the information given in the question or directive. If plausible but incorrect information is present in the text, it tends not to be located near the correct information.	Tasks in this level tend to require the respondent either to locate a piece of information based on a literal match or to enter information from personal knowledge onto a document. Little, if any, distracting information is present.	Tasks in this level require the respondent to show an understanding of basic numerical ideas by completing simple tasks in concrete, familiar contexts where the mathematical content is explicit with little text. Tasks consist of simple, one-step operations such as counting, sorting dates, performing simple arithmetic operations or understanding common and simple percents such as 50%.
Level 2 (226-275)	Some tasks in this level require respondents to locate a single piece of information in the text; however, several distractors or plausible but incorrect pieces of information may be present, or low-level inferences may be required. Other tasks require the respondent to integrate two or more pieces of information or to compare and contrast easily identifiable information based on a criterion provided in the question or directive.	Tasks in this level are more varied than those in Level 1. Some require the respondents to match a single piece of information; however, several distractors may be present, or the match may require low-level inferences. Tasks in this level may also ask the respondent to cycle through information in a document or to integrate information from various parts of a document.	Tasks in this level are fairly simple and relate to identifying and understanding basic mathematical concepts embedded in a range of familiar contexts where the mathematical content is quite explicit and visual with few distractors. Tasks tend to include one-step or two-step processes and estimations involving whole numbers, benchmark percents and fractions, interpreting simple graphical or spatial representations, and performing simple measurements.
Level 3 (276-325)	Tasks in this level tend to require respondents to make literal or synonymous matches between the text and information given in the task, or to make matches that require low-level inferences. Other tasks ask respondents to integrate information from dense or lengthy text that contains no organizational aids such as headings. Respondents may also be asked to generate a response based on information that can be easily identified in the text. Distracting information is present, but is not located near the correct information.	Some tasks in this level require the respondent to integrate multiple pieces of information from one or more documents. Others ask respondents to cycle through rather complex tables or graphs which contain information that is irrelevant or inappropriate to the task.	Tasks in this level require the respondent to demonstrate understanding of mathematical information represented in a range of different forms, such as in numbers, symbols, maps, graphs, texts, and drawings. Skills required involve number and spatial sense, knowledge of mathematical patterns and relationships and the ability to interpret proportions, data and statistics embedded in relatively simple texts where there may be distractors. Tasks commonly involve undertaking a number of processes to solve problems.
Level 4 (326-375)	These tasks require respondents to perform multiple-feature matches and to integrate or synthesize information from complex or lengthy passages. More complex inferences are needed to perform successfully. Conditional information is frequently present in tasks at this level and must be taken into consideration by the respondent.	Tasks in this level, like those at the previous levels, ask respondents to perform multiple-feature matches, cycle through documents, and integrate information; however, they require a greater degree of inferencing. Many of these tasks require respondents to provide numerous responses but do not designate how many responses are needed. Conditional information is also present in the document tasks at this level and must be taken into account by the respondent.	Tasks at this level require respondents to understand a broad range of mathematical information of a more abstract nature represented in diverse ways, including in texts of increasing complexity or in unfamiliar contexts. These tasks involve undertaking multiple steps to find solutions to problems and require more complex reasoning and interpretation skills, including comprehending and working with proportions and formulas or offering explanations for answers.
Level 5 (376-500)	Some tasks in this level require the respondent to search for information in dense text which contains a number of plausible distractors. Others ask respondents to make high-level inferences or use specialized background knowledge. Some tasks ask respondents to contrast complex information.	Tasks in this level require the respondent to search through complex displays that contain multiple distractors, to make high-level text-based inferences, and to use specialized knowledge.	Tasks in this level require respondents to understand complex representations and abstract and formal mathematical and statistical ideas, possibly embedded in complex texts. Respondents may have to integrate multiple types of mathematical information, draw inferences, or generate mathematical justification for answers.

TABLE I.2

Four levels of difficulty for the problem solving domain

	Problem Solving
Level 1 (0-250)	Tasks in this level typically require the respondent to make simple inferences, based on limited information stemming from a familiar context. Tasks in this level are rather concrete with a limited scope of reasoning. They require the respondent to make simple connections, without having to check systematically any constraints. The respondent has to draw direct consequences, based on the information given and on his/her previous knowledge about a familiar context.
Level 2 (251-300)	Tasks in this level often require the respondent to evaluate certain alternatives with regard to well-defined, transparent, explicitly stated criteria. The reasoning however may be done step by step, in a linear process, without loops or backtracking. Successful problem solving may require to combine information from different sources, as e.g. from the question section and the information section of the test booklet.
Level 3 (301-350)	Some tasks in this level require the respondent to order several objects according to given criteria. Other tasks require him/her to determine a sequence of actions/events or to construct a solution by taking non-transparent or multiple interdependent constraints into account. The reasoning process goes back and forth in a non-linear manner, requiring a good deal of self-regulation. At this level respondents often have to cope with multi-dimensional or ill-defined goals.
Level 4 (351-500)	Items in this level require the respondent to judge the completeness, consistency and/or dependency among multiple criteria. In many cases, he/she has to explain how the solution was reached and why it is correct. The respondent has to reason from a meta-perspective, taking into account an entire system of problem solving states and possible solutions. Often the criteria and the goals have to be inferred from the given information before actually starting the solution process.

Data collection

The ALL assessment was administered in homes by experienced interviewers. The study design combined educational testing techniques with those of household survey research. Respondents were first asked a series of questions to obtain background information on a range of variables thought to influence the formation of skill and in turn impact on a range of educational, social and health outcomes. Annex B describes in more detail the survey design used for ALL, including details about survey methods, coverage, sample sizes and key indicators of quality.

Once this background questionnaire was completed the interviewer presented a booklet containing six simple tasks. If the respondent failed to complete two of these tasks correctly, the interview was adjourned. Respondents who completed two or more tasks correctly were then given a much larger variety of tasks drawn from a pool of 170 items, printed in one of eight test booklets. Test booklets were randomly assigned to respondents to ensure good representation of the domains of interest. The assessment was not timed and respondents were given maximum opportunity to demonstrate their skill proficiency.

Organization of the report

The main goal of this first ALL report is to present initial findings on the level and distribution of skills, and the relationships between skills and important background variables. The findings are presented in 11 chapters.

Chapter 1 presents an overview of the ALL study.

Chapter 2 compares the basic distributions of skill by age, gender and country. The chapter also presents evidence on how rapidly skill profiles have changed over time for those countries where such analyses could be conducted[1].

Chapter 3 explores the relationship between each skill domain and education at various levels.

Chapter 4 documents the role skill plays in formal adult education and training markets and the effects of education and skill on continuing learning in informal and non-formal settings at home and at work.

Chapter 5 traces the influence of skill on employment and unemployment and on the transition from school to work.

Chapter 6 explores connections between the emergence of the knowledge economy, reading, writing and numeracy practices at work, and mismatch between observed skill and skill requirements at work.

Chapter 7 presents evidence on the profound effects of skill on earnings from work and investment income.

Chapter 8 focuses on the relationships between familiarity and use of information and communication technologies, labour market outcomes and the social distribution of ICT use and familiarity.

Chapter 9 sheds light on the relative skill levels of immigrants and on the implications of between-country differences in immigration patterns.

Chapter 10 concentrates on the relationship between parents' education and skills, patterns of skill use and how engagement in various activities at home, at work and during leisure can vary by skill level.

Chapter 11 examines the relationship between skill and summary measures of physical and mental health and overall life satisfaction.

Annex A provides a detailed overview of the ALL proficiency scales – how they are defined, how they were measured, how proficiency was summarized and how proficiency estimates should be interpreted. Readers requiring additional technical information on the psychometric aspects of the study are referred to The Adult Literacy and Life Skills Survey: Aspects of Design, Development and Validation (Statistics Canada, 2004), The International Adult Literacy Survey: A Technical Report (NCES, 1997) and The Adult Literacy and Life Skills Survey: A Technical Report (Statistics Canada, 2005).

Annex B documents key aspects of survey administration, response and data quality.

Finally, Annex C identifies the experts, researchers and analysts who were involved in developing the ALL instruments, in implementing the national data collections, and in the writing, analytical and editorial work that made publication of this report possible.

Endnotes

1. Comparable prose literacy and document literacy scores are available from the 1994 IALS study for Canada, Switzerland (German and French-speaking populations) and the United States, and from the 1998 IALS study for Norway, Italy and Switzerland (Italian-speaking population). The data sets thus allow for the analysis of changes in skill profiles over a nine and five-year period respectively.
2. Results are presented separately for the three Swiss language groups when considering changes in prose and document literacy skills between the IALS and ALL survey periods. This is because the IALS data for the German and French-speaking communities were collected in 1994 and for the Italian-speaking community in 1998. Estimates for the three Swiss language groups are also presented separately in Chapter 11 because of a high degree of variance among the three language groups with respect to health outcomes. Otherwise, the results present the three population groups combined into a single estimate for the whole country of Switzerland. This report also features estimates for the Mexican state of Nuevo Leon in Chapter 2 and a few other analyses when data were made available.

References

NCES (1997), *The International Adult Literacy Survey: A Technical Report,* National Centre for Educational Statistics, Washington, DC.

Statistics Canada (2004), *The Adult Literacy and Life Skills Survey: Aspects of Design, Development and Validation,* Ottawa.

Statistics Canada (2005), *The Adult Literacy and Life Skills Survey: A Technical Report,* Ottawa.

Note to Readers

> Throughout this report graphs are employed to convey study results in a non-technical manner and to provide a source of informative displays that readers may use for their own purposes. To satisfy the more technical reader data tables for all displays are provided in a statistical annex at the end of each corresponding chapter.

The skill proficiency results from the 2003 ALL study are reported separately for four scales – prose literacy, document literacy, numeracy, and problem solving – rather than on a single scale. Although it is desirable to maintain separate scales for the majority of more complex analyses, the theoretical and empirical properties also allow for creating composite skill scales. The prose and document literacy scales are combined into a composite literacy scale for some analyses in this book. Results of multivariate analysis are usually presented for a specific scale. Unless otherwise noted, the results for other scales exhibit the same pattern and magnitude of relationships.

Multiple sources of uncertainty and error are a fact of life in social science research. Given the comparative nature of the ALL study, those responsible for the design of the study and its implementation went to great lengths to establish the validity, reliability, comparability and interpretability of estimates, and to control and quantify errors that might interfere with or bias interpretation. Statistics Canada, the Educational Testing Service and the national study teams have performed comprehensive analyses to understand the nature and extent of errors associated with subtle differences in design and implementation. Notes to figures and tables are used to alert readers whenever errors have been detected that might affect interpretation.

The data values presented in this volume are estimated from representative but complex samples of adults from each country. Consequently there is a degree of sampling error that must be taken into account. Additionally, there is a degree of error associated with the measurement of skills because they are estimated on the basis of responses to samples of test items. Thus a statistic, called the standard error, is used to express the degree of uncertainty associated with both sampling and measurement error.

Country abbreviations used in this report[2]

OECD countries		Non-OECD countries	
Canada	CAN	Bermuda	BER
Italy	ITA	Nuevo Leon	NL
Norway	NOR		
Switzerland	CHE		
United States	USA		

Chapter 1

The Why, What and How of the ALL Survey

Table of Contents

1

The Why, What and How of the ALL Survey

1.1 Goals of the ALL survey

The first and most important goal of the study is to shed light on the twin processes of skill gain and loss in adult populations. For the countries for which repeat measures are available, research can explore changes that may have occurred in the level and distribution of skills since the IALS data were collected; and identify concomitant changes in population groups whose level of prose and document skills place them at a relative disadvantage in the labour market and other life contexts.

In general, one expects the quality of the skills supply to increase over time in response to increases in the incidence, average duration and quality of initial and post-secondary education as well as adult learning. The IALS data confirms this expectation — the quality of the skill supply is determined by a host of factors that influence the rate of skill acquisition over the life course, from before birth through old age. An important insight is the fact that education and experience do not "fix" a person's skill level for life. Personal choice and differences in the nature of skill demand can lead to skill acquisition, skill maintenance or significant skill loss in adulthood . The IALS data indeed suggest that a significant skill loss in adulthood can occur — losses that may be related to low levels of skill demand at work, at home and in the community.

Skill loss represents a serious problem for individuals, social institutions and governments because it erodes the economic and social return on educational investments and hampers productivity and economic growth. With the ALL data, these important assumptions and hypotheses about the presence, likely causes and possible social and economic consequences of skill loss and deterioration can finally be explored empirically for Canada, Italy, Norway, Switzerland and the United States.

The second major goal of the ALL is to profile and compare, for the first time, the level and distribution of directly assessed numeracy skills among adult populations in participating countries. The ALL assessment replaces the quantitative literacy domain used in IALS with a broader and more robust numeracy measure that reflects better the range of numerate behaviours that confront adults in their daily lives.

The third major goal pursued by the ALL study is to profile and compare the level and distribution of problem solving skills among the adult populations of the countries surveyed. The Definition and Selection of Key Competencies (DeSeCo) programme of work (Rychen and Salganik, 2001, 2003) identified several clusters of distinct skill domains on the basis of theoretical extrapolation. This pioneering work concludes that a wider range of skills, attitudes and values about learning should be considered in international comparative surveys. Accordingly, beyond introducing an improved measure of numeracy skill, a key goal of ALL was to develop a theoretical framework that could serve as a basis for measuring additional skill domains. A substantive effort was made to develop frameworks and measures for team work skills, practical cognition, and information and communication technology (ICT) skills. But only the problem solving domain was shown to meet the high empirical standards set for directly assessing skills in the ALL study. Indirect measures of ICT skills were nevertheless retained in the final design (Statistics Canada, 2005).

A final set of goals relate to the design of the background questionnaire used to collect information on the antecedents of skill and their outcomes. The IALS study was the first international study to collect comparable data on participation in formal adult education. The analysis of this data advanced our understanding of the importance of adult learning in building skills but interpretation was hindered by the lack of measures capturing the broader contexts of life long and life wide learning. Accordingly the ALL background questionnaire was deliberately designed to profile formal, non-formal and informal adult learning and its social distribution.

Information on skill demand was also collected through questions asking about skill use at work, at home and in the community. These measures can reveal the importance of the skills measured, but only if the appropriate outcome measures are also available. Hence the final goal of the ALL study was to collect data that allows for an analysis of the relationships between skill and outcomes ranging from labour market participation and earnings, to physical and mental health, and engagement in community activities.

1.2 The conceptual approach to the ALL survey

The ALL study embodies a conceptual approach that includes elements of skill demand, skill supply and markets for skill. Adopting such an approach allows one to profile the nature of skill supply and demand. An important assumption is that different life contexts – work, home and the community – impose skill demands on individuals. Directly observed measures of skill such as those in ALL reflect the supply of economically and socially important skills. ALL also seeks to understand how skills influence the level and distribution of outcomes, whether economic, social or environmental. See *Measuring Adult Literacy and Life Skills: new Framework for Assessment* (2005) for further details on the conceptual framework used in the ALL study.

Changes in skill demand can be traced to two sources – externally imposed and internally imposed changes. Externally imposed ones result from changes in technology and work organization, consumer markets and social institutions. While there is a consensus that skill demand is rising in all life contexts – work, home and the community – it is also the result of individual life circumstances. Internally motivated changes in skill demand flow from two sources –

modifications in individual and collective aspirations and as a natural consequence of a person's passage through stages of life.

Changes in skill supply are a consequence of demographic shifts and trends in the social systems that support skill acquisition and maintenance. Education reform is the most obvious factor contributing to changes in the supply of skill. However, other factors also play an important role (OECD and HRDC, 1997). These include socio-economic development, participation in tertiary education and its quality, as well as adult education and training. All these factors have a marked impact on the quality of the skill supply.

The ALL approach allows one to gauge the efficiency of markets, which match the supply of, and demand for skills. The notion of markets embodied in the study extends beyond goods, services and labour. It also includes health care delivery and the exchange of social goods and services such as unpaid work in the family and the community. The available evidence suggests that markets for skill are reasonably efficient in recognizing and rewarding skill. However, the degree to which skills impact outcomes can vary depending on the country.

Skill loss is also an observed reality. It is assumed that this loss is related to variations in skill use in differing life contexts. Individual and collective choices can also play a role. Differences exist in the extent to which countries nurture life long learning. Skill loss implies educational opportunity costs and leads one to reflect on the need to balance supply-side intervention with measures to increase skill demand. The phenomenon of skill loss justifies the need to repeatedly measure adult skills. If initial education fixed skills for life then student assessments, such as the one organised under the auspices of the Programme of International Student Assessment (PISA), would be all that would be required.

Policy makers want to understand the nature of skill deficits and devise mitigating strategies. The predominance of change requires policy makers to better appreciate the rates at which skills evolve, the forces that underlie change and the impact that change will have on key outcomes. In summary, ALL seeks to add to what is known about the scope of public policy in influencing the level and distribution of skills in society.

References

OECD and HRDC (1997), *Literacy Skills for the Knowledge Society: Further Results from the International Adult Literacy Survey,* Paris and Hull.

Rychen, D.S. and Salganik, L.H. (eds.) (2001), *Defining and Selecting Key Competencies,* Hogrefe and Huber Publishers, Göttingen.

Rychen, D.S. and Salganik, L.H. (eds.) (2003), *Key Competencies for a Successful Life and a Well-functioning Society,* Hogrefe and Huber Publishers, Göttingen.

Statistics Canada (2005), *Measuring Adult Literacy and Life Skills: New Frameworks for Assessment,* Ottawa.

Contributor

T. Scott Murray, *Statistics Canada*

Chapter 2

2

Comparative Profiles of Adult Skills

Summary

This chapter presents a comparative perspective on the levels and distributions of adult skills in four domains – prose literacy, document literacy, numeracy and problem solving – for the countries that collected data in the first round of the Adult Literacy and Life Skills Survey (ALL). The first part of the analysis displays the basic country distributions for each skill domain. The second tracks changes in the distributions of prose and document literacy skills over time for the countries that participated in both ALL and its predecessor, the International Adult Literacy Survey (IALS) – Canada, Norway, Switzerland and the United States. Finally, the analysis focuses on how skill distributions interact with key demographic variables such as age and gender.

Table of Contents

Comparative Profiles of Adult Skills

2

2.1 Overview and highlights

This chapter presents a comparative perspective on the levels and distributions of adult skills in four domains – prose literacy, document literacy, numeracy and problem solving – for the countries that collected data in the first round of the Adult Literacy and Life Skills Survey (ALL). The first part of the analysis displays the basic country distributions for each skill domain. The second tracks changes in the distributions of prose and document literacy skills over time for the countries that participated in both ALL and its predecessor, the International Adult Literacy Survey (IALS) – Canada, Norway, Switzerland and the United States. Finally, the analysis focuses on how skill distributions interact with key demographic variables such as age and gender.

Key findings presented in this chapter are:

- The ALL results confirm the IALS findings that many adults have difficulties coping with literacy and numeracy related demands that are common in modern life and work. Although relative proportions vary, there are significant numbers of adults with low skills in all the countries surveyed.
- Depending on the country, between one-third and over two-thirds of adult populations do not attain skill Level 3, the level considered by experts as a suitable minimum level for coping with the increasing demands of the emerging knowledge society and information economy (OECD and Statistics Canada, 1995).
- Both the average performance levels and the distributions of skills among adult populations differ substantially between countries. Some perform better than others in terms of average performance, with Norway performing among the highest on all four scales.
- The spread in literacy scores between adults at the lowest and highest skill levels is significantly smaller in some countries (Norway and Switzerland) and larger in others (Italy and the United States).

- Some countries have a relative advantage in a particular skill domain. For example, Switzerland performs comparatively well on the numeracy scale whereas Bermuda scores better on the prose scale. Norway is a country that does consistently well in all four skills domains.
- Measured by the difference in average scores between the 5th and 95th percentiles, all countries in ALL display less inequality in skill between the highest and lowest performing groups than in IALS. The exception is Norway, where skill inequality was already low in IALS.
- Changes in mean country performance are not substantial, but the results show some improvement among the five per cent of adults with the lowest scores.
- Only the German speaking population in Switzerland has recorded an increase in its average performance on the prose and document literacy scale between the IALS and ALL survey periods.
- Age and skills are inversely related in all countries. Younger cohorts tend to score higher on average and have larger proportions at higher levels of skills. Even after controlling for educational attainment the relationship remains negative. There is also wider variation in performance among older cohorts.
- The relationship between age and skills is complex because age represents an accumulation of life experiences that are likely to impact on the development and even loss of skills throughout the lifespan.
- Gender interacts with the distribution of adult skills and confirms previously observed patterns. In general, men tend to display an advantage in numeracy and document literacy skills, while women tend to display an advantage in prose literacy. Although women in Bermuda show a noticeable advantage in problem solving, these types of skill appear gender neutral in Canada, Italy, Norway and Switzerland (German and French speaking populations).

2.2 Comparative distributions of adult skills

This section presents the key comparative findings with respect to the levels and distributions of adult skills. Figures 2.1, 2.2 and 2.3 present complementary information. The first set of charts in Figure 2.1 focus on the mean proficiency scores of populations aged 16 to 65. Because the information is derived from sample data, there is a measurable degree of error present in the estimates. This error must be taken into account when comparing differences in performance. Therefore, the charts indicate whether the average performance of countries differs in a statistically significant way. Indeed there are many cases where the mean scores are higher or lower but these differences are not meaningful in a statistical sense (this is indicated by a dot in the small squares of the charts).

Countries differ in their ranking from scale to scale. Norway, for example, ranks highest on the prose, document and problem solving scales, whereas Switzerland tops the numeracy scale. Moreover, while Bermuda's average performance is not statistically different than Norway's on the prose literacy scale, the average performance of Bermudans is significantly lower on the other three scales. Canada's average performance is in the middle on all four scales, and it is not statistically different from Bermuda's on the document, numeracy and problem solving scales. While Switzerland's average performance is the highest on numeracy scale and only Norway has a higher mean on the problem solving scale, its average performance is lower than Bermuda, Canada, and Norway on the prose scale, and lower than Canada and Norway on the document scale. The United States' average performance is higher than Italy's on the prose, document and numeracy scales, and the Mexican State of Nuevo Leon on the prose and document scales.

Country comparisons based solely on mean scores are not that revealing. Although of interest for other reasons, a mean score does not offer any insight into within-country variation in skill proficiency. The charts in Figure 2.2 display the mean scores as well as the 5th, 25th, 75th, and 95th percentile scores of a country's distribution. Estimates are shown using gradation bars. These are useful because they indicate the degree of inequality in the distribution of skills. In particular they show the extent of discrepancy between those scoring among the lowest (5th) and those scoring among the highest (95th) percentiles. The extent of skill difference is an important indicator because it is associated with the distribution of social, economic, health and educational outcomes in a country.

The varying lengths of the bars indicate that countries differ in skills inequality among their adult populations. Norway has the least inequality in the distribution of prose (144 points), numeracy (153 points) and problem solving (162 points) skills, whereas Switzerland has the least on the document (157 points) scale. Norway and Switzerland also display consistently small ranges. For Nuevo Leon it varies, with a small range (149 points) on the prose scale and the largest range (193 points) on the document scale. Italy has the widest range in the distribution of prose (183 points) and problem solving (189 points) skills. Bermuda, Canada and the United States display consistently medium to wide ranges.

FIGURE 2.1

Multiple comparisons of skills proficiencies

Comparisons of countries based on average scores, populations aged 16 to 65, 2003

A. Prose literacy scale

COUNTRY	Norway	Bermuda	Canada	Switzerland	United States	Italy
Norway		●	▲	▲	▲	▲
Bermuda	●		▲	▲	▲	▲
Canada	▼	▼		▲	▲	▲
Switzerland	▼	▼	▼		●	▲
United States	▼	▼	▼	●		▲
Italy	▼	▼	▼	▼	▼	

B. Document literacy scale

COUNTRY	Norway	Canada	Bermuda	Switzerland	United States	Italy
Norway		▲	▲	▲	▲	▲
Canada	▼		●	▲	▲	▲
Bermuda	▼	●		●	▲	▲
Switzerland	▼	▼	●		▲	▲
United States	▼	▼	▼	▼		▲
Italy	▼	▼	▼	▼	▼	

C. Numeracy scale

COUNTRY	Switzerland	Norway	Canada	Bermuda	United States	Italy
Switzerland		▲	▲	▲	▲	▲
Norway	▼		▲	▲	▲	▲
Canada	▼	▼		●	▲	▲
Bermuda	▼	▼	●		▲	▲
United States	▼	▼	▼	▼		▲
Italy	▼	▼	▼	▼	▼	

D. Problem solving scale

COUNTRY	Norway	Switzerland	Canada	Bermuda	Italy
Norway		▲	▲	▲	▲
Switzerland	▼		▲	▲	▲
Canada	▼	▼		●	▲
Bermuda	▼	▼	●		▲
Italy	▼	▼	▼	▼	

Note: Switzerland (Italian) and United States did not field the problem solving skills domain.

▲ Mean proficiency significantly* higher than comparison country
● No statistically significant* difference from comparison country
▼ Mean proficiency significantly* lower than comparison country

Countries are ranked by mean proficiency across the heading and down the rows.

* Statistically significant at 0.5 level, adjusted for multiple comparisons.

Source: Adult Literacy and Life Skills Survey, 2003.

Instruction: Read across the row for a country to compare performance with the countries listed in the heading of the chart. The symbols indicate whether the mean proficiency of the country in the row is significantly lower than that of the comparison country, significantly higher than that of the comparison country, or if there is no statistically significant difference between the two countries.

Norway has the twin advantage of having relatively high average scores and low inequalities in all skill domains. In contrast, Italy tends to exhibit relatively low average scores and high inequalities. In general however, the range is somewhat independent of the average. For example, Nuevo Leon has both a low average score and low inequality in the distribution of prose scores. Bermuda and Canada are examples of countries with relatively high average scores and high inequalities.

The charts in Figure 2.2 also reveal significant differences in overall performance between countries. For example, the average prose scores in Bermuda and Norway are higher than the 75th percentile scores in Italy and Nuevo Leon.

To facilitate interpretation the proficiency scores with a range from 0 to 500 points are grouped into four levels. Each level corresponds to successive ranges of scores denoting increased task difficulty. The proficiency levels for each skill domain are described in detail in Annex A. The charts in Figure 2.3 show estimates of the proportion of the adult population scoring at each proficiency level on each of the four scales.

Each level can be described in terms of what persons at that level can do. For example, persons proficient at Level 4/5 on the prose scale are capable of making medium to high level text-based inferences by integrating or contrasting abstract pieces of information in relatively lengthy texts that contain several to many distractors. Figure 2.3a indicates that about one in four persons are at this level in Bermuda. This falls to approximately one in five in Canada and Norway, one in eight in Switzerland and the United States and one in 28 in Italy.

At Level 3 on the prose scale, persons can make low-level text-based inferences by locating several pieces of information from a few to a number of different sentences or paragraphs, and integrating or contrasting information across sections of text that contain few to several distractors. This level is deemed as a minimum for persons to understand and use information contained in the increasingly difficult texts and tasks that characterize the emerging knowledge society and information economy. More than two thirds of Norwegians are at this level or higher. This falls to approximately 60 per cent of persons in Bermuda and Canada, just under 50 per cent of persons in Switzerland and the United States, around 20 per cent in Italy and 11 per cent in Nuevo Leon.

Those scoring at Level 2 on the prose scale are capable of making low-level text-based inferences by locating one or more pieces of information, and integrating or contrasting two or more pieces of information across sections of text that contain some distractors. Thus, persons at this level may not be able to consistently understand more difficult texts and tasks that are increasingly prevalent in modern societies. Approximately one in four persons is at this level in Bermuda, Canada and Norway. This rises to around one in three persons in Italy, Switzerland and the United States. Just over 45 per cent of adults in Nuevo Leon are at this level.

FIGURE 2.2

Comparative distributions of skills scores

Mean scores with .95 confidence interval and scores at the 5th, 25th, 75th and 95th percentiles on skills scales ranging from 0 to 500 points, populations aged 16 to 65, 2003

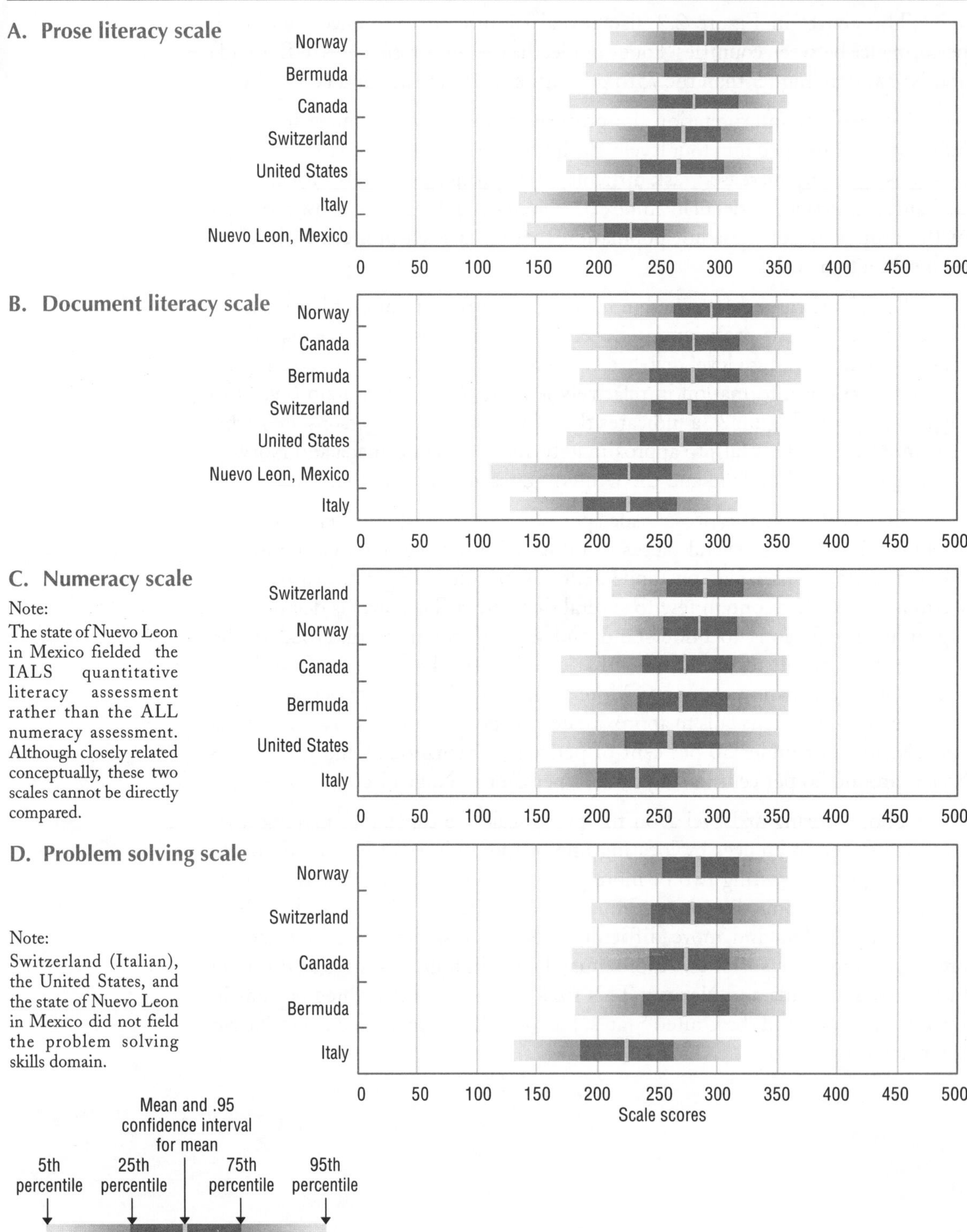

Countries are ranked by mean scores.

Source: Adult Literacy and Life Skills Survey, 2003.

Proficiency at Level 1 indicates that persons may be able to locate one piece of information that is identical or synonymous with the information given in a directive but in general they have difficulty making low-level text-based inferences. Norway has the fewest adults at this level – approximately eight per cent. The proportion rises to just over 12 per cent in Bermuda, around 15 per cent in Canada and Switzerland, 20 per cent in the United States and over 43 and 47 per cent in Nuevo Leon and Italy, respectively.

The interpretation of proficiency levels on the document, numeracy and problem solving scales is similar to that on the prose scale. See Annex A for a full description of the different levels for each of the skill domains.

Figure 2.3b displays the proportion of the adult population at each of the four levels on the document literacy scale. The results show that country rankings based on the proportion of adults at Levels 3 and 4/5 vary by skill domain. The most substantial difference occurs in Bermuda, where approximately eight per cent fewer adults attain Level 3 or higher on the document scale compared with the prose scale. In contrast, the proportion of adults scoring at Levels 3 and 4/5 on the document scale increases by approximately three and five per cent in Switzerland and Nuevo Leon, respectively.

Comparing Figures 2.3a-d shows that overall, Switzerland performs much better on the numeracy scale than on the prose, document or problem solving scales. While there are about six per cent fewer Norwegians at Level 3 or higher on the numeracy scale than the prose scale, Switzerland has nearly 13 per cent more. Bermuda shows the sharpest drop in the proportion of adults at Levels 3 and 4/5, from nearly 62 per cent on the prose scale to 46 per cent on the numeracy scale. Similarly, Canada and the United States perform relatively better in the prose and document skills domains than in numeracy. Countries tend to perform better on prose and document than on numeracy and problem solving. Norway, however, is the only country to have 60 per cent or more of adults performing at Levels 3 and 4/5 on the prose, document and numeracy scales.

FIGURE 2.3

Comparative distributions of skills levels

Per cent of populations aged 16 to 65 at each skills level, 2003

A. Prose literacy scale

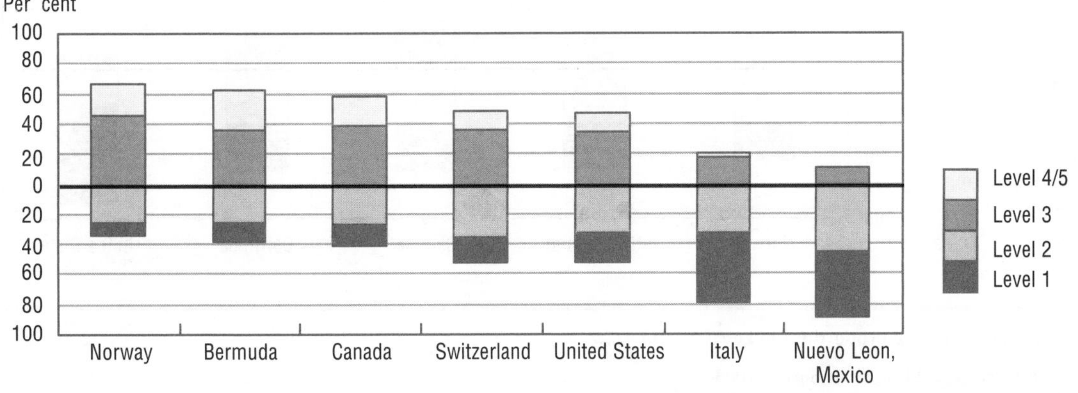

FIGURE 2.3 (concluded)

Comparative distributions of skills levels

Per cent of populations aged 16 to 65 at each skills level, 2003

B. Document literacy scale

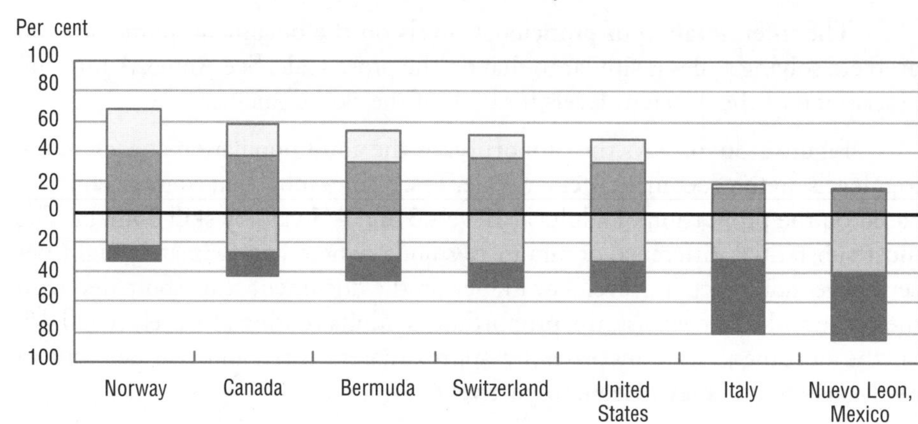

Level 4/5
Level 3
Level 2
Level 1

C. Numeracy scale

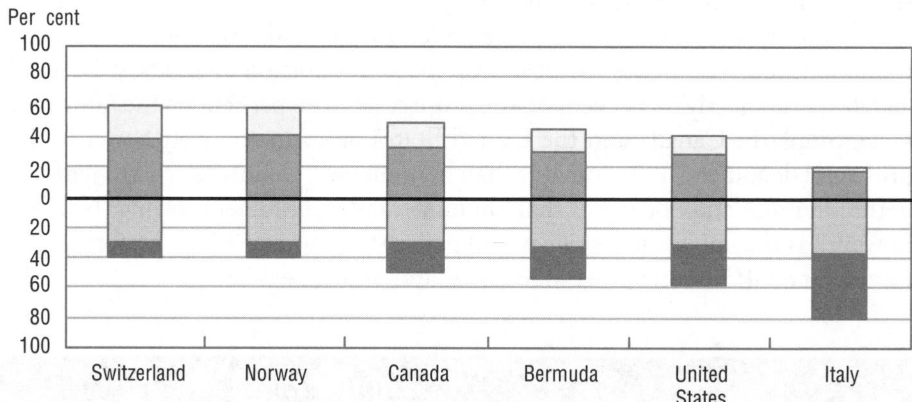

Note:
The state of Nuevo Leon in Mexico fielded the IALS quantitative literacy assessment rather than the ALL numeracy assessment. Although closely related conceptually, these two scales cannot be directly compared.

D. Problem solving scale

Per cent
100
80
60
40
20
0
20
40
60
80
100
Norway
Switzerland
Canada
Bermuda
United States

Note:
Switzerland (Italian), the United States, and the state of Nuevo Leon in Mexico did not field the problem solving skills domain.

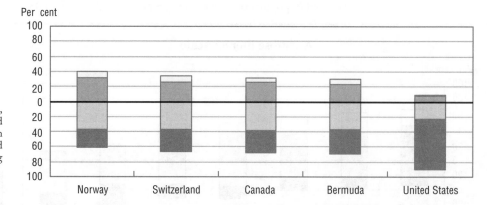

Countries are ranked by the proportions in Levels 3 and 4/5.

Source: Adult Literacy and Life Skills Survey, 2003.

2.3 Changes in skills profiles from IALS to ALL

The ALL and the IALS assessed prose and document literacy skills using identical methods and metrics. This was done so as to permit comparable and reliable estimates of changes in skill profiles between the two survey periods. IALS data for Canada, the French and German speaking populations of Switzerland, and the United States were collected in 1994 as part of the first wave of IALS countries. Data for Norway and the Italian speaking population of Switzerland were collected in 1998 as part of the third and final wave of countries participating in IALS. The ALL data were collected in 2003. Thus the time elapsed between the two surveys is approximately nine years for the first set of countries and five years for the second.

Figures 2.4a-b compare the ALL gradation bars with similar bars derived from IALS data. In general, changes in country mean performance are not substantial (see Figure 2.5). But the comparatively higher 5th percentile scores in ALL than in IALS indicate improvements among the lowest scoring adults. Countries or regions showing the largest improvements among the low-skilled are German speaking Switzerland (+47 points), French speaking Switzerland (+42 points) and the United States (+38 points) on the prose scale; and Canada (+51 points), German speaking Switzerland (+82 points) and the United States (+50 points) on the document scale.

The results also show that in a few countries or regions the performance of the top five per cent is somewhat lower in ALL than in IALS. The 95th percentile scores are significantly lower in Canada (-10 points), Italian speaking Switzerland (-16 points) and the United States (-23 points) on the prose scale; and Canada (-18 points), French speaking Switzerland (-9 points), Italian speaking Switzerland (-14 points) and the United States (-15 points) on the document scale. Most of the five-year score differences between high and low performers in Norway are not statistically significant, except for a small improvement in the 95th percentile on the prose scale (see Table 2.4 in Annex 2).

Moreover, improvements in performance at the lower end and reductions at the upper ends of distributions imply less inequality in the distribution of prose and document skills. Reductions in the range of scores from the 5th to the 95th percentiles are substantial in all countries and regions, except in Norway, which already had a low level of inequality in 1998.

There is little change in the inter-quartile range (difference between 75th and 25th percentiles). Overall, changes in the 25th percentiles are negligible and changes in the 75th percentiles are few. Notable on the prose scale are lower 75th percentiles in Italian speaking Switzerland (-13 points) and the United States (-15 points), while in German speaking Switzerland it is higher (+6 points). It is also lower on the document scale in Italian speaking Switzerland (-12 points).

Norway and the German speaking population in Switzerland show some improvement in the distribution of prose scores, although it is marginal for the former. Otherwise, the results show overall improvements among low scoring adults and lower performances among some high scoring adults. This combination produces mixed results when comparing changes in mean proficiency over time. Figure 2.5 shows that German speaking Switzerland has statistically improved its mean performance on both the prose and document literacy scales, and Norway has improved on the prose scale. The overall performance of Italian speaking Switzerland has decreased on both scales, while the United States has decreased only on the prose scale. Other changes are not statistically significant.

FIGURE 2.4

Changes in distributions of skills scores

Mean scores with .95 confidence interval and scores at the 5th, 25th, 75th and 95th percentiles on skills scales ranging from 0 to 500 points, populations aged 16 to 65, IALS 1994/1998 and ALL 2003

A. Prose literacy scale

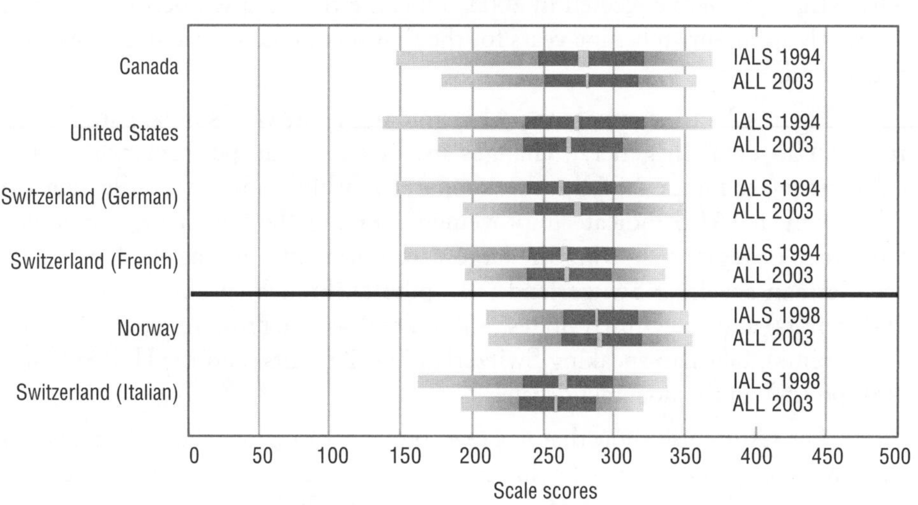

B. Document literacy scale

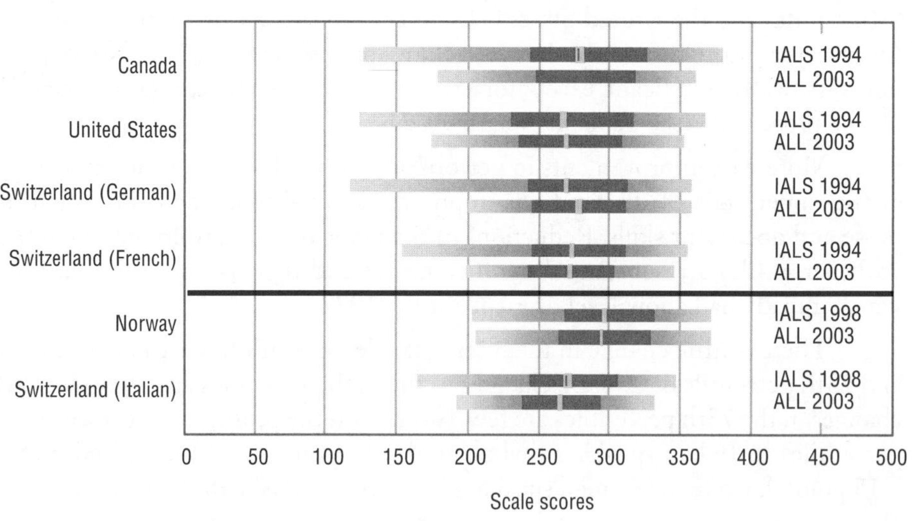

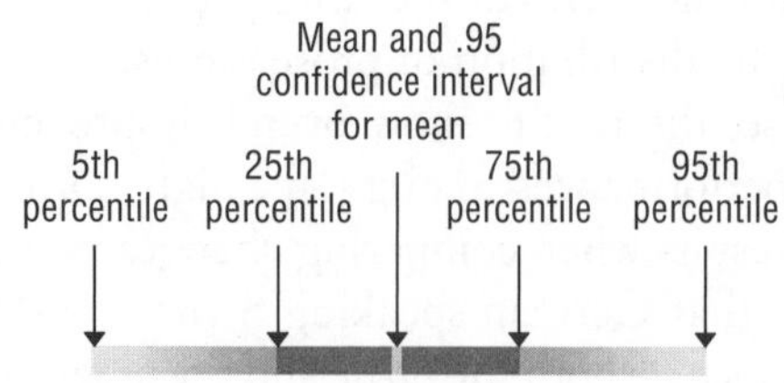

Sources: Adult Literacy and Life Skills Survey, 2003.
International Adult Literacy Survey, 1994-1998.

FIGURE 2.5

Changes in mean scores from IALS to ALL

Summary of changes in mean scores from IALS to ALL, by statistical significance at the five per cent level, populations aged 16 to 65, IALS 1994/1998 and ALL 2003

Increase in mean proficiency significant	No change/Change not significant	Decrease in mean proficiency significant
A. Prose literacy scale		
Switzerland-German (+11.2)	Norway Canada Switzerland-French	United States (-5.1) Switzerland-Italian (-4.8)
B. Document literacy scale		
Switzerland-German (+8.9)	Norway Canada United States Switzerland-French	Switzerland-Italian (-5.4)

Changes in skill scores do not necessarily imply changes in skill levels, since the latter refer to ranges of scores. Higher scores within levels imply better performance, but not necessarily a high enough improvement to consistently succeed on tasks at the next level of difficulty. Figures 2.6a-b display changes in the proportions of adults at each skill level. There are no statistically significant changes at any level in Canada and Norway on the prose scale, and Norway on the document scale.

German speaking Switzerland displays the most success in reducing the proportion of adults at Level 1 (-4.3 per cent) on both the prose and document scales. But while this percentage shifts into Level 2 on the document scale, a broader change occurs on the prose scale, where the net increase is primarily in the proportion at Levels 4/5. The latter result implies an upward shift in the entire distribution, whereas the former implies an improvement at the lower end of the distribution only. Accordingly, German speaking Switzerland has significantly increased the proportion of adults at prose literacy Levels 4/5 (+4.4 per cent). The net change between low (Levels 1 and 2) and medium to high (Levels 3 and 4/5) skilled adults remains unchanged on the document scale.

The United States has also reduced the percentage of adults at Level 1 on the document scale (-3.4 per cent); but there is also a marked reduction in the proportion at document Level 4/5 (-5.0 per cent). The net result is an increase of persons at Level 2 (7.5 per cent). The pattern is similar on the prose scale but with an even sharper reduction at Level 4/5 (-9.1 per cent) as well as a larger increase at Level 2 (+8.1 per cent). Therefore, on the prose scale, it appears that there is a small improvement among low-skilled adults only, and a comparatively high decline among high skilled adults. The result is a lower proportion (-7.3 per cent) of adults with medium to high skills (Levels 3 and 4/5) on the prose scale.

The French and Italian speaking populations of Switzerland display a pattern similar to the United States. There are overall reductions in the proportion of adults at Levels 3 and 4/5 and increases at Levels 1 and 2. Italian speaking Switzerland shows the highest net decrease in the proportion of medium to high skilled adults on both the prose (-9.7 per cent) and document (-11.8 per cent) scales.

FIGURE 2.6

Changes in distributions of skills levels

Differences between IALS 1994/1998 and ALL 2003 in the per cent of adults aged 16 to 65 at each skills level

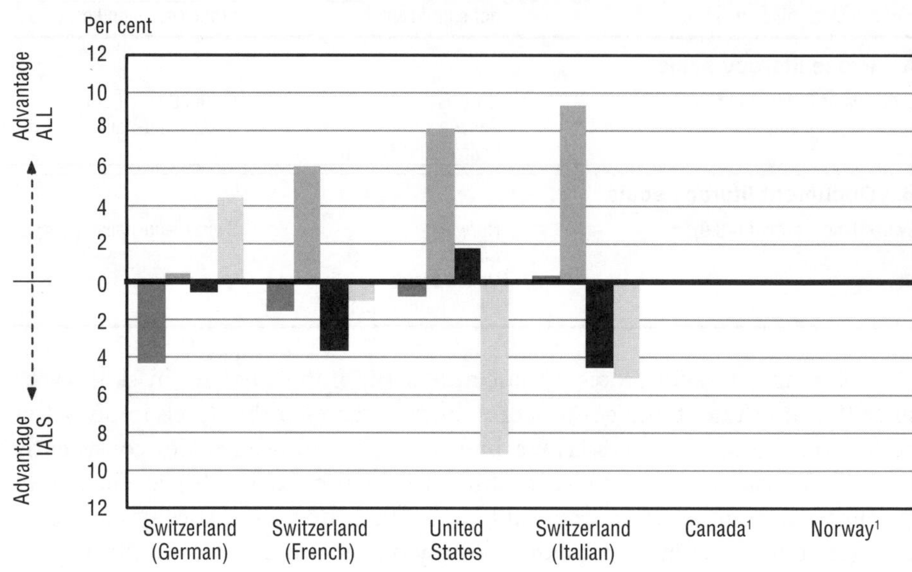

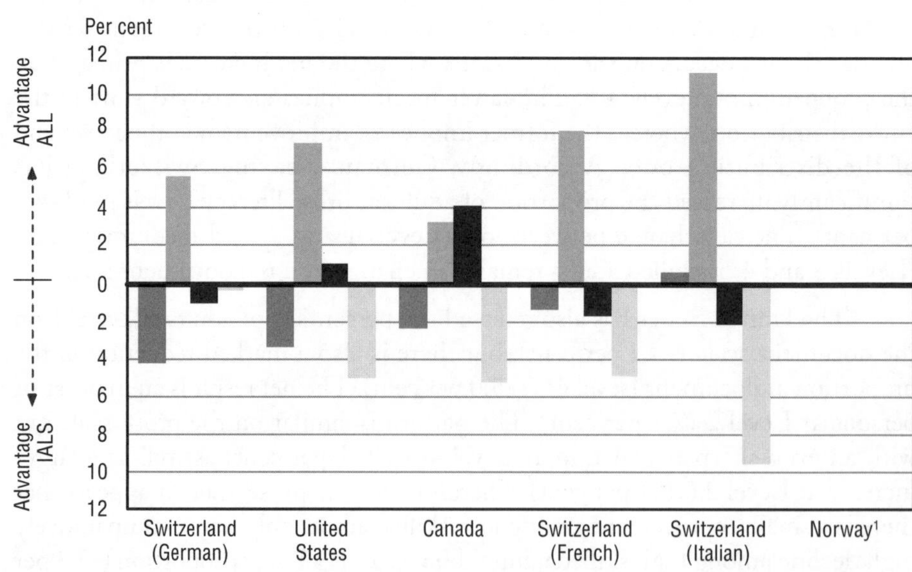

Countries are ranked by the difference in per cent in the advantage of IALS at level 1.

1. For countries that do not have statistically significant changes observed at any level, there are no changes reported in the graphic. But if change is statistically significant for at least one level in a country, changes for all levels are reported in the graphic.

Sources: Adult Literacy and Life Skills Survey, 2003.
International Adult Literacy Survey, 1994-1998.

2.4 Adult skills and age

Skills can be acquired, developed, maintained and lost over the lifespan, making the relationship between skills and age complex. Aside from the possible effects of ageing, the influence of age on skills does not operate in isolation. Rather it is influential in so far as it denotes typical life experiences that occur at various stages of the life span such as those in early childhood, schooling and transition to work, life career and other daily activities. The features of life experiences that influence the development of skills, positively or negatively, are not yet well understood. This section presents empirical findings on the relationship between age and skills and introduces some of the interactions that may explain the patterns observed.

Figures 2.7a-b show that compared to older age cohorts, younger cohorts tend to score higher and have larger proportions at higher levels of skill on the document scale. This result is consistent with previously reported findings for IALS (OECD and Statistics Canada, 2000: 34; OECD and HRDC, 1997: 30). The findings are also similar for the prose, numeracy and problem solving scales, which are not reported here. Thus age is an important demographic factor to consider when drawing conclusions about skill profiles of regions or countries and for devising strategies to improve skills.

In every country, the relationship between age and document skills is negative as indicated by the downward sloping trend lines in Figure 2.7a. Moreover, a comparison of the gradation bars for different age cohorts reveals that the difference between those with the lowest and those with the highest proficiency scores tends to be higher among older adults aged 46 to 65. This implies that there is a wider variability in performance among older persons. Accumulation of differing life experiences is likely to be an important factor explaining higher variations in performance among older cohorts.

Without considering the influence of other factors, the findings show a negative association between age and cognitive skills. An explanation put forth in the scholarly literature suggests that as time progresses, adults may experience reduced cognitive performance, which is attributable to *ageing* effects, or alternatively stated, to declines in *cognitive mechanics* such as attentional capacity, processing speed, reasoning, working memory capacity and spatial ability (Smith and Marsiske, 1997).

At the same time, however, research suggests that depending on life experiences, cognitive performance may be enhanced over time (Baltes, 1987). Indeed, a number of studies suggest that experiences can lead to an accumulation of knowledge and skills until an advanced age, when they may level off (Horn and Hofer, 1992; Schaie, 1994; Marsiske and Smith, 1998). The latter phenomenon is referred to as *practice* effect. The outcome of the interaction between ageing and practice effects invariably depends on the extent and nature of life experiences.

FIGURE 2.7 A B

Age and adult skills

A. Mean scores with .95 confidence interval and scores at the 5th, 25th, 75th and 95th percentiles on the document scale, population aged 16 to 25, 26 to 45 and 46 to 65, 2003

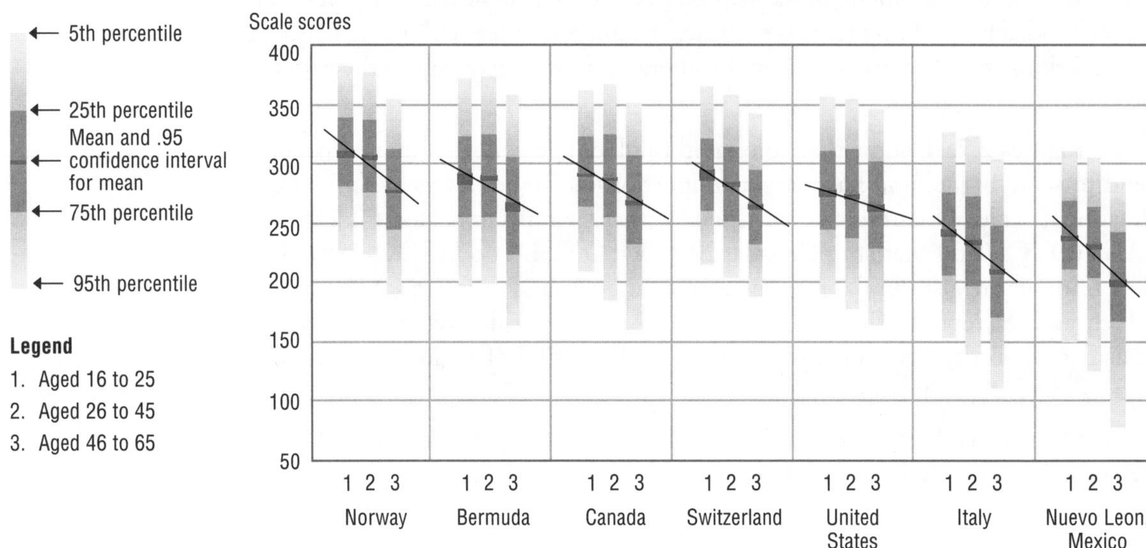

B. Per cent of populations aged 16 to 25, 26 to 45 and 46 to 65 at each level on the document scale, 2003

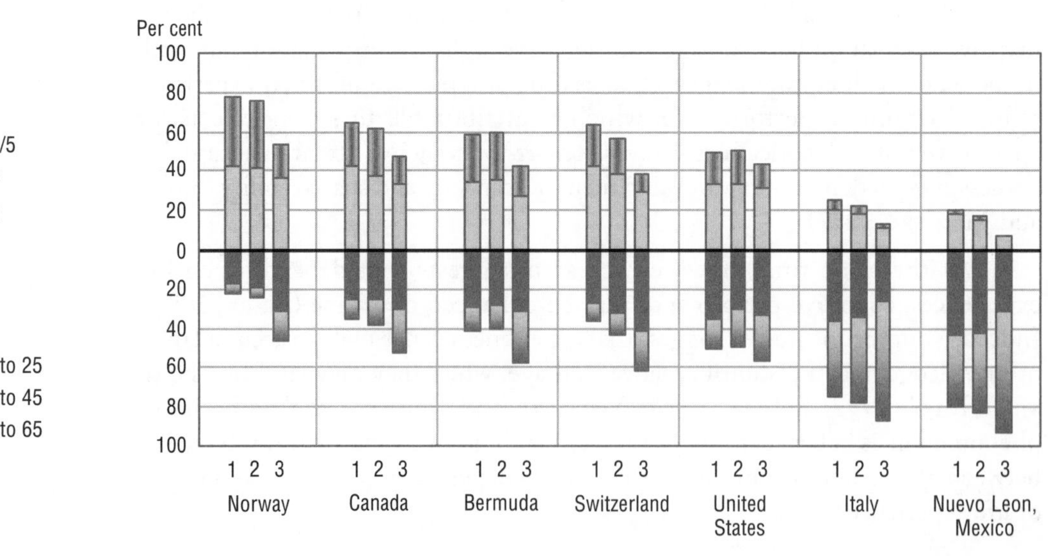

A. **Countries are ranked by the mean of age group 26 to 45.**

B. **Countries are ranked by the proportions in Levels 3 and 4/5 in age 26 to 45.**

Source: Adult Literacy and Life Skills Survey, 2003.

Lower skills among older age groups may also be attributable to other types of effects such as *cohort* and *period* effects (see Portrait, Alessie and Deeg, 2003). In particular, younger cohorts have received extended formal schooling compared to older cohorts, and more emphasis may be placed on the acquisition of cognitive skills now than in earlier periods. But younger adults also benefit from more recent schooling. This may be referred to as the recency effect, which is closely related to the ageing effect. It suggests that as time advances, cognitive skills can diminish from what they were at the time of school completion. Whether they actually diminish will depend on the interaction of ageing and practice effects over time. The widely perceived impact of education on skill development is discussed further in Chapter 3.

There are wide differences in educational attainment among age cohorts, making this particular life experience a potentially major factor influencing the relationship between age and skills, and perhaps the most important cohort effect. To adjust for these differences, Figure 2.8 depicts the relationship between age and skills after taking into account levels of educational attainment. The results show that skill differences among age cohorts remain, which provides some evidence that skills are related to age independently from education. Findings are similar for all the skill domains assessed.

FIGURE 2.8

Skills-age profiles controlling for educational attainment

Relationship between age and literacy scores on the document literacy scale, with adjustment for level of education and language status, populations aged 16 to 65, 2003

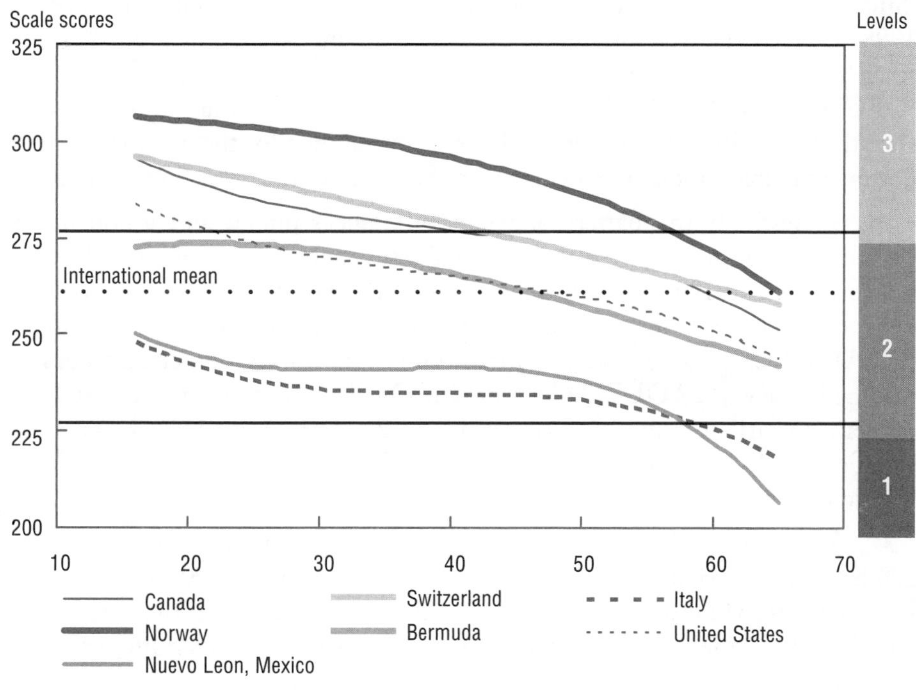

Source: Adult Literacy and Life Skills Survey, 2003.

In general, however, it is impossible to separate cohort, period, ageing, and practice effects when working with cross-sectional data. While the ALL survey measures a number of important life experiences, they are only at a particular age. The information needed to assess the cumulative impact of individual life experiences on the development of skills is not captured in the survey. Addressing this would require complex and costly longitudinal designs involving repeated cognitive assessments of the same individuals over time.

It is also important to consider changes in the quality of education over time, or the *quality* effects of education. Findings presented in Figure 2.8 adjust for the quantity of education only, not the quality of education. But it is likely that gradual improvement in education systems over time explains at least part of the skills-age relationship observed. Thus changes in quality must be assessed and included in this type of analysis in order to properly ascertain the observed skills-age relationship.

Beyond education there are differing life experiences such as individual labour market experiences, the extent of engagement in adult learning and other practices that are likely to have a significant influence on the skills-age relationship. Although cumulative measures are not available, the ALL survey is a rich and unique source of information that allows these types of practice effects to be considered further. This is done in subsequent chapters.

2.5 Adult skills and gender

Another key issue to consider are differences between men and women. It is possible that variations in overall performance stem from gender differences in adult skill distributions. Until recently, men have typically obtained more education than women; and because education is an important determinant of skills development (see Chapter 3), differences in education may be responsible for differences in the skills of men and women. But evidence from IALS (1994-1998) suggests that the differences between men and women in adult skills are small and, in some countries, negligible, even after controlling for education (OECD and HRDC, 1997: 34-35). In IALS, when the gender differences are statistically significant, they tend to be in favour of men for the quantitative and document literacy domains, and in favour of women for the prose literacy domain.

Interestingly, this pattern of gender differences among similar domains is consistent with findings from international assessments of school-aged children at age 14 for the 1991 IEA Reading Literacy Study (see OECD and HRDC, 1997: 33) and age 15 for the Programme for International Student Assessment (PISA) (OECD, 2001) study. In PISA, girls significantly outperform boys in reading literacy in 28 OECD and four non-OECD countries. In contrast, boys outperform girls in mathematical literacy in 26 OECD countries (results are significant in 13 countries) and three non-OECD countries (results are significant in 2 countries).

Again, the results presented in Figures 2.9a-b confirm previously observed gender patterns. Men tend to display an advantage in numeracy and document literacy skills, while women tend to display an advantage in prose literacy. In addition, ALL offers the opportunity to examine whether gender interacts with the problem solving skills domain. Only in Bermuda and Norway do the results suggest that women have an advantage in problem solving, but the result for Norway is not statistically significant. In the other countries, performance on problem solving appears to be gender neutral.

Explanations for these types of findings remain elusive. But findings indicate that differences arise already at an early age. Preferences in general are likely to play an important role, but there are also other factors (see Miller *et al.*, 2004). For example, differences in occupational choices, course enrolment and training can lead to differing pathways over the lifespan that influence the development and maintenance of skills in specific domains.

FIGURE 2.9

Gender differences in skills

Standard score differences in mean skills proficiencies between men and women on the prose, document, numeracy and problem solving scales, 2003

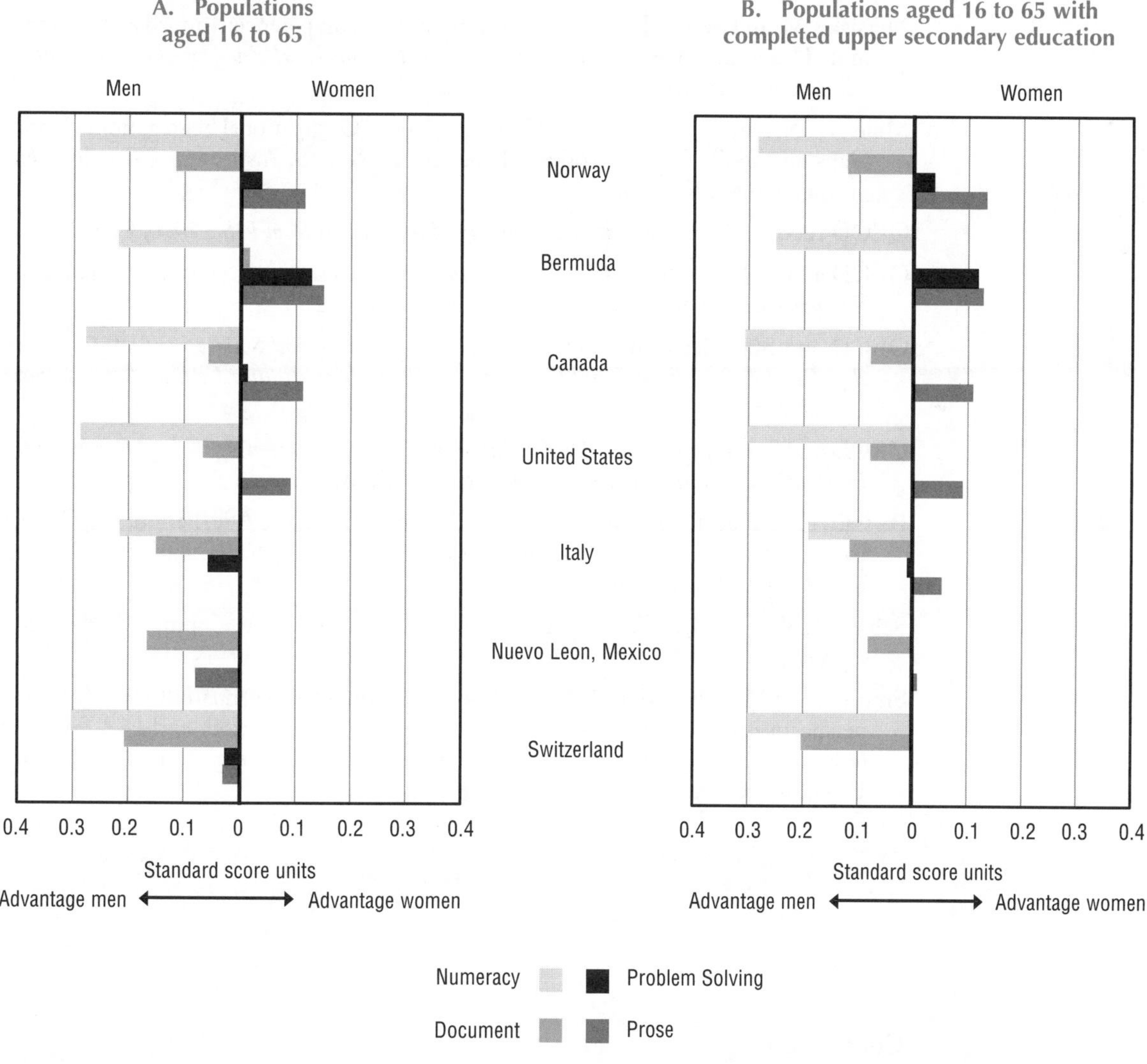

Countries are ranked by the difference in standard score units on the prose scale in panel B.

Notes: The state of Nuevo Leon in Mexico fielded the IALS quantitative literacy assessment rather than the ALL numeracy assessment. Although closely related conceptually, these two scales cannot be directly compared.

Switzerland (Italian), the United States, and the state of Nuevo Leon in Mexico did not field the problem solving skills domain.

Source: Adult Literacy and Life Skills Survey, 2003.

References

Baltes, P.B. (1987), "Theoretical Propositions of Life-span Developmental Psychology: On the dynamics between growth and decline", *Developmental Psychology*, Vol. 23(5), pp. 611-626.

Horn, J.L. and Hofer, S.M. (1992), "Major Abilities and Development in the Adult Period", in R.J. Sternberg and C.A. Berg (eds.), *Intellectual Development*, Cambridge University Press, New York, pp. 44-49.

Marsiske, M. and Smith, J. (1998), "Development of Competence: Toward a taxonomy", in T. Husén and T.N. Postlethwaite (eds.), *International Encyclopedia of Education* (Electronic edition), Pergamon Press, Oxford.

Miller, L., Neathy, F., Pollard, E. and Hill, D. (2004), "Occupational Segregation, Gender Gaps and Skills Gaps", Working Paper Series No. 15, Institute for Employment Studies, United Kingdom.

OECD (2001), *Knowledge and Skills for Life: First Results from PISA 2000,* Paris.

OECD and HRDC (1997), *Literacy Skills for the Knowledge Society: Further Results from the International Adult Literacy Survey,* Paris and Hull.

OECD and Statistics Canada (1995), *Literacy, Economy and Society in the Information Age: Results of the First Final Report on the International Adult Literacy Survey,* Paris and Ottawa.

OECD and Statistics Canada (2000), *Literacy in the Information Age: Final Report on the International Adult Literacy Survey,* Paris and Ottawa.

Portrait, F., Alessie, R. and Deeg, D. (2003), "Disentangling the Age, Period, and Cohort Effects Using a Modeling Approach", Discussion paper, Timbergen Institute, University of Amsterdam.

Schaie, K.W. (1994), "The Course of Adult Intellectual Development", *American Psychologist*, Vol. 49(4), pp. 304-313.

Smith, J. and Marsiske, M. (1997), "Abilities and Competencies in Adulthood: Lifespan perspectives on workplace skills", in A.C. Tuijnman, I.S. Kirsch and D.A. Wagner (eds.), *Adult Basic Skills: Innovations in Measurement and Policy Analysis,* Hampton Press, Inc., Cresskill, NJ, pp. 73-114.

Contributor

Richard Desjardins, *Statistics Canada*

Annex 2

2

Data Values for the Figures

TABLE 2.1 For data values of FIGURE 2.1 see TABLE 2.2

TABLE 2.2

Mean scores with .95 confidence interval and scores at the 5th, 25th, 75th and 95th percentiles on skills scales ranging from 0 to 500 points, populations aged 16 to 65, 2003

	5th percentile		25th percentile		Mean		75th percentile		95th percentile	
A. Prose literacy scale										
Bermuda	192.0	(4.4)	255.6	(2.7)	289.8	(1.3)	328.4	(1.8)	374.1	(2.5)
Canada	178.1	(2.1)	250.6	(1.3)	280.8	(0.7)	318.0	(0.7)	358.7	(1.2)
Italy	135.8	(3.9)	192.3	(2.8)	229.1	(1.7)	267.2	(1.9)	318.7	(2.2)
Norway	211.5	(3.4)	263.5	(1.4)	290.1	(1.0)	320.5	(0.8)	355.8	(1.0)
Nuevo Leon, Mexico	143.3	(4.2)	206.1	(0.9)	228.3	(0.7)	255.8	(0.9)	292.0	(1.7)
Switzerland	193.8	(2.7)	242.1	(2.2)	272.1	(1.3)	303.7	(1.5)	346.0	(4.0)
United States	175.9	(3.5)	235.5	(1.6)	268.6	(1.3)	306.1	(1.9)	346.9	(2.2)
B. Document literacy scale										
Bermuda	185.1	(3.5)	243.9	(2.4)	280.0	(1.5)	318.3	(1.8)	369.9	(2.2)
Canada	178.3	(2.1)	248.1	(1.0)	280.6	(0.6)	318.8	(0.8)	361.5	(1.7)
Italy	127.9	(3.4)	187.9	(2.3)	225.8	(1.7)	265.6	(2.2)	317.1	(2.9)
Norway	205.8	(3.1)	264.0	(1.6)	295.1	(0.9)	329.7	(1.0)	372.3	(1.9)
Nuevo Leon, Mexico	111.6	(5.0)	199.6	(1.4)	226.2	(1.1)	261.9	(1.0)	304.6	(2.2)
Switzerland	198.8	(2.3)	244.3	(2.3)	276.6	(1.6)	309.1	(2.4)	355.3	(3.1)
United States	174.3	(3.6)	235.5	(1.7)	269.8	(1.5)	308.7	(2.2)	352.5	(2.4)
C. Numeracy scale										
Bermuda	176.8	(2.5)	233.3	(2.4)	269.7	(1.6)	308.5	(2.0)	359.4	(2.8)
Canada	170.4	(2.5)	237.2	(1.3)	272.3	(0.7)	311.9	(1.2)	357.7	(2.0)
Italy	148.8	(3.9)	200.4	(2.1)	233.3	(1.4)	267.1	(1.6)	313.9	(2.0)
Norway	204.9	(3.0)	255.2	(1.5)	284.9	(1.0)	316.2	(1.4)	357.8	(2.5)
Switzerland	212.4	(3.0)	257.8	(1.8)	289.8	(1.0)	322.2	(2.0)	368.9	(4.1)
United States	162.8	(2.6)	222.4	(2.1)	260.9	(1.5)	302.2	(2.1)	351.5	(3.0)
D. Problem solving scale										
Bermuda	182.3	(3.3)	237.8	(2.2)	272.8	(1.4)	309.6	(2.2)	356.7	(2.4)
Canada	178.8	(2.2)	243.3	(1.5)	273.8	(1.1)	309.5	(1.5)	352.8	(2.4)
Italy	130.7	(4.1)	186.1	(2.4)	224.9	(1.5)	263.4	(1.5)	319.5	(3.2)
Norway	197.0	(3.8)	254.2	(2.6)	284.2	(1.7)	318.3	(1.4)	358.6	(1.5)
Switzerland	194.6	(5.3)	244.8	(2.4)	279.0	(1.2)	313.0	(1.6)	360.5	(2.7)

Notes: The state of Nuevo Leon in Mexico fielded the IALS quantitative literacy assessment rather than the ALL numeracy assessment. Although closely related conceptually, these two scales cannot be directly compared.

Switzerland (Italian), the United States, and the state of Nuevo Leon in Mexico did not field the problem solving skills domain.

Source: Adult Literacy and Life Skills Survey, 2003.

TABLE 2.3

Per cent of populations aged 16 to 65 at each skills level, 2003

	Level 1		Level 2		Level 3		Level 4/5	
A. Prose literacy scale								
Bermuda	12.5	(0.8)	25.6	(1.4)	35.6	(1.4)	26.3	(1.1)
Canada	14.6	(0.4)	27.3	(0.7)	38.6	(0.9)	19.5	(0.8)
Italy	47.0	(1.5)	32.5	(1.1)	17.0	(0.8)	3.5	(0.4)
Norway	7.9	(0.7)	26.2	(1.1)	45.3	(1.4)	20.6	(0.7)
Nuevo Leon, Mexico	43.2	(1.2)	45.8	(1.4)	10.3	(0.5)	0.7[1]	(0.2)
Switzerland	15.9	(1.2)	36.3	(1.1)	35.7	(1.9)	12.1	(0.9)
United States	20.0	(0.8)	32.6	(1.1)	34.6	(1.2)	12.8	(1.0)
B. Document literacy scale								
Bermuda	16.6	(1.0)	29.5	(1.7)	32.7	(1.7)	21.1	(0.9)
Canada	15.6	(0.4)	27.0	(0.7)	36.9	(1.0)	20.5	(0.6)
Italy	49.2	(1.4)	31.4	(1.2)	15.8	(1.0)	3.6	(0.4)
Norway	8.9	(0.5)	23.5	(1.1)	39.7	(1.1)	27.9	(0.8)
Nuevo Leon, Mexico	43.8	(0.9)	40.3	(0.9)	14.2	(0.8)	1.7	(0.2)
Switzerland	14.5	(0.9)	34.5	(1.5)	35.8	(1.8)	15.1	(1.4)
United States	20.2	(1.0)	32.3	(1.4)	32.6	(1.1)	15.0	(1.0)
C. Numeracy scale								
Bermuda	21.4	(1.0)	32.7	(1.7)	29.9	(1.5)	16.0	(0.9)
Canada	19.5	(0.5)	30.3	(0.7)	33.4	(0.9)	16.9	(0.6)
Italy	43.5	(1.2)	36.7	(1.1)	16.8	(0.8)	3.0	(0.4)
Norway	10.6	(0.6)	29.6	(1.0)	41.5	(1.5)	18.4	(0.9)
Switzerland	8.6	(0.7)	30.7	(1.5)	37.8	(1.3)	22.9	(1.2)
United States	26.8	(0.9)	31.8	(1.1)	28.8	(1.0)	12.7	(1.1)
D. Problem solving scale								
Bermuda	33.1	(1.4)	36.8	(2.0)	23.6	(1.3)	6.5	(0.6)
Canada	29.7	(0.8)	38.8	(0.9)	26.2	(0.8)	5.4	(0.5)
Italy	67.8	(0.9)	22.8	(0.8)	8.1	(0.6)	1.2	(0.2)
Norway	23.3	(1.3)	37.5	(1.0)	32.0	(1.2)	7.2	(0.5)
Switzerland	28.8	(1.3)	37.3	(1.5)	26.5	(1.0)	7.3	(0.7)

1. Unreliable estimate.

Notes: The state of Nuevo Leon in Mexico fielded the IALS quantitative literacy assessment rather than the ALL numeracy assessment. Although closely related conceptually, these two scales cannot be directly compared.

Switzerland (Italian), the United States, and the state of Nuevo Leon in Mexico did not field the problem solving skills domain.

Source: Adult Literacy and Life Skills Survey, 2003.

TABLE 2.4

Mean scores with .95 confidence interval and scores at the 5th, 25th, 75th and 95th percentiles on skills scales ranging from 0 to 500 points, populations aged 16 to 65, IALS 1994/1998 and ALL 2003

		5th percentile		25th percentile		Mean		75th percentile		95th percentile	
A. Prose literacy scale											
Canada	IALS 1994	146.9	(15.3)	246.5	(5.9)	278.8	(3.1)	321.7	(3.9)	369.0	(6.3)
	ALL 2003	178.2	(2.1)	250.7	(1.3)	280.8	(0.7)	318.0	(0.7)	358.7	(1.2)
United States	IALS 1994	137.1	(5.8)	236.7	(2.4)	273.7	(1.6)	321.0	(2.1)	369.6	(3.2)
	ALL 2003	175.9	(3.5)	235.5	(1.6)	268.6	(1.3)	306.1	(1.9)	346.9	(2.2)
Switzerland (German)	IALS 1994	147.2	(5.4)	238.9	(1.7)	263.3	(1.4)	300.5	(2.0)	339.7	(3.4)
	ALL 2003	193.8	(3.7)	244.3	(2.7)	274.5	(1.6)	306.9	(2.0)	349.1	(4.4)
Switzerland (French)	IALS 1994	152.5	(7.5)	239.6	(3.3)	264.8	(1.7)	301.7	(1.6)	338.3	(1.6)
	ALL 2003	194.2	(5.8)	237.9	(2.5)	267.1	(1.5)	297.9	(2.1)	336.5	(2.2)
Norway	IALS 1998	209.4	(3.5)	264.6	(1.9)	288.5	(1.0)	317.8	(0.9)	352.4	(1.1)
	ALL 2003	211.5	(3.4)	263.5	(1.4)	290.1	(1.0)	320.5	(0.8)	355.8	(1.0)
Switzerland (Italian)	IALS 1998	161.7	(5.7)	235.6	(2.5)	264.3	(2.1)	300.2	(2.4)	338.0	(3.8)
	ALL 2003	192.0	(4.3)	232.8	(1.8)	259.5	(1.0)	286.8	(1.5)	322.0	(3.1)
B. Document literacy scale											
Canada	IALS 1994	127.4	(20.4)	244.1	(5.5)	279.3	(3.0)	327.4	(3.2)	379.6	(5.2)
	ALL 2003	178.3	(2.1)	248.1	(1.0)	280.6	(0.6)	318.8	(0.8)	361.5	(1.7)
United States	IALS 1994	124.0	(4.1)	230.1	(2.4)	267.9	(1.7)	317.5	(2.2)	367.9	(3.0)
	ALL 2003	174.3	(3.6)	235.5	(1.7)	269.8	(1.5)	308.7	(2.2)	352.5	(2.4)
Switzerland(German)	IALS 1994	117.1	(4.4)	242.3	(2.2)	269.7	(1.9)	314.0	(1.7)	358.3	(5.7)
	ALL 2003	199.7	(3.7)	245.4	(3.4)	278.6	(2.1)	312.4	(2.6)	358.9	(3.6)
Switzerland (French)	IALS 1994	153.7	(7.8)	245.5	(2.5)	274.1	(1.7)	311.5	(2.7)	355.1	(3.6)
	ALL 2003	198.7	(3.3)	243.0	(2.4)	272.6	(1.5)	303.5	(1.5)	345.7	(4.3)
Norway	IALS 1998	203.3	(4.1)	268.4	(2.4)	296.9	(1.2)	332.1	(1.5)	371.9	(2.6)
	ALL 2003	205.8	(3.1)	264.0	(1.6)	295.1	(0.9)	329.7	(1.0)	372.3	(1.9)
Switzerland (Italian)	IALS 1998	164.6	(8.9)	243.5	(2.8)	271.0	(2.2)	307.0	(2.3)	347.2	(3.8)
	ALL 2003	192.6	(5.4)	238.5	(2.2)	265.7	(1.1)	294.5	(1.8)	332.8	(2.3)

Sources: Adult Literacy and Life Skills Survey, 2003.
International Adult Literacy Survey, 1994-1998.

See FIGURE 2.5 in CHAPTER 2 page 41

TABLE 2.6

Differences between IALS 1994/1998 and ALL 2003 in the per cent of adults aged 16 to 65 at each skills level

	Level 1	Level 2	Level 3	Level 4/5	Levels 1 and 2	Levels 3 and 4/5
A. Prose literacy scale						
Canada	-2.0	+2.5	+2.2	-2.8	+0.5	-0.6
United States	-0.8	+8.1 [1]	+1.8	-9.1 [1]	+7.3 [1]	-7.3 [1]
Switzerland (German)	-4.3 [1]	+0.4	-0.5	4.4 [1]	-3.9	+3.9
Switzerland (French)	-1.6	+6.1 [1]	-3.7	-1.0	+4.5	-4.7
Switzerland (Italian)	+0.3	+9.3 [1]	-4.6	-5.1 [1]	+9.6 [1]	-9.7 [1]
Norway	-0.6	+1.4	-2.9	2.1	0.8	-0.8
B. Document literacy scale						
Canada	-2.4	+3.3	+4.2	-5.2 [1]	+0.9	-1.0
United States	-3.4 [1]	+7.5 [1]	+1.0	-5.0 [1]	+4.1	-4.0
Switzerland (German)	-4.3 [1]	+5.7 [1]	-1.0	-0.4	+1.4	-1.4
Switzerland (French)	-1.4	+8.1 [1]	-1.7	-4.9 [1]	+6.7 [1]	-6.6 [1]
Switzerland (Italian)	+0.6	+11.2 [1]	-2.2	-9.6 [1]	+11.8 [1]	-11.8 [1]
Norway	0.2	+2.4	-0.8	-1.8	+2.6	-2.6

1. p<.05 statistically significant

Sources: Adult Literacy and Life Skills Survey, 2003.
International Adult Literacy Survey, 1994-1998.

TABLE 2.7 A

Mean scores with .95 confidence interval and scores at the 5th, 25th, 75th, and 95th percentiles on the document scale, population aged 16 to 25, 26 to 45 and 46 to 65, 2003

	Age	5th percentile		25th percentile		Mean		75th percentile		95th percentile	
Bermuda	16 to 25	197.0	(10.6)	255.5	(8.5)	286.9	(4.6)	322.3	(6.7)	372.1	(10.3)
	26 to 45	198.0	(4.5)	254.2	(1.9)	288.4	(1.8)	324.7	(2.5)	374.1	(3.4)
	46 to 65	164.6	(4.8)	223.6	(4.2)	263.5	(2.7)	304.9	(5.1)	358.3	(5.9)
Canada	16 to 25	208.8	(4.3)	262.6	(2.4)	290.7	(1.6)	323.3	(1.6)	361.8	(3.2)
	26 to 45	184.6	(3.7)	255.2	(1.6)	287.0	(1.3)	325.3	(1.4)	366.8	(2.6)
	46 to 65	160.5	(4.1)	231.9	(2.8)	266.9	(1.4)	307.6	(1.5)	351.7	(2.0)
Italy	16 to 25	153.4	(5.5)	205.2	(3.5)	240.9	(2.6)	276.5	(3.2)	326.6	(5.8)
	26 to 45	139.3	(4.5)	197.0	(2.4)	233.7	(2.1)	271.8	(3.6)	322.9	(4.0)
	46 to 65	110.5	(4.3)	170.4	(3.8)	209.2	(2.3)	248.2	(2.9)	304.3	(3.7)
Norway	16 to 25	226.2	(7.6)	281.1	(5.0)	308.4	(2.3)	338.8	(3.1)	382.2	(6.7)
	26 to 45	223.8	(4.4)	276.6	(2.0)	305.0	(1.7)	337.2	(2.5)	377.0	(3.6)
	46 to 65	189.8	(6.4)	244.9	(2.0)	276.8	(1.4)	312.0	(2.3)	355.0	(3.1)
Nuevo Leon, Mexico	16 to 25	150.1	(9.9)	210.7	(2.1)	237.3	(1.8)	269.3	(2.4)	311.6	(4.7)
	26 to 45	124.9	(7.2)	204.6	(2.0)	230.3	(1.5)	263.0	(1.8)	305.3	(3.1)
	46 to 65	78.7	(5.6)	166.9	(5.1)	200.3	(2.7)	242.3	(2.6)	284.7	(4.2)
Switzerland	16 to 25	214.3	(17.5)	259.7	(5.6)	291.0	(4.6)	321.3	(7.5)	365.3	(9.5)
	26 to 45	204.1	(5.4)	250.6	(2.9)	282.1	(1.9)	314.3	(2.8)	357.6	(3.8)
	46 to 65	188.2	(4.2)	232.4	(2.2)	263.4	(2.1)	294.4	(2.7)	341.8	(5.9)
United States	16 to 25	189.4	(6.0)	244.5	(2.8)	275.3	(2.8)	310.5	(3.8)	356.8	(5.9)
	26 to 45	178.5	(4.8)	236.9	(1.9)	272.7	(2.0)	311.8	(2.4)	355.3	(4.5)
	46 to 65	164.0	(6.1)	228.0	(3.0)	262.8	(2.2)	302.6	(3.4)	345.7	(3.5)

Source: Adult Literacy and Life Skills Survey, 2003.

TABLE 2.7 B

Per cent of populations aged 16 to 25, 26 to 45 and 46 to 65 at each level on the document scale, 2003

	Age	Level 1		Level 2		Level 3		Level 4/5	
Bermuda	16 to 25	12.3	(3.3)	29.3	(4.9)	34.8	(4.3)	23.6	(3.3)
	26 to 45	11.8	(1.4)	28.5	(2.0)	35.2	(2.1)	24.5	(1.3)
	46 to 65	26.3	(1.8)	31.2	(2.1)	27.7	(2.6)	14.7	(2.1)
Canada	16 to 25	9.5	(1.1)	25.4	(2.0)	42.1	(2.0)	23.0	(1.5)
	26 to 45	13.0	(0.7)	25.1	(0.9)	37.4	(1.4)	24.5	(1.0)
	46 to 65	22.2	(1.1)	30.4	(1.2)	33.3	(1.5)	14.1	(0.8)
Italy	16 to 25	38.5	(2.4)	36.2	(2.5)	20.2	(1.8)	5.1	(1.0)
	26 to 45	43.7	(1.7)	33.9	(2.2)	17.9	(1.9)	4.5	(0.7)
	46 to 65	60.9	(1.6)	26.1	(1.6)	11.2	(1.1)	1.8	(0.5)
Norway	16 to 25	5.0	(1.1)	17.0	(2.3)	42.3	(2.7)	35.7	(2.2)
	26 to 45	5.4	(0.6)	19.1	(1.3)	41.2	(2.0)	34.3	(1.5)
	46 to 65	15.0	(1.0)	31.8	(2.3)	36.7	(2.1)	16.5	(1.0)
Nuevo Leon, Mexico	16 to 25	36.2	(1.7)	43.6	(2.1)	18.3	(1.9)	1.9	(0.5)
	26 to 45	40.9	(1.6)	42.4	(1.6)	14.7	(1.1)	2.1	(0.3)
	46 to 65	61.8	(2.1)	30.9	(2.2)	7.0	(1.0)	0.4	(0.3)
Switzerland	16 to 25	8.5	(2.6)	27.6	(4.3)	42.0	(3.9)	22.0	(4.0)
	26 to 45	11.6	(1.3)	31.9	(1.7)	38.8	(2.4)	17.7	(1.8)
	46 to 65	20.9	(1.1)	41.0	(1.8)	29.3	(2.2)	8.9	(1.6)
United States	16 to 25	15.7	(2.2)	35.0	(2.3)	33.6	(2.4)	15.6	(2.0)
	26 to 45	19.5	(1.1)	30.4	(1.4)	33.3	(1.4)	16.8	(1.5)
	46 to 65	23.7	(1.8)	33.0	(2.4)	31.0	(1.6)	12.3	(1.1)

Source: Adult Literacy and Life Skills Survey, 2003.

TABLE 2.8

Relationship between age and literacy scores on the document literacy scale, with adjustment for level of education and language status, populations aged 16 to 65, 2003

	Unstandardized coefficients		Standardized coefficients		
	B	Standard error	β	t-value	Significance
Bermuda					
(Constant)	0.02	0.04		0.45	0.66
Age (40 years = 0)					
Linear	-0.01	0.00	-0.17	-3.62	0.00
Quadratic	-0.25	0.17	-0.04	-1.42	0.17
Cubic	3.80	8.09	0.02	0.47	0.64
Years of education (Grade 12 = 0)	0.14	0.01	0.48	18.87	0.00
Test langauge (Same as mother tongue = 0)	-0.14	0.08	-0.04	-1.72	0.10
Canada					
(Constant)	0.21	0.02		9.31	0.00
Age (40 years = 0)					
Linear	-0.01	0.00	-0.10	-3.55	0.00
Quadratic	-0.08	0.08	-0.01	-0.99	0.33
Cubic	-14.02	4.41	-0.08	-3.18	0.00
Years of education (Grade 12 = 0)	0.13	0.00	0.47	34.78	0.00
Test langauge (Same as mother tongue = 0)	-0.48	0.03	-0.21	-15.78	0.00

TABLE 2.8 (concluded)

Relationship between age and literacy scores on the document literacy scale, with adjustment for level of education and language status, populations aged 16 to 65, 2003

	Unstandardized coefficients		Standardized coefficients		
	B	Standard error	β	t-value	Significance
Italy					
(Constant)	-0.53	0.04		-14.60	0.00
Age (40 years = 0)					
Linear	0.00	0.00	-0.01	-0.32	0.75
Quadratic	-0.03	0.10	0.00	-0.27	0.79
Cubic	-16.47	8.02	-0.09	-2.05	0.05
Years of education (Grade 12 = 0)	0.11	0.01	0.43	18.55	0.00
Test langauge (Same as mother tongue = 0)	-0.14	0.18	-0.01	-0.75	0.46
Norway					
(Constant)	0.55	0.03	0.00	19.98	0.00
Age (40 years = 0)					
Linear	-0.01	0.00	-0.19	-5.41	0.00
Quadratic	-0.34	0.10	-0.06	-3.36	0.00
Cubic	-4.73	5.60	-0.03	-0.84	0.30
Years of education (Grade 12 = 0)	0.11	0.01	0.36	17.27	0.00
Test langauge (Same as mother tongue = 0)	-0.43	0.06	-0.12	-6.67	0.08
Nuevo Leon, Mexico					
(Constant)	-0.41	0.03		-13.83	0.00
Age (40 years = 0)					
Linear	0.00	0.00	0.00	0.11	0.91
Quadratic	-0.34	0.09	-0.06	-3.80	0.00
Cubic	-26.23	7.54	-0.14	-3.48	0.00
Years of education (Grade 12 = 0)	0.13	0.00	0.57	34.15	0.00
Test langauge (Same as mother tongue = 0)	-0.28	1.14	-0.01	-0.25	0.80
Switzerland					
(Constant)	0.24	0.03		9.04	0.00
Age (40 years = 0)					
Linear	-0.01	0.00	-0.22	-3.18	0.01
Quadratic	-0.04	0.14	-0.01	-0.28	0.95
Cubic	0.16	9.59	0.00	0.02	0.90
Years of education (Grade 12 = 0)	0.09	0.01	0.36	14.17	0.00
Test langauge (Same as mother tongue = 0)	-0.40	0.06	-0.19	-7.19	0.00
United States					
(Constant)	0.00	0.03		-0.03	0.00
Age (40 years = 0)					
Linear	-0.01	0.00	-0.11	-2.75	0.30
Quadratic	-0.01	0.10	0.00	-0.12	0.40
Cubic	-10.30	6.60	-0.06	-1.56	0.00
Years of education (Grade 12 = 0)	0.15	0.01	0.51	22.18	0.00
Test langauge (Same as mother tongue = 0)	-0.67	0.08	-0.25	-8.82	0.27

Source: Adult Literacy and Life Skills Survey, 2003.

TABLE 2.9 A

Mean skills proficiencies between men and women on the prose, document, numeracy and problem solving scales, 2003

	Population aged 16 to 65				
	Men mean		Women mean		Standard deviation
Prose literacy scale					
Bermuda	285.7	(1.6)	293.6	(2.1)	53.2
Canada	277.7	(1.3)	283.8	(1.0)	53.2
Italy	229.2	(2.3)	229.1	(1.7)	53.2
Norway	287.1	(1.2)	293.3	(1.5)	53.2
Nuevo Leon, Mexico	230.4	(1.1)	226.1	(1.0)	53.2
Switzerland	272.9	(1.1)	271.3	(2.0)	53.2
United States	266.1	(1.8)	271.0	(1.6)	53.2
Document literacy scale					
Bermuda	279.5	(1.7)	280.5	(2.3)	56.9
Canada	282.2	(1.3)	279.0	(0.9)	56.9
Italy	230.1	(2.2)	221.5	(1.8)	56.9
Norway	298.4	(1.5)	291.7	(1.3)	56.9
Nuevo Leon, Mexico	231.0	(1.7)	221.5	(1.4)	56.9
Switzerland	282.5	(1.8)	270.8	(2.1)	56.9
United States	271.8	(2.1)	267.9	(1.6)	56.9
Numeracy scale					
Bermuda	275.7	(1.5)	264.1	(2.5)	52.5
Canada	279.6	(1.5)	265.0	(0.8)	52.5
Italy	239.0	(1.6)	227.6	(1.8)	52.5
Norway	292.4	(1.5)	277.1	(1.3)	52.5
Switzerland	297.8	(1.1)	281.8	(1.5)	52.5
United States	268.6	(2.0)	253.5	(1.9)	52.5
Problem solving scale					
Bermuda	269.4	(2.0)	276.1	(2.2)	53.0
Canada	273.4	(1.4)	274.1	(1.3)	53.0
Italy	226.5	(2.1)	223.4	(2.2)	53.0
Norway	283.2	(2.6)	285.2	(1.6)	53.0
Switzerland	279.7	(1.3)	278.2	(2.3)	53.0

Notes: The state of Nuevo Leon in Mexico fielded the IALS quantitative literacy assessment rather than the ALL numeracy assessment. Although closely related conceptually, these two scales cannot be directly compared.

Switzerland (Italian), the United States, and the state of Nuevo Leon in Mexico did not field the problem solving skills domain.

Source: Adult Literacy and Life Skills Survey, 2003.

TABLE 2.9 B

Mean skills proficiencies between men and women on the prose, document, numeracy and problem solving scales, 2003

	Population aged 16 to 65 with completed upper secondary education				
	Men mean		Women mean		Standard deviation
Prose					
Bermuda	291.3	(1.8)	298.0	(2.1)	53.2
Canada	287.9	(1.4)	293.6	(0.9)	53.2
Italy	250.7	(2.7)	253.5	(2.1)	53.2
Norway	292.5	(1.1)	299.6	(1.6)	53.2
Nuevo Leon, Mexico	252.7	(1.4)	253.3	(1.1)	53.2
Switzerland	278.8	(1.2)	279.0	(2.4)	53.2
United States	276.3	(1.9)	281.0	(1.6)	53.2
Document					
Bermuda	284.8	(1.8)	285.0	(2.3)	56.9
Canada	293.1	(1.3)	288.8	(1.0)	56.9
Italy	251.3	(2.9)	244.8	(2.8)	56.9
Norway	305.0	(1.6)	298.6	(1.4)	56.9
Nuevo Leon, Mexico	258.7	(2.0)	254.1	(1.6)	56.9
Switzerland	288.2	(1.7)	276.8	(2.2)	56.9
United States	281.7	(2.1)	277.3	(1.8)	56.9
Numeracy					
Bermuda	281.7	(1.5)	268.5	(2.6)	52.5
Canada	290.7	(1.5)	274.5	(0.8)	52.5
Italy	259.7	(2.3)	249.9	(2.1)	52.5
Norway	298.2	(1.2)	283.3	(1.4)	52.5
Switzerland	303.7	(1.6)	287.9	(1.7)	52.5
United States	279.0	(2.1)	263.1	(1.9)	52.5
Problem solving					
Bermuda	274.3	(2.2)	280.5	(2.3)	53.0
Canada	283.3	(1.6)	283.5	(1.3)	53.0
Italy	248.8	(2.3)	248.3	(2.1)	53.0
Norway	290.3	(2.2)	292.4	(1.8)	53.0
Switzerland	283.6	(1.4)	283.6	(2.7)	53.0

Notes: The state of Nuevo Leon in Mexico fielded the IALS quantitative literacy assessment rather than the ALL numeracy assessment. Although closely related conceptually, these two scales cannot be directly compared.

Switzerland (Italian), the United States, and the state of Nuevo Leon in Mexico did not field the problem solving skills domain.

Source: Adult Literacy and Life Skills Survey, 2003.

Chapter 3

3

Education and Skills

Summary

This chapter examines the relationship between individual educational experiences and observed measures of skill. First, evidence of a strong positive association between skills and educational attainment is established. Both theory and evidence suggest that education plays a key role in the formation of the skills measured in ALL, but the imperfect association between education and skills also suggests that other factors are implicated in the development of skills over the lifespan. Second, the analysis focuses on comparing the skills of younger adults with varying experiences of upper secondary education. In particular, the skills of early school leavers are considered (youth and young adults aged 16 to 30 who have not completed upper secondary education and have not been in school for at least one year). Finally, the relationships between individual skills and additional years and levels of post secondary schooling are studied in detail.

Table of Contents

Education and Skills

3

3.1 Overview and highlights

This chapter examines the relationship between individual educational experiences and observed measures of skill. First, evidence of a strong positive association between skills and educational attainment is established. Both theory and evidence suggest that education plays a key role in the formation of the skills measured in ALL, but the imperfect association between education and skills also suggests that other factors are implicated in the development of skills over the lifespan. Second, the analysis focuses on comparing the skills of younger adults with varying experiences of upper secondary education. In particular, the skills of early school leavers are considered (youth and young adults aged 16 to 30 who have not completed upper secondary education and have not been in school for at least one year). Finally, the relationships between individual skills and additional years and levels of post-secondary schooling are studied in detail.

The main findings presented in this chapter are:

- There is a strong positive relationship between educational attainment and skills on all domains measured in ALL. But there are also substantial variations in performance within each level of education, with as many as 25 per cent of adults who completed tertiary education scoring less than over 25 per cent of those who completed less than upper secondary.
- Age differences do not explain the variation within levels of education. In fact, comparisons between younger and older age cohorts reveal that skill dispersions are more pronounced among older cohorts. On the one hand, this suggests that the predictive capacity of education can, for many persons, diminish over time. On the other hand, the stability of the average trend among younger and older age cohorts suggests that education has a strong and persistent effect on skills over time.
- Despite the strong relationship between education and skills, it is imperfect. This suggests that relying on measures of educational attainment to predict adult skills will lead to considerable

measurement error. It also suggests that the development and maintenance of cognitive skills is more complex than simply attending school or achieving a certificate of completion, and that education does not "fix" skill levels for life. There are other factors that play an important role in the acquisition, development, maintenance and loss of skills over the lifespan.

- Individual differences in upper secondary education status are strongly related to differences in observed skills. In all countries, early school leavers are the most likely to score at Levels 1 or 2 when compared to those who have stayed in school, or completed upper secondary education or higher.
- In all countries, youth and young adults aged 16 to 35 with more years of post-secondary schooling, on average, consistently show higher skill proficiencies than those with fewer or no years of post-secondary schooling.
- Compared to other countries, Norway and Switzerland display, on average, the highest skill proficiencies associated with each additional year of schooling beyond upper secondary education. Switzerland also displays the sharpest average differences in skill proficiencies for every additional year of post-secondary schooling.

3.2 The relationship between education and cognitive skills

Previous research suggests that educational attainment is a key determinant of cognitive skills proficiency including adult literacy and numeracy (e.g., Kirsch *et al.*, 1993; OECD and Statistics Canada, 2000; Boudard, 2001; Desjardins, 2004). This is not surprising since, in most societies, a principal and widely accepted goal of educational systems is to produce a population able to read, write and count. But despite the strong relationship, it is imperfect; hence supporting the assertion that the development and maintenance of cognitive skills is more complex than simply attending school or achieving a certificate of completion.

Figures 3.1a-b depict the strong positive relationship between education and skills. In all countries considered, higher levels of educational attainment are associated with higher average proficiency scores. Beyond average scores, however, higher levels of education do not necessarily imply higher proficiencies for all. As the gradation bars depict in Figures 3.1a-b, sizeable proportions of persons attaining higher levels of education obtain lower scores than persons with less education. For example, in Canada, Italy and Switzerland, 25 per cent of persons (below the 25th percentile) who completed some kind of tertiary education score less than over 25 per cent of persons (over the 75th percentile) who completed less than upper secondary education.

It was suggested in Chapter 2 that differences in the quality of educational provision among age cohorts may systematically contribute to the above mentioned pattern. For example, younger persons who may have benefited from better educational provision may consistently score above average for each level of educational attainment; and vice-versa, older persons may consistently score below average. But Figures 3.2a-b show that the general pattern holds even among groups aged 26 to 35 and 56 to 65, respectively.

One notable difference among those aged 26 to 35 and 56 to 65 is the dispersion in proficiency scores within the levels of educational attainment. The extent of the dispersion is indicated by the length of the gradation bars in Figures 3.2a-b. Comparisons reveal that dispersions are more pronounced among older cohorts. Hence the predictive capacity of education diminishes over time. This is consistent with the findings of previous research and the proposition from Chapter 2 that as age related processes play out with time, some older adults gain skills while many others lose them, independent of education. On the other hand the stability of the average trend amongst the two age groups suggests that education has a strong and persistent effect over time.

In summary, although education and skills are strongly related, exclusive reliance on measures of educational attainment to predict adult skills will lead to considerable error. This is consistent with the long standing observation that the impact of education cannot be measured only in terms of the number of years an individual has been exposed to it (Coombs and Ahmed, 1974). Hence other factors are implicated in the acquisition, development, maintenance and loss of skills over the lifespan. Some of these are explored in further detail in subsequent chapters.

FIGURE 3.1 A and B

Educational attainment and skills proficiencies

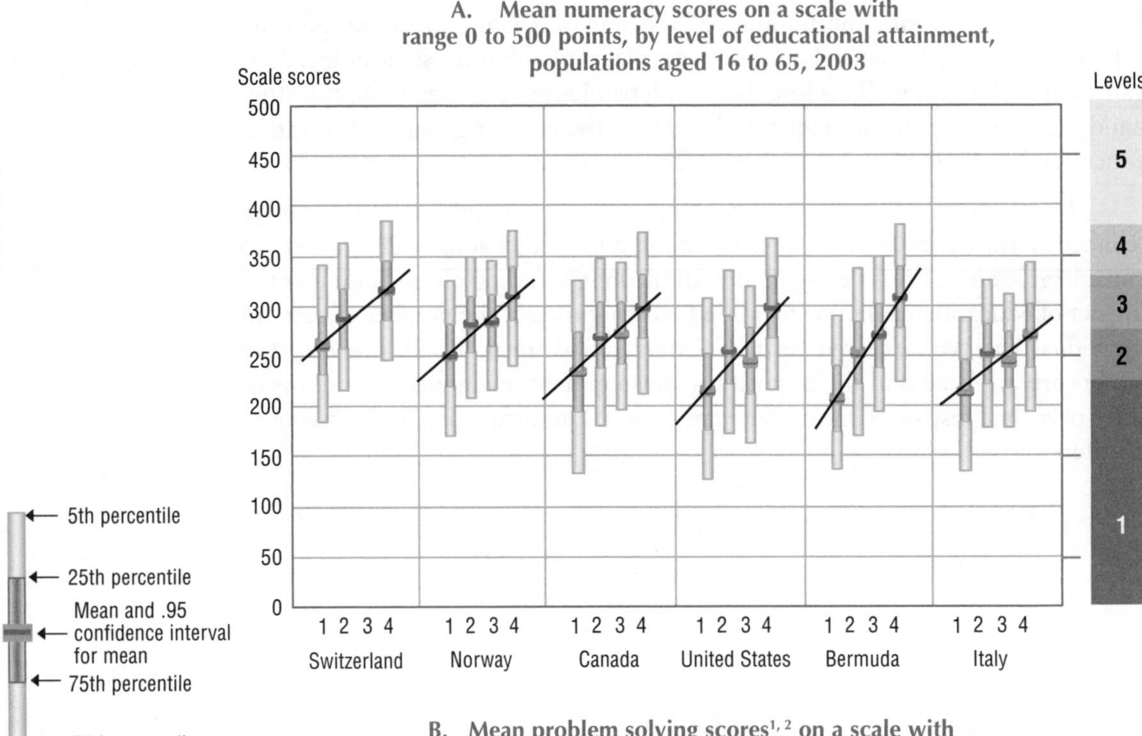

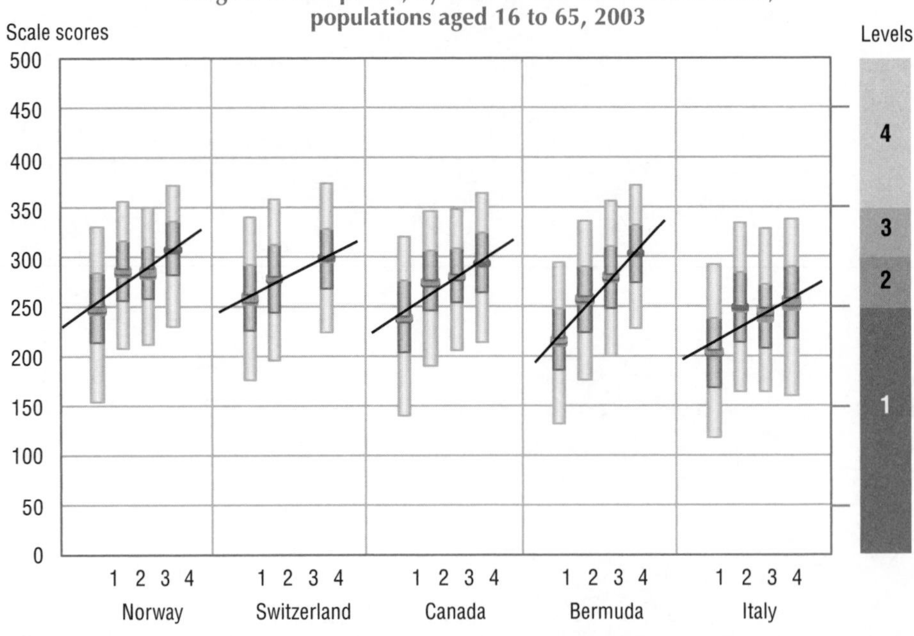

Legend
1. Less than upper secondary
2. Upper secondary
3. Post-secondary, non-tertiary
4. Tertiary type B or higher

A. The countries are ranked by the mean of the numeracy score of those completed upper secondary.

B. The countries are ranked by the mean of the problem solving score of those who completed upper secondary.

1. United States did not field the problem solving skills domain.
2. The problem solving skills scores for Switzerland apply to the German and French speaking communities only since they did not field the problem solving skills domain in the Italian speaking community.

Source: Adult Literacy and Life Skills Survey, 2003.

FIGURE 3.2 A and B

Age, educational attainment and skills proficiencies

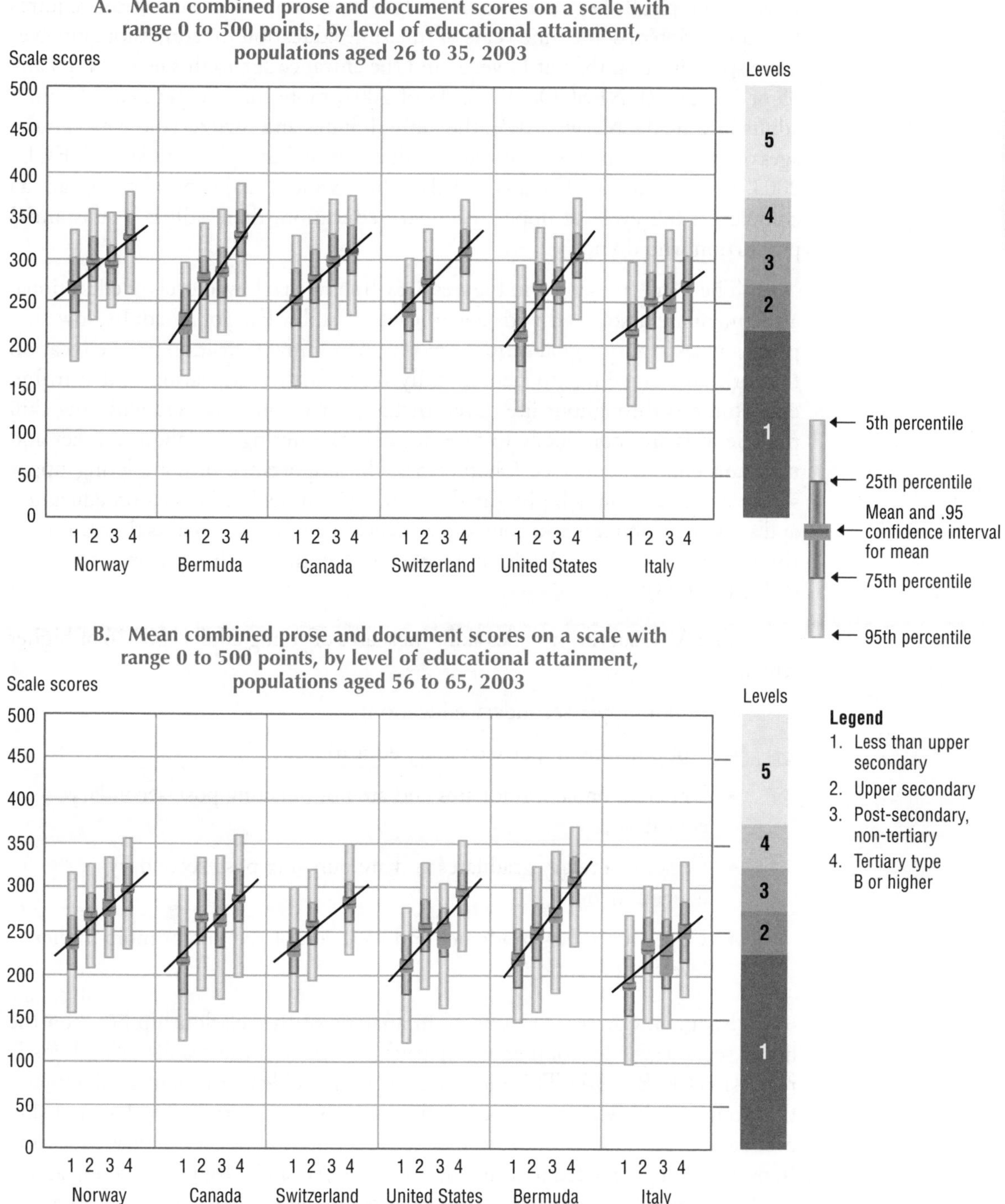

The countries are ranked by the mean of the combined prose and document skills score of those who completed upper secondary.

Source: Adult Literacy and Life Skills Survey, 2003.

3.3 Skills of upper secondary graduates

This section examines the skills of those with varying experiences of upper secondary education. According to the 1997 International Standard Classification of Education (ISCED 1997), upper secondary education corresponds to ISCED Level 3. It typically begins at the end of full-time compulsory education, requires the completion of some nine years of full-time education for admission, involves more specialization than at Level 2, and the entrance age to this level is typically 15 or 16 years (UNESCO, 1997). As of 2001, more than 70 per cent of young adults in Canada, Norway, Italy, the United States and Switzerland between the ages of 15 to 19 attend upper secondary education and complete this level (OECD, 2003, p. 40; Statistics Canada, 2003). Thus while a majority of young adults complete a full cycle of upper secondary education, there still is a substantial proportion who do not.

The results presented in Figures 3.1a-b show that lower levels of educational attainment are associated with lower levels of skills. For young adults, low skill proficiencies in turn signal serious risks in their initial transition from education to work and of failing to benefit fully from further education and learning opportunities throughout life. Even further, early school leavers with low skill proficiencies are more likely to face difficulties entering the labour market and maintain employment (see Chapter 5). The importance of completing upper secondary education is highlighted by OECD's annual indicators on education and associated labour market outcomes, which suggest that it marks the minimum threshold for successful labour market entry and continued employability (OECD, 2003).

The ALL survey provides skills measures of young adults aged 16 or higher who are:

- Still in upper secondary education;
- Not pursuing upper secondary education;
- Upper secondary graduates and are not pursuing post-secondary education;
- Upper secondary graduates and are pursuing post-secondary education; or
- Upper secondary graduates and have completed one or more higher levels of education.

Figure 3.3 presents results of an analysis of the relationship between the upper secondary education status of young adults and their skills using logistic regression (see Box 3A). This method makes it possible to estimate the likelihood that young adults with varying education status will perform at low levels of skill proficiency. The results indicate that differences in upper secondary education status are strongly related to differences in observed skills. Youth and young adults aged 16 to 30 who have not completed upper secondary education and have not been in school for at least one year are dubbed early school leavers. In all countries, early school leavers are the most likely to score at Levels 1 or 2 when compared to those who have stayed in school, or completed upper secondary or higher.

As shown in Figure 3.3a, the likelihood of Canadian and Swiss early school leavers scoring at Levels 1 or 2 on the problem solving scale is about seven times that of those who have completed an educational level higher than upper secondary.

In Italy and Norway it is about six and four times, respectively. Similarly, young adults completing upper secondary but who do not pursue post-secondary education are more likely to score at Levels 1 or 2 than those completing higher levels of education. Results presented in Figure 3.3b also suggest that early school leavers are much more likely to score at low levels of numeracy.

FIGURE 3.3 A and B

Likelihood of scoring at low skill levels by upper secondary education status

A. Odds of scoring at Levels 1 or 2 on the problem solving scale by upper secondary education status, adjusted for age and native language status, persons aged 16 to 30, 2003

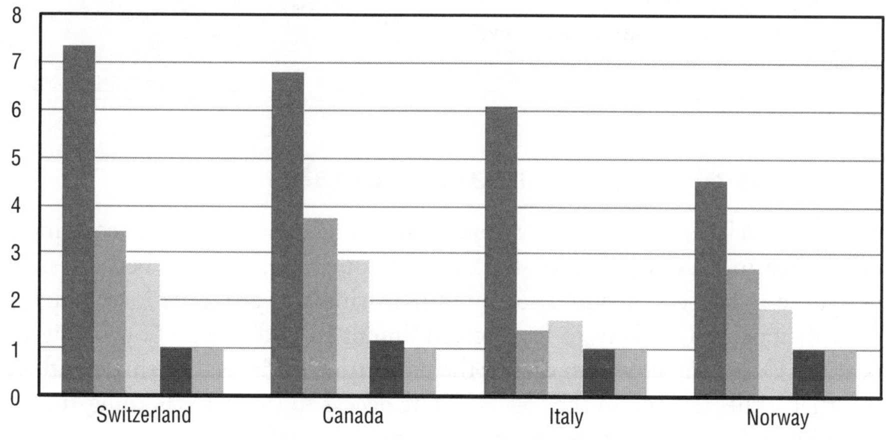

B. Odds of scoring at Levels 1 or 2 on the numeracy scale by upper secondary education status, adjusted for age and native language status, persons aged 16 to 30, 2003

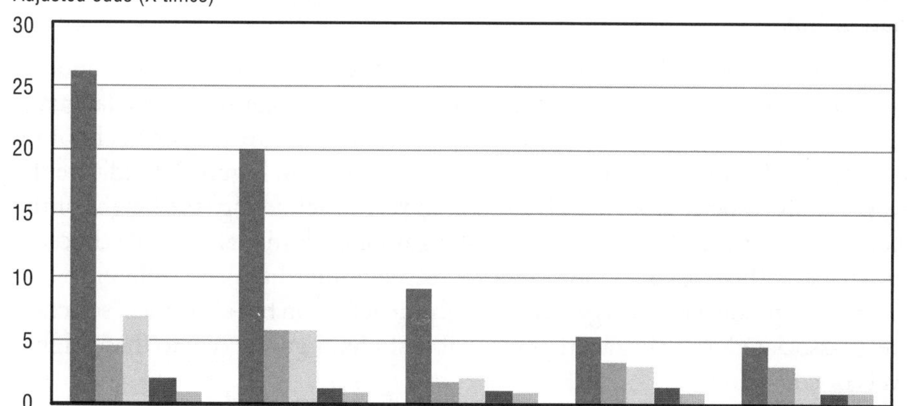

Less than upper secondary, not in school
Less than upper secondary, still in school
Completed upper secondary, not in school
Completed upper secondary, still in school
Completed higher than upper secondary (reference group = 1)

The countries are ranked by the odds ratio of those who completed less than upper secondary and not in school.

1. United States did not field the problem solving skills domain.
2. The problem solving skills scores for Switzerland apply to the German and French speaking communities only since they did not field the problem solving skills domain in the Italian speaking community.

Note: Data for Bermuda are not reported due to low sample sizes for this indicator.

Source: Adult Literacy and Life Skills Survey, 2003.

Box 3A

Using odds ratios

Odds ratios reflect the relative likelihood of an event occurring for a particular group compared to a reference group. An odds ratio of one represents equal chances of an event occurring for a particular group vis-à-vis the reference group. Coefficients with a value below one indicate less chance of the event occurring for a particular group compared to the reference group, and coefficients greater than one represent increased chances (Hosmer and Lemeshow, 1989).

For the purpose of the analyses presented in Figures 3.3, the likelihood or odds of adults scoring at Levels 1 and 2 was set to one for adults who have completed higher than upper secondary education. Odds greater than one for persons completing less education indicate that those persons have increased chances to score at Levels 1 and 2.

3.4 Skills of post-secondary graduates

Previous research suggests that education is a major factor affecting the acquisition, maintenance and development of skills. At the same time, however, because skills are required to succeed in education, and increasingly so at higher levels, higher skill proficiencies are likely to lead to enrolment in and completion of higher education. Often these two aspects of the education-skills relationship reinforce each other: skills learned in schools facilitate access to further schooling that in turn builds skill. It is impossible to separate these two effects when working with cross-sectional data. Because without a longitudinal design there is no way to know for sure that the skills of post-secondary graduates are not the same as they were before they entered post-secondary. Nevertheless, the survey results provide compelling evidence confirming the strong and positive education-skills relationship.

Figures 3.4a-f show the relationship between post-secondary schooling and skill proficiencies after controlling for the effects of age and native language status (see Box 3B). On average, individuals with more years of schooling consistently show higher skill proficiencies. The charts in Figure 3.4 indicate the level of skills associated with each additional year of schooling (the height of the line), as well as the difference in level of skills among additional years of schooling (the shape of the line). It is important to keep in mind that these differences are not only the product of skills gained through participation but also reflect selection effects associated with the fact that more able students gain access to these higher levels of education.

The height and shape of lines differ among countries. For example, Norway and Switzerland have the highest lines; that is, each additional year of schooling is associated with higher skill proficiencies compared to other countries. Norway displays a steady increase between 12 and 20 years of schooling, whereas Switzerland displays a sharper increase between 12 and 18 years. By contrast, the line for Italy is low and flattens out after 16 years of schooling, implying that most persons who report additional years of post-secondary schooling beyond 16 years do not perform better on the problem solving scale.

Note that there are country differences in the average number of years taken to complete comparable levels of education. Each education level point is mapped according to the average number of years associated with completing that level and the average skill proficiencies associated with that level as predicted by the regression (See Box 3B). Education level points above the trend line indicate that, on average, persons completing this level score better than is predicted by the mean years of formal education associated with completing the level. Points on the trend line indicate no additional effect and points below indicate that, on average, persons completing this level perform less than is otherwise predicted by the mean years of formal education associated with completing the level.

For example, one reason for the observed difference in the shape of the line between Norway and Switzerland appears to be a skill premium associated with completing a higher level of schooling. Those who complete tertiary level programs in Norway score higher than those who report having completed the same average years of schooling but have not completed the corresponding level of education. This partly reflects differences in access to and progression in tertiary education, repeated years of schooling as well as completion rates associated with tertiary programs.

Box 3B

Reading the figures on skills of post-secondary graduates

The graphs in Figures 3.4a-f show the effect of formal education on skill scores for persons aged 16 to 35 who have completed at least upper secondary education. The effect of education is separated into two additive components, namely years of formal education and highest level of education ever completed.

The trend line indicates the effect of years of formal education on problem solving scores. The values plotted are those predicted by a regression equation reflecting the country specific relationship between years of formal education and problem solving proficiency. The observed relationship is independent of the highest levels of education ever completed and adjusted for respondents' age and native language status.

Separately, education level points indicate the additional skill effect of the highest level of education ever completed. The values are plotted according to this additional effect, which is predicted by the same regression, and the country specific mean years of formal education associated with each level. Education level points above the trend line indicate that, on average, persons completing this level score better than is predicted by the mean years of formal education associated with completing the level. Points on the trend line indicate no additional effect and points below indicate that, on average, persons completing this level perform less than is otherwise predicted by the mean years of formal education associated with completing the level.

Skills-education profiles are also compared to the ALL international mean score on the problem solving scale for the same population. The international mean score is 284. Scale scores above or below the 284 reference line indicate differences to the international mean that are statistically significant at conventional levels.

FIGURE 3.4 A to F

Skills of post-secondary graduates

ALL skills-education profiles for persons aged 16 to 35 who have completed at least upper secondary education, adjusted for age and native language status, problem solving scale (United States[1] on combined prose and document scale), 2003

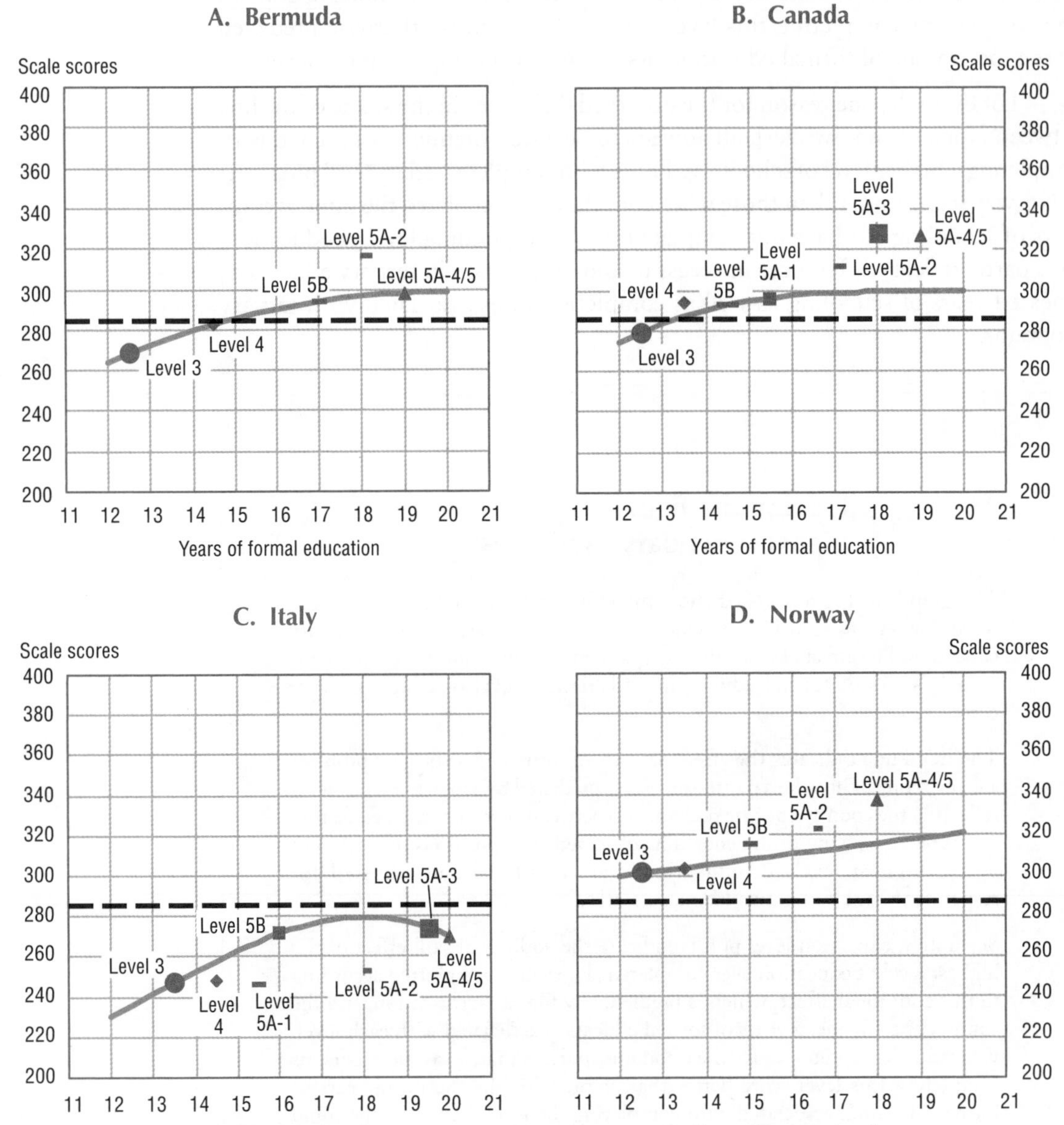

FIGURE 3.4 A to F (concluded)

Skills of post-secondary graduates

ALL skills-education profiles for persons aged 16 to 35 who have completed at least upper secondary education, adjusted for age and native language status, problem solving scale (United States[1] on combined prose and document scale), 2003

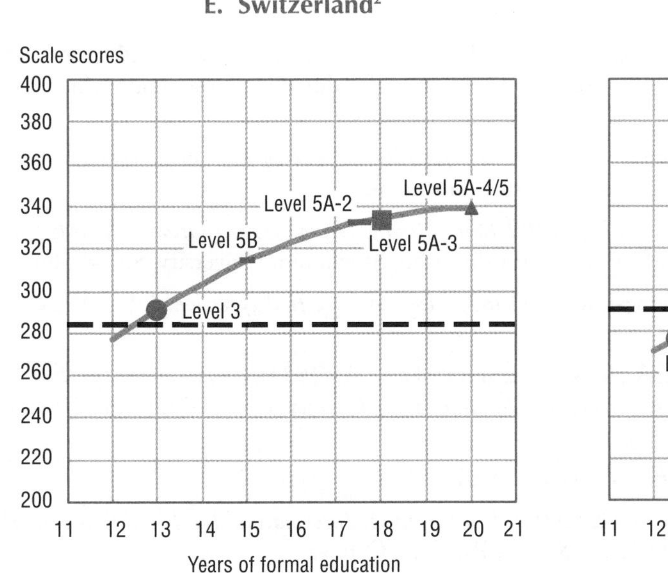

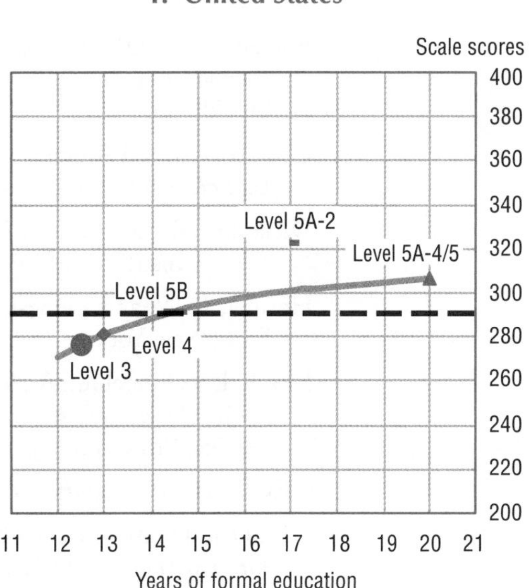

1. The skills scores for the United States are combined prose and document scale since they did not field the problem solving skills domain.
2. The problem solving skills scores for Switzerland apply to the German and French speaking communities only since they did not field the problem solving skills domain in the Italian speaking community.

Notes: The international mean is calculated for persons aged 16 to 35 who have completed at least upper secondary education.

Upper secondary completion is set as a reference group.

The international means years of formal education corresponding to upper secondary completion is 13 years.

The trend line reflects the observed relationship between years of formal education and problem solving skills, adjusting for completed levels of education, age and native language status.

Education level points are mapped according to the additional effect of having completed the level and the mean years of formal education for persons who completed this level. This is done within each country.

Education level points above the trend line indicate that on average persons completing this level perform better than is predicted by the mean years of formal education associated with completing the level.

Education level points on the trend line indicate that on average persons completing this level do not perform better than is predicted by the mean years of formal education associated with completing the level.

Education level points below the trend line indicate that on average persons completing this level perform less than is predicted by the mean years of formal education associated with completing the level.

Source: Adult Literacy and Life Skills Survey, 2003.

References

Boudard, E. (2001), *Literacy Proficiency, Earnings and Recurrent Training: A Ten Country Comparative Study,* Institute of International Education, Stockholm University, Stockholm.

Coombs, P.A. and Ahmed, M. (1974), *Attacking Rural Poverty: How Nonformal Education Can Help,* John Hopkins University, Baltimore.

Desjardins, R. (2004), *Learning for Well Being: Studies Using the International Adult Literacy Survey,* Institute of International Education, Stockholm University, Stockholm.

Hosmer, D.W. and Lemeshow, S. (1989), *Applied Logistic Regression,* John Wiley and Sons, New York.

Kirsch, I. S., Jungeblut, A., Jenkins, L. and Kolstad, A. (1993), *Adult Literacy in America: A First Look at the Results of the National Adult Literacy Survey,* Educational Testing Service, Princeton, NJ.

OECD (2003). *Education at a Glance.* Paris.

OECD and Statistics Canada (2000), *Literacy in the Information Age: Final Report on the International Adult Literacy Survey,* Paris and Ottawa.

Statistics Canada (2003), *Education Indicators in Canada,* Ottawa.

UNESCO (1997), *International Standard Classification of Education - 1997 version,* Paris.

Contributor

Richard Desjardins, *Statistics Canada*

Annex 3

Data Values for the Figures

3

TABLE 3.1 A

Mean numeracy scores on a scale with range 0 to 500 points, by level of educational attainment, populations aged 16 to 65, 2003

Level of educational attainment	5th percentile		25th percentile		Mean		75th percentile		95th percentile	
Bermuda										
Less than upper secondary	137.2	(8.8)	174.6	(4.7)	207.5	(3.0)	239.8	(5.6)	289.0	(9.8)
Upper secondary	170.1	(5.6)	222.3	(3.9)	253.5	(2.8)	284.5	(4.8)	337.5	(4.7)
Post-secondary, non-tertiary	193.9	(6.1)	238.0	(3.4)	270.1	(2.3)	302.1	(3.3)	348.9	(5.0)
Tertiary type B or higher	224.8	(7.9)	277.8	(2.3)	307.6	(1.5)	339.9	(1.6)	380.9	(5.4)
Canada										
Less than upper secondary	133.9	(4.5)	195.3	(3.2)	233.9	(1.6)	274.1	(2.5)	326.1	(5.7)
Upper secondary	180.9	(3.3)	237.5	(2.6)	268.6	(1.4)	302.9	(1.5)	346.4	(3.5)
Post-secondary, non-tertiary	196.1	(5.4)	241.9	(2.5)	271.6	(2.1)	303.4	(3.9)	343.0	(2.7)
Tertiary type B or higher	211.9	(4.0)	267.9	(2.0)	297.9	(1.7)	332.1	(2.3)	372.4	(3.3)
Italy										
Less than upper secondary	134.7	(3.0)	183.6	(2.6)	213.7	(1.8)	245.2	(1.7)	287.5	(2.5)
Upper secondary	177.8	(6.2)	223.2	(2.8)	252.5	(1.8)	282.6	(2.2)	324.5	(2.3)
Post-secondary, non-tertiary	179.2	(7.9)	218.2	(8.9)	245.6	(5.1)	274.7	(6.8)	312.0	(73.6)
Tertiary type B or higher	195.2	(6.9)	238.9	(5.4)	270.7	(3.4)	301.4	(4.6)	343.2	(8.8)
Norway										
Less than upper secondary	171.1	(5.6)	219.6	(3.5)	250.5	(1.9)	282.3	(2.6)	326.2	(3.3)
Upper secondary	208.9	(5.3)	254.5	(2.6)	281.8	(1.5)	309.7	(1.9)	349.4	(4.0)
Post-secondary, non-tertiary	215.9	(6.0)	259.8	(1.9)	284.1	(2.4)	311.1	(3.6)	345.0	(7.7)
Tertiary type B or higher	240.8	(3.0)	286.3	(1.5)	310.8	(1.1)	338.5	(1.0)	374.2	(2.6)
Switzerland										
Less than upper secondary	184.5	(8.9)	231.2	(3.2)	261.8	(3.2)	290.3	(5.5)	340.8	(11.2)
Upper secondary	215.9	(3.4)	258.4	(2.3)	288.2	(1.5)	317.7	(2.8)	362.9	(4.4)
Post-secondary, non-tertiary	...	...	...	...	...	...	...	...	...	...
Tertiary type B or higher	245.9	(5.2)	285.1	(3.0)	315.6	(1.9)	345.9	(2.6)	384.4	(5.8)
United States										
Less than upper secondary	127.1	(4.6)	176.9	(2.9)	215.0	(2.6)	251.7	(2.8)	307.8	(7.2)
Upper secondary	173.0	(3.5)	222.2	(2.1)	255.0	(1.9)	289.0	(2.1)	335.0	(4.0)
Post-secondary, non-tertiary	162.9	(14.9)	213.1	(10.3)	244.4	(4.4)	278.6	(4.7)	319.2	(5.7)
Tertiary type B or higher	217.0	(7.1)	268.3	(3.3)	297.8	(2.6)	329.7	(3.1)	367.9	(3.9)

... Not applicable

Source: Adult Literacy and Life Skills Survey, 2003.

TABLE 3.1 B

Mean problem solving[1] scores on a scale with range 0 to 500 points, by level of educational attainment, populations aged 16 to 65, 2003

Level of educational attainment	5th percentile		25th percentile		Mean		75th percentile		95th percentile	
Bermuda										
Less than upper secondary	133.0	(11.7)	185.7	(3.5)	215.5	(3.0)	247.8	(4.7)	294.2	(8.0)
Upper secondary	176.0	(5.2)	224.4	(4.7)	256.6	(2.9)	290.8	(3.2)	335.4	(6.2)
Post-secondary, non-tertiary	199.2	(6.5)	248.7	(4.4)	279.0	(2.6)	310.2	(3.7)	355.9	(5.3)
Tertiary type B or higher	228.7	(5.4)	274.7	(2.7)	302.9	(1.8)	332.9	(2.8)	372.7	(5.9)
Canada										
Less than upper secondary	140.3	(6.0)	203.3	(2.8)	237.6	(1.7)	275.8	(1.9)	319.5	(3.9)
Upper secondary	189.5	(4.4)	245.4	(1.9)	273.7	(1.8)	306.1	(2.0)	346.2	(3.7)
Post-secondary, non-tertiary	205.5	(5.9)	253.7	(2.4)	279.8	(2.4)	308.6	(4.0)	348.2	(6.3)
Tertiary type B or higher	213.2	(4.9)	264.8	(2.4)	293.2	(1.5)	324.5	(1.7)	364.9	(2.6)
Italy										
Less than upper secondary	117.8	(5.2)	167.4	(2.7)	203.7	(2.1)	238.4	(2.5)	291.9	(3.0)
Upper secondary	163.7	(4.2)	213.4	(2.9)	248.0	(1.8)	283.7	(2.4)	334.2	(3.6)
Post-secondary, non-tertiary	163.2	(12.8)	207.5	(11.4)	242.3	(6.1)	273.0	(7.7)	328.6	(15.9)
Tertiary type B or higher	160.5	(14.9)	218.1	(6.1)	252.9	(5.3)	289.5	(6.4)	337.9	(7.2)
Norway										
Less than upper secondary	154.4	(12.0)	213.5	(4.4)	247.0	(2.7)	284.8	(3.4)	330.3	(2.9)
Upper secondary	207.6	(4.4)	255.3	(3.4)	285.0	(2.2)	316.7	(2.1)	356.1	(2.5)
Post-secondary, non-tertiary	213.0	(7.0)	258.3	(5.3)	283.7	(4.2)	311.0	(4.9)	350.4	(8.0)
Tertiary type B or higher	230.2	(5.8)	282.2	(1.3)	306.6	(1.1)	335.2	(1.4)	371.2	(2.0)
Switzerland[2]										
Less than upper secondary	176.2	(18.0)	226.4	(7.9)	257.9	(3.4)	292.3	(4.4)	340.3	(10.4)
Upper secondary	196.1	(5.3)	244.1	(2.8)	277.6	(1.7)	311.1	(1.9)	358.8	(3.8)
Post-secondary, non-tertiary	...	...	...	...	...	...	...	...	...	...
Tertiary type B or higher	223.1	(4.3)	268.9	(3.0)	298.5	(2.1)	327.9	(2.9)	374.8	(10.3)

... Not applicable

1. United States did not field the problem solving skills domain.
2. The problem solving skills scores for Switzerland apply to the German and French speaking communities only since they did not field the problem solving skills domain in the Italian speaking community.

Source: Adult Literacy and Life Skills Survey, 2003.

TABLE 3.2 A

Mean combined prose and document scores on a scale with range 0 to 500 points, by level of educational attainment, populations aged 26 to 35, 2003

Level of educational attainment	5th percentile		25th percentile		Mean		75th percentile		95th percentile	
Bermuda										
Less than upper secondary	164.5 [1]	(8.0)	191.5 [1]	(14.5)	226.5 [1]	(11.0)	265.0 [1]	(16.7)	295.5 [1]	(70.9)
Upper secondary	209.1	(14.1)	253.9	(9.2)	278.5	(4.4)	302.7	(7.6)	340.9	(16.7)
Post-secondary, non-tertiary	215.5	(13.0)	254.2	(4.8)	285.4	(4.2)	313.6	(6.6)	357.9	(8.3)
Tertiary type B or higher	257.1	(8.3)	303.7	(4.3)	328.3	(3.5)	356.8	(5.7)	388.2	(10.6)
Canada										
Less than upper secondary	152.8	(13.1)	222.1	(9.3)	252.8	(4.3)	288.8	(5.3)	326.8	(8.6)
Upper secondary	187.8	(9.8)	249.2	(5.2)	277.5	(2.9)	311.5	(3.8)	346.2	(7.9)
Post-secondary, non-tertiary	219.1	(11.1)	269.8	(5.9)	297.9	(4.9)	329.4	(5.7)	369.5	(85.9)
Tertiary type B or higher	235.7	(5.6)	283.1	(4.6)	309.6	(2.6)	338.7	(4.4)	373.5	(5.5)
Italy										
Less than upper secondary	130.2	(7.8)	185.0	(5.1)	216.4	(3.3)	250.6	(3.9)	297.8	(7.1)
Upper secondary	174.8	(5.8)	220.0	(3.5)	251.4	(3.0)	284.7	(5.0)	327.4	(5.2)
Post-secondary, non-tertiary	183.6	(9.4)	213.9	(16.6)	250.2	(9.4)	285.3	(23.2)	335.2	(74.5)
Tertiary type B or higher	198.5	(6.3)	230.1	(13.6)	269.9	(5.2)	305.4	(10.5)	345.0	(9.6)
Norway										
Less than upper secondary	180.2	(24.1)	236.6	(8.8)	266.4	(6.1)	302.2	(10.7)	333.9	(73.8)
Upper secondary	229.4	(10.2)	273.4	(4.2)	296.9	(2.9)	324.5	(4.8)	356.9	(6.4)
Post-secondary, non-tertiary	243.1	(5.9)	268.8	(7.5)	294.2	(4.0)	315.6	(4.3)	354.0	(10.8)
Tertiary type B or higher	258.6	(9.1)	305.4	(2.7)	325.0	(1.7)	350.7	(2.0)	378.2	(3.6)
Switzerland										
Less than upper secondary	169.5	(14.4)	216.7	(14.8)	242.1	(7.5)	266.4	(8.9)	301.5	(68.1)
Upper secondary	205.3	(10.7)	248.2	(4.4)	274.2	(2.9)	303.0	(3.2)	336.1	(4.3)
Post-secondary, non-tertiary	...	...	...	...	...	...	...	...	...	...
Tertiary type B or higher	241.5	(11.9)	283.6	(4.7)	308.8	(3.6)	336.3	(6.4)	369.6	(7.0)
United States										
Less than upper secondary	124.8	(10.7)	176.3	(8.9)	211.0	(5.0)	244.5	(7.7)	292.4	(12.4)
Upper secondary	194.0	(9.9)	242.2	(3.8)	268.5	(2.9)	297.9	(3.3)	337.8	(5.1)
Post-secondary, non-tertiary	198.1	(24.0)	248.4	(11.9)	268.0	(7.2)	292.1	(6.4)	328.2	(18.7)
Tertiary type B or higher	230.7	(9.5)	278.3	(6.0)	304.4	(3.6)	331.7	(6.8)	371.3	(8.4)

... Not applicable

1. Unreliable estimate.

Source: Adult Literacy and Life Skills Survey, 2003.

TABLE 3.2 B

Mean combined prose and document scores on a scale with range 0 to 500 points, by level of educational attainment, populations aged 56 to 65, 2003

Level of educational attainment	5th percentile		25th percentile		Mean		75th percentile		95th percentile	
Bermuda										
Less than upper secondary	146.3	(14.7)	184.6	(6.2)	219.6	(5.7)	253.2	(6.8)	301.2	(69.0)
Upper secondary	157.1	(20.2)	217.3	(10.2)	249.4	(5.6)	282.7	(8.0)	324.0	(14.1)
Post-secondary, non-tertiary	180.0	(15.4)	239.2	(11.0)	270.5	(6.7)	303.6	(7.6)	342.1	(19.9)
Tertiary type B or higher	234.1	(33.4)	283.3	(12.8)	307.7	(5.3)	335.7	(8.5)	369.7	(85.1)
Canada										
Less than upper secondary	122.9	(4.5)	176.8	(7.3)	216.1	(3.3)	255.9	(3.9)	300.5	(6.1)
Upper secondary	180.3	(9.4)	239.6	(5.2)	266.6	(2.7)	298.9	(4.1)	334.9	(6.7)
Post-secondary, non-tertiary	171.5	(37.7)	231.2	(4.2)	262.6	(5.5)	299.2	(4.6)	337.1	(6.2)
Tertiary type B or higher	196.3	(16.7)	260.7	(5.2)	287.7	(2.4)	320.1	(3.1)	360.1	(6.2)
Italy										
Less than upper secondary	98.6	(4.3)	153.4	(4.6)	188.0	(2.5)	222.1	(3.5)	268.7	(6.9)
Upper secondary	145.4	(13.1)	204.1	(10.7)	232.7	(6.2)	267.9	(8.3)	303.4	(12.0)
Post-secondary, non-tertiary	139.1	(10.3)	184.9	(31.9)	225.4	(21.6)	265.0	(15.0)	304.2	(74.6)
Tertiary type B or higher	175.6	(14.2)	215.1	(8.6)	251.9	(6.9)	284.7	(9.0)	330.8	(10.2)
Norway										
Less than upper secondary	156.0	(7.8)	205.7	(6.6)	236.2	(4.5)	267.4	(7.2)	317.0	(8.6)
Upper secondary	208.1	(14.7)	246.0	(6.6)	267.5	(3.7)	292.1	(5.3)	326.4	(9.9)
Post-secondary, non-tertiary	219.5	(13.3)	255.0	(12.4)	276.5	(7.5)	305.0	(11.1)	335.5	(78.9)
Tertiary type B or higher	229.5	(15.4)	273.4	(5.6)	298.2	(3.0)	327.2	(3.6)	356.1	(5.4)
Switzerland										
Less than upper secondary	157.0	(22.7)	201.4	(12.1)	229.8	(7.3)	253.9	(9.0)	301.3	(64.9)
Upper secondary	192.7	(8.6)	235.1	(3.2)	257.8	(3.0)	282.7	(5.8)	321.2	(5.4)
Post-secondary, non-tertiary	...	...	...	...	...	...	...	...	...	...
Tertiary type B or higher	223.4	(13.7)	261.7	(6.7)	283.7	(4.8)	306.0	(5.6)	350.9	(78.5)
United States										
Less than upper secondary	122.2	(20.0)	177.7	(10.9)	210.7	(5.9)	245.4	(9.3)	277.6	(16.1)
Upper secondary	184.0	(18.1)	227.0	(4.6)	255.3	(4.1)	286.3	(5.9)	328.0	(11.2)
Post-secondary, non-tertiary	161.3[1]	(28.0)	220.9[1]	(22.1)	245.5[1]	(13.2)	277.2[1]	(22.9)	304.0[1]	(71.5)
Tertiary type B or higher	227.2	(13.4)	269.6	(6.6)	294.6	(3.3)	321.3	(4.3)	354.2	(9.1)

... Not applicable

1. Unreliable estimate.

Source: Adult Literacy and Life Skills Survey, 2003.

TABLE 3.3 A

Odds of scoring at Levels 1 or 2 on the problem solving[1] scale by upper secondary education status, adjusted for age and native language status, persons aged 16 to 30, 2003

	Less than upper secondary, not in school		Less than upper secondary, still in school		Completed upper secondary, not in school		Completed upper secondary, still in school		Completed higher than upper secondary
Canada	6.77***	(0.33)	3.73***	(0.27)	2.84***	(0.18)	1.19	(0.17)	1.00
Italy	6.08**	(0.79)	1.38	(0.58)	1.58	(0.47)	0.53	(0.41)	1.00
Norway	4.51***	(0.27)	2.67*	(0.45)	1.83**	(0.24)	0.75	(0.25)	1.00
Switzerland[2]	7.33***	(0.60)	3.43**	(0.54)	2.75**	(0.36)	0.97	(0.39)	1.00

TABLE 3.3 B

Odds of scoring at Levels 1 or 2 on the numeracy scale by upper secondary education status, adjusted for age and native language status, persons aged 16 to 30, 2003

	Less than upper secondary, not in school		Less than upper secondary, still in school		Completed upper secondary, not in school		Completed upper secondary, still in school		Completed higher than upper secondary
Canada	5.29***	(0.25)	3.30***	(0.22)	2.94***	(0.19)	1.38*	(0.16)	1.00
Italy	9.04***	(0.39)	1.73	(0.59)	1.98*	(0.32)	1.02	(0.37)	1.00
Norway	4.58***	(0.31)	2.97***	(0.35)	2.13***	(0.22)	1.01	(0.29)	1.00
Switzerland	19.94***	(0.74)	5.73*	(0.82)	5.78**	(0.60)	1.18	(0.60)	1.00
United States	26.03***	(0.37)	4.46***	(0.34)	6.93***	(0.23)	1.98**	(0.32)	1.00

* $p<0.10$, statistically significant at the 10 per cent level

** $p<0.05$, statistically significant at the 5 per cent level

*** $p<0.01$, statistically significant at the 1 per cent level

1. United States did not field the problem solving skills domain.
2. The problem solving skills scores for Switzerland apply to the German and French speaking communities only since they did not field the problem solving skills domain in the Italian speaking community.

Notes: Data for Bermuda are not reported due to low sample sizes for this indicator.
See Box 3A in text for further information on odds ratios.
Odds ratios are adjusted for the age and native language status.
Standard errors are of the logarithm of the odds ratios.

Source: Adult Literacy and Life Skills Survey, 2003.

TABLE 3.4

ALL skills-education profiles for persons aged 16 to 35 who have completed at least upper secondary education, adjusted for age and native language status, problem solving scale (United States[1] on combined prose and document scale), 2003

	Unstandardized coefficients			
	B	Standard error	t-value	Significance
A. Bermuda				
(Constant)	-0.25	0.05	-4.95	0.00
Years of education (13 years = 0)				
Linear	0.16	0.03	5.42	0.00
Quadratic	-0.12	0.05	-2.43	0.01
Cubic	--	--	--	--
Highest level of education completed (Level 3 upper secondary = 0)				
Level 4 post-secondary, non-tertiary	--	--	--	--
Level 5B tertiary	--	--	--	--
Level 5A tertiary, Intermediate	--	--	--	--
Level 5A tertiary, First degree, 3 to 5 years	0.42	0.09	4.62	0.00
Level 5A tertiary, First degree, 5+ years	--	--	--	--
Level 5A/6 tertiary, Second or higher degree	--	--	--	--
Test language (Same as mother tongue = 0)	-0.20	0.10	-1.96	0.06
Age (25 years = 0)				
Linear	0.03	0.02	1.50	0.10
Quadratic	--	--	--	--
Cubic	0.00	0.00	--	0.07
B. Canada				
(Constant)	-0.02	0.04	-0.49	0.60
Years of education (13 years = 0)				
Linear	0.17	0.02	8.46	0.00
Quadratic	-0.28	0.08	-3.56	0.00
Cubic	0.02	0.01	1.58	0.02
Highest level of education completed (Level 3 upper secondary = 0)				
Level 4 post-secondary, non-tertiary	0.15	0.05	2.98	0.01
Level 5B tertiary	0.07	0.08	0.89	0.36
Level 5A tertiary, Intermediate	--	--	--	--
Level 5A tertiary, First degree, 3 to 5 years	0.28	0.10	2.81	0.01
Level 5A tertiary, First degree, 5+ years	0.61	0.15	4.07	0.00
Level 5A/6 tertiary, Second or higher degree	0.57	0.17	3.34	0.00
Test language (Same as mother tongue = 0)	-0.56	0.04	-14.00	0.00
Age (25 years = 0)				
Linear	-0.02	0.01	-1.62	0.07
Quadratic	0.04	0.01	3.89	0.00
Cubic	0.00	0.00	--	0.15

TABLE 3.4 (continued)

ALL skills-education profiles for persons aged 16 to 35 who have completed at least upper secondary education, adjusted for age and native language status, problem solving scale (United States[1] on combined prose and document scale), 2003

	Unstandardized coefficients			
	B	Standard error	t-value	Significance
C. Italy				
(Constant)	-0.89	0.09	-9.93	0.00
Years of education (13 years = 0)				
Linear	0.24	0.04	5.91	0.00
Quadratic	--	--	--	--
Cubic	-0.03	0.01	-3.08	0.02
Highest level of education completed (Level 3 upper secondary = 0)				
Level 4 post-secondary, non-tertiary	-0.21	0.12	-1.78	0.09
Level 5B tertiary	--	--	--	--
Level 5A tertiary, Intermediate	-0.44	0.23	-1.91	0.07
Level 5A tertiary, First degree, 3 to 5 years	-0.56	0.12	-4.70	0.00
Level 5A tertiary, First degree, 5+ years	--	--	--	--
Level 5A/6 tertiary, Second or higher degree	0.86	0.71	1.21	0.24
Test language (Same as mother tongue = 0)	--	--	--	--
Age (25 years = 0)				
Linear	--	--	--	--
Quadratic	0.06	0.03	1.85	0.09
Cubic	0.00	0.00	--	0.18
D. Norway				
(Constant)	0.38	0.03	12.62	0.00
Years of education (13 years = 0)				
Linear	0.06	0.02	2.80	0.00
Quadratic	--	--	--	--
Cubic	--	--	--	--
Highest level of education completed (Level 3 upper secondary = 0)				
Level 4 post-secondary, non-tertiary	--	--	--	--
Level 5B tertiary	0.17	0.08	2.08	0.05
Level 5A tertiary, Intermediate	--	--	--	--
Level 5A tertiary, First degree, 3 to 5 years	0.24	0.08	3.01	0.00
Level 5A tertiary, First degree, 5+ years	--	--	--	--
Level 5A/6 tertiary, Second or higher degree	0.45	0.11	4.08	0.00
Test language (Same as mother tongue = 0)	-0.43	0.08	-5.41	0.00
Age (25 years = 0)				
Linear	-0.03	0.01	-3.15	0.01
Quadratic	-0.03	0.01	-2.50	0.01
Cubic	0.00	0.00	--	0.05

TABLE 3.4 (concluded)

ALL skills-education profiles for persons aged 16 to 35 who have completed at least upper secondary education, adjusted for age and native language status, problem solving scale (United States[1] on combined prose and document scale), 2003

	Unstandardized coefficients			
	B	Standard error	t-value	Significance
E. Switzerland[2]				
(Constant)	0.15	0.07	2.15	0.04
Years of education (13 years = 0)				
Linear	0.28	0.03	9.20	0.00
Quadratic	-0.19	0.06	-3.19	0.00
Cubic	--	--	--	--
Highest level of education completed (Level 3 upper secondary = 0)				
Level 4 post-secondary, non-tertiary	--	--	--	--
Level 5B tertiary	--	--	--	--
Level 5A tertiary, Intermediate	--	--	--	--
Level 5A tertiary, First degree, 3 to 5 years	--	--	--	--
Level 5A tertiary, First degree, 5+ years	--	--	--	--
Level 5A/6 tertiary, Second or higher degree	--	--	--	--
Test language (Same as mother tongue = 0)	-0.26	0.17	-1.51	0.15
Age (25 years = 0)				
Linear	-0.04	0.01	-4.10	0.00
Quadratic	--	--	--	--
Cubic	--	--	--	--
F. United States				
(Constant)	-0.16	0.04	-4.09	0.00
Years of education (13 years = 0)				
Linear	0.20	0.03	6.54	0.00
Quadratic	-0.29	0.09	-3.20	0.00
Cubic	0.02	0.01	1.75	0.02
Highest level of education completed (Level 3 upper secondary = 0)				
Level 4 post-secondary, non-tertiary	--	--	--	--
Level 5B tertiary	--	--	--	--
Level 5A tertiary, Intermediate	--	--	--	--
Level 5A tertiary, First degree, 3 to 5 years	0.49	0.09	5.40	0.00
Level 5A tertiary, First degree, 5+ years	--	--	--	--
Level 5A/6 tertiary, Second or higher degree	0.66	0.62	1.07	0.29
Test language (Same as mother tongue = 0)	-0.82	0.11	-7.49	0.00
Age (25 years = 0)				
Linear	-0.02	0.00		0.00
Quadratic	--	--	--	--
Cubic	--	--	--	--

-- Estimate was not statistically different from zero at the five per cent level of significance in the first step of the analysis. Hence this parameter was not estimated in the country specific model.

1. The skills scores for the United States are combined prose and document scale since they did not field the problem solving skills domain.
2. The problem solving skills scores for Switzerland apply to the German and French speaking communities only since they did not field the problem solving skills domain in the Italian speaking community.

Source: Adult Literacy and Life Skills Survey, 2003.

Chapter 4

Skills and Adult Learning

4

Summary

This chapter embraces an expanded understanding of adult learning by examining participation in organised forms of adult education and training as well as engagement in informal learning. Findings on adult education and training participation for ALL are presented and compared, where possible, to the results from IALS. Thus one can assess whether the increased importance given to adult learning by policy makers, the business community and other sectors of society has translated into increased readiness by adults to actively engage in various forms of learning. This is followed by an analysis of some key characteristics of participating adults, and whether these have changed in the intervening years. This permits an assessment of whether inequalities in adult learning patterns are shifting. Next, patterns of informal learning are compared, and in particular, an analysis of active versus passive modes of informal learning is presented. Finally, the role of employers, governments and individuals in financially supporting adult learning is considered.

Table of Contents

Skills and Adult Learning

4

4.1 Overview and highlights

This chapter embraces an expanded understanding of adult learning by examining participation in organised forms of adult education and training as well as engagement in informal learning. Findings on adult education and training participation for ALL are presented and compared, where possible, to the results from IALS. Thus one can assess whether the increased importance given to adult learning by policy makers, the business community and other sectors of society has translated into increased readiness by adults to actively engage in various forms of learning. This is followed by an analysis of some key characteristics of participating adults, and whether these have changed in the intervening years. This permits an assessment of whether inequalities in adult learning patterns are shifting. Next, patterns of informal learning are compared, and in particular, an analysis of active versus passive modes of informal learning is presented. Finally, the role of employers, governments and individuals in financially supporting adult learning is considered.

The analysis on adult learning presented in this chapter offers some interesting and clear messages, including:

- There is a broad and growing acceptance of the principles of lifelong learning in most countries, as evidenced by a marked increase in the rate of participation in adult education and training between the IALS and ALL survey periods.
- A large proportion of adults with poor foundation skills are still not being reached by organized forms of adult education and training. But there are significant differences in participation patterns among countries, which suggest that differences in adult learning policy do matter.
- Engagement in passive modes of informal learning is an almost universal activity while active modes of adult learning, although frequent, are more unequally distributed both within and between

country populations. This suggests that there are important factors contributing to certain forms of informal learning. In particular, levels of formal education and adult skills of the type measured in ALL are strongly related to the extent of active engagement in informal learning.

- Employer financing plays a central role in supporting opportunities to engage in lifelong learning in all countries but countries differ markedly in the share of the total adult learning effort which is employer supported. Furthermore, the levels of worker engagement in literacy and numeracy practices on the job are strongly associated with the likelihood of benefiting from employer-sponsored adult education and training.

4.2 Participation in organised forms of adult education and training[1]

Over the last decade, adult learning has progressed from being a form of policy rhetoric promoted by intergovernmental organisations to a central issue in national policies on education, economy and welfare. In 1996, the OECD conference of ministers of education proposed that member countries adopt the policy of "making lifelong learning a reality for all" and to make it a priority for the ensuing five year period (OECD, 1996). A similar policy was promoted by the European Commission in 2000 when it confirmed lifelong learning as a basic component of the European social model. This is reflected among others in the European employment strategy, the European social agenda, the skills and mobility action plan and the e-learning initiative. More recently, national policy documents are increasingly referring to concrete measures that promote a lifelong learning culture (see EU, 2001; OECD, 2003). Using the ALL and IALS data, this section examines the extent to which these policies have translated into increased participation in adult learning.

Like IALS, the ALL survey collected data on participation in adult education and training that are representative of populations aged 16 to 65 and comparable across countries. Figure 4.1 shows that, with the exception of Italy, the results reflect a broad acceptance of the principles of lifelong learning. Close to or over half of adult populations are enrolling in some form of organised adult education or training during the year preceding the interview. In Italy, however, less than 20 per cent participate in some form of organized adult education and training.

Figure 4.1 further distinguishes between participation in courses, programs or other forms of training (e.g., workshops). Apart from Italy, the rate of participation in programs varies little among countries – from a low of 16 per cent in Canada to a high of 20 per cent in Norway. Thus, disparities in overall country participation rates appear to be driven by the rate of participation in courses and other forms of training. Course participation varies from a low of about 21 per cent in the United States to a high of 40 per cent in Switzerland. Note that the relatively low rate of participation in courses in the United States may be related to the fact that Americans report a high rate of participation (17 per cent) in other forms of training (e.g., workshops).

FIGURE 4.1

Adult education and training participation rates

Per cent of populations aged 16 to 65 receiving adult education and training during the year preceding the interview, by type of participation, 2003

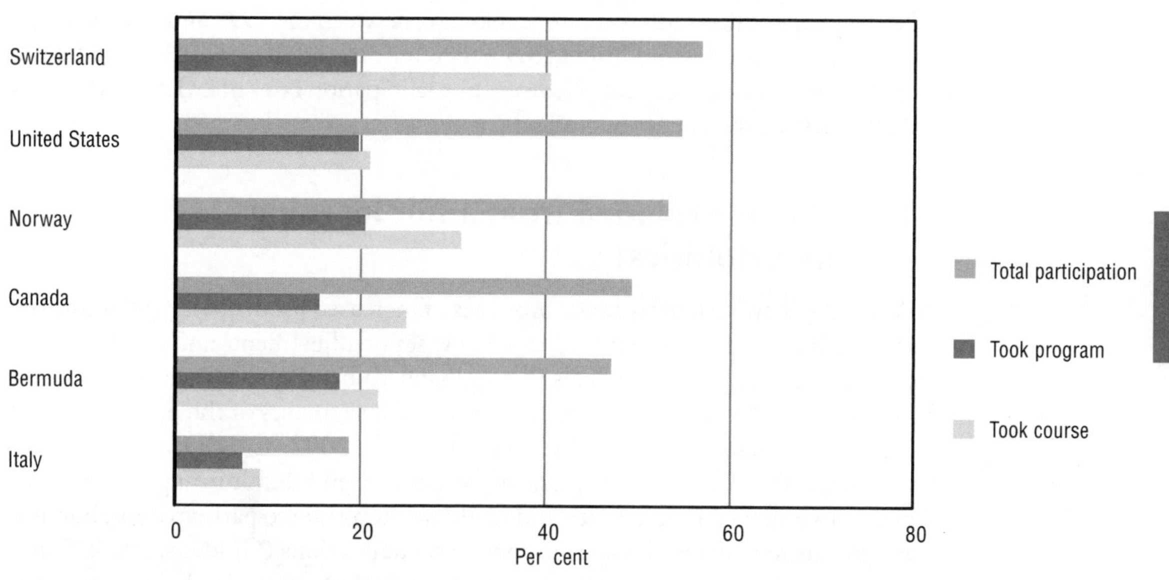

Countries are ranked by the total participation rate.

Source: Adult Literacy and Life Skills Survey, 2003.

FIGURE 4.2

Changes in adult education and training participation rates

Per cent of populations aged 16 to 65 receiving adult education and training during the year preceding the interview, IALS 1994/1998 and ALL 2003

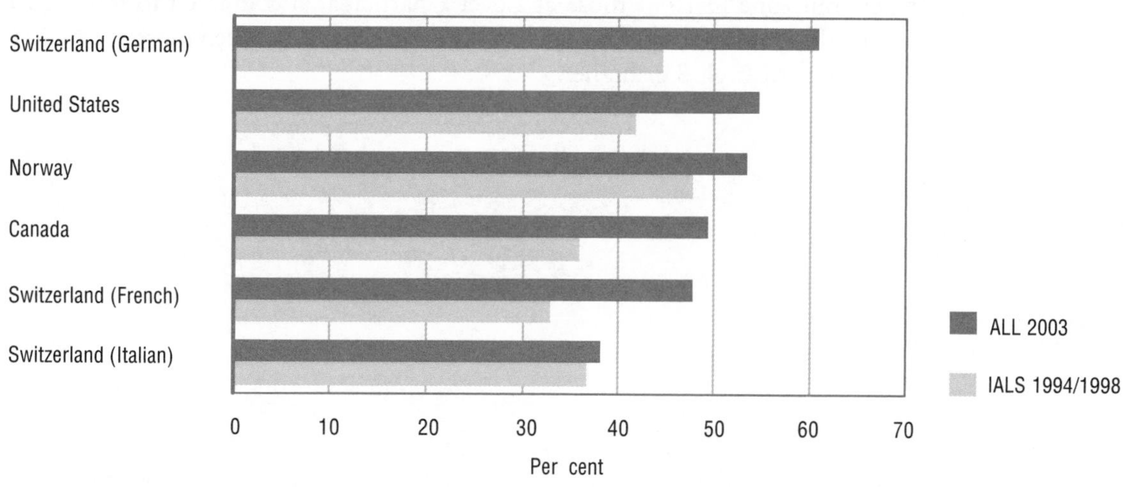

Countries are ranked by the per cent of respondents receiving adult education and training in ALL 2003.

Sources: Adult Literacy and Life Skills Survey, 2003.
International Adult Literacy Survey, 1994-1998.

It is encouraging to note that the increased importance awarded to adult learning in policy circles corresponds to sizeable increases in participation rates. Figure 4.2 compares participation rates derived from IALS[2] in 1994 (1998 in Norway) and ALL in 2003. In the German and French speaking populations of Switzerland, about 15 per cent more adults participated in some form of organized adult education and training in 2003 compared to 1994. Similarly, Canada and the United States had approximately 13 per cent more persons participating. Norway experienced a slower rate of increase, between the 1998 and 2003 surveys, which accounts for an additional 5.5 per cent of the adult population aged 16 to 65. This might be expected as Norwegian participation rates in IALS were among the highest of the countries studied.

4.3 Who is excluded from adult learning opportunities?

While the "new" economy holds promises of increased productivity and improved standards of living, it also introduces a new set of adjustments and challenges for society, industry and individuals (Gaskell and Rubenson, 2004). In particular, it may increase the exclusion or marginalisation of segments of the population and exacerbate socio-economic divisions (HRDC, 2002; OECD and Statistics Canada, 2000). Consequently, it is important to view adult learning not only as a means to enhance productivity and facilitate labour force participation, but also as a means to assist individuals in their everyday actions (Giddens, 1994: 7) and promote active citizenship (Esping-Andersen, 1996: 260). In this context, it is important to monitor how learning opportunities are distributed across different segments of the population, especially as the promotion of, and investment in, lifelong learning expands.

Adult literacy skills are critical for citizens to function in a learning society (Sen, 1982). Thus, it is particularly important to assess the extent of adult learning among those with limited literacy skills. Figure 4.3 presents participation in adult education and training by document literacy skills. Two findings stand out. First, in all countries there is a substantial difference between the participation rates of those with the lowest and highest levels of literacy. This is accentuated in Italy where only one in 10 of those at Level 1 participated compared to four in 10 among those at Level 4/5. Second, there is a sharp divide between those at Levels 1 and those at Levels 3 or higher.

FIGURE 4.3

Literacy and adult education participation

Per cent of population aged 16 to 65 receiving adult education and training during the year preceding the interview, by document literacy levels, 2003

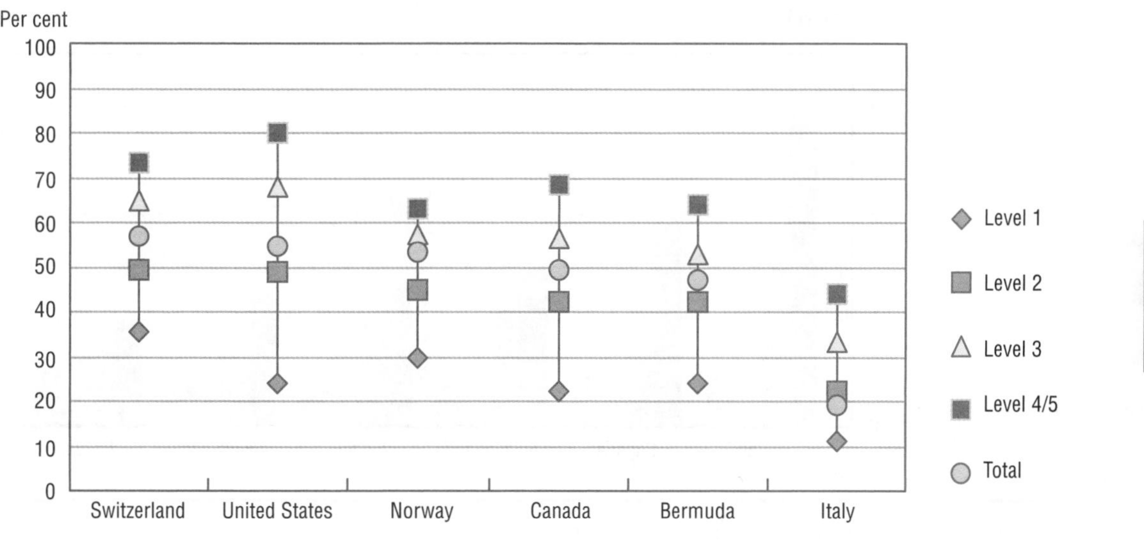

Countries are ranked by the total participation rate.

Source: Adult Literacy and Life Skills Survey, 2003.

Results in Figure 4.4 extend the analysis of the relationship between document literacy and participation in adult education and training using logistic regression analysis. This method makes it possible to obtain comparable estimates of inequalities even though the actual participation rates vary between countries (see Box 4A). Inequalities are expressed by differences in the likelihood of participating compared to adults scoring at Level 1, while controlling for education, gender and labour force participation. Findings show that Americans at document literacy Level 4/5 are about six times more likely to participate than those at Level 1. Comparable estimates are only two times in Norway. This confirms the existence of sharp differences in inequality between countries. Low inequality in Norway corresponds with a long tradition of adult education including popular adult education, as well as recent reforms that continue to aim efforts toward increasing participation among low skilled adults who are hard to reach (OECD, 2001).

While large differences remain between low and high skilled adults, it is worth noting that in some countries, the most vulnerable have benefited substantially. Figure 4.5 shows that in Norway, Switzerland (German and French speaking populations) and the United States, participation rates have increased more among those with the lowest level of literacy than any other levels. These results are consistent with overall improvements in the lower end of the skills distribution between the ALL and IALS survey period, as presented in Section 2.3.

FIGURE 4.4

Likelihood of participation by literacy levels

Adjusted odds ratios showing the likelihood of adults aged 16 to 65 receiving adult education and training during the year preceding the interview, by document literacy levels, 2003

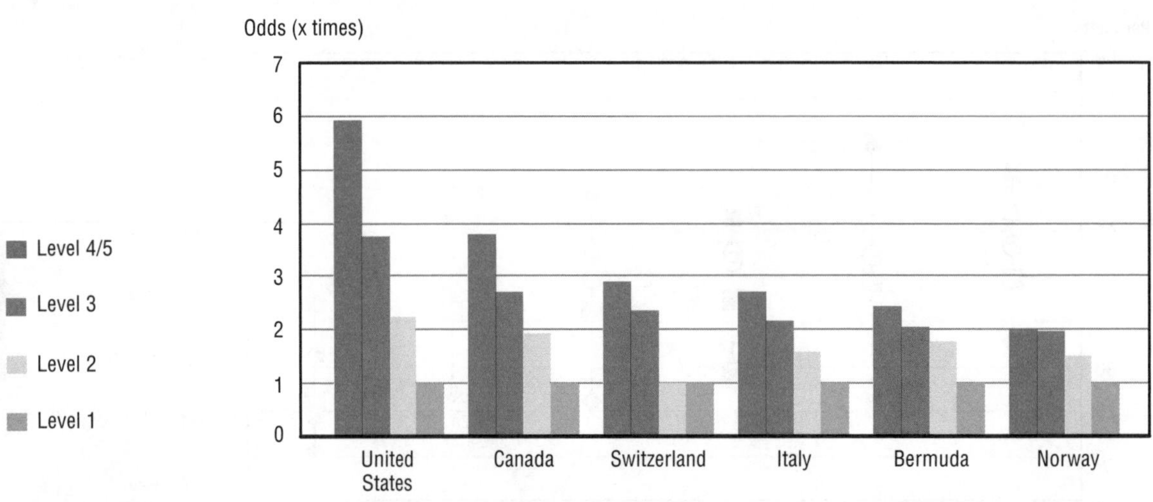

Countries are ranked according to the odds of persons who score at Level 4/5.

1. Odds estimates that are not statistically different from one at conventional levels of significance are reported as one in the figure. For the actual estimate and its corresponding significance, see Table 4.4 in the annex to this chapter.

Source: Adult Literacy and Life Skills Survey, 2003.

FIGURE 4.5

Changes in participation rates by literacy levels

Changes in the per cent of adults aged 16 to 65 in adult education and training between IALS 1994/1998 and ALL 2003, by document literacy levels

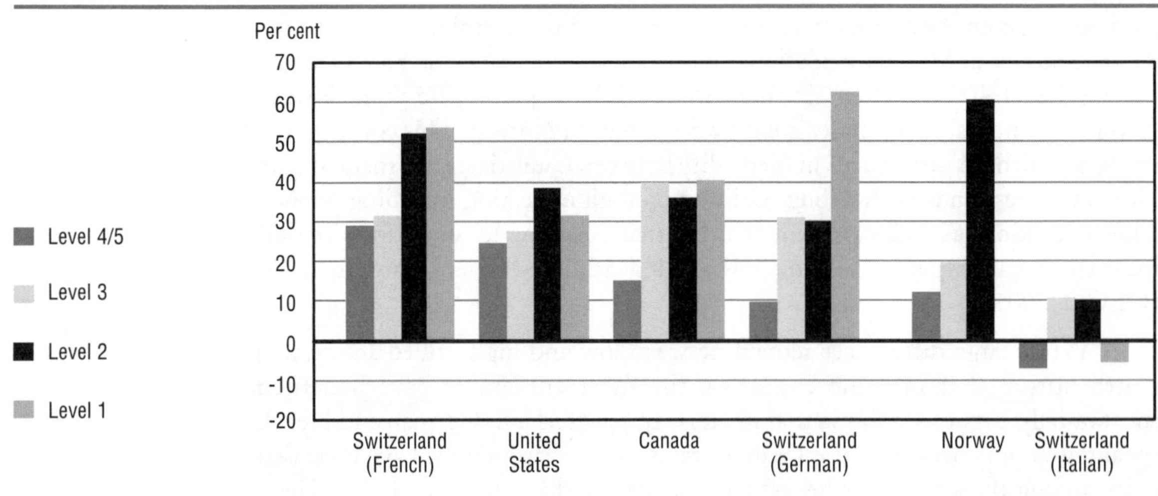

Countries are ranked by the change in the per cent at Level 4/5.

Note: Changes in participation rates are calculated by taking the difference between the ALL and the IALS rates and dividing by the average participation rates of the two periods, i.e., (ALL rate - IALS rate) / ((ALL rate +IALS rate)/2).

Source: Adult Literacy and Life Skills Survey, 2003.
International Adult Literacy Survey, 1994-1998.

Box 4A

Interpreting odds ratios in Figures 4.4 and 4.8

For the purpose of the analyses presented in Figures 4.4 and 4.8, the likelihood or odds of adults scoring at Level 1 was set at one for all countries. Thus, odds greater than one for persons at Levels 2, 3 and 4/5 indicate that those persons have increased chances compared to persons scoring at Level 1 of receiving adult education and training.

4.4 Patterns of informal learning[3]

According to the underlying philosophy of lifelong learning, participation is not limited to organised forms of adult education and training but also includes informal learning. Interestingly, studies have shown differing patterns of engagement in adult education and training compared to informal learning (e.g., Livingstone, 1999; Statistics Canada, 2001). It is well documented, for example, that opportunities and readiness to engage in organised forms of adult learning are unequally distributed across different segments of the population (see OECD, 1997; OECD 2003; and the previous section). In contrast, some studies suggest that conventional inequalities that exist among social or ethnic groups, or those with differing levels of educational attainment, may not apply to informal learning. This section explores this issue further by analyzing the informal learning data collected in the ALL survey.

As expected, results presented in Figure 4.6 confirm previous findings (see Livingstone, 1999), which suggest that informal learning is more or less a universal activity. Nearly 95 per cent of the population in five of six countries report that they engaged in some kind of informal learning activity over the cycle of one year. In Italy, however, engagement in activities of the type included in the ALL survey is less common, with fewer than 60 per cent reporting that they participated in some kind of informal learning activity.

Figure 4.6 also introduces the distinction between active and passive modes of informal learning, which reveals some interesting results. The former relates to activities such as learning by oneself, trying things out and learning by watching or getting help, while the latter refers to going on guided tours and learning by being sent to organizations. The results show that engagement in active modes remains frequent, particularly in Bermuda and Switzerland, but it is more variable among countries, with fewer than 40 per cent participating in Italy compared with nearly 80 per cent in Switzerland. Note that engagement in passive modes remains almost universal (i.e., over 90 per cent with the exception of Italy). These findings suggest that inequalities are more prevalent when active forms of informal learning are considered.

FIGURE 4.6

Engagement in informal learning

Per cent of populations aged 16 to 65 participating in informal learning activities during the year preceding the interview, by mode of engagement, 2003

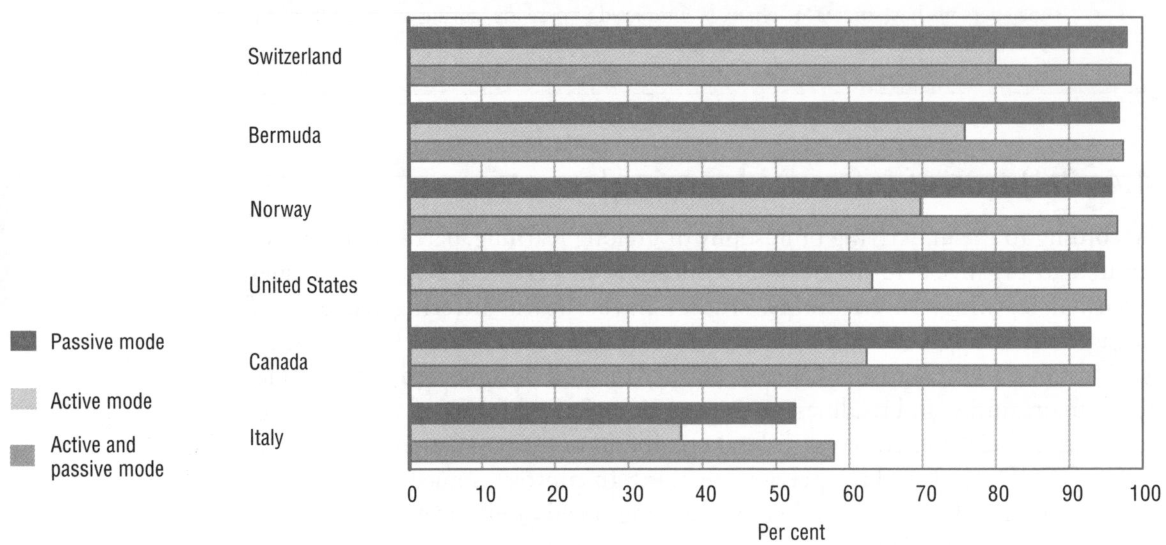

Countries are ranked by the active and passive mode.

Source: Adult Literacy and Life Skills Survey, 2003.

In general, the research literature suggests that well-educated adults benefit the most from organised forms of learning. Findings presented in Figure 4.7 show a similar pattern between educational attainment and participation in active modes of informal learning. In all of the countries, the rate of active engagement in informal learning increases sharply with rising levels of educational attainment. In the United States, only about 30 per cent of those who did not complete upper secondary education report that they engaged in active modes of informal learning compared to more than 80 per cent among those with a university education (tertiary type A or higher). Nevertheless, participation among those with the lowest levels of education is comparatively high in Bermuda, Norway and Switzerland (German and French speaking populations); with around 50 per cent reporting some engagement in active forms of informal learning.

Similarly, Figure 4.8 shows that the likelihood of engaging in active modes of informal learning is closely linked to adult skills, even after controlling for educational attainment, age, labour force participation and gender. Overall, adjusted odds increase markedly by level of skill. Adults scoring at the highest level in Italy and Switzerland are around four times more likely to engage in active modes of informal learning than those scoring at Level 1 on the document scale. In Canada, high skilled adults are nearly five times more likely to be active informal learners than low skilled adults.

FIGURE 4.7

Informal learning by level of education

Per cent of populations aged 16 to 65 participating in active modes of informal learning in the year preceding the interview, by educational attainment, 2003

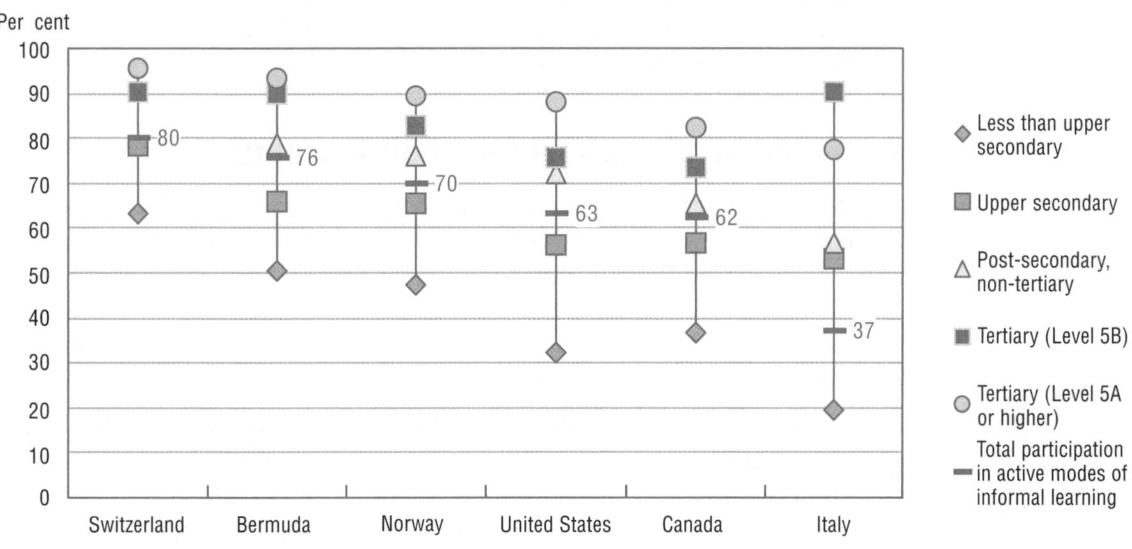

Source: Adult Literacy and Life Skills Survey, 2003.

FIGURE 4.8

Likelihood of participation in active modes of informal learning by literacy levels

Adjusted odds ratios[1] showing the likelihood of adults aged 16 to 65 participating in active modes of informal adult learning during the year preceding the interview, by document literacy levels, 2003

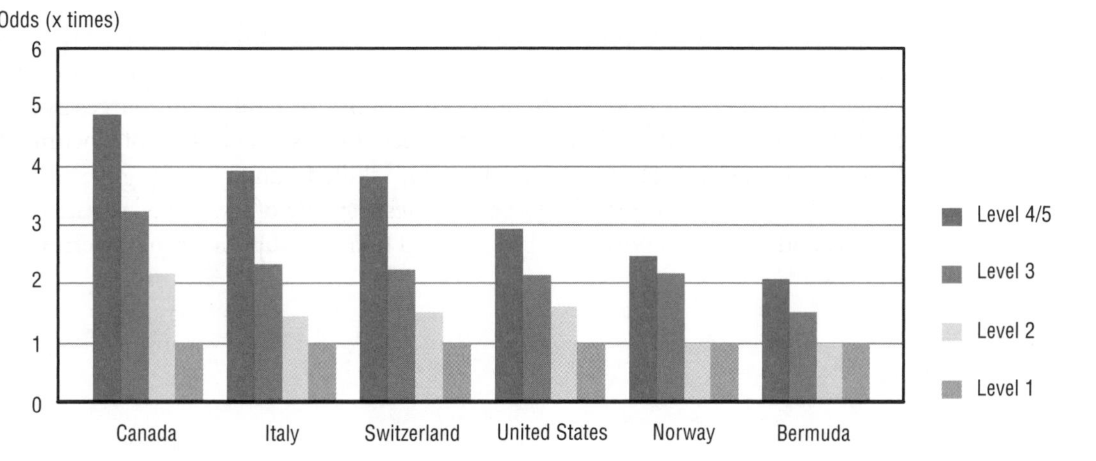

Countries are ranked according to the odds of persons who score at Level 4/5.

1. Odds estimates that are not statistically different from one at conventional levels of significance are reported as one in the figure. For the actual estimate and its corresponding significance, see Table 4.8 in the annex to this chapter.

Source: Adult Literacy and Life Skills Survey, 2003.

These findings suggest that initial formal education and foundation skills are major factors influencing active forms of informal learning, including learning by oneself, trying things out and learning by watching or getting help. It also implies that it may not be wise to rely on informal learning alone to substitute for low levels of initial education, or adult education and training. Merely learning in the course of daily life without some systematic prior reinforcement, such as formal education, may not be sufficient for gaining knowledge and skills. It is probably also more difficult to convert what is learned passively into economic and social value (Svensson, Ellström and Åberg, 2004).

4.5 Financial support for adult learning

Investing in adult learning is important for several reasons including, among others, to enhance productivity, facilitate participation in labour markets, promote active citizenship and democracy, and to assist individuals in their everyday actions. Accordingly, governments, firms and individuals alike have vested interests to financially support adult learning. This section examines the role of each in supporting organised forms of adult education and training.

Figure 4.9 confirms findings from IALS (OECD and HRDC, 1997) that show the important role of employers in providing financial support for adult education and training. This is most prevalent in Norway, where more than half of participating men as well as women receive financial support from their employers. Furthermore, employers are the most common source of financial support among men in Bermuda, Canada, Norway, Switzerland, and the United States, and among women in Norway and the United States. But compared to men, the data show that in all countries self or family financing is a more common source of financing for women.

Overall, direct financial support from government sources is less common. In Italy and Norway, governments are able to extend direct support to a larger number of participants compared to other countries, with over 13 per cent of all participants obtaining this type of financial support. In other countries, fewer than 10 per cent of participants are able to support their adult learning through direct government financing.

It is interesting to consider the extent to which government support reaches vulnerable groups such as those with low literacy skills. Figure 4.10 shows the proportion of persons who obtain financial support from different sources by low (Levels 1 and 2) and medium to high levels (Levels 3 and 4/5) of document literacy. Overall, a higher proportion of low skilled adults obtain government financial support. Nearly 16 and 11 per cent, respectively, of low skilled participants in Italy and Norway report that they received financial support from government sources.

FIGURE 4.9

Sources of financial support for adult education and training

A. Per cent of men participating in adult education and training who receive financial support from various sources, populations aged 16 to 65, 2003

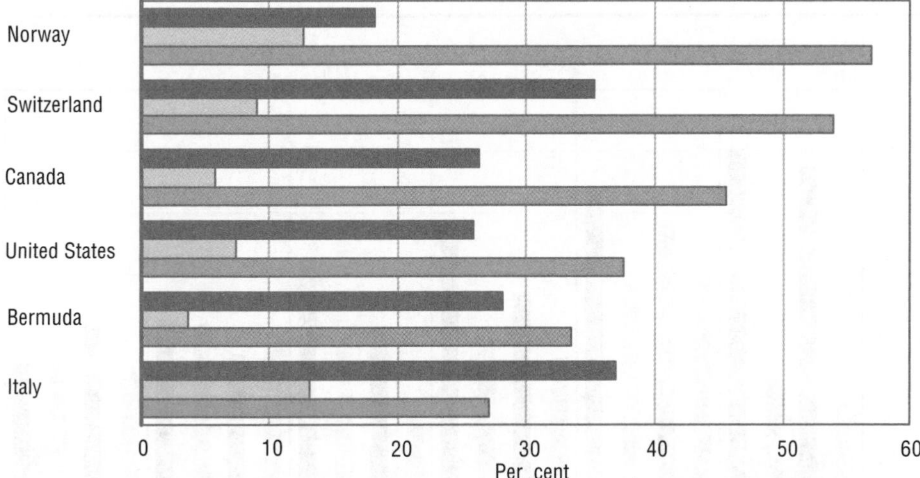

B. Per cent of women participating in adult education and training who receive financial support from various sources, populations aged 16 to 65, 2003

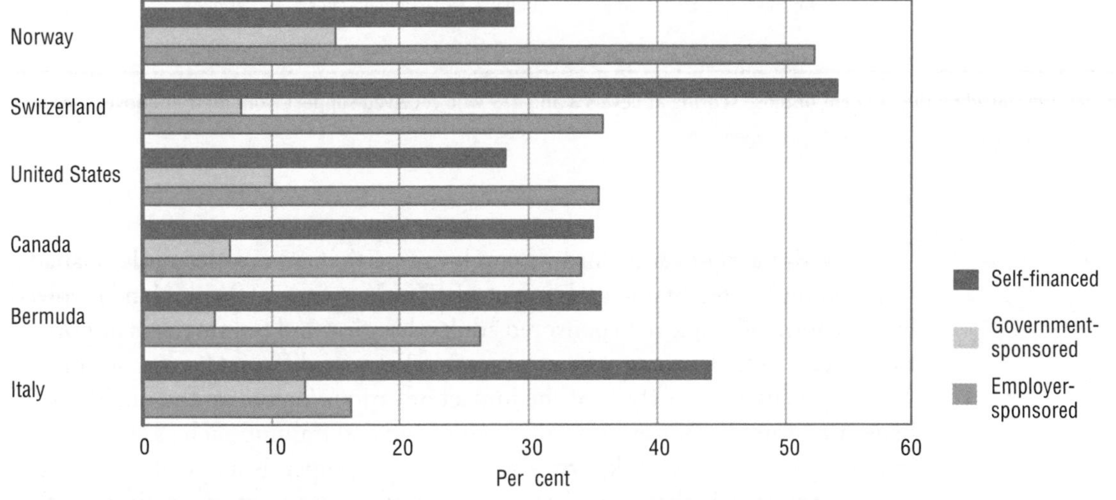

A. Countries are ranked by the per cent of men who received support from their employer.

B. Countries are ranked by the per cent of women who received support from their employer.

Source: Adult Literacy and Life Skills Survey, 2003.

Figure 4.10 also shows that in Bermuda, Italy, Norway and Switzerland, low skilled adults who participate in adult education and training are nearly as likely to receive employer financing than those who are more skilled. The differences are larger in Canada and the United States, where there are about 8 and 11 per cent more medium to high skilled participants who obtain employer financing. It is noteworthy that in Switzerland about 48 per cent, and in Norway more than 50 per cent of low skilled participants were able to secure financial support from their employers. Finally, in all countries it is slightly more common for medium to high skilled participants to draw on self or family sources of financing.

FIGURE 4.10

Sources of financing by document literacy levels

Per cent of participants in adult education and training who received financial support from various sources, by document literacy, populations aged 16 to 65 who worked in the last 12 months, 2003

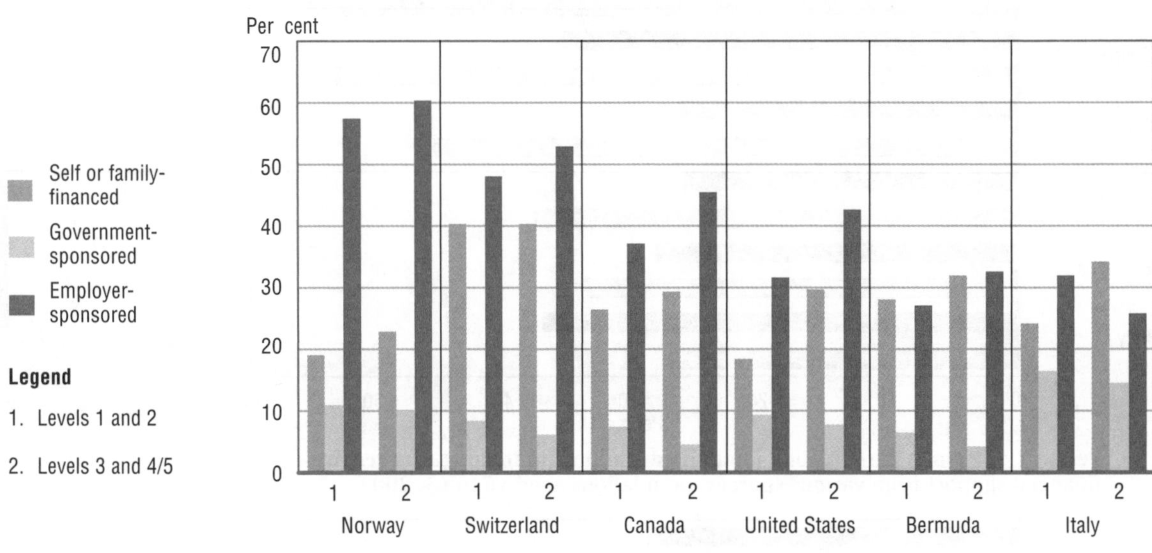

Countries are ranked by the per cent of those scoring at Levels 3 and 4/5 who received support from their employer.

Source: Adult Literacy and Life Skills Survey, 2003.

With nearly over a third of employed participants in Bermuda, Canada, Italy and the United States, and over one half in Norway and Switzerland involved in some form of employer-sponsored adult education and training, it is important to take a closer look at how opportunities vary between different groups of workers. Not surprisingly, an analysis of the impact of various factors on the likelihood of benefiting from employer-sponsored education and training such as engagement in literacy practices at work, firm size, occupation, supervisory position and type of industry, reveals that the combined level of engagement in reading, writing and numeracy practices at work is one of the strongest factors predicting employer support. Firm size is also a strong determinant of participation in employer-sponsored adult education and training (see Table 4.11 in Data Values for the Figures, Annex 4). Larger firms tend to invest in adult learning more than small and medium sized firms.

FIGURE 4.11

Employer-sponsored training by level of practice engagement

Adjusted odds ratios[1] showing the likelihood of receiving employer-sponsored adult education and training during the year preceding the interview, by combined levels of engagement in reading, writing and numeracy practices at work, populations aged 16 to 65, 2003

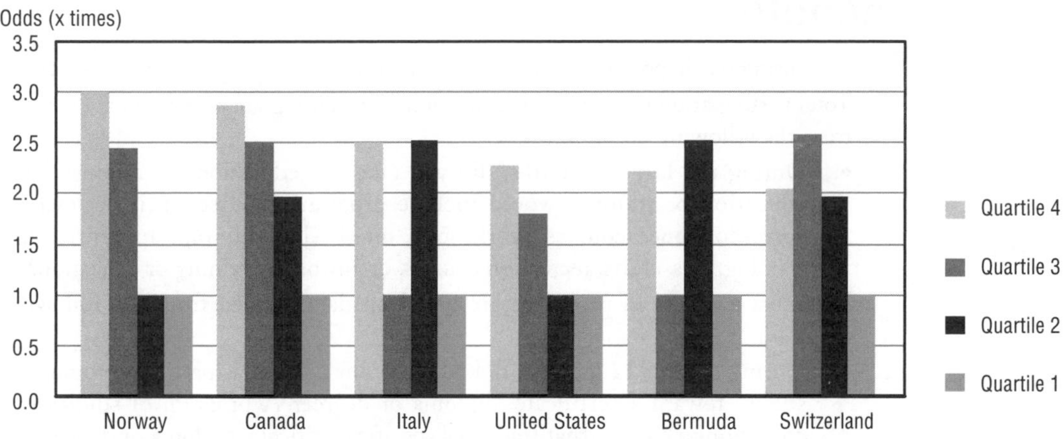

Countries are ranked by the adjusted odds ratios of those who are in 4th quartile.

1. Odds estimates that are not statistically different from one at conventional levels of significance are reported as one in the figure. For the actual estimate and its corresponding significance, see Table 4.11 in the annex to this chapter.

Source: Adult Literacy and Life Skills Survey, 2003.

Figure 4.11 shows the likelihood of receiving employer-sponsored training by the extent of engagement in literacy and numeracy practices at work. The frequency and variety of engagement in these types of job tasks are considered as good indirect measures of skill requirements at work. The results are obtained while holding variation in gender, age and educational attainment constant. In all countries, employees who engage the most in literacy practices at work (quartile 4) are over two to three times more likely to enrol in employer-sponsored training than those with the lowest engagement (quartile 1). The differences are most pronounced in Norway, with a difference of three times.

Endnotes

1. Measuring participation in adult education and training programs and courses.

   Total participation rates in adult education and training are based on data derived from the following question:

   - During the last 12 months, did you take any education or training? This education or training would include programs, courses, private lessons, correspondence courses, workshops, on-the-job training, apprenticeship training, arts, crafts, recreation courses, or any other training or education?

   Participation rates in programs are based on data derived from the following question:

   - During the last 12 months, did you take any courses as part of a program of studies toward a certificate, diploma or degree? A program of studies is a collection of courses that leads to a specific certificate, diploma or degree.

   Participation rates in courses are based on data derived from the following question:

   - During the last 12 months, did you participate in any courses that were not part of a program of studies?

2. To allow comparisons between participation rates in IALS and ALL the calculations exclude all full-time students under 25 years of age.

3. Measuring participation in active and passive modes of informal learning

   Participation rates in passive forms of informal learning are based on whether sampled adults responded yes to one of the following questions:

   - During the last 12 months, did you learn by going on guided tours such as museums, art galleries, or other locations?
   - During the last 12 months, did you learn by being sent around an organization to learn different aspects of that organization?
   - During the last 12 months, did you visit trade fairs, professional conferences or congresses?
   - During the last 12 months, did you attend short lectures, seminars, workshops or special talks that were not part of a course?

   Participation rates in active forms of informal learning are based on whether sampled adults responded yes to one of the following questions:

   - During the last 12 months, did you learn by watching, getting help from or advice from others but not from course instructors?
   - During the last 12 months, did you learn by yourself by trying things out, doing things for practice, trying different approaches to doing things?
   - During the last 12 months, did you use video, television, tapes to learn but not as part of the course?
   - During the last 12 months, did you use computers or the Internet to learn but not as part of a course?
   - During the last 12 months, did you read manuals, reference books, journals or other written materials but not as part of a course?

References

European Union (2001), *National Actions to Implement Lifelong Learning in Europe*, Eurydice, Brussel.

Esping-Andersen, G. (1996), "Positive-sum Solutions in a World of Trade Offs?", in G. Esping-Andersen (ed.), *Welfare States in Transition: National Adaptations in Global Economies,* Oxford University Press, Oxford.

Gaskell, J. and Rubenson, K. (2004), "Introduction: Towards a Research Program in Education and Training", in J. Gaskell and K. Rubenson (eds.), *Educational Outcomes for the Canadian Workplace: New Frameworks for Policy and Research,* University of Toronto Press, Toronto.

Giddens, A. (1994), *Beyond Left and Right,* Standford University Press, Stanford, CA.

HRDC (2002), *Knowledge Matters: Skills and Learning for Canadians,* Human Resources Development Canada, Ottawa.

Livingstone, D.W. (1999), "Exploring the Icebergs of Adult Learning; Findings of the first Canadian survey of informal learning practices", *Canadian Journal for the Study of Adult Education*, Vol. 13(2), pp. 49-72.

OECD (1996), *Lifelong Learning for All,* Paris.

OECD (2001), *Thematic Review of Adult Learning: Norway Country Report,* Paris.

OECD (2003), *Beyond Rhetoric: Adult Learning Policies and Practices,* Paris.

OECD and HRDC (1997), *Literacy Skills for the Knowledge Society: Further Results from the International Adult Literacy Survey,* Paris and Hull.

OECD and Statistics Canada (2000*), Literacy in the Information Age: Final Report on the International Adult Literacy Survey,* Paris and Ottawa.

Sen, A. (1982), *Choice, Welfare and Measurement,* MIT Press, Cambridge, Massachusetts.

Statistics Canada (2001), *A Report on Adult Education and Training in Canada,* Ottawa.

Svensson, L., Ellström, P.-E. and Åberg, C. (2004), "Integrating Formal and Informal Learning at Work", *Journal of Workplace Learning*, Vol. 16(8), pp. 479-491.

Contributor

Kjell Rubenson, *University of British Columbia*

Annex 4

Data Values for the Figures

4

TABLE 4.1

Per cent of populations aged 16 to 65 receiving adult education and training during the year preceding the interview, by type of participation, 2003

	Total participation		Took program		Took course	
Bermuda	47.0	(1.4)	18.0	(0.8)	22.1	(1.1)
Canada	49.3	(0.7)	15.8	(0.6)	24.9	(0.6)
Italy	18.9	(0.9)	7.4	(0.4)	9.2	(0.7)
Norway	53.3	(0.9)	20.7	(0.8)	30.9	(0.8)
Switzerland	56.9	(1.1)	19.5	(1.3)	40.5	(0.9)
United States	54.6	(1.4)	19.9	(0.9)	21.0	(0.9)

Source: Adult Literacy and Life Skills Survey, 2003.

TABLE 4.2

Per cent of populations aged 16 to 65 receiving adult education and training during the year preceding the interview, IALS 1994/1998 and ALL 2003

	IALS 1994/1998		ALL 2003	
Canada	36.0	(1.4)	49.3	(0.7)
Norway	47.8	(1.4)	53.3	(0.9)
Switzerland (French)	32.9	(1.9)	47.8	(1.4)
Switzerland (German)	44.5	(1.1)	60.8	(1.3)
Switzerland (Italian)	36.8	(1.7)	38.2	(1.7)
United States	41.7	(1.3)	54.6	(1.4)

Sources: Adult Literacy and Life Skills Survey, 2003.
International Adult Literacy Survey, 1994-1998.

TABLE 4.3

Per cent of populations aged 16 to 65 receiving adult education and training during the year preceding the interview, by document literacy levels, 2003

	Level 1		Level 2		Level 3		Level 4/5		Total	
Bermuda	23.9	(3.0)	42.3	(2.9)	53.0	(2.2)	63.9	(3.1)	47.0	(1.4)
Canada	22.1	(1.8)	42.4	(1.4)	56.3	(1.0)	68.6	(2.4)	49.3	(0.7)
Italy	10.9	(1.0)	22.4	(2.0)	33.5	(2.5)	44.2	(4.1)	18.9	(0.9)
Norway	29.9	(3.7)	44.7	(2.9)	57.5	(2.5)	63.0	(3.1)	53.3	(0.9)
Switzerland	35.6	(3.9)	49.4	(3.1)	64.9	(2.3)	73.2	(3.6)	56.9	(1.1)
United States	24.0	(2.1)	48.7	(2.9)	68.2	(2.4)	79.9	(2.9)	54.6	(1.4)

Source: Adult Literacy and Life Skills Survey, 2003.

TABLE 4.4

Adjusted odds ratios showing the likelihood of adults aged 16 to 65 receiving adult education and training during the year preceding the interview, by document literacy levels, 2003

	Level 1	Level 2		Level 3		Level 4/5	
Bermuda	1.00	1.77**	(0.25)	2.04***	(0.22)	2.42**	(0.31)
Canada	1.00	1.93***	(0.12)	2.72***	(0.11)	3.78***	(0.14)
Italy	1.00	1.60***	(0.16)	2.16***	(0.17)	2.69***	(0.25)
Norway	1.00	1.52**	(0.19)	1.97***	(0.18)	2.00**	(0.25)
Switzerland	1.00	1.53	(0.25)	2.37***	(0.22)	2.90***	(0.26)
United States	1.00	2.24***	(0.19)	3.75***	(0.16)	5.91***	(0.23)

* $p<0.10$, statistically significant at the 10 per cent level.

** $p<0.05$, statistically significant at the 5 per cent level.

*** $p<0.01$, statistically significant at the 1 per cent level.

Notes: Odds are adjusted for gender, age, educational attainment and labour force participation status.
Standard errors are of the logarithm of the odds ratios.

Source: Adult Literacy and Life Skills Survey, 2003.

TABLE 4.5

Changes in the per cent of adults aged 16 to 65 in adult education and training between IALS 1994/1998 and ALL 2003, by document literacy levels

	Level 1		Level 2		Level 3		Level 4/5		Total	
Canada										
IALS 1994/1998	14.7	(5.0)	29.5	(2.7)	37.6	(3.7)	58.9	(3.2)	36.0	(1.4)
ALL 2003	22.1	(1.8)	42.4	(1.4)	56.3	(1.0)	68.6	(2.4)	49.3	(0.7)
Norway										
IALS 1994/1998	16.0	(1.9)	36.7	(2.7)	50.8	(1.5)	63.1	(2.3)	47.8	(1.4)
ALL 2003	29.9	(3.7)	44.7	(2.9)	57.5	(2.5)	63.0	(3.1)	53.3	(0.9)
Switzerland (French)										
IALS 1994/1998	19.2	(3.5)	25.5	(3.7)	38.9	(2.0)	47.0	(4.4)	32.9	(1.9)
ALL 2003	33.2	(7.1)	43.5	(3.9)	53.4	(2.3)	63.0	(6.3)	47.8	(1.4)
Switzerland (German)										
IALS 1994/1998	19.7	(3.5)	39.1	(2.9)	50.6	(2.0)	68.4	(3.5)	44.5	(1.1)
ALL 2003	37.7	(4.4)	52.8	(4.3)	69.2	(3.4)	75.5	(3.6)	60.8	(1.3)
Switzerland (Italian)										
IALS 1994/1998	19.8	(4.2)	27.9	(2.8)	46.3	(3.0)	65.0	(3.1)	36.8	(1.7)
ALL 2003	18.7	(5.4)	30.9	(2.3)	51.6	(3.1)	60.4	(5.4)	38.2	(1.7)
United States										
IALS 1994/1998	17.5	(1.7)	33.1	(2.2)	51.8	(1.9)	62.5	(2.7)	41.7	(1.3)
ALL 2003	24.0	(2.1)	48.7	(2.9)	68.2	(2.4)	79.9	(2.9)	54.6	(1.4)

Note: Estimates are based on adult population with full-time students aged 16 to 24 excluded.
Sources: Adult Literacy and Life Skills Survey, 2003.
International Adult Literacy Survey, 1994-1998.

TABLE 4.6

Per cent of populations aged 16 to 65 participating in informal learning activities during the year preceding the interview, by mode of engagement, 2003

	Active and passive mode		Active mode		Passive mode	
Bermuda	97.4	(0.4)	75.8	(1.0)	96.8	(0.5)
Canada	93.4	(0.3)	62.4	(0.6)	92.9	(0.3)
Italy	57.9	(1.4)	37.1	(0.9)	52.7	(1.4)
Norway	96.6	(0.2)	69.8	(1.0)	95.8	(0.3)
Switzerland	98.4	(0.3)	79.9	(1.4)	98.0	(0.3)
United States	95.0	(0.4)	63.2	(1.0)	94.7	(0.4)

Source: Adult Literacy and Life Skills Survey, 2003.

TABLE 4.7

Per cent of populations aged 16 to 65 participating in active modes of informal learning in the year preceding the interview, by education attainment, 2003

	Active mode		Passive mode	
Bermuda				
Less than upper secondary	50.6	(3.6)	89.3	(1.6)
Upper secondary	65.9	(2.2)	95.3	(1.0)
Post-secondary, non-tertiary	78.7	(1.7)	98.4	(0.5)
Tertiary (Level 5B)	89.8	(2.1)	99.5	(0.4)
Tertiary (Level 5A or higher)	93.5	(1.5)	98.7	(0.5)
Total participation in active modes of informal learning	75.8	(1.0)	96.8	(0.5)
Canada				
Less than upper secondary	36.8	(1.8)	84.3	(1.1)
Upper secondary	56.7	(1.2)	91.8	(0.7)
Post-secondary, non-tertiary	65.4	(1.7)	95.6	(0.9)
Tertiary (Level 5B)	73.5	(1.7)	96.7	(0.5)
Tertiary (Level 5A or higher)	82.5	(1.3)	97.7	(0.4)
Total participation in active modes of informal learning	62.4	(0.6)	92.9	(0.3)
Italy				
Less than upper secondary	19.3	(1.1)	35.8	(1.9)
Upper secondary	53.0	(1.7)	69.3	(2.1)
Post-secondary, non-tertiary	56.6	(4.0)	65.8	(6.5)
Tertiary (Level 5B)	90.4	(7.5)	91.7	(7.1)
Tertiary (Level 5A or higher)	77.5	(2.3)	84.5	(2.3)
Total participation in active modes of informal learning	37.1	(0.9)	52.7	(1.4)
Norway				
Less than upper secondary	47.4	(2.4)	88.9	(1.2)
Upper secondary	65.3	(1.7)	95.6	(0.4)
Post-secondary, non-tertiary	76.2	(2.1)	96.5	(1.0)
Tertiary (Level 5B)	82.9	(1.4)	98.5	(0.5)
Tertiary (Level 5A or higher)	89.4	(0.8)	99.7	(0.1)
Total participation in active modes of informal learning	69.8	(1.0)	95.8	(0.3)
Switzerland				
Less than upper secondary	63.1	(4.6)	95.3	(2.2)
Upper secondary	78.3	(2.0)	98.1	(0.3)
Tertiary (Level 5B)	90.1	(1.9)	98.2	(1.1)
Tertiary (Level 5A or higher)	95.4	(1.0)	99.9	(0.1)
Total participation in active modes of informal learning	79.9	(1.4)	98.0	(0.3)
United States				
Less than upper secondary	32.4	(1.9)	82.9	(1.8)
Upper secondary	56.3	(1.7)	95.4	(0.6)
Post-secondary, non-tertiary	72.0	(3.9)	98.4	(1.3)
Tertiary (Level 5B)	75.6	(2.7)	97.3	(1.2)
Tertiary (Level 5A or higher)	87.9	(1.4)	98.7	(0.5)
Total participation in active modes of informal learning	63.2	(1.0)	94.7	(0.4)

Source: Adult Literacy and Life Skills Survey, 2003.

TABLE 4.8

Adjusted odds ratios showing the likelihood of adults aged 16 to 65 participating in active modes of informal adult learning during the year preceding the interview, by document literacy levels, 2003

	Level 1	Level 2		Level 3		Level 4/5	
Bermuda	1.00	1.16	(0.18)	1.53*	(0.21)	2.09**	(0.28)
Canada	1.00	2.17***	(0.10)	3.23***	(0.08)	4.88***	(0.12)
Italy	1.00	1.46***	(0.12)	2.34***	(0.17)	3.91***	(0.32)
Norway	1.00	1.45	(0.22)	2.18***	(0.18)	2.47***	(0.20)
Switzerland	1.00	1.53**	(0.17)	2.25***	(0.19)	3.82***	(0.37)
United States	1.00	1.60**	(0.17)	2.14***	(0.13)	2.95***	(0.19)

* p<0.10, statistically significant at the 10 per cent level.

** p<0.05, statistically significant at the 5 per cent level.

*** p<0.01, statistically significant at the 1 per cent level.

Notes: Odds ratios are adjusted for gender, age, educational attainment and labour force participation status. Standard errors are of the logarithm of the odds ratios.

Source: Adult Literacy and Life Skills Survey, 2003.

TABLE 4.9

Per cent of men and women participating in adult education and training who receive financial support from various sources, populations aged 16 to 65, 2003

	Employer-sponsored		Government-sponsored		Self-financed	
Bermuda						
Women	26.3	(2.3)	5.5	(1.0)	35.7	(2.4)
Men	33.5	(2.1)	3.6	(0.8)	28.2	(1.9)
Canada						
Women	34.1	(1.2)	6.8	(0.7)	35.0	(1.1)
Men	45.5	(1.7)	5.7	(0.6)	26.4	(1.2)
Italy						
Women	16.3	(1.6)	12.6	(1.8)	44.2	(2.3)
Men	27.1	(3.1)	13.1	(2.7)	36.9	(2.7)
Norway						
Women	52.3	(2.3)	15.0	(1.8)	28.8	(1.7)
Men	57.0	(2.1)	12.7	(1.6)	18.2	(1.7)
Switzerland						
Women	35.8	(2.3)	7.6	(1.5)	54.2	(2.1)
Men	54.0	(2.4)	9.1	(1.1)	35.3	(2.4)
United States						
Women	35.5	(1.6)	10.1	(1.4)	28.2	(1.4)
Men	37.6	(1.7)	7.4	(1.2)	26.0	(1.1)

Source: Adult Literacy and Life Skills Survey, 2003.

TABLE 4.10

Per cent of participants in adult education and training who received financial support from various sources, by document literacy, populations aged 16 to 65 who worked in the last 12 months, 2003

	Employer-sponsored		Government-sponsored		Self or family-financed	
Bermuda						
Levels 1 and 2	27.1	(2.4)	6.3	(1.7)	28.1	(3.0)
Levels 3 and 4/5	32.7	(2.0)	4.1	(0.8)	31.9	(2.3)
Total	30.7	(1.5)	4.9	(0.7)	30.6	(1.5)
Canada						
Levels 1 and 2	37.2	(2.2)	7.3	(1.1)	26.6	(1.9)
Levels 3 and 4/5	45.5	(1.3)	4.5	(0.7)	29.5	(1.1)
Total	43.0	(1.0)	5.3	(0.5)	28.6	(0.7)
Italy						
Levels 1 and 2	31.8	(3.4)	16.5	(3.8)	24.1	(2.6)
Levels 3 and 4/5	25.7	(4.9)	14.4	(3.4)	34.3	(4.2)
Total	29.5	(2.4)	15.7	(2.1)	27.8	(2.5)
Norway						
Levels 1 and 2	57.4	(3.8)	10.9	(2.0)	18.9	(2.2)
Levels 3 and 4/5	60.3	(1.7)	9.9	(1.1)	22.8	(1.3)
Total	59.6	(1.7)	10.2	(0.8)	21.8	(0.9)
Switzerland						
Levels 1 and 2	48.0	(4.2)	8.3	(2.1)	40.2	(2.4)
Levels 3 and 4/5	53.0	(3.1)	6.2	(1.1)	40.4	(2.4)
Total	51.1	(1.5)	6.9	(0.7)	40.4	(1.7)
United States						
Levels 1 and 2	31.7	(2.3)	9.2	(1.6)	18.3	(2.3)
Levels 3 and 4/5	42.5	(1.7)	7.7	(1.4)	29.8	(1.4)
Total	38.6	(1.3)	8.3	(1.1)	25.6	(0.9)

Source: Adult Literacy and Life Skills Survey, 2003.

TABLE 4.11

Adjusted odds ratios showing the likelihood of receiving employer-sponsored adult education and training during the year preceding the interview, by combined levels of engagement in reading, writing and numeracy practices at work, populations aged 16 to 65, 2003

	Literacy engagement at work						
	Quartile 1	Quartile 2		Quartile 3		Quartile 4	
Bermuda	1.00	2.53*	(0.51)	2.33	(0.50)	2.21*	(0.45)
Canada	1.00	1.97***	(0.20)	2.51***	(0.18)	2.87***	(0.18)
Italy	1.00	2.53***	(0.33)	1.10	(0.46)	2.50**	(0.41)
Norway	1.00	1.69	(0.43)	2.44**	(0.42)	3.01**	(0.41)
Switzerland	1.00	1.97*	(0.38)	2.59***	(0.33)	2.04**	(0.32)
United States	1.00	1.45	(0.28)	1.79**	(0.23)	2.27***	(0.24)

	Firm size								
	Less than 20	20 to 99		100 to 499		500 to 999		1,000 and over	
Bermuda	1.00	2.16***	(0.21)	2.12***	(0.26)	2.66***	(0.35)	2.38**	(0.33)
Canada	1.00	1.58***	(0.13)	2.92***	(0.12)	3.02***	(0.19)	3.09***	(0.12)
Italy	1.00	3.32	(0.87)	9.83***	(0.74)	1.68	(0.85)	4.71**	(0.60)
Norway	1.00	2.42***	(0.32)	2.14**	(0.29)	1.90*	(0.36)	1.86**	(0.28)
Switzerland	1.00	2.93***	(0.30)	4.49***	(0.37)	2.74***	(0.32)	4.15***	(0.21)
United States	1.00	2.62***	(0.24)	3.12***	(0.21)	3.30***	(0.33)	3.19***	(0.17)

* $p<0.10$, statistically significant at the 10 per cent level.

** $p<0.05$, statistically significant at the 5 per cent level.

*** $p<0.01$, statistically significant at the 1 per cent level.

Notes: Odds are adjusted for gender and age, educational attainment, supervisory role, type of occupation, type of industry and firm size. Standard errors are of the logarithm of the odds ratios.

Source: Adult Literacy and Life Skills Survey, 2003.

Chapter 5

Skills and the Labour Force

5

Summary

This chapter focuses on the skills of labour force participants. First, the difference in workers' skills between the top and bottom 25 per cent of performers is compared. This allows for a comparative assessment of the skills supplied in the labour market. Second, the employability of working-age adults is studied. This is done by comparing the likelihood of experiencing labour force inactivity and unemployment over the cycle of one year for persons who are at low and medium to high levels of skill. Finally, the employability analysis is extended to also include younger and older workers.

Table of Contents

Skills and the Labour Force

5

5.1 Overview and highlights

This chapter focuses on the skills of labour force participants. First, the difference in workers' skills between the top and bottom 25 per cent of performers is compared. This allows for a comparative assessment of the skills supplied in the labour market. Second, the employability of working-age adults is studied. This is done by comparing the likelihood of experiencing labour force inactivity and unemployment over the cycle of one year for persons who are at low and medium to high levels of skill. Finally, the employability analysis is extended to also include younger and older workers.

Several key findings arise from the analysis presented in this chapter:

- The Norwegian labour force has the highest top and bottom 25 per cent of performers on the prose, document and problem solving scales. The Swiss labour force is best qualified on the numeracy scale.
- The highest scoring working adults tend to be the most numerous in the group aged 26 to 45 and fewest among older workers aged 46 to 65. The group aged 16 to 25 lies somewhere in between. Many adults aged 26 to 45 have been exposed to learning opportunities at work that reinforce the development of their skills. This may explain why workers in early to mid career display the best skills among the top end of workforces.
- Adults with higher levels of skill of the types measured in ALL tend to be more employable than adults with low skills, but not necessarily. The findings show that low skilled adults are more likely than medium to high skilled adults to experience unemployment in half of the countries and to experience labour force inactivity for six or more months in all countries except Bermuda.
- Among adults who experience unemployment, those who score at higher levels on the document literacy scale have a higher likelihood of re-entering employment sooner. The results are similar for all the skills measured in ALL.

- Proficiency in foundation skills such as document literacy and numeracy is strongly associated with the probability of young adults to find employment. Young adults who score at Levels 1 and 2 have a lower chance of exiting unemployment and tend to be unemployed longer than the more highly skilled.
- Even though unemployment rates tend to be higher among young labour force participants, younger adults are able to exit unemployment more quickly than older adults. In fact, low skilled younger adults have better chances of finding a job than low skilled older adults. This highlights the difficulties that displaced workers face when searching for job at an older age. Even so, older adults with higher skills find it easier to obtain employment than those with lower skills.

5.2 Competitiveness of labour force populations

The challenges of competing in global markets and adopting technological, process and organizational innovations place a premium on the capacity of individuals to adapt to changes in the workplace. Many workers who are faced with these challenges are expected to be highly skilled, not least in foundation skills such as literacy and numeracy, but at all levels they are also increasingly expected to solve problems and create ways to improve the methods they use (Bailey, 1997). Thus the skills measured in ALL, among others, are important for work organisations and countries to adapt and succeed. This section takes a closer look at the distribution of skills among the labour force[1] in each country assessed.

Figures 5.1a-c compare the scores that are at the 75th percentile of each country's skill distribution. This highlights differences among the top 25 per cent of highest scorers. The scores are displayed relative to the ALL international average 75th percentile. Thus countries with higher 75th percentile scores have workers who tend to display higher average levels of ability in the relevant skills domain when comparing the top end of distributions among countries. This would imply that relative to the size of labour force populations, these countries have better "pools of skills" to draw from for market-oriented activities. Presumably, such countries are in a better position to compete for "high-skills" jobs (Brown, Green and Lauder, 2001).

The data indicate that on the combined prose and document literacy scale[2], Norway and Bermuda score highest at the top end of the distribution. On the numeracy and problem solving scale, the patterns are similar to those observed in Chapter 2, with Switzerland's top performers scoring the highest on the numeracy scale and doing better on the problem solving scale than on the prose and document scales.

FIGURE 5.1 A to C

Skills among labour force populations in the top 25 per cent

Score differences to the 75th percentile of the ALL international population on a scale with range 0 to 500 points, labour force populations aged 16 to 65, 2003

A. Prose and document literacy scales combined

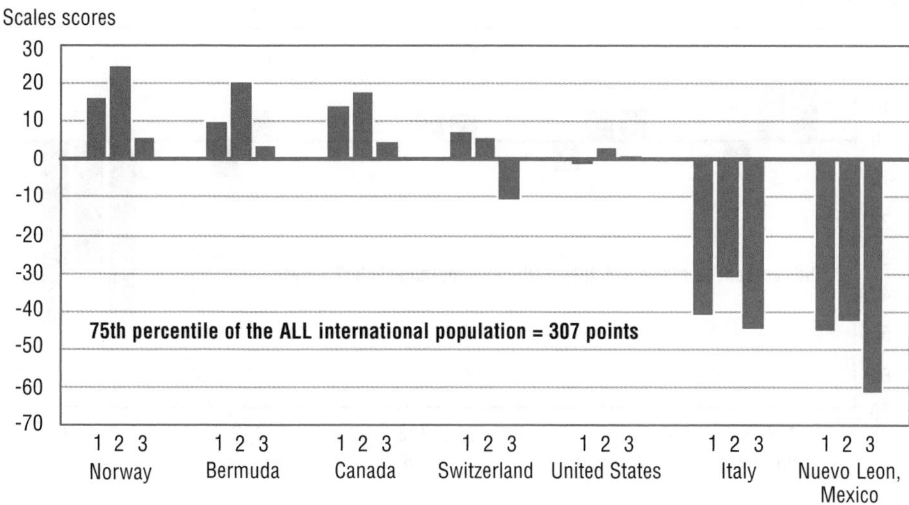

Legend
1. 16 to 25
2. 26 to 45
3. 46 to 65

B. Numeracy[1] scale

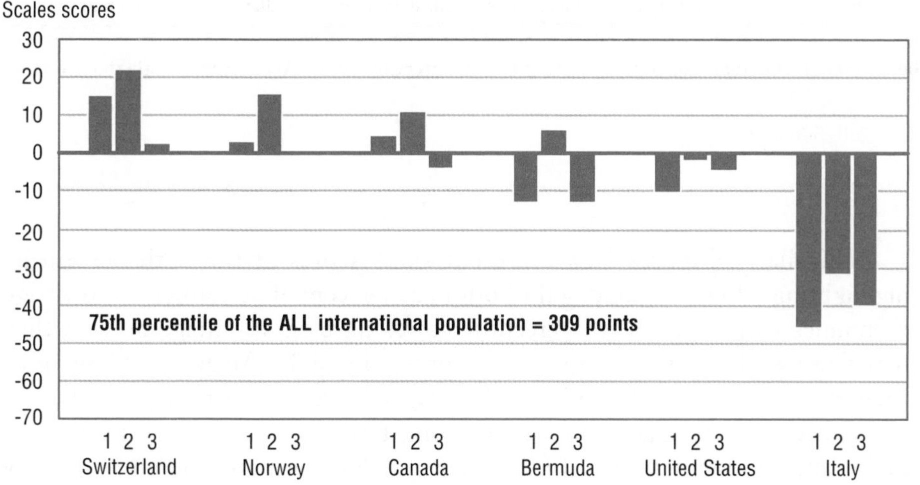

1. The state of Nuevo Leon in Mexico fielded the IALS quantitative literacy assessment rather than the ALL numeracy assessment. Although closely related conceptually, these two scales cannot be directly compared.

Countries are ranked by the difference of persons aged 26 to 45 to the 75th percentile of the ALL international labour force population aged 16 to 65.

Source: Adult Literacy and Life Skills Survey, 2003.

FIGURE 5.1 A to C (concluded)

Skills among labour force populations in the top 25 per cent

Score differences to the 75th percentile of the ALL international population on a scale with range 0 to 500 points, labour force populations aged 16 to 65, 2003

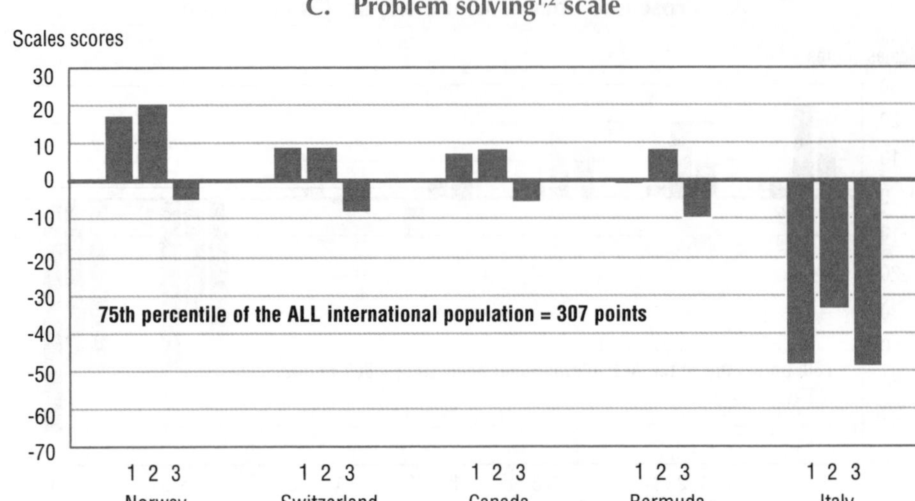

1. United States and Nuevo Leon, Mexico did not field the problem solving skills domain.
2. The problem solving skills scores for Switzerland apply to the German and French speaking communities only since they did not field the problem solving skills domain in the Italian speaking community.

Countries are ranked by the difference of persons aged 26 to 45 to the 75th percentile of the ALL international labour force population aged 16 to 65.

Source: Adult Literacy and Life Skills Survey, 2003.

Similarly, Figures 5.2a-c present skills scores at the 25th percentile, highlighting differences among the bottom 25 per cent of performers. Knowledge economies with higher 25th percentile scores have an advantage because they have fewer workers with low information processing skills. Analysis by Coulombe, Tremblay and Marchand (Statistics Canada, 2004) reveals that the proportion of low skilled workers appears to suppress long-term rates of growth in GDP per capita and productivity in OECD countries. Furthermore, the employability analysis below indicates that workers with higher skills are more employable because they display a lower likelihood of being unemployed, and when they do experience unemployment they have a higher likelihood of re-entering employment sooner.

FIGURE 5.2 A to C

Skills among labour force populations in the bottom 25 per cent

Score differences to the 25th percentile of the ALL international population on a scale with range 0 to 500 points, labour force populations aged 16 to 65, 2003

A. Prose and document literacy scales combined

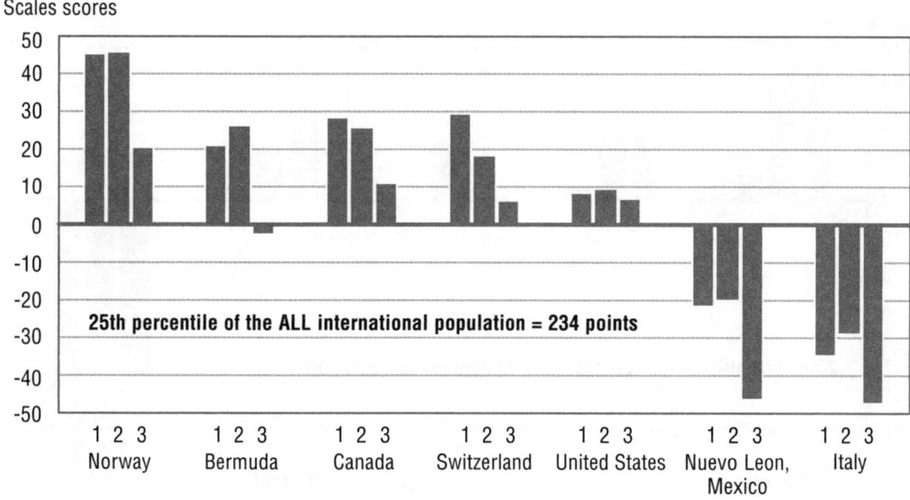

Legend

1. 16 to 25
2. 26 to 45
3. 46 to 65

B. Numeracy[1] scale

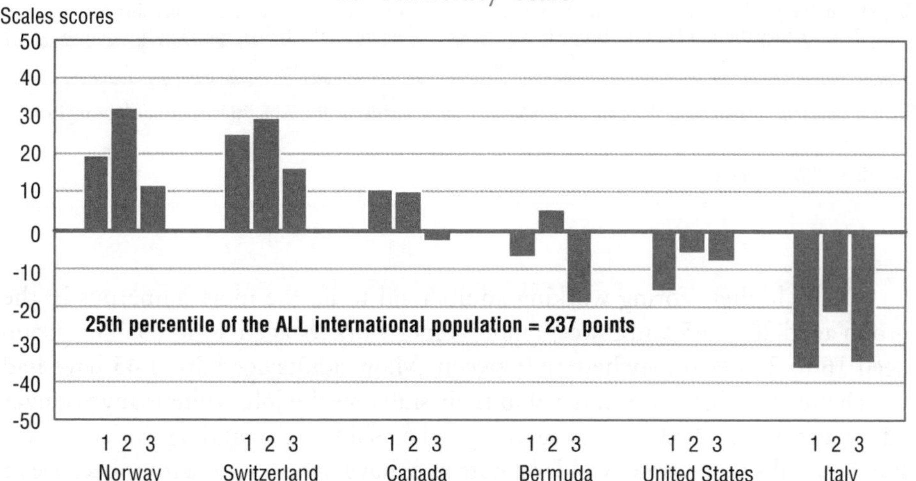

1. The state of Nuevo Leon in Mexico fielded the IALS quantitative literacy assessment rather than the ALL numeracy assessment. Although closely related conceptually, these two scales cannot be directly compared.

Countries are ranked by the difference of persons aged 26 to 45 to the 25th percentile of the ALL international labour force population aged 16 to 65.

Source: Adult Literacy and Life Skills Survey, 2003.

FIGURE 5.2 A to C (concluded)

Skills among labour force populations in the bottom 25 per cent

Score differences to the 25th percentile of the ALL international population on a scale with range 0 to 500 points, labour force populations aged 16 to 65, 2003

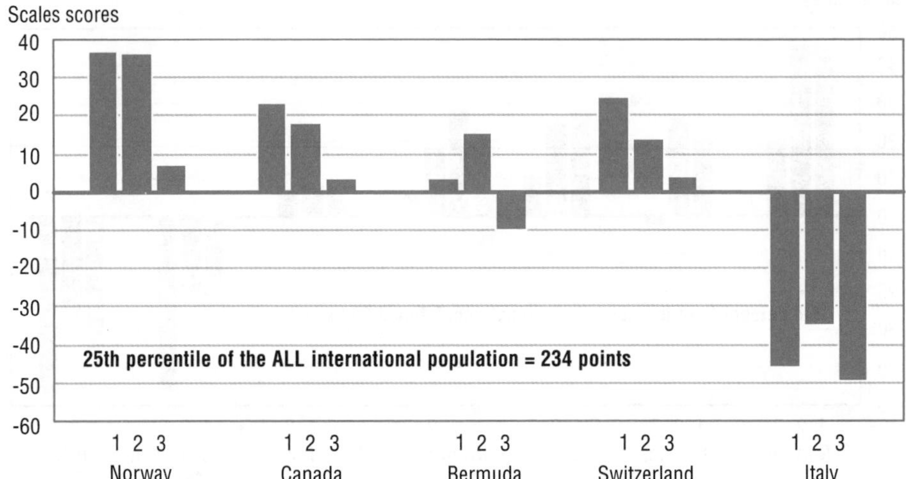

1. United States and Nuevo Leon, Mexico did not field the problem solving skills domain.
2. The problem solving skills scores for Switzerland apply to the German and French speaking communities only since they did not field the problem solving skills domain in the Italian speaking community.

Countries are ranked by the difference of persons aged 26 to 45 to the 25th percentile of the ALL international labour force population aged 16 to 65.

Source: Adult Literacy and Life Skills Survey, 2003.

The higher scoring working adults tend to be the most numerous in the group aged 26 to 45 and fewest among older workers aged 46 to 65. The group aged 16 to 25 lies somewhere in between. Many adults aged 26 to 45 have had the chance to reinforce and develop their skills on the job, while many younger adults have not yet had the chance to apply their skills in demanding work contexts. Further, skills among many older adults may have deteriorated either because of lack of use or because they have become obsolete due to the introduction of new work routines or other innovations. This may explain why workers in early to mid career display the best skills among the top end of the labour force.

5.3 Employability of working-age populations

Employability and *employability skills* are terms increasingly used by researchers and policy makers alike. While there are many definitions, employability essentially refers to the capability of adults to obtain and maintain satisfactory work. Naturally, this involves the skills and knowledge relating to jobs, which are referred to as employability skills. These are numerous, but many efforts have been made to identify and list key employability skills that apply in varying degrees to all jobs (e.g., Carnevale, Gainer, and Meltzer, 1990; SCANS, 1991, HRDC, 2001). Not surprisingly, most lists feature foundation skills such as literacy, numeracy and problem solving near the top. Accordingly, this section considers the relationship between the skills measured in ALL and the employability of adults.

Even though they are termed "foundation skills", the findings presented in Chapter 2 suggest that many adults have difficulties coping with literacy and numeracy related activities that are common in modern workplaces. Additionally, there is some evidence suggesting that most OECD economies continue to witness a general shift in labour demand from lower to higher levels of skills (Dickerson and Green, 2004; Machin, 2001). Thus adults with low skills, of the type measured in ALL, are likely to face increasing difficulties in gaining access to and securing gainful employment. They are also more likely than high skilled adults to experience unemployment and to not participate in the labour force at all.

Results presented in Figure 5.3 show that compared to persons who score at Levels 3 or higher on the numeracy scale, low scorers have a higher chance of experiencing six or more months of labour force inactivity than being employed all year (see Box 3A – Using odds ratios). In most countries, persons who score at Levels 1 and 2 are two to three times more likely to be outside the labour force for six or more months than those who score at Levels 3 or higher. Only in Bermuda do low and medium to high skilled adults have nearly the same odds of experiencing six or more months of labour force inactivity and being employed all year.

FIGURE 5.3

Likelihood of labour force inactivity by skills levels

Odds ratios[1] showing the likelihood of experiencing labour force inactivity for 6 months or more in the last 12 months compared to being employed all year, by numeracy levels, populations aged 16 to 65, excluding students and retirees, 2003

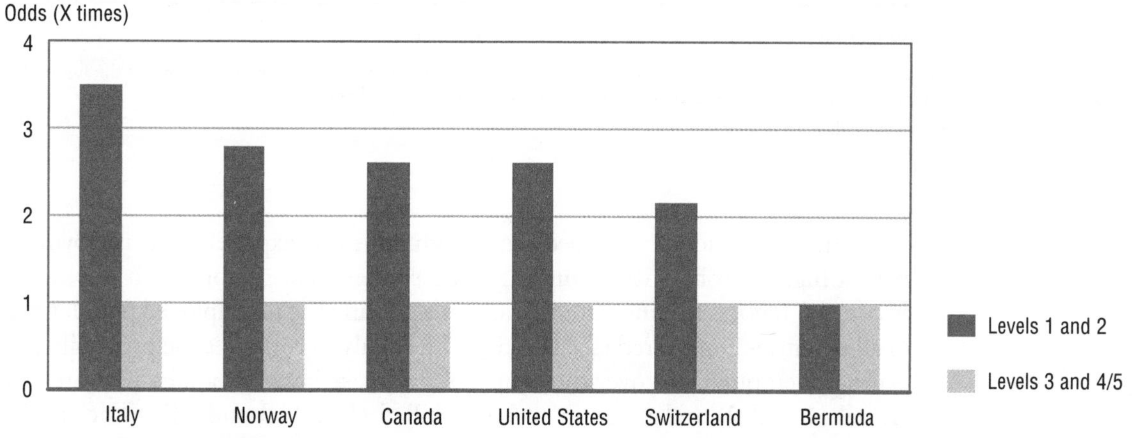

Countries are ranked according to the odds of persons who score at Levels 1 and 2.

1. Odds estimates that are not statistically different from one at conventional levels of significance are reported as one in the figure. For the actual estimate and its corresponding significance, see Table 5.3 in the annex to this chapter.

Source: Adult Literacy and Life Skills Survey, 2003.

Furthermore, Figure 5.4 shows that in half of the countries, low skilled adults are more likely than high skilled adults to experience unemployment lasting six or more months. But note that the overall labour market conditions, including the balance between the demand and supply of skilled workers and the economic cycle, which are specific to a country or region, are important to consider in this type of analysis (De Grip, van Loo and Sanders, 2004). For example, in areas where the demand for low skilled workers exceeds the supply, low skilled adults are less likely to be outside the labour force or in unemployment.

FIGURE 5.4

Likelihood of experiencing unemployment by skills levels

Odds ratios[1] showing the likelihood of experiencing unemployment for 6 months or more in the last 12 months compared to being employed all year, by numeracy levels, labour force populations aged 16 to 65, 2003

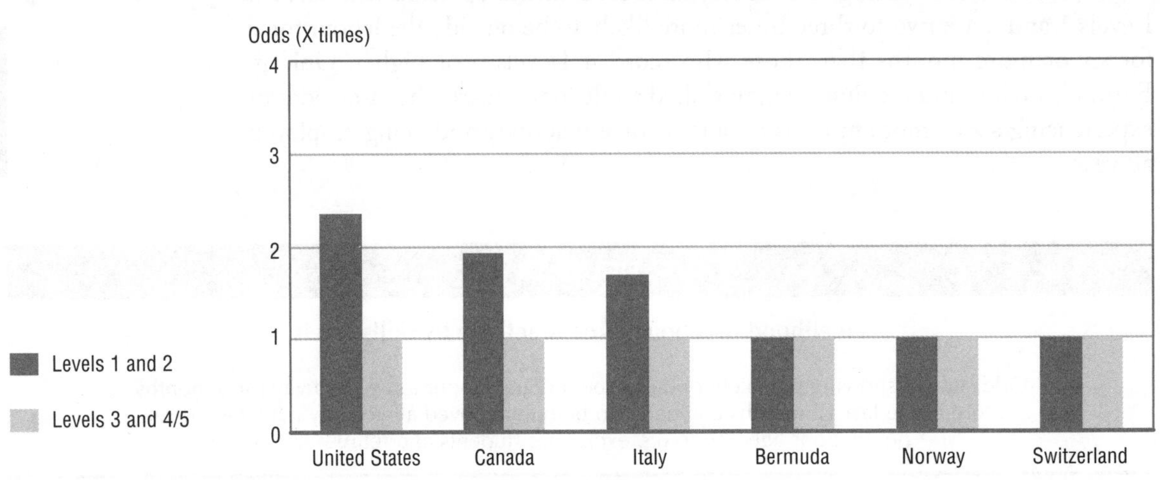

Countries are ranked according to the odds of persons who score at Levels 1 and 2.

1. Odds estimates that are not statistically different from one at conventional levels of significance are reported as one in the figure. For the actual estimate and its corresponding significance, see Table 5.4 in the annex to this chapter.

Source: Adult Literacy and Life Skills Survey, 2003.

In general, adults with medium to high skills who experience unemployment have a higher probability of finding a job sooner than persons with low skills. Figure 5.5 reports findings from an analysis pooling the unemployed populations of all countries considered (see Box 5A). The analysis contrasts the probability of exiting unemployment over the course of 52 weeks between adults who are low (Levels 1 and 2) and medium to high skilled (Levels 3 and 4/5). The results clearly indicate that persons with higher proficiency in document literacy are capable of finding employment sooner. For example, after 16 weeks of unemployment, persons scoring at Levels 3 and 4/5 have a 60 per cent chance of exiting unemployment. This increases to 70 per cent after 48 weeks. In contrast, adults who score at Levels 1 and 2 still only have a 50 per cent chance of finding a job even after 52 weeks of unemployment. The results are similar in other skills domains, although labour markets appear to recognize document and numeracy skills the most.

FIGURE 5.5

Probability of exiting unemployment by skills levels

The probabilities of unemployed adults aged 16 to 65 to exit unemployment over a 52 week period, by low (Levels 1 and 2) and medium to high (Levels 3 and 4/5) skills, document scale, 2003

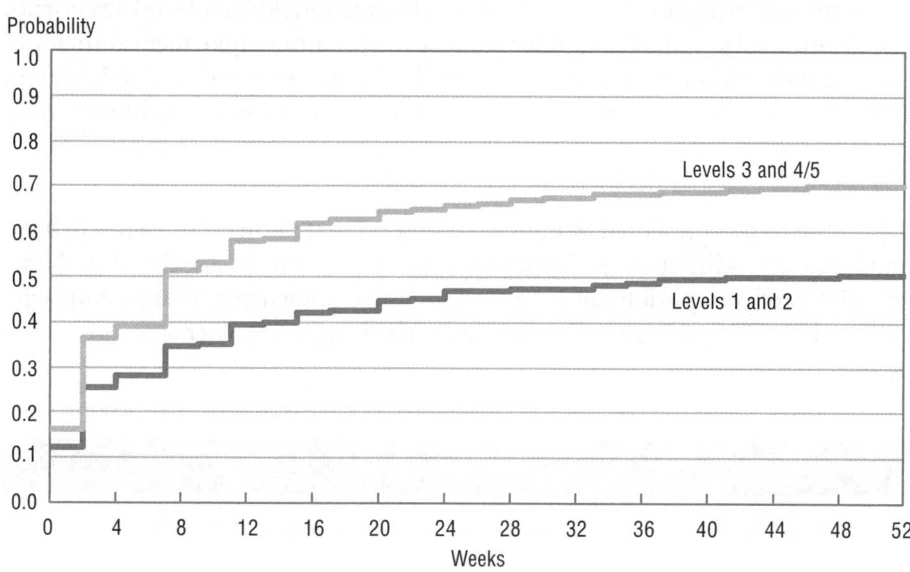

Source: Adult Literacy and Life Skills Survey, 2003.

Box 5A

Measuring the probabilities of exiting unemployment

The probabilities of exiting unemployment that are presented in Figures 5.5, 5.6 and 5.7 are estimated using survival analysis. In particular, the Kaplan and Meier (1958) estimator is used. This type of analysis considers the duration before or after an event occurs as well as the duration of the event itself. The ALL skills survey collected data that describes the duration and frequency of unemployment in the 52 weeks preceding the data collection as well as whether individuals were unemployed at the time of the survey.

In this context, the survival analysis allows for an estimation of the probability that persons will exit unemployment after a certain number of weeks. The survival function is graphed so that the probability of exiting unemployment begins at 0.0 where all persons are unemployed, and approaches 1.0 as time elapses. Notice that some adults leave unemployment very quickly while others remain for up to 52 weeks or longer. But the probability of exiting unemployment rises as the number of weeks in unemployment increases. Eventually, by 52 weeks most persons have left unemployment. Accordingly, the probability of exiting unemployment is very high (close to 1.0) at 52 weeks, but there are still some who remain unemployed more than one year.

5.4 Employability of younger and older working-age populations

When it comes to employment, age can be seen as a barrier. Both younger and older workers can face substantial difficulties in the labour market. The successful integration of young adults into the labour market remains a major political concern in most OECD countries (OECD, 2002). Often, young adults are disadvantaged by their lack of qualifications, foundation skills and work experience (UK Youth, 2002). Similarly, older adults can run into employment difficulties because their skills have become obsolete (De Grip and van Loo, 2002; Dubin, 1972; Rosen, 1975), and employers may be less inclined to invest in retraining for older workers (Heckman, 1999). This section considers the employability of younger and older adults by their levels of skill.

The results presented in Figure 5.6 suggest that higher proficiency in basic employability skills such as document literacy is strongly associated with the probability of young adults aged 16 to 30 to find employment. Young adults who score at Levels 1 and 2 have a lower chance of exiting unemployment and tend to be unemployed longer.

FIGURE 5.6

Probability of younger workers exiting unemployment by skills levels

The probabilities of unemployed adults aged 16 to 30 to exit unemployment over a 52 week period, by low (Levels 1 and 2) and medium to high (Levels 3 and 4/5) skills, document scale, 2003

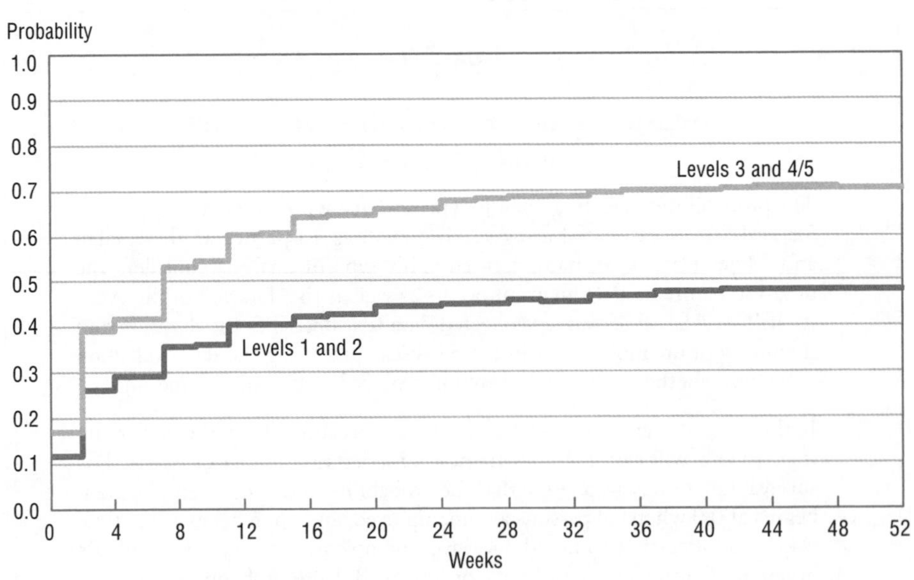

Source: Adult Literacy and Life Skills Survey, 2003.

Many older unemployed workers face difficulties finding a new job. In general, the average duration of unemployment tends to be higher among older labour force participants, even though the rate of unemployment is higher among younger adults (Ryan, 2001). This is because younger labour force participants are able to exit unemployment more quickly than older adults. Comparing the probability trajectories of exiting unemployment that are presented in Figures 5.6 and 5.7 supports this tendency. In fact, low skilled younger adults appear to have better chances of finding a job than low skilled older adults. This highlights the difficulties that displaced workers face when searching for a job at an older age.

Even so, older adults with higher skills find it easier to obtain employment. Figure 5.7 shows that older labour force participants who score at Levels 3 and 4/5 on the document literacy scale have a higher probability of finding employment more quickly when compared to those scoring at Levels 1 and 2. But note that while this analysis is done using pooled international data, the results are likely to vary according to the relative demand and supply for low skills in specific regions. It is expected that relatively high demand for, and/or low supply of, skilled workers will reduce the difference between the employability of low and medium to high skilled workers.

FIGURE 5.7

Probability of older workers exiting unemployment by skills levels

The probabilities of unemployed adults aged 50 to 65 to exit unemployment over a 52 week period, by low (Levels 1 and 2) and medium to high (Levels 3 and 4/5) skills, document scale, 2003

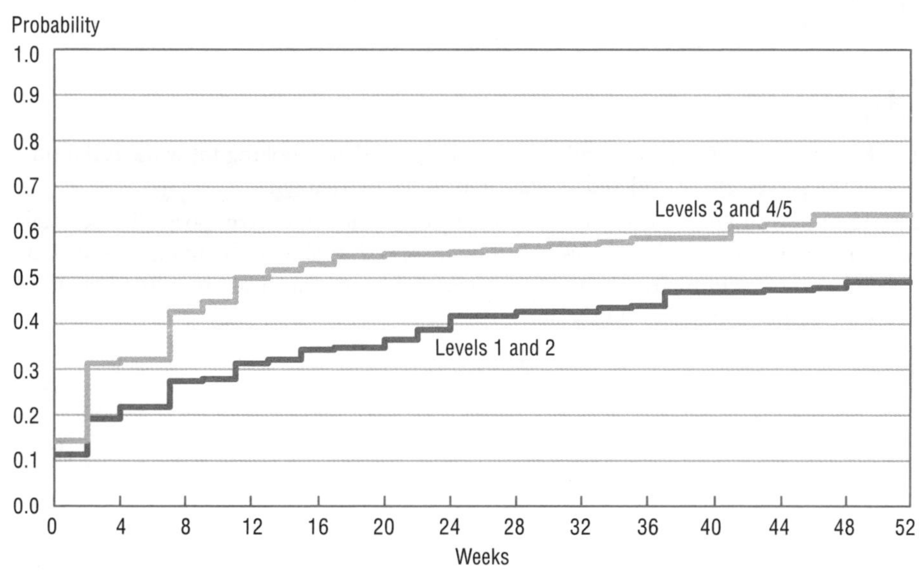

Source: Adult Literacy and Life Skills Survey, 2003.

For many, the link between foundation skills and employability is not necessarily direct. Employability also depends on the willingness and capacity of workers to participate in training. But adults aged 56 to 65 are the least likely to participate in adult education and training (OECD, 2003). Moreover, participation itself is linked to foundation skills (see Figure 4.4 in Chapter 4). Many lack the basic skills to engage in training that maintains their employability, including younger and older workers.

Those working in jobs requiring predominantly firm-specific or technology-specific skills for extended periods of time are likely to be the most vulnerable. Evidence suggests that working in an environment with limited complexity or repetitive tasks leads to skills loss over time (Krahn and Lowe, 1998). In particular, low requirements for literacy and numeracy skills at work may be associated with loss of these skills (See Chapter 6). Therefore it is expected that adults with this type of labour force experience face increased difficulties to participate in training courses that are otherwise needed to keep up with changes in skill requirements.

Endnotes

1. Persons who were either employed or unemployed and looking for work at the time of the survey are considered active labour force participants.
2. The prose and document literacy scales are combined into a composite literacy scale for the purposes of this analysis. Although, it is desirable to maintain two separate literacy scales for many analyses, the theoretical and empirical properties also allow for creating composite skill scales.

References

Bailey, T. (1997), "Changes in the Nature of Work: Implications for Skills and Assessment", in H.F. O'Neil (ed.), *Workforce Readiness: Competencies and Assessment,* Lawrence Erlbaum Associates, Mahwah, NJ.

Brown, P., Green, A. and Lauder, H. (eds.) (2001), *High Skills,* Oxford University Press, Oxford.

Carnevale, A.P., Gainer, L.J. and Meltzer, A.S. (1990), *Workplace Basics: The Essential Skills Employers Want,* Jossey-Bass, San Francisco.

Dickerson, A. and Green, F. (2004), "The Growth and Valuation of Computing and Other Generic Skills", *Oxford Economic Papers,* Vol. 56(3), pp. 371-406.

De Grip, A. and van Loo, J. (2002), "The Economics of Skills Obsolescence: A review", *Research in Labor Economics,* Vol. 21, pp. 1-26.

De Grip, A., van Loo, J. and Sanders, J. (2004), "The Industry Employability Index: Taking account of supply and demand characteristics", *International Labour Review,* Vol. 143(3), pp. 211-233.

Dubin, S. (1972), "Obsolescence or Lifelong Education", *American Psychologist,* Vol. 27, pp. 486-498.

Heckman, J. (1999), "Policies to Foster Human Capital", NBER Working Paper 7288, Cambridge, Massachussetts.

HRDC (2001, October 12), "Readers' Guide to Essential Skills Profiles, Skills Information Division", Human Resources and Skills Development Canada, Hull, Quebec. Retrieved from http://www15.hrdc-drhc.gc.ca/english/readers_guide_whole.asp.

Judy, R. and D'Amico, C. (1997), *Workforce 2020: Work and Workers in the 21st Century,* Hudson Institute, Indianapolis, IN.

Kaplan, E.L. and Meier, P. (1958), "Nonparametric Estimation from Incomplete Observations", *Journal of the American Statistical Association,* Vol. 53, pp. 457-458.

Krahn, H. and Lowe, G.S. (1998), *Literacy Utilization in Canadian Workplaces,* Statistics Canada and Human Resource Development Canada, Ottawa and Hull.

Machin, S. (2001), "The Changing Nature of Labour Demand in the New Economy and Skill-biased Technology Change", *Oxford Bulletin of Economics and Statistics,* Vol. 63, pp. 753-776.

OECD (2002), *Employment Outlook,* Paris.

OECD (2003), *Employment Outlook,* Paris.

Rosen, S. (1975), "Measuring the Obsolescence of Knowledge", in F.T. Juster (ed.), *Education, Income and Human Behavior,* McGraw-Hill, New York, pp. 199-232.

Ryan, P. (2001), "The School-to-Work Transition: A Cross-National Perspective", *Journal of Economic Literature,* Vol. 39(1), pp. 34-92.

Secretary's Commission on Achieving Necessary Skills (1991), *What Work Requires of Schools: A SCANS Report for America 2000,* U.S. Department of Labor, Washington, DC.

Statistics Canada (2004), *Literacy Scores, Human Capital and Growth Across Fourteen OECD Countries*, Ottawa.

UK Youth (2002), *Basic Skills and Young Adults,* London.

Contributors

Patrick Werquin, *OECD*

Isabelle Recotillet, *Centre d'études et de recherches sur les qualifications, Marseilles*

Richard Desjardins, *Statistics Canada*

Annex 5

Data Values for the Figures

5

TABLE 5.1

Score of the 75th percentile on a scale with range 0 to 500 points, labour force populations aged 16 to 25, 26 to 45 and 46 to 65, 2003

	Age	75th percentile	
A. Prose and document literacy scales combined			
Bermuda	16 to 25	317.3	(5.2)
	26 to 45	327.8	(3.0)
	46 to 65	311.2	(3.6)
Canada	16 to 25	321.3	(2.7)
	26 to 45	324.8	(1.5)
	46 to 65	312.1	(1.6)
Italy	16 to 25	265.8	(3.2)
	26 to 45	275.8	(2.8)
	46 to 65	262.2	(2.8)
Norway	16 to 25	323.7	(3.3)
	26 to 45	332.1	(2.2)
	46 to 65	313.0	(2.5)
Nuevo Leon, Mexico	16 to 25	261.5	(2.0)
	26 to 45	264.3	(2.0)
	46 to 65	245.7	(3.3)
Switzerland	16 to 25	314.8	(7.1)
	26 to 45	313.1	(1.7)
	46 to 65	296.0	(2.9)
United States	16 to 25	305.8	(4.9)
	26 to 45	310.6	(2.8)
	46 to 65	308.4	(3.4)

TABLE 5.1 (concluded)

Score of the 75th percentile on a scale with range 0 to 500 points, labour force populations aged 16 to 25, 26 to 45 and 46 to 65, 2003

	Age	75th percentile	
B. Numeracy[1] scale			
Bermuda	16 to 25	296.3	(7.7)
	26 to 45	315.5	(2.3)
	46 to 65	296.0	(4.2)
Canada	16 to 25	313.9	(3.1)
	26 to 45	320.5	(1.7)
	46 to 65	305.0	(1.9)
Italy	16 to 25	262.9	(4.8)
	26 to 45	277.5	(2.4)
	46 to 65	268.8	(2.5)
Norway	16 to 25	312.2	(3.4)
	26 to 45	324.7	(1.5)
	46 to 65	308.5	(2.2)
Switzerland	16 to 25	324.5	(12.3)
	26 to 45	331.0	(3.1)
	46 to 65	311.9	(2.7)
United States	16 to 25	298.9	(4.5)
	26 to 45	307.1	(2.7)
	46 to 65	304.4	(2.8)
C. Problem solving[2] scale			
Bermuda	16 to 25	306.2	(5.9)
	26 to 45	315.6	(2.4)
	46 to 65	297.6	(4.5)
Canada	16 to 25	314.8	(4.6)
	26 to 45	316.0	(1.6)
	46 to 65	301.6	(1.8)
Italy	16 to 25	258.5	(3.7)
	26 to 45	273.5	(3.0)
	46 to 65	258.3	(3.6)
Norway	16 to 25	324.8	(3.6)
	26 to 45	327.8	(1.9)
	46 to 65	301.9	(3.1)
Switzerland[3]	16 to 25	316.1	(5.7)
	26 to 45	316.5	(2.4)
	46 to 65	299.1	(3.9)

1. The state of Nuevo Leon in Mexico fielded the IALS quantitative literacy assessment rather than the ALL numeracy assessment. Although closely related conceptually, these two scales cannot be directly compared.
2. United States and Nuevo Leon, Mexico did not field the problem solving skills domain.
3. The problem solving skills scores for Switzerland apply to the German and French speaking communities only since they did not field the problem solving skills domain in the Italian speaking community.

Source: Adult Literacy and Life Skills Survey, 2003.

TABLE 5.2

Score of the 25th percentile on a scale with range 0 to 500 points, labour force populations aged 16 to 25, 26 to 45 and 46 to 65, 2003

	Age	25th percentile	
A. Prose and document scales combined			
Bermuda	16 to 25	254.9	(9.7)
	26 to 45	259.9	(3.1)
	46 to 65	231.1	(4.1)
Canada	16 to 25	262.1	(3.7)
	26 to 45	259.5	(2.0)
	46 to 65	244.5	(3.1)
Italy	16 to 25	198.6	(4.2)
	26 to 45	204.7	(2.7)
	46 to 65	186.4	(4.4)
Norway	16 to 25	278.9	(4.4)
	26 to 45	279.4	(1.8)
	46 to 65	254.4	(2.1)
Nuevo Leon, Mexico	16 to 25	212.2	(4.1)
	26 to 45	213.5	(2.9)
	46 to 65	187.3	(5.4)
Switzerland	16 to 25	263.2	(10.9)
	26 to 45	252.1	(2.8)
	46 to 65	240.0	(2.5)
United States	16 to 25	242.1	(4.0)
	26 to 45	243.3	(2.3)
	46 to 65	240.4	(3.2)
B. Numeracy[1] scale			
Bermuda	16 to 25	229.6	(8.5)
	26 to 45	242.0	(3.3)
	46 to 65	217.4	(3.7)
Canada	16 to 25	247.6	(2.7)
	26 to 45	247.0	(2.1)
	46 to 65	234.0	(2.1)
Italy	16 to 25	200.2	(4.8)
	26 to 45	214.8	(2.1)
	46 to 65	202.1	(3.4)
Norway	16 to 25	256.5	(7.1)
	26 to 45	268.9	(2.3)
	46 to 65	248.3	(2.9)
Switzerland	16 to 25	262.3	(9.7)
	26 to 45	266.4	(2.4)
	46 to 65	253.0	(4.2)
United States	16 to 25	220.7	(5.4)
	26 to 45	230.4	(2.4)
	46 to 65	228.6	(4.1)

TABLE 5.2 (concluded)

Score of the 25th percentile on a scale with range 0 to 500 points, labour force populations aged 16 to 25, 26 to 45 and 46 to 65, 2003

	Age	25th percentile	
C. Problem solving[2] scale			
Bermuda	16 to 25	237.1	(10.5)
	26 to 45	249.5	(3.5)
	46 to 65	223.5	(3.8)
Canada	16 to 25	257.3	(2.7)
	26 to 45	251.7	(2.2)
	46 to 65	237.1	(2.1)
Italy	16 to 25	187.5	(7.2)
	26 to 45	198.6	(3.3)
	46 to 65	184.3	(4.1)
Norway	16 to 25	270.3	(5.0)
	26 to 45	270.1	(2.5)
	46 to 65	242.8	(3.1)
Switzerland[3]	16 to 25	258.8	(8.9)
	26 to 45	247.6	(3.3)
	46 to 65	237.6	(3.4)

1. The state of Nuevo Leon in Mexico fielded the IALS quantitative literacy assessment rather than the ALL numeracy assessment. Although closely related conceptually, these two scales cannot be directly compared.
2. United States and Nuevo Leon, Mexico did not field the problem solving skills domain.
3. The problem solving skills scores for Switzerland apply to the German and French speaking communities only since they did not field the problem solving skills domain in the Italian speaking community.

Source: Adult Literacy and Life Skills Survey, 2003.

TABLE 5.3

Odds ratios showing the likelihood of experiencing labour force inactivity for 6 months or more in the last 12 months compared to being employed all year, by numeracy levels, populations aged 16 to 65, excluding students and retirees, 2003

	Levels 1 and 2		Levels 3 and 4/5
	Not in labour force for 6 months or more		Employed all year
Bermuda	1.29	(0.24)	1.00
Canada	2.62***	(0.08)	1.00
Italy	3.49***	(0.16)	1.00
Norway	2.80***	(0.21)	1.00
Switzerland	2.17***	(0.19)	1.00
United States	2.61***	(0.17)	1.00

* $p<0.10$, statistically significant at the 10 per cent level.
** $p<0.05$, statistically significant at the 5 per cent level.
*** $p<0.01$, statistically significant at the 1 per cent level.
Note: Standard errors are of the logarithm of the odds ratios.
Source: Adult Literacy and Life Skills Survey, 2003.

TABLE 5.4

Odds ratios showing the likelihood of experiencing unemployment for 6 months or more in the last 12 months compared to being employed all year, by numeracy levels, labour force populations aged 16 to 65, 2003

	Levels 1 and 2		Levels 3 and 4/5
	Unemployed for 6 months or more		Employed all year
Bermuda	2.04	(0.74)	1.00
Canada	1.92***	(0.19)	1.00
Italy	1.68**	(0.25)	1.00
Norway	2.55	(0.58)	1.00
Switzerland	3.02	(0.64)	1.00
United States	2.36**	(0.37)	1.00

* p<0.10, statistically significant at the 10 per cent level.
** p<0.05, statistically significant at the 5 per cent level.
*** p<0.01, statistically significant at the 1 per cent level.
Note: Standard errors are of the logarithm of the odds ratios.
Source: Adult Literacy and Life Skills Survey, 2003.

TABLE 5.5

The probabilities of unemployed adults aged 16 to 65 to exit unemployment over a 52 week period, by low (Levels 1 and 2) and medium to high (Levels 3 and 4/5) skills, document scale, 2003

	Levels 1 and 2	Levels 3 and 4/5
Weeks	Probability	
0	0.124	0.161
2	0.253	0.363
4	0.281	0.392
7	0.345	0.511
9	0.350	0.530
11	0.395	0.578
13	0.397	0.583
15	0.420	0.621
17	0.423	0.626
20	0.448	0.643
22	0.453	0.647
24	0.468	0.660
26	0.469	0.663
28	0.474	0.673
30	0.475	0.675
33	0.484	0.683
35	0.485	0.683
37	0.494	0.687
39	0.495	0.687
41	0.500	0.694
43	0.500	0.696
46	0.502	0.700
48	0.502	0.701
50	0.502	0.701
52	0.502	0.701

Source: Adult Literacy and Life Skills Survey, 2003.

TABLE 5.6

The probabilities of unemployed adults aged 16 to 30 to exit unemployment over a 52 week period, by low (Levels 1 and 2) and medium to high (Levels 3 and 4/5) skills, document scale, 2003

Weeks	Levels 1 and 2	Levels 3 and 4/5
	Probability	
0	0.116	0.169
2	0.262	0.391
4	0.292	0.420
7	0.357	0.531
9	0.363	0.546
11	0.404	0.604
13	0.404	0.607
15	0.425	0.643
17	0.428	0.647
20	0.445	0.661
22	0.447	0.661
24	0.451	0.675
26	0.451	0.679
28	0.457	0.686
30	0.454	0.687
33	0.468	0.696
35	0.469	0.698
37	0.475	0.698
39	0.475	0.699
41	0.480	0.704
43	0.481	0.705
46	0.482	0.707
48	0.482	0.705
50	0.482	0.705
52	0.482	0.705

Source: Adult Literacy and Life Skills Survey, 2003.

TABLE 5.7

The probabilities of unemployed adults aged 50 to 65 to exit unemployment over a 52 week period, by low (Levels 1 and 2) and medium to high (Levels 3 and 4/5) skills, document scale, 2003

	Levels 1 and 2	Levels 3 and 4/5
Weeks	Probability	
0	0.113	0.143
2	0.192	0.313
4	0.215	0.323
7	0.273	0.426
9	0.280	0.450
11	0.315	0.499
13	0.322	0.516
15	0.342	0.532
17	0.349	0.548
20	0.367	0.552
22	0.387	0.553
24	0.417	0.558
26	0.419	0.563
28	0.427	0.568
30	0.427	0.574
33	0.435	0.579
35	0.438	0.587
37	0.468	0.587
39	0.470	0.588
41	0.471	0.613
43	0.472	0.616
46	0.477	0.637
48	0.491	0.639
50	0.491	0.639
52	0.491	0.639

Source: Adult Literacy and Life Skills Survey, 2003.

Chapter 6

Skills and the Nature of the Workplace

Summary

This chapter explores the relationship between different types of jobs, job tasks, and skills. First, the skill distributions of the workforce in technology- and knowledge-intensive industries are compared to other sectors. Similarly, the skills of workers in knowledge-intensive occupations are compared to those in other types of occupations. Second, the relationships between literacy and numeracy engagement at work and the skills measured by ALL are considered. Third, it is shown that the extent of engagement in literacy and numeracy activities is strongly linked to the types of occupations in which adults are employed. The last section looks at the match and mismatch between the skills of workers and the extent to which they engage in job tasks that require those skills.

6

Table of Contents

Skills and the Nature of the Workplace

6

6.1 Overview and highlights

This chapter explores the relationship between different types of jobs, job tasks, and skills. First, the skill distributions of the workforce in technology- and knowledge-intensive industries are compared to other sectors. Similarly, the skills of workers in knowledge-intensive occupations are compared to those in other types of occupations. Second, the relationships between literacy and numeracy engagement at work and the skills measured by ALL are considered. Third, it is shown that the extent of engagement in literacy and numeracy activities is strongly linked to the types of occupations in which adults are employed. The last section looks at the match and mismatch between the skills of workers and the extent to which they engage in job tasks that require those skills.

The highlights of the chapter are as follows:

- High skills industries including knowledge-intensive market service activities; high and medium-high technology manufacturing; and public administration, defense, education and health feature comparatively high proportions of adults at skill Levels 3 and 4/5.
- High and medium-high technology compared with low and medium-low technology manufacturing industries have comparatively higher proportions of skilled workers. Thus continued growth in the high technology sector is likely to cause upward pressure on the demand for skills.
- Occupations with high requirements for the use of cognitive skills including expert, management, and high-skill information types of jobs tend to feature higher proportions of workers with medium to high levels of the skills measured in ALL.
- "Old economy" types of occupations including low-skill services and goods-related types of jobs employ a limited proportion of workers with medium to high literacy and numeracy skills.
- There is a significant association between literacy and numeracy related practices at work and the skills measured in ALL. Workers

scoring at higher levels of literacy and numeracy skills also engage more frequently in literacy and numeracy related practices at work.

- All countries show apparent skills deficits as measured by the difference between observed skills and the extent to which those skills are required at work. That is, workers with low skills who are employed in jobs requiring comparatively high engagement in literacy and numeracy related job tasks. This applies to about 10 to 30 per cent of the workforce depending on the country.
- All countries show apparent skills surpluses as measured by the difference between observed skills and the extent to which those skills are required at work. That is, workers with medium to high skills who are employed in jobs requiring comparatively low engagement in literacy and numeracy related job tasks. This is good for growing knowledge economies in the long run, but a lack of skills use in the workplace may be problematic in the short run. This follows from the "use it or lose it" hypothesis.

6.2 Skills in knowledge economies

Various processes including globalisation, technological and labour force changes as well as the increased use of flexible work practices have caused major structural changes in OECD economies and are likely to continue to do so (OECD and Statistics Canada, 2000; OECD 2001a; OECD 2001b; Judy and D'Amico, 1997). Many developments linked to such processes have led to more jobs that require higher levels of knowledge and skills. These are the types of jobs that form knowledge economies and raise the importance of skills such as those measured in the ALL survey. Accordingly this section reports on distributions of adult skills among different types of jobs. Findings are presented by two key variables often used to monitor growth in knowledge economies but also to describe the nature of one's employment, namely reclassifications of the International Standard Industry Classification (ISIC) and International Standard Classification of Occupations (ISCO).

Box 6A

Measuring technology- and knowledge-intensive industries

All industries are to some extent dependent on technology and knowledge inputs. However, some industries rely more on these than others. Recent efforts drawing on methodological work carried out at the OECD and by others have led to a categorization used in this section that delimits industries according to their relative intensity of technology in the case of manufacturing industries, and knowledge in the case of market service industries. See *Science, Technology and Industry Scoreboard* (OECD, 1999, pp. 18, 60, 137-140; and 2001b, p. 124) for further details.

In summary, all manufacturing industries are classified according to technology intensity into four categories as follows: high technology manufacturing, medium-high technology manufacturing, medium-low technology manufacturing, and low technology manufacturing. But note that due to sample size limitations for some countries the first and last two categories are collapsed when reporting skill distributions.

The knowledge-intensive market service activities category includes post and telecommunications (ISIC division 64), finance and insurance (ISIC divisions 65-67), and business activities excluding real estate (ISIC divisions 71-74).

In general, high-skill industries feature higher proportions of adults with medium to high levels of skill. In particular, Figure 6.1 shows that industries related to knowledge-intensive market service activities; public administration, defense, education and health; and high and medium-high technology manufacturing tend to have relatively higher proportions of adults at Levels 3 and 4/5 on the document scale than other types of industries (see Box 6A). The results, however, vary substantially by country.

For example, primary type industries in Norway feature comparatively high rates of medium to high skilled workers, reaching over 85 per cent. Bermuda and Canada also have about 50 per cent of those working in primary industries at Levels 3 and 4/5. Consequently, these countries are likely to have a comparative advantage in implementing technological, process and organizational innovations in the primary sector. Note that Norway has a high proportion of skilled workers in every type of industry, with at least 60 per cent of workers in each type of industry scoring at Levels 3 and 4/5. Canada also has high proportions in all types of industries, where only low and medium-low technology manufacturing industries have less than 50 per cent of workers with medium to high levels of document literacy skills.

In every country, high and medium-high technology compared to low and medium-low technology manufacturing industries have comparatively more skilled workers. Results are similar for other skill domains but are not reported here. High-technology industries account for a growing share of OECD-wide value added and international trade and are expected to play a significant role in economic growth (OECD, 2004). Therefore, this is an expanding sector that is likely to put upward pressure on the demand for skills.

Industry classifications are relevant to skills analysis (and vice versa) because they are useful in delimiting the extent and nature of particular technologies and work practices that are prevailing in different industry sectors. But skills represent much of the know-how used to carry out job tasks and therefore, are likely to be more closely associated with occupational classifications. After all, occupational classifications are partly based on descriptions of work tasks and the skills needed to complete those successfully.

FIGURE 6.1

Knowledge- and technology-based industry classification by skills

Per cent of labour force populations aged 16 to 65 at document literacy Levels 3 and 4/5, by type of industry, 2003

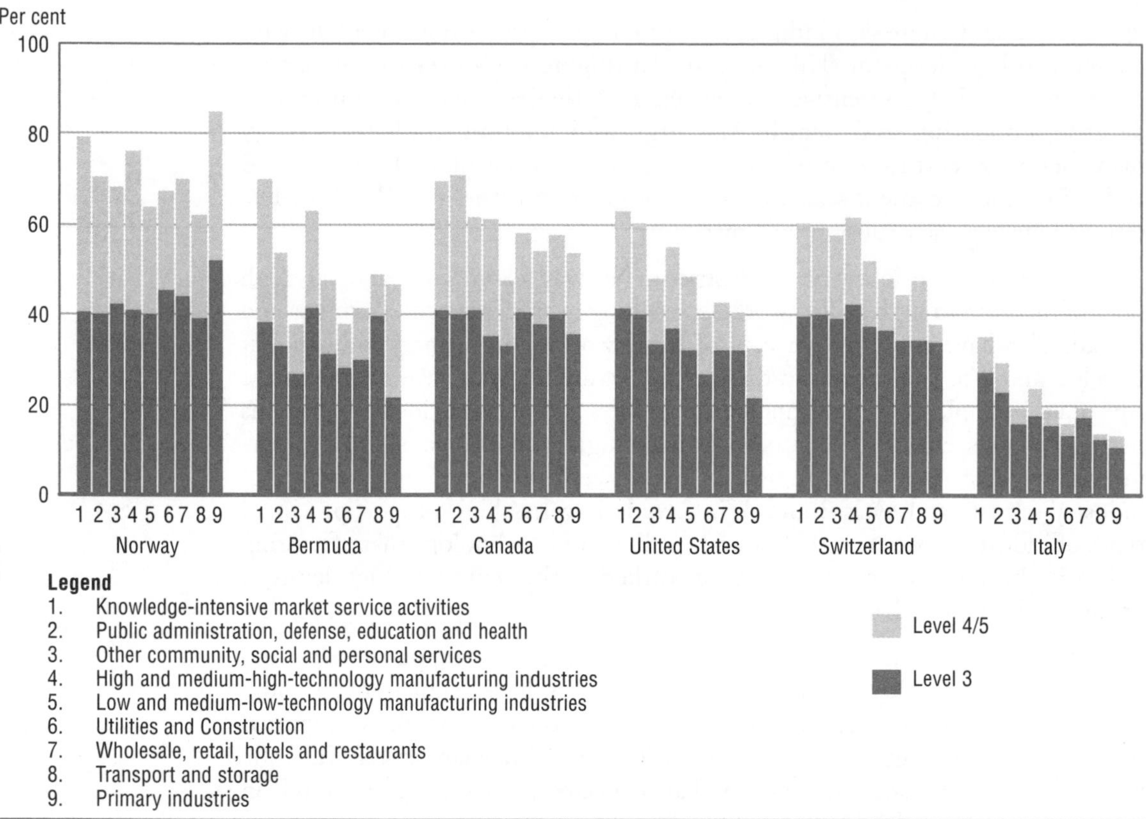

Countries are ranked by the combined proportion of persons at Levels 3 and 4/5 in knowledge-intensive market service activities.

Source: Adult Literacy and Life Skills Survey, 2003.

Box 6B

Measuring knowledge-based occupations

A number of recent efforts reclassify the International Standard Classification of Occupations (ISCO) into fewer occupational groups (e.g., Osberg, Wolff and Baumol, 1989; Lavoie and Roy, 1998; Boothby, 1999). These efforts attempt to delimit types of occupations on the basis of knowledge content and common skills requirements including cognitive, communication, management and motor skills. Many skills are required in varying degrees to carry out typical tasks associated with different jobs, but some preliminary evidence suggests that occupations tend to cluster according to relatively few mixes of skill requirements and accordingly few occupational types (Béjaoui, 2000). Note that the types of skills measured in ALL are considered to be associated with cognitive skills only.

In this section, all ISCO occupations are classified according to different types of job tasks that require varying skills as follows: knowledge expert, management, information high-skill, information low-skill, services low-skill, and goods-related.

See Boothby (1999) and Béjaoui (2000) for a more detailed description of the relative requirements of different skills by occupational types. In summary, knowledge expert types of occupations require the most use of cognitive skills, more than average management and communication skills as well as fine motor skills. Although managers are required to use cognitive skills slightly less intensively than experts, they are required to use management and communication skills the most often, making their required skills set the most balanced. Similar to experts, high-skill information occupations require the use of cognitive, management and communication skills more than the average. Although lower, low-skill information occupations also require the use of these skills slightly more than average. Low-skill services and good-related occupations require the use of these types of skills comparatively less often.

Figure 6.2a-c reports on skill distributions by the occupational types described in Box 6B. In general, occupational types that have higher requirements for the use of cognitive skills also tend to feature higher proportions of persons with medium to high levels (Levels 3 and 4/5) of the skills measured in ALL. This is the case for all domains including prose and document literacy, numeracy and problem solving. Within countries, the pattern of distributions are very similar. Occupations that form knowledge economies including expert, management, high-skill and low-skill information types, have higher proportions of skilled workers than "old economy" types of occupations such as low-skill services and goods-related. Moreover, the supply of skills in the "old economy" appears to be limited.

Following an economic downturn in the early 2000s, many OECD countries are placing even more emphasis on the development of knowledge economies (European Communities, 2004). The aim is to increase competitiveness, create 'good' jobs and sustain long-term economic growth. At the same time there is a major concern in most OECD countries about ageing populations (OECD, 2003). This combined with other upward pressures on the demand for skill, has many suggesting that labour markets cannot rely solely on higher graduation rates and quality improvements in initial education systems. Accordingly, many OECD countries also emphasize lifelong learning policies that aim to raise the skill levels of the current workforce. But as noted in Chapter 4, marked increases in the rate of participation in adult education and training experienced in most participating countries are also accompanied by strong indications that many people with low skills continue to be excluded from further education and training.

FIGURE 6.2 A to C

Knowledge-based occupational classification by skills

Per cent of labour force populations aged 16 to 65 at skills Levels 3 and 4/5, by type of occupation, 2003

A. Combined prose and document literacy scale

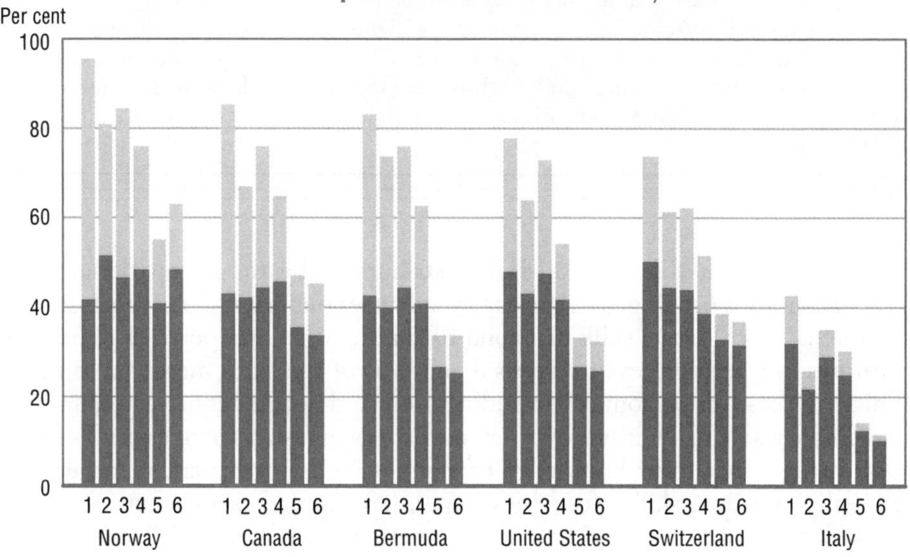

B. Numeracy scale

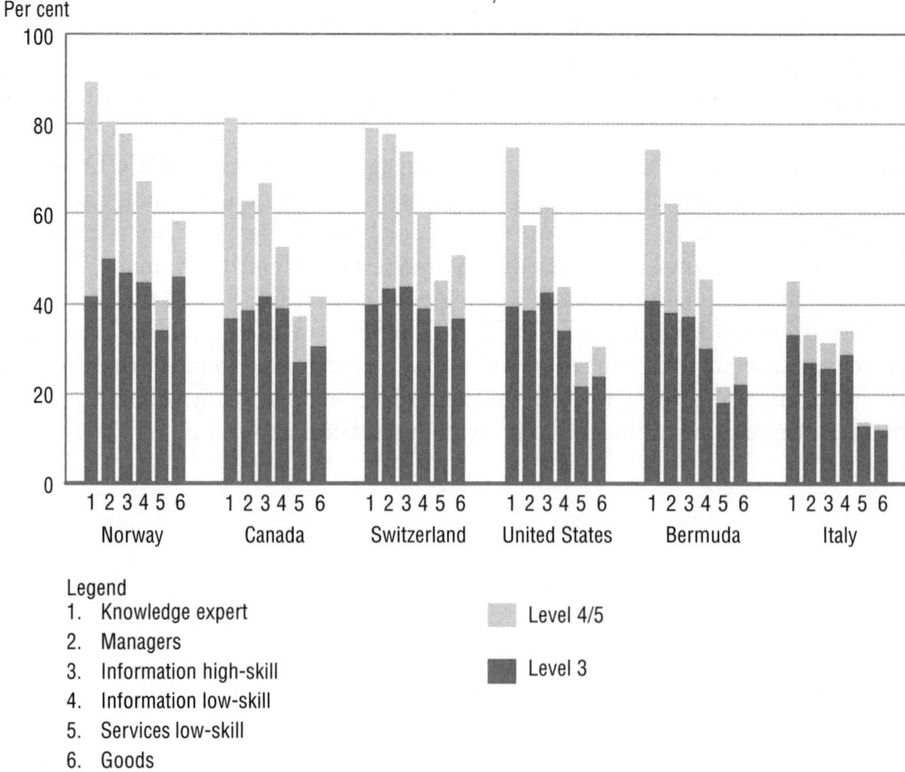

Legend
1. Knowledge expert
2. Managers
3. Information high-skill
4. Information low-skill
5. Services low-skill
6. Goods

Level 4/5

Level 3

Countries are ranked by the combined proportion of persons at Levels 3 and 4/5 in knowledge expert occupations.

Source: Adult Literacy and Life Skills Survey, 2003.

FIGURE 6.2 A to C (concluded)

Knowledge-based occupational classification by skills

Per cent of labour force populations aged 16 to 65 at skills Levels 3 and 4/5, by type of occupation, 2003

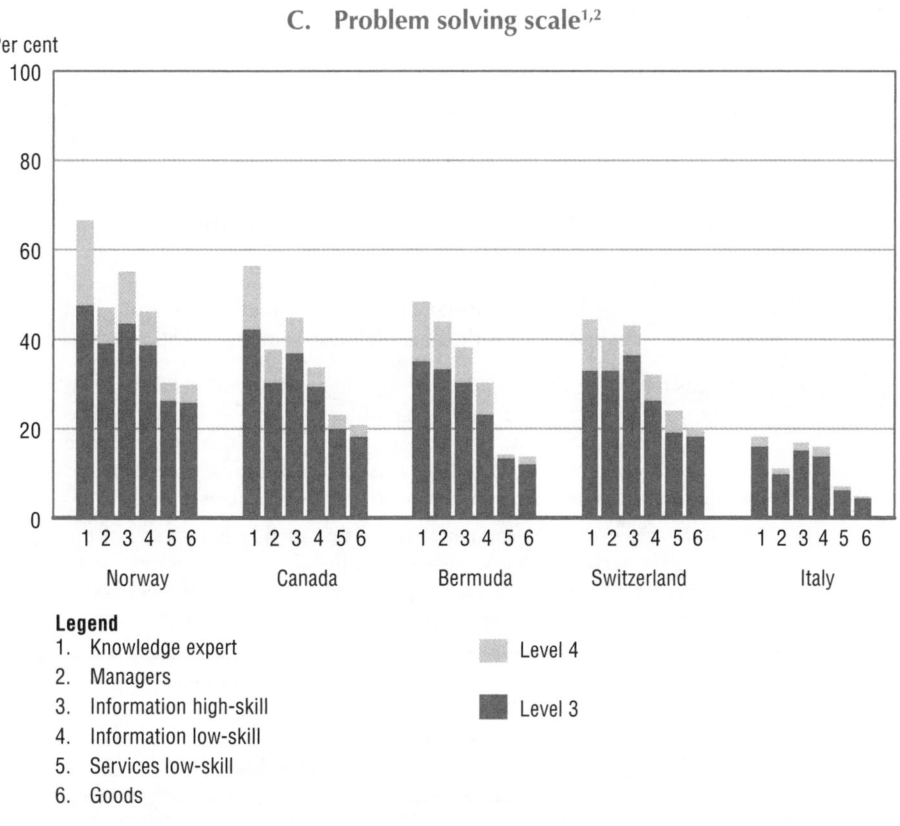

Countries are ranked by the combined proportion of persons at Levels 3 and 4 in knowledge expert occupations.

1. United States did not field the problem solving skills domain.
2. The problem solving skills scores for Switzerland apply to the German and French speaking communities only since they did not field the problem solving skills domain in the Italian speaking community.

Source: Adult Literacy and Life Skills Survey, 2003.

6.3 The relationship between job tasks and skills

The various tasks that workers engage in on a day to day basis require different types of skills to complete them in a satisfactory manner. Thus certain skills are closely related to specific job tasks. Accordingly, the ALL survey collected information on select job tasks that are relevant to the skills assessed. These data are used to create measures that gauge the extent to which adults engage in reading, writing and numeracy related activities at work (see Box 6C). This section considers such job tasks in relation to skills and the occupational types described in the previous section.

As expected, there is a clear association between literacy and numeracy related practices at work and the skills measured in ALL. Figures 6.3a-d show that persons scoring at higher levels of skill engage more in these practices. The data also offer other insights into the distribution of skills. The case of Italy provides an example of how the average level of engagement among all employed adults has an impact on the overall skills performance of the country as measured by ALL. In relation to other countries, Italians on average engage the least in literacy and numeracy related practices at work. Yet Italian adults who engage more also score higher just like in comparison countries.

Box 6C

Measuring engagement in literacy and numeracy related tasks at work

The ALL survey gathered information on select reading, writing and numeracy related activities at work. This includes 17 items as follows:

- Six items regarding the frequency of reading or using information from each of the following as part of the respondent's main job: letters, memos or e-mails; reports, articles, magazines or journals; manuals or reference books including catalogues; diagrams or schematics; directions or instructions; bills, invoices, spreadsheets or budget tables.
- Five items regarding the frequency of writing or filling out each of the following as part of the respondent's main job: letters, memos or e-mails; reports, articles, magazines or journals; manuals or reference books including catalogues; directions or instructions; bills, invoices, spreadsheets or budget tables.
- Six items regarding the frequency of doing each of the following as part of the respondent's main job: measure or estimate the size or weight of objects; calculate prices, costs or budgets; count or read numbers to keep track of things; manage time or prepare timetables; give or follow directions or use maps or street directories; use statistical data to reach conclusions.

Using these items, reading, writing and numeracy indices were created. This involved a three step process. First, Exploratory Factor Analysis (EFA) was used to explore and model the data. Second, Confirmatory Factor Analysis (CFA) was used to validate the models chosen and hence the indices. Third, items were selected and scaled according to the CFA using the Rasch item response model. The scale score is a weighted maximum likelihood estimate, and countries were given equal weight in the scaling process. Indices are standardized so the mean of the index value for the combined sample of all participating countries is two and the standard deviation is one. But for the purpose of the analyses reported in Figures 6.3, 6.4 and 6.5, the index scores are reported as ranging from zero to four in order to facilitate the interpretation of the scale. The scale values roughly correspond as follows: one is "never"; two is "rarely"; three is "less than once a week"; and four is "at least once a week".

FIGURE 6.3 A to D

Practice engagement at work by skills levels

Index scores of reading, writing and numeracy engagement at work on a standardized scale (centred on 2), by skills levels, labour force populations aged 16 to 65, 2003

A. Reading engagement at work index by document literacy levels

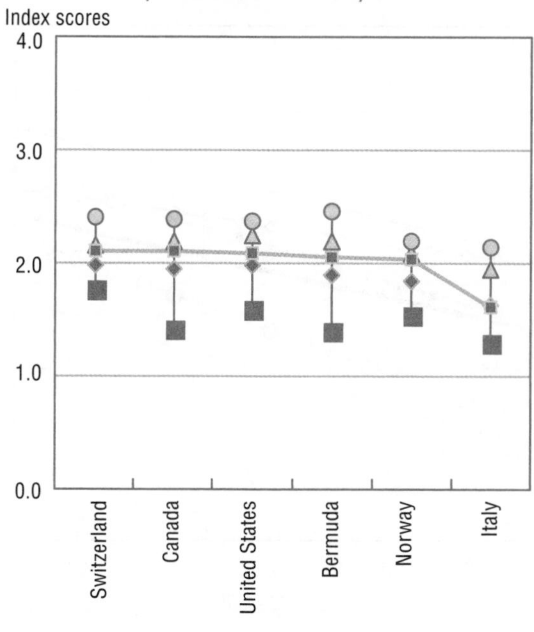

B. Writing engagement at work index by prose literacy levels

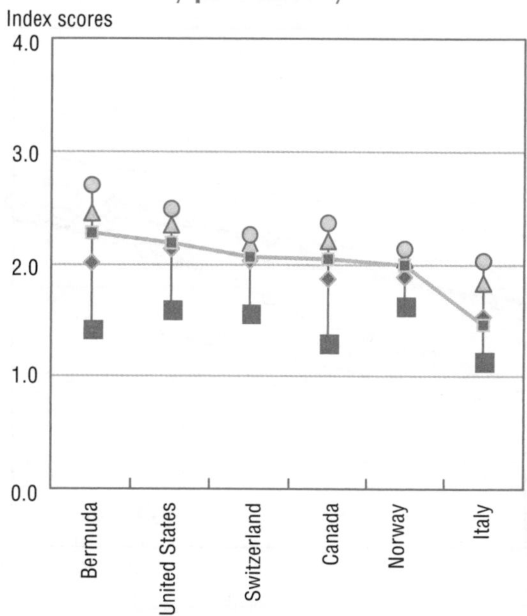

C. Numeracy engagement at work index by numeracy levels

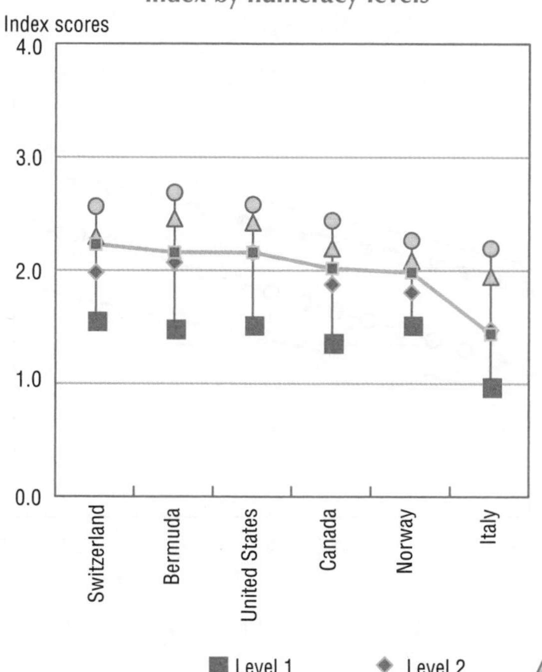

D. Combined engagement at work index by problem solving levels

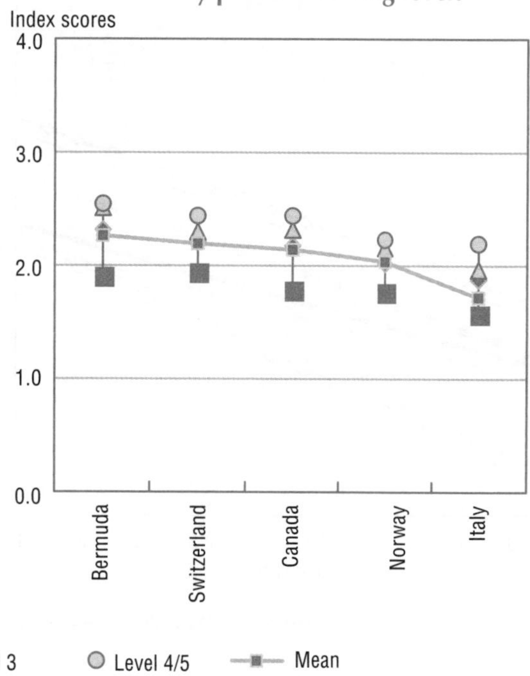

Level 1 Level 2 Level 3 Level 4/5 Mean

Countries are ranked by the mean of the index scale.

Source: Adult Literacy and Life Skills Survey, 2003.

FIGURE 6.4 A to D

Practice engagement at work and skills, controlling for education

Relationship between combined index scores of reading, writing and numeracy engagement at work on a standardized scale (centred on 2) and skills scores on scales 0 to 500 points, adjusted for years of schooling and native language status, labour force populations aged 16 to 65, 2003

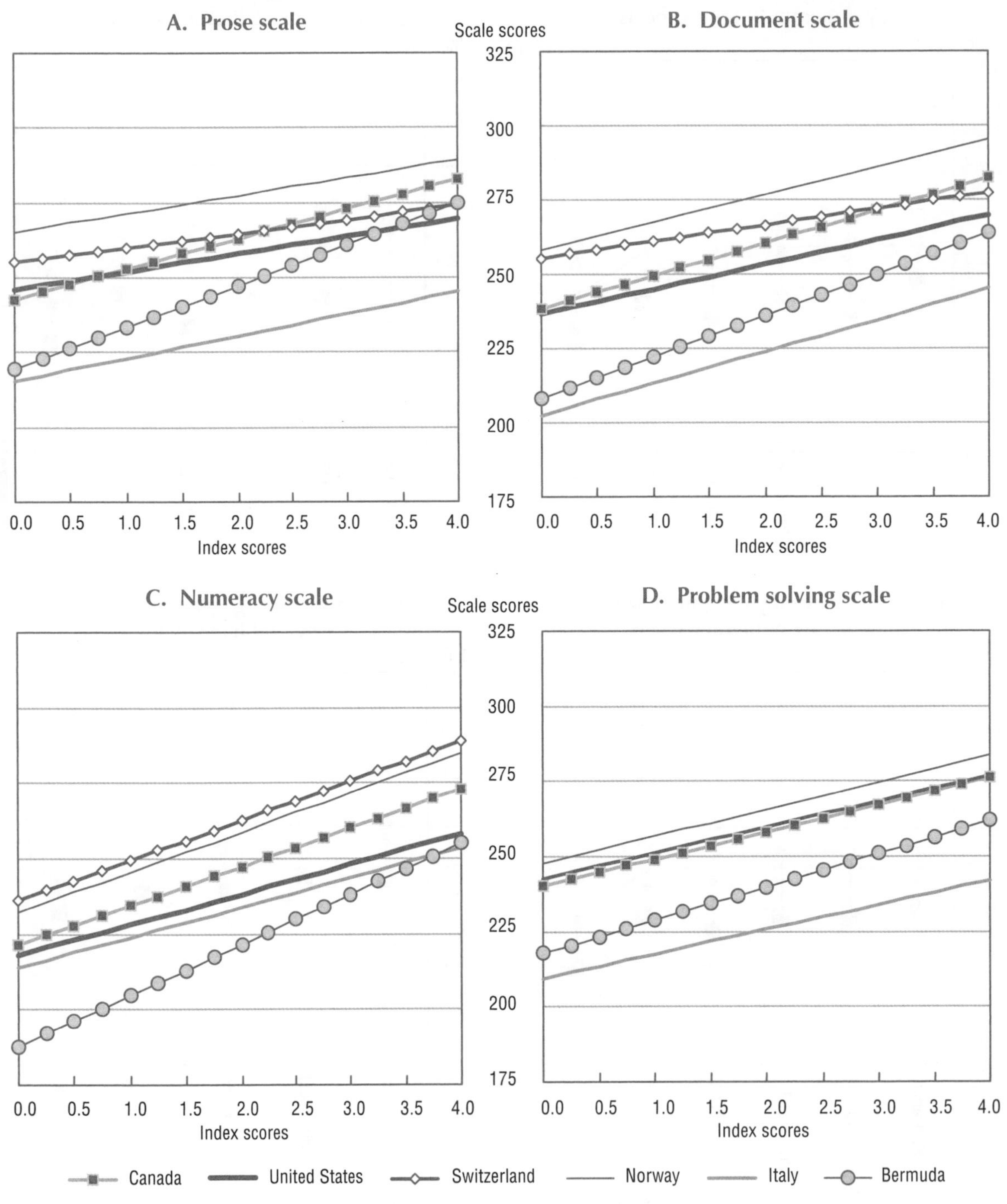

1. United States did not field the problem solving skills domain.
2. The problem solving skills scores for Switzerland apply to the German and French speaking communities only since they did not field the problem solving skills domain in the Italian speaking community.

Source: Adult Literacy and Life Skills Survey, 2003.

An important question is whether engagement in these practices leads to the formation of skills or whether persons are engaging in these tasks because they already have high levels of skill. This is a difficult question that is impossible to answer with certainty when working with cross-sectional data. But the answer has important implications for initial education and adult education and training systems. In reality, both possibilities are likely to be significant and vary according to individual life experiences. Figures 6.4a-d consider the relationships between practice engagement and skills, after taking into account completed years of schooling and whether the respondents mother tongue is the same as the test language. The results show that in every country, practice engagement maintains a strong positive relation with skills. Only in Switzerland is the extent of engagement in reading at work not related to skills after adjusting for education and native language status.

These findings imply that even after taking into account initial schooling experiences, practice engagement tends to have a significant relation to skills. This is not surprising, since learning by doing (or practice engagement or informal learning) in the work place and in daily life involves processes that play an important role in the formation of skills. Previous findings and research based on IALS also assert that skills are like muscles that need to be exercised in order to be developed and maintained (Statistics Canada and OECD, 1995).

Processes of informal learning as well as the formation, transmission, storage and dissemination of knowledge are increasingly managed by firms in a proactive manner (Mårtensson, 2000). In general, there is an increased emphasis on viewing the work place as a learning place. Hence the reason for slogans such as "learning while working, and working while learning" and "learning organizations" that have gained currency in recent years. Few doubt the importance of learning at work but many questions merit further investigation and support. Major issues at the level of the firm are to understand better the nature of skills required for developing high performance work practices, how firms recruit these skills, and how to develop them through training and work organization.

At a macro level, these issues take on added urgency because of the growing share of knowledge-intensive jobs in labour markets and associated possible skills shortages. More knowledge intensive jobs imply an increased demand for literacy and numeracy related skills, including increased use of information and communication technologies. This is because many of the jobs forming knowledge economies require higher engagement in the processing of information including reading, writing and numeracy practices. Figures 6.5a-c show that the extent of engagement in literacy and numeracy practices at work is strongly associated with the occupational types introduced in the previous section (see Box 6B). Results display a consistent pattern which suggests that knowledge related occupations including experts, managers and high-skill information workers tend to engage more in these types of practices. Another major issue at the macro level is to understand better how different models of lifelong learning articulate with different competition strategies in sectors and economies as a whole.

FIGURE 6.5 A to C

Practice engagement at work by occupational types

Index scores of reading, writing and numeracy engagement at work on a standardized scale (centred on 2) by aggregated occupational types, labour force populations aged 16 to 65, 2003

A. Writing engagement at work

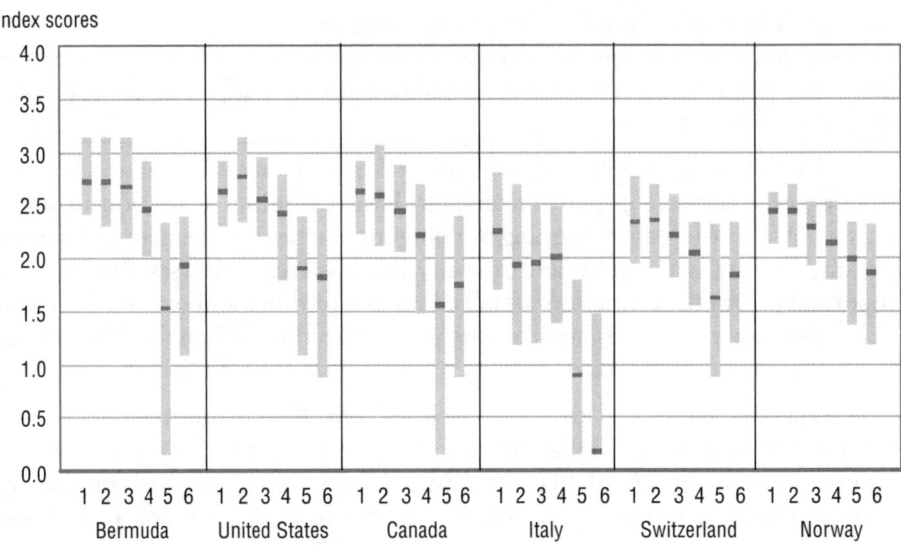

B. Reading engagement at work

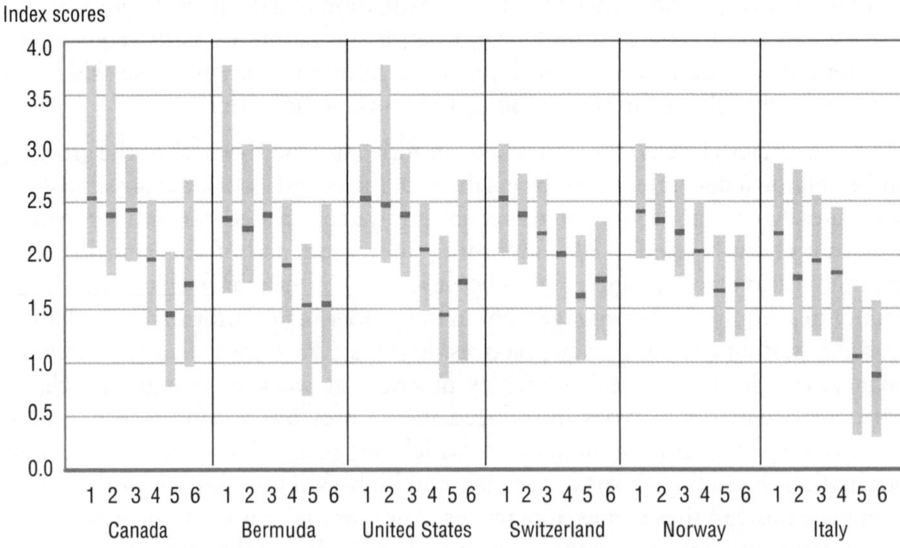

Legend

1. Knowledge expert
2. Managers
3. Information high-skill
4. Information low-skill
5. Services low-skill
6. Goods

A. Countries are ranked by the mean of the 75th percentile in knowledge expert occupations.

B. Countries are ranked by the mean of the 75th percentile in knowledge expert occupations, if tied, then ranked by the means of the 50th/25th pecentiles in knowledge expert occupations.

Source: Adult Literacy and Life Skills Survey, 2003.

FIGURE 6.5 A to C (concluded)

Practice engagement at work by occupational types

Index scores of reading, writing and numeracy engagement at work on a standardized scale (centred on 2) by aggregated occupational types, labour force populations aged 16 to 65, 2003

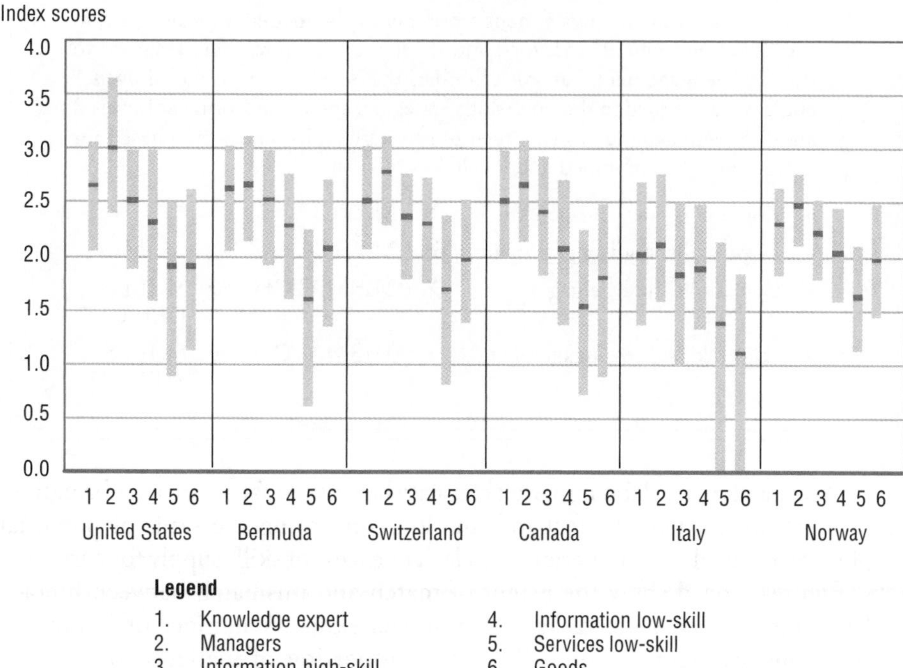

C. **Countries are ranked by the mean of the 75th percentile in knowledge expert occupations, if tied, then ranked by the mean of the 50th pecentile in knowledge expert occupations.**

Source: Adult Literacy and Life Skills Survey, 2003.

6.4 Match and mismatch between job tasks and observed skills

This section considers how workers actually use their skills in their jobs. Specifically it examines the match and mismatch between the day to day literacy and numeracy related requirements of workers and their actual skills as measured by ALL (See Box 6D). This is important for several reasons. First, there is a tendency to focus on individual deficits and remedial training, but the issue is broader than this. Deficits and the need for training depend on the requirements of the job. Also, skills are under-utilized in many labour markets (see Krahn and Lowe, 1998; Boothby, 1999). That is, many workers have high literacy and numeracy skills but do not use them at work. This is referred to as a "skills surplus". On the other hand, there are also many workers who have low skills but engage relatively often in literacy and numeracy related activities for productive purposes. This is referred to as a "skills deficit".

Box 6D

"Match" and "mismatch" between job tasks and skills

Match and mismatch is determined on the basis of reported engagement in literacy and numeracy related tasks at work and measured skills. The approach in this section is based on a methodology developed by Krahn and Lowe (1998). Persons with engagement scores below the median were assigned to the "low-engagement" category, and those scoring above were assigned to the "high-engagement" category. Similarly, persons scoring at skills Levels 1 and 2 were assigned to the "low-skills" category, and those scoring at Levels 3 and 4/5 were assigned to the "medium to high skills" category. These four categories were combined and labeled as follows:

- Low-skills, low-engagement → MATCH
- High-skills, high-engagement → MATCH
- Low-skills, high-engagement → MISMATCH → SKILLS DEFICIT
- High-skills, low-engagement → MISMATCH → SKILLS SURPLUS

Mismatch in the labour market can arise because of asymmetric information. Employers do not have perfect information concerning the skills of potential employees. It can also occur because of a lack or excess of skills supply for particular jobs. Figures 6.6a-d show the extent of match and mismatch between literacy and numeracy related job tasks and observed skills. A number of important observations are worth noting. First, the proportion of matches consistently exceeds 50 per cent of workers in every country and ranges up to over 60 per cent in all countries for the case of numeracy skills and numeracy engagement (see Figure 6.6c). This is not surprising, since one would expect that over time workers with higher skills would find their way into jobs requiring more skills, whereas those with few skills would not move up.

Skills deficits are apparent in every country, but the extent of the problem varies. Approximately 10 to 30 per cent of the workforce can fall into this category, depending on the country. Some countries have a comparatively high skills deficit. This is indicated by a high proportion of workers with low document and problem solving skills who are working in jobs that require high-engagement in literacy and numeracy related tasks. Presumably, a certain level of mismatch is expected in the labour market but whether 10 per cent, for example, is normal cannot be answered with certainty. Higher rates, however, are likely to suggest a need for adjustment; in particular, the need for an increased effort to train persons in those jobs.

The reserve of skills, or skills surplus, as defined by the number of workers with medium to high skills employed in jobs requiring low-engagement also varies substantially by country. For example, Norway has a reserve of skills in the document literacy domain equivalent to approximately 30 per cent of working adults whereas Italy's reserve is around 10 per cent. Overall country performances as measured by ALL tend to be related to the size of skill reserves. While a skills surplus is good for growing knowledge economies in the long run, a lack of skills use in the workplace may be problematic in the short run because it exposes workers to the risk of skill loss. This follows from the "use it or lose it" hypothesis (OECD and HRDC, 1997; Krahn and Lowe, 1998). The previous section suggested that practice engagement is important to nurture and develop skills. Some evidence suggests that the opposite may also be true. Workers who are deprived of the opportunity to perform complex literacy and numeracy tasks may lose some of their skills proficiency.

FIGURE 6.6 A to D

"Match" and "mismatch" between individual skills and practice engagement in the workplace

Per cent of labour force populations aged 16 to 65 whose skills match or mismatch their level of practice engagement at work, 2003

A. Prose literacy skills and writing engagement at work

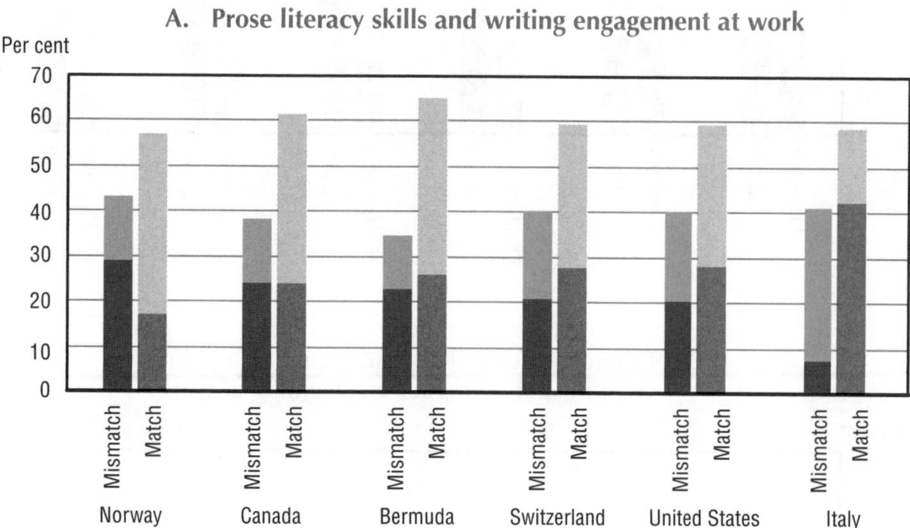

B. Document literacy skills and reading engagement at work

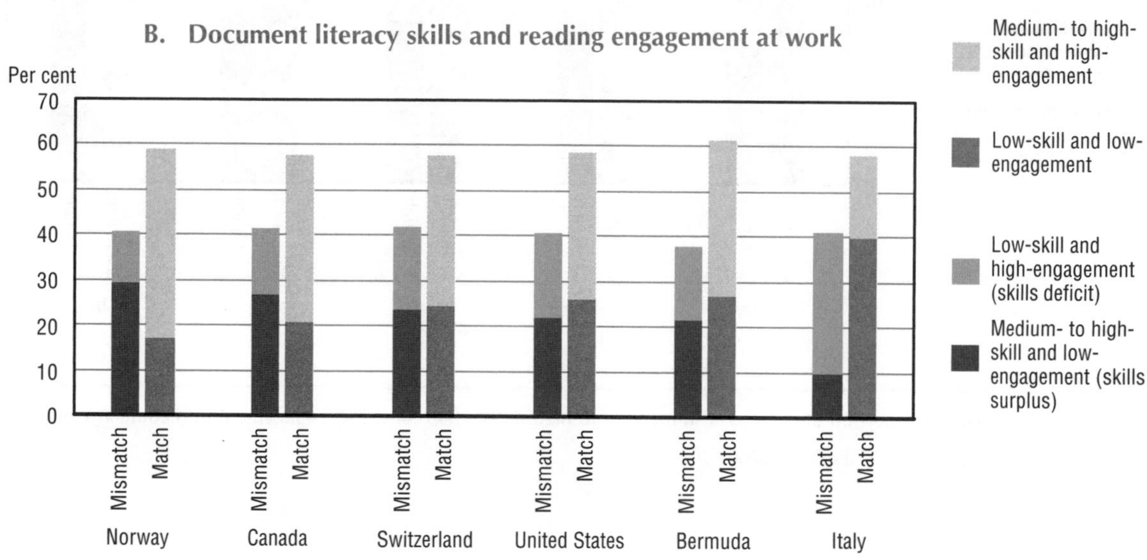

Countries are ranked by proportion of persons with medium to high skills who report low engagement in reading at work.

Source: Adult Literacy and Life Skills Survey, 2003.

FIGURE 6.6 A to D (concluded)

"Match" and "mismatch" between individual skills and practice engagement in the workplace

Per cent of labour force populations aged 16 to 65 whose skills match or mismatch their level of practice engagement at work, 2003

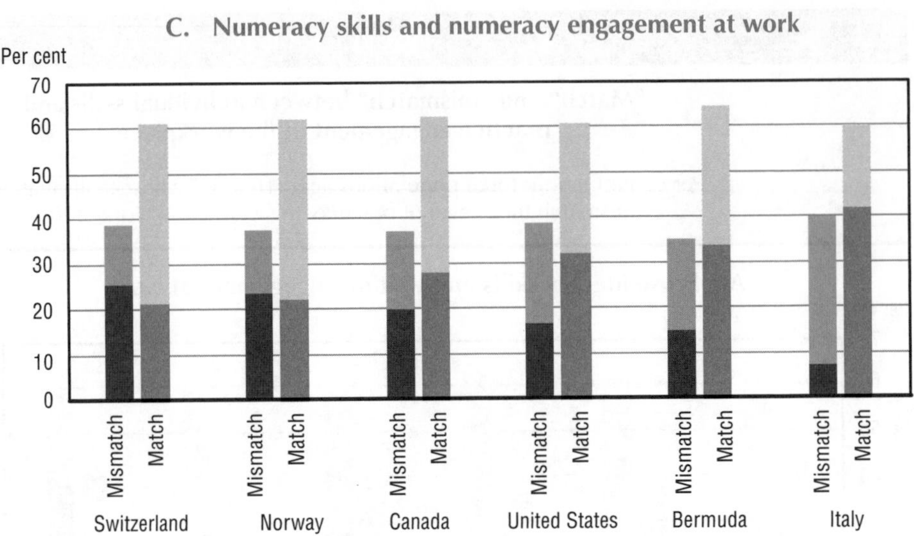

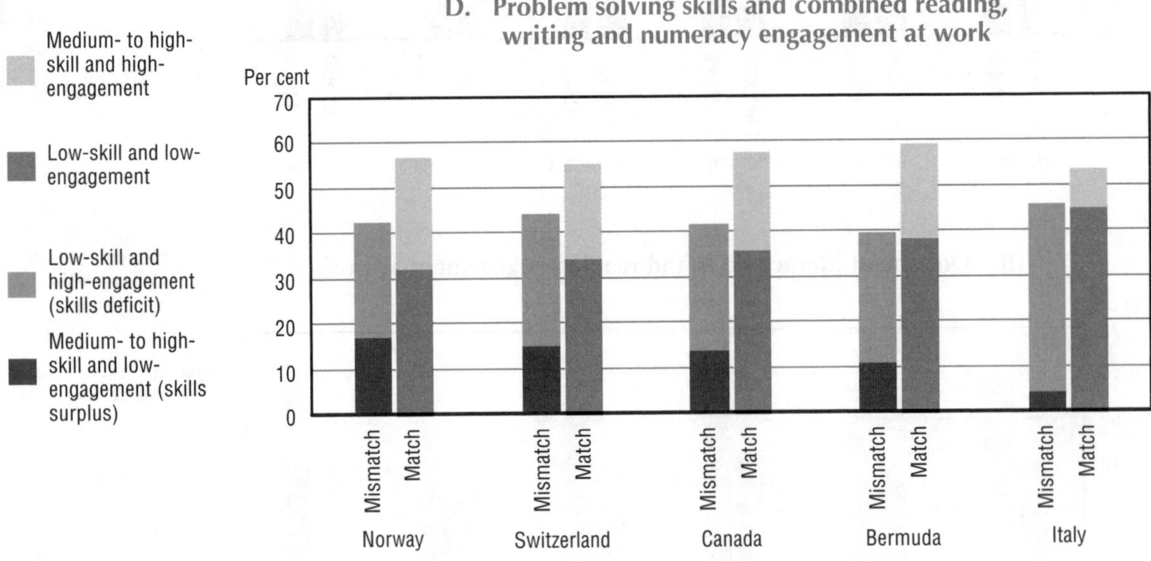

Countries are ranked by proportion of persons with medium to high skills who report low engagement in reading at work.

Source: Adult Literacy and Life Skills Survey, 2003.

References

Béjaoui, A. (2000), *L'évolution de la prime associée aux qualifications et son implication quant aux changements de la structures des salaires,* Université de Montréal, Montréal.

Boothby, D. (1999), "Literacy Skills, the Knowledge Content of Occupations and Occupational Mismatch", Working Paper 99-3E, Applied Research Branch, Human Resource Development Canada, Hull, Quebec.

European Communities (2004), *Facing the Challenge – The Lisbon Strategy for Growth and Employment,* Report from the High Level Group chaired by Wim Kok, November.

Judy, R. and D'Amico, C. (1997), *Workforce 2020: Work and Workers in the 21st Century,* Hudson Institute, Indianapolis, IN.

Krahn, H. and Lowe, G.S. (1998), *Literacy Utilization in Canadian Workplaces,* Statistics Canada and Human Resource Development Canada, Ottawa and Hull.

Lavoie, M. and Roy, R. (1998), "Employment in the Knowledge-based Economy: A growth accounting exercise for Canada", Research Paper, Applied Research Branch, Human Resources Development Canada, Hull, Quebec.

Mårtensson, M. (2000), "A Critical Review of Knowledge Management as a Management Tool", *Journal of Knowledge Management,* Vol. 4(3), pp. 204-216.

OECD (1994), *The OECD jobs study – Facts, analysis and strategies,* Paris.

OECD (1999), *Science, Technology and Industry Scoreboard: Benchmarking Knowledge-Based Economies,* Paris.

OECD (2001a), *Education Policy Analysis,* Paris.

OECD (2001b), *Science, Technology and Industry Scoreboard: Towards a Knowledge-Based Economy,* Paris.

OECD (2003), *Ageing, Housing and Urban Development,* Paris.

OECD (2004), *Science, Technology and Industry Outlook,* Paris.

OECD and HRDC (1997), *Literacy Skills for the Knowledge Society: Further Results from the International Adult Literacy Survey,* Paris and Hull.

OECD and Statistics Canada (2000), *Literacy in the Information Age: Final Report on the International Adult Literacy Survey,* Paris and Ottawa.

Osberg, L., Wolff, E.N. and Baumol, W.J. (1989), *The Information Economy: The Implications of Unbalanced Growth,* Institute for Research on Public Policy, Halifax.

Contributors

Richard Desjardins, *Statistics Canada*

Patrick Werquin, *OECD*

Annex 6

Data Values for the Figures

TABLE 6.1

Per cent of labour force populations aged 16 to 65 at document literacy Levels 3 and 4/5, by type of industry, 2003

	Level 3		Level 4/5	
Bermuda				
Knowledge-intensive market service activities	38.5	(4.8)	31.7	(2.6)
Public administration, defense, education and health	33.2	(4.2)	20.6	(2.8)
Other community, social and personal services	27.0	(5.4)	11.0	(3.1)
High and medium-high-technology manufacturing industries	41.4	(10.1)	21.4	(6.6)
Low and medium-low-technology manufacturing industries	31.3	(9.9)	16.4	(6.1)
Utilities and Construction	28.1	(4.8)	10.0	(2.9)
Wholesale, retail, hotels and restaurants	30.1	(4.3)	11.5	(2.1)
Transport and storage	39.6	(8.3)	9.4	(5.3)
Primary industries	21.4	(7.1)	25.3	(8.9)
Canada				
Knowledge-intensive market service activities	41.1	(2.0)	28.5	(2.0)
Public administration, defense, education and health	40.0	(1.8)	31.0	(1.8)
Other community, social and personal services	41.1	(4.7)	20.6	(4.1)
High and medium-high-technology manufacturing industries	35.2	(4.8)	26.1	(4.7)
Low and medium-low-technology manufacturing industries	32.9	(3.2)	14.8	(2.2)
Utilities and Construction	40.6	(4.6)	17.5	(2.9)
Wholesale, retail, hotels and restaurants	38.0	(2.2)	16.1	(1.4)
Transport and storage	40.2	(5.7)	17.6	(3.4)
Primary industries	35.8	(4.2)	18.0	(3.0)
Italy				
Knowledge-intensive market service activities	27.5	(3.6)	7.9	(2.2)
Public administration, defense, education and health	23.1	(2.3)	6.5	(1.3)
Other community, social and personal services	15.7	(4.9)	3.8	(1.6)
High and medium-high-technology manufacturing industries	17.8	(4.2)	5.8	(3.4)
Low and medium-low-technology manufacturing industries	15.6	(5.2)	3.3	(1.4)
Utilities and Construction	13.1	(3.2)	2.9	(1.5)
Wholesale, retail, hotels and restaurants	17.4	(2.3)	2.2	(1.0)
Transport and storage	12.3	(3.9)	1.4	(0.9)
Primary industries	10.7	(3.1)	2.6	(1.8)

TABLE 6.1 (concluded)

Per cent of labour force populations aged 16 to 65 at document literacy Levels 3 and 4/5, by type of industry, 2003

	Level 3		Level 4/5	
Norway				
Knowledge-intensive market service activities	40.7	(3.9)	38.7	(2.7)
Public administration, defense, education and health	40.1	(2.1)	30.4	(2.0)
Other community, social and personal services	42.1	(7.5)	26.3	(7.1)
High and medium-high-technology manufacturing industries	41.1	(7.1)	34.9	(5.9)
Low and medium-low-technology manufacturing industries	40.2	(5.6)	23.6	(4.3)
Utilities and Construction	45.2	(4.7)	22.4	(4.1)
Wholesale, retail, hotels and restaurants	44.0	(4.9)	26.0	(3.2)
Transport and storage	39.0	(5.9)	22.9	(4.8)
Primary industries	52.1	(8.5)	32.8	(7.6)
Switzerland				
Knowledge-intensive market service activities	39.8	(5.0)	20.7	(3.2)
Public administration, defense, education and health	39.9	(3.4)	19.4	(2.7)
Other community, social and personal services	39.3	(10.7)	18.5	(7.7)
High and medium-high-technology manufacturing industries	42.1	(8.6)	19.7	(4.9)
Low and medium-low-technology manufacturing industries	37.3	(7.4)	14.5	(4.8)
Utilities and Construction	36.4	(10.2)	11.7	(4.0)
Wholesale, retail, hotels and restaurants	34.5	(3.7)	9.8	(2.7)
Transport and storage	34.4	(7.5)	13.1	(5.4)
Primary industries	33.9	(10.5)	4.2	(3.5)
United States				
Knowledge-intensive market service activities	41.2	(3.8)	21.7	(3.4)
Public administration, defense, education and health	39.9	(3.1)	20.6	(2.2)
Other community, social and personal services	33.3	(6.1)	14.8	(3.5)
High and medium-high-technology manufacturing industries	37.0	(6.2)	17.9	(3.0)
Low and medium-low-technology manufacturing industries	32.3	(4.4)	16.0	(3.8)
Utilities and Construction	26.8	(3.9)	12.9	(3.5)
Wholesale, retail, hotels and restaurants	32.2	(2.5)	10.4	(1.8)
Transport and storage	32.2	(8.0)	8.2	(4.0)
Primary industries	21.7	(12.0)	11.0	(6.8)

Source: Adult Literacy and Life Skills Survey, 2003.

TABLE 6.2

Per cent of labour force populations aged 16 to 65 at skills Levels 3 and 4/5, by type of occupation, 2003

	Level 3		Level 4/5	
A. Combined prose and document literacy scale				
Bermuda				
Knowledge expert	42.6	(4.3)	40.7	(4.5)
Managers	40.1	(2.7)	33.6	(3.3)
Information high-skill	44.4	(4.9)	31.4	(4.4)
Information low-skill	40.8	(4.2)	22.0	(2.5)
Services low-skill	26.6	(4.2)	7.1	(3.2)
Goods	25.5	(3.3)	8.3	(1.6)
Canada				
Knowledge expert	43.0	(3.1)	42.5	(3.2)
Managers	42.4	(3.0)	24.8	(2.5)
Information high-skill	44.3	(2.6)	31.5	(2.0)
Information low-skill	45.6	(2.2)	19.2	(1.7)
Services low-skill	35.5	(2.9)	11.7	(1.9)
Goods	33.8	(2.1)	11.7	(1.5)
Italy				
Knowledge expert	31.9	(5.7)	10.6	(2.6)
Managers	21.6	(4.5)	4.4	(2.4)
Information high-skill	28.8	(3.1)	6.3	(2.3)
Information low-skill	25.1	(2.6)	5.3	(1.9)
Services low-skill	12.3	(2.3)	1.9	(0.8)
Goods	10.4	(1.1)	1.3	(0.6)
Norway				
Knowledge expert	41.6	(4.3)	54.1	(4.1)
Managers	51.4	(5.3)	29.7	(3.9)
Information high-skill	46.5	(2.1)	38.1	(1.9)
Information low-skill	48.5	(3.5)	27.5	(3.4)
Services low-skill	41.0	(3.8)	14.0	(3.2)
Goods	48.4	(4.3)	14.5	(3.1)
Switzerland				
Knowledge expert	50.4	(5.0)	23.3	(3.8)
Managers	44.4	(3.3)	17.1	(3.9)
Information high-skill	43.8	(4.9)	18.5	(3.4)
Information low-skill	38.5	(3.5)	13.0	(2.4)
Services low-skill	33.1	(3.2)	5.4	(2.5)
Goods	31.4	(3.4)	5.4	(1.9)
United States				
Knowledge expert	47.9	(5.1)	29.9	(4.8)
Managers	43.3	(2.8)	20.5	(2.7)
Information high-skill	47.7	(4.1)	25.1	(3.2)
Information low-skill	41.7	(2.4)	12.7	(1.7)
Services low-skill	26.8	(3.3)	6.6	(1.4)
Goods	25.9	(2.4)	6.5	(1.6)

Source: Adult Literacy and Life Skills Survey, 2003.

TABLE 6.2 (continued)

Per cent of labour force populations aged 16 to 65 at skills Levels 3 and 4/5, by type of occupation, 2003

	Level 3		Level 4/5	
B. Numeracy scale				
Bermuda				
Knowledge expert	40.8	(5.7)	33.5	(3.4)
Managers	38.0	(3.5)	24.3	(3.9)
Information high-skill	37.1	(5.8)	17.1	(3.4)
Information low-skill	30.0	(3.1)	15.7	(1.4)
Services low-skill	18.2	(3.8)	3.4	(1.1)
Goods	22.0	(3.6)	6.2	(1.5)
Canada				
Knowledge expert	36.7	(3.0)	44.7	(3.7)
Managers	38.5	(2.7)	24.4	(2.2)
Information high-skill	41.6	(2.0)	25.0	(1.8)
Information low-skill	39.1	(1.8)	13.5	(1.2)
Services low-skill	26.9	(2.8)	10.2	(1.5)
Goods	30.7	(1.8)	10.8	(1.7)
Italy				
Knowledge expert	33.3	(4.3)	11.7	(3.7)
Managers	26.8	(5.9)	6.3	(2.7)
Information high-skill	25.7	(5.3)	5.9	(1.9)
Information low-skill	28.7	(2.2)	5.5	(1.5)
Services low-skill	12.7	(2.4)	1.0	(0.9)
Goods	11.9	(1.5)	1.3	(0.5)
Norway				
Knowledge expert	41.4	(5.8)	47.8	(5.1)
Managers	50.2	(3.5)	30.4	(3.0)
Information high-skill	47.1	(3.2)	30.6	(3.2)
Information low-skill	44.9	(3.3)	22.5	(3.0)
Services low-skill	33.9	(3.4)	6.7	(2.6)
Goods	45.9	(3.2)	12.4	(1.7)
Switzerland				
Knowledge expert	39.8	(4.6)	39.5	(5.4)
Managers	43.3	(4.6)	34.5	(3.6)
Information high-skill	43.6	(4.0)	30.1	(2.9)
Information low-skill	39.1	(4.9)	21.0	(3.1)
Services low-skill	34.9	(4.4)	10.3	(3.1)
Goods	36.7	(3.1)	14.2	(3.0)
United States				
Knowledge expert	39.2	(4.2)	35.5	(4.5)
Managers	38.3	(3.9)	19.4	(2.9)
Information high-skill	42.3	(2.5)	19.2	(2.0)
Information low-skill	34.0	(3.0)	10.0	(1.7)
Services low-skill	21.9	(2.7)	5.3	(1.4)
Goods	23.9	(2.0)	6.5	(1.6)

Source: Adult Literacy and Life Skills Survey, 2003.

TABLE 6.2 (concluded)

Per cent of labour force populations aged 16 to 65 at skills Levels 3 and 4/5, by type of occupation, 2003

	Level 3		Level 4	
C. Problem solving scale[1]				
Bermuda				
Knowledge expert	35.0	(4.7)	13.5	(3.3)
Managers	33.2	(2.9)	10.8	(2.0)
Information high-skill	30.1	(5.8)	8.3	(2.4)
Information low-skill	23.2	(3.1)	6.9	(1.4)
Services low-skill	13.2	(2.8)	1.2	(0.9)
Goods	11.9	(2.7)	2.1	(1.4)
Canada				
Knowledge expert	42.1	(3.8)	14.4	(2.7)
Managers	30.3	(2.7)	7.7	(1.9)
Information high-skill	36.8	(2.2)	8.2	(1.3)
Information low-skill	29.3	(2.0)	4.6	(1.1)
Services low-skill	19.9	(2.0)	3.3	(1.3)
Goods	18.4	(1.6)	2.4	(0.7)
Italy				
Knowledge expert	16.2	(3.8)	2.2	(1.0)
Managers	9.8	(3.0)	1.5	(1.5)
Information high-skill	15.1	(3.2)	1.8	(1.4)
Information low-skill	13.6	(2.4)	2.4	(1.0)
Services low-skill	6.2	(1.9)	1.1	(0.6)
Goods	4.5	(1.4)	0.4	(0.3)
Norway				
Knowledge expert	47.6	(5.6)	18.9	(3.2)
Managers	38.9	(5.5)	8.1	(2.1)
Information high-skill	43.6	(2.9)	11.6	(1.5)
Information low-skill	38.5	(4.2)	7.6	(1.9)
Services low-skill	26.3	(3.0)	3.9	(1.4)
Goods	25.9	(3.4)	3.8	(1.0)
Switzerland[2]				
Knowledge expert	32.9	(5.2)	11.7	(3.0)
Managers	33.0	(3.5)	6.9	(2.2)
Information high-skill	36.5	(2.4)	6.4	(1.8)
Information low-skill	26.3	(4.1)	5.9	(2.0)
Services low-skill	18.9	(4.0)	5.0	(2.7)
Goods	18.1	(4.1)	2.1	(1.2)

1. United States did not field the problem solving skills domain.
2. The problem solving skills scores for Switzerland apply to the German and French speaking communities only since they did not field the problem solving skills domain in the Italian speaking community.

Source: Adult Literacy and Life Skills Survey, 2003.

TABLE 6.3

Index scores of reading, writing and numeracy engagement at work on a standardized scale (centred on 2), by skills levels, labour force populations aged 16 to 65, 2003

	Level 1		Level 2		Level 3		Level 4/5	
A. Reading engagement at work index by document literacy levels								
Bermuda	1.4	(0.1)	1.9	(0.1)	2.2	(0.1)	2.5	(0.1)
Canada	1.4	(0.1)	1.9	(0.0)	2.2	(0.0)	2.4	(0.0)
Italy	1.3	(0.1)	1.6	(0.1)	1.9	(0.1)	2.1	(0.1)
Norway	1.5	(0.1)	1.9	(0.0)	2.1	(0.0)	2.2	(0.0)
Switzerland	1.8	(0.1)	2.0	(0.1)	2.2	(0.0)	2.4	(0.1)
United States	1.6	(0.1)	2.0	(0.1)	2.2	(0.1)	2.4	(0.1)
B. Writing engagement at work index by prose literacy levels								
Bermuda	1.4	(0.1)	2.0	(0.1)	2.5	(0.1)	2.7	(0.0)
Canada	1.3	(0.1)	1.9	(0.0)	2.2	(0.0)	2.4	(0.0)
Italy	1.2	(0.0)	1.5	(0.1)	1.8	(0.1)	2.0	(0.2)
Norway	1.6	(0.1)	1.9	(0.0)	2.0	(0.0)	2.1	(0.0)
Switzerland	1.6	(0.1)	2.0	(0.1)	2.2	(0.0)	2.3	(0.1)
United States	1.6	(0.1)	2.1	(0.1)	2.4	(0.0)	2.5	(0.1)
C. Numeracy engagement at work index by numeracy levels								
Bermuda	1.5	(0.1)	2.1	(0.1)	2.5	(0.1)	2.7	(0.0)
Canada	1.4	(0.0)	1.9	(0.0)	2.2	(0.0)	2.4	(0.0)
Italy	1.0	(0.1)	1.5	(0.1)	1.9	(0.1)	2.2	(0.1)
Norway	1.5	(0.1)	1.8	(0.0)	2.1	(0.0)	2.3	(0.0)
Switzerland	1.6	(0.1)	2.0	(0.1)	2.3	(0.0)	2.6	(0.1)
United States	1.5	(0.1)	2.2	(0.1)	2.4	(0.0)	2.6	(0.1)
D. Combined engagement at work index by problem solving[1] levels								
Bermuda	1.9	(0.0)	2.3	(0.0)	2.5	(0.1)	2.5	(0.1)
Canada	1.8	(0.0)	2.2	(0.0)	2.3	(0.0)	2.4	(0.1)
Italy	1.6	(0.0)	1.9	(0.1)	2.0	(0.1)	2.2	(0.3)
Norway	1.8	(0.0)	2.0	(0.0)	2.2	(0.0)	2.2	(0.1)
Switzerland[2]	1.9	(0.1)	2.2	(0.0)	2.3	(0.1)	2.4	(0.1)

1. United States did not field the problem solving skills domain.
2. The problem solving skills scores for Switzerland apply to the German and French speaking communities only since they did not field the problem solving skills domain in the Italian speaking community.

Source: Adult Literacy and Life Skills Survey, 2003.

TABLE 6.4

Relationship between combined index scores of reading, writing and numeracy engagement at work on a standardized scale (centred on 2) and skills scores on scales 0 to 500 points, adjusted for years of schooling and native language status, labour force populations aged 16 to 65, 2003

	Unstandardized coefficients			
	B	Standard error	t-value	Significance
A. Prose scale				
Bermuda				
(Constant)	-0.53	0.06	-8.83	0.00
Combined index scores (scale 2 = 0)	0.27	0.03	9.00	0.00
Years of education (Grade 12 = 0)	0.14	0.01	14.00	0.00
Test language (Same as mother tongue = 0)	-0.20	0.07	-2.86	0.01
Canada				
(Constant)	-0.23	0.04	-5.75	0.00
Combined index scores (scale 2 = 0)	0.20	0.02	10.00	0.00
Years of education (Grade 12 = 0)	0.11	0.00		0.00
Test language (Same as mother tongue = 0)	-0.51	0.04	-12.75	0.00
Italy				
(Constant)	-0.86	0.05	-17.20	0.00
Combined index scores (scale 2 = 0)	0.15	0.03	5.00	0.00
Years of education (Grade 12 = 0)	0.08	0.01	8.00	0.00
Test language (Same as mother tongue = 0)	--	--	--	--
Norway				
(Constant)	0.06	0.05	1.20	0.28
Combined index scores (scale 2 = 0)	0.12	0.03	4.00	0.00
Years of education (Grade 12 = 0)	0.10	0.01	10.00	0.00
Test language (Same as mother tongue = 0)	-0.33	0.06	-5.50	0.00
Switzerland				
(Constant)	-0.19	0.06	-3.17	0.01
Combined index scores (scale 2 = 0)	0.09	0.02	4.50	0.00
Years of education (Grade 12 = 0)	0.10	0.00		0.00
Test language (Same as mother tongue = 0)	-0.44	0.06	-7.33	0.00
United States				
(Constant)	-0.33	0.05	-6.60	0.00
Combined index scores (scale 2 = 0)	0.11	0.02	5.50	0.00
Years of education (Grade 12 = 0)	0.13	0.01	13.00	0.00
Test language (Same as mother tongue = 0)	-0.84	0.06	-14.00	0.00

-- Estimate was not statistically different from zero at the five per cent level of significance in the first step of the analysis. Hence this parameter was not estimated in the country specific model.

Source: Adult Literacy and Life Skills Survey, 2003.

TABLE 6.4

Relationship between combined index scores of reading, writing and numeracy engagement at work on a standardized scale (centred on 2) and skills scores on scales 0 to 500 points, adjusted for years of schooling and native language status, labour force populations aged 16 to 65, 2003

	Unstandardized coefficients			
	B	Standard error	t-value	Significance
B. Document scale				
Bermuda				
(Constant)	-0.72	0.07	-10.29	0.00
Combined index scores (scale 2 = 0)	0.26	0.03	8.67	0.00
Years of education (Grade 12 = 0)	0.13	0.01	13.00	0.00
Test language (Same as mother tongue = 0)	-0.15	0.07	-2.14	0.05
Canada				
(Constant)	-0.26	0.04	-6.50	0.00
Combined index scores (scale 2 = 0)	0.21	0.02	10.50	0.00
Years of education (Grade 12 = 0)	0.11	0.00		0.00
Test language (Same as mother tongue = 0)	-0.44	0.05	-8.80	0.00
Italy				
(Constant)	-0.95	0.04	-23.75	0.00
Combined index scores (scale 2 = 0)	0.20	0.03	6.67	0.00
Years of education (Grade 12 = 0)	0.07	0.01	7.00	0.00
Test language (Same as mother tongue = 0)	--	--	--	--
Norway				
(Constant)	0.04	0.07	0.57	0.53
Combined index scores (scale 2 = 0)	0.18	0.03	6.00	0.00
Years of education (Grade 12 = 0)	0.10	0.01	10.00	0.00
Test language (Same as mother tongue = 0)	-0.30	0.05	-6.00	0.00
Switzerland				
(Constant)	-0.15	0.04	-3.75	0.00
Combined index scores (scale 2 = 0)	0.10	0.02	5.00	0.00
Years of education (Grade 12 = 0)	0.09	0.01	9.00	0.00
Test language (Same as mother tongue = 0)	-0.36	0.05	-7.20	0.00
United States				
(Constant)	-0.40	0.05	-8.00	0.00
Combined index scores (scale 2 = 0)	0.16	0.02	8.00	0.00
Years of education (Grade 12 = 0)	0.12	0.01	12.00	0.00
Test language (Same as mother tongue = 0)	-0.72	0.07	-10.29	0.00

-- Estimate was not statistically different from zero at the five per cent level of significance in the first step of the analysis. Hence this parameter was not estimated in the country specific model.

Source: Adult Literacy and Life Skills Survey, 2003.

TABLE 6.4

Relationship between combined index scores of reading, writing and numeracy engagement at work on a standardized scale (centred on 2) and skills scores on scales 0 to 500 points, adjusted for years of schooling and native language status, labour force populations aged 16 to 65, 2003

	Unstandardized coefficients			
	B	Standard error	t-value	Significance
C. Numeracy scale				
Bermuda				
(Constant)	-0.99	0.06	-16.50	0.00
Combined index scores (scale 2 = 0)	0.33	0.02	16.50	0.00
Years of education (Grade 12 = 0)	0.12	0.01	12.00	0.00
Test language (Same as mother tongue = 0)	--	--	--	--
Canada				
(Constant)	-0.48	0.04	-12.00	0.00
Combined index scores (scale 2 = 0)	0.25	0.02	12.50	0.00
Years of education (Grade 12 = 0)	0.11	0.00		0.00
Test language (Same as mother tongue = 0)	-0.38	0.04	-9.50	0.00
Italy				
(Constant)	-0.75	0.04	-18.75	0.00
Combined index scores (scale 2 = 0)	0.20	0.02	10.00	0.00
Years of education (Grade 12 = 0)	0.07	0.01	7.00	0.00
Test language (Same as mother tongue = 0)	--	--	--	--
Norway				
(Constant)	-0.26	0.05	-5.20	0.00
Combined index scores (scale 2 = 0)	0.26	0.03	8.67	0.00
Years of education (Grade 12 = 0)	0.09	0.01	9.00	0.00
Test language (Same as mother tongue = 0)	-0.25	0.06	-4.17	0.00
Switzerland				
(Constant)	-0.18	0.05	-3.60	0.01
Combined index scores (scale 2 = 0)	0.26	0.03	8.67	0.00
Years of education (Grade 12 = 0)	0.09	0.01	9.00	0.00
Test language (Same as mother tongue = 0)	-0.41	0.05	-8.20	0.00
United States				
(Constant)	-0.66	0.05	-13.20	0.00
Combined index scores (scale 2 = 0)	0.20	0.02	10.00	0.00
Years of education (Grade 12 = 0)	0.15	0.01	15.00	0.00
Test language (Same as mother tongue = 0)	-0.64	0.08	-8.00	0.00

-- Estimate was not statistically different from zero at the five per cent level of significance in the first step of the analysis. Hence this parameter was not estimated in the country specific model.

Source: Adult Literacy and Life Skills Survey, 2003.

TABLE 6.4

Relationship between combined index scores of reading, writing and numeracy engagement at work on a standardized scale (centred on 2) and skills scores on scales 0 to 500 points, adjusted for years of schooling and native language status, labour force populations aged 16 to 65, 2003

	Unstandardized coefficients			
	B	Standard error	t-value	Significance
D. Problem solving scale[1]				
Bermuda				
(Constant)	-0.56	0.07	-8.00	0.00
Combined index scores (scale 2 = 0)	0.22	0.03	7.33	0.00
Years of education (Grade 12 = 0)	0.11	0.01	11.00	0.00
Test language (Same as mother tongue = 0)	--	--	--	--
Canada				
(Constant)	-0.21	0.04	-5.25	0.00
Combined index scores (scale 2 = 0)	0.18	0.02	9.00	0.00
Years of education (Grade 12 = 0)	0.10	0.00	0.00	0.00
Test language (Same as mother tongue = 0)	-0.51	0.04	-12.75	0.00
Italy				
(Constant)	-0.84	0.04	-21.00	0.00
Combined index scores (scale 2 = 0)	0.16	0.03	5.33	0.00
Years of education (Grade 12 = 0)	0.06	0.01	6.00	0.00
Test language (Same as mother tongue = 0)	--	--	--	--
Norway				
(Constant)	-0.06	0.06	-1.00	0.30
Combined index scores (scale 2 = 0)	0.18	0.03	6.00	0.00
Years of education (Grade 12 = 0)	0.11	0.01	11.00	0.00
Test language (Same as mother tongue = 0)	-0.37	0.08	-4.63	0.00
Switzerland[2]				
(Constant)	-0.18	0.10	-1.80	0.09
Combined index scores (scale 2 = 0)	0.17	0.04	4.25	0.00
Years of education (Grade 12 = 0)	0.08	0.01	8.00	0.00
Test language (Same as mother tongue = 0)	-0.28	0.08	-3.50	0.00

-- Estimate was not statistically different from zero at the five per cent level of significance in the first step of the analysis. Hence this parameter was not estimated in the country specific model.

1. United States did not field the problem solving skills domain.
2. The problem solving skills scores for Switzerland apply to the German and French speaking communities only since they did not field the problem solving skills domain in the Italian speaking community.

Source: Adult Literacy and Life Skills Survey, 2003.

TABLE 6.5

Index scores of reading, writing and numeracy engagement at work on a standardized scale (centred on 2) by aggregated occupational types, labour force populations aged 16 to 65, 2003

	25th percentile		50th percentile		75th percentile	
A. Writing engagement at work						
Bermuda						
Knowledge expert	2.4	(0.1)	2.7	(0.1)	3.1	(0.1)
Managers	2.3	(0.1)	2.7	(0.1)	3.1	(0.1)
Information high-skill	2.2	(0.1)	2.7	(0.1)	3.1	(0.1)
Information low-skill	2.0	(0.1)	2.4	(0.1)	2.9	(0.1)
Services low-skill	0.2	(0.0)	1.5	(0.1)	2.3	(0.1)
Goods	1.1	(0.1)	1.9	(0.1)	2.4	(0.0)
Canada						
Knowledge expert	2.2	(0.0)	2.6	(0.0)	2.9	(0.0)
Managers	2.1	(0.0)	2.6	(0.0)	3.1	(0.1)
Information high-skill	2.1	(0.0)	2.4	(0.0)	2.9	(0.0)
Information low-skill	1.5	(0.1)	2.2	(0.0)	2.7	(0.0)
Services low-skill	0.2	(0.0)	1.5	(0.1)	2.2	(0.1)
Goods	0.9	(0.2)	1.7	(0.1)	2.4	(0.0)
Italy						
Knowledge expert	1.7	(0.1)	2.2	(0.1)	2.8	(0.1)
Managers	1.2	(0.4)	1.9	(0.1)	2.7	(0.1)
Information high-skill	1.2	(0.2)	1.9	(0.1)	2.5	(0.1)
Information low-skill	1.4	(0.1)	2.0	(0.1)	2.5	(0.1)
Services low-skill	0.2	(0.0)	0.9	(0.3)	1.8	(0.1)
Goods	0.2	(0.0)	0.2	(0.0)	1.5	(0.1)
Norway						
Knowledge expert	2.1	(0.1)	2.4	(0.0)	2.6	(0.0)
Managers	2.1	(0.1)	2.4	(0.0)	2.7	(0.1)
Information high-skill	1.9	(0.0)	2.3	(0.0)	2.5	(0.0)
Information low-skill	1.8	(0.0)	2.1	(0.0)	2.5	(0.1)
Services low-skill	1.4	(0.1)	2.0	(0.1)	2.3	(0.0)
Goods	1.2	(0.1)	1.8	(0.1)	2.3	(0.1)
Switzerland						
Knowledge expert	2.0	(0.1)	2.3	(0.1)	2.8	(0.1)
Managers	1.9	(0.0)	2.3	(0.1)	2.7	(0.0)
Information high-skill	1.8	(0.0)	2.2	(0.1)	2.6	(0.1)
Information low-skill	1.6	(0.1)	2.0	(0.0)	2.3	(0.1)
Services low-skill	0.9	(0.2)	1.6	(0.1)	2.3	(0.1)
Goods	1.2	(0.1)	1.8	(0.1)	2.3	(0.1)
United States						
Knowledge expert	2.3	(0.1)	2.6	(0.0)	2.9	(0.0)
Managers	2.3	(0.0)	2.7	(0.1)	3.1	(0.1)
Information high-skill	2.2	(0.1)	2.5	(0.0)	3.0	(0.0)
Information low-skill	1.8	(0.1)	2.4	(0.0)	2.8	(0.1)
Services low-skill	1.1	(0.1)	1.9	(0.1)	2.4	(0.0)
Goods	0.9	(0.2)	1.8	(0.1)	2.5	(0.1)

Source: Adult Literacy and Life Skills Survey, 2003.

TABLE 6.5

Index scores of reading, writing and numeracy engagement at work on a standardized scale (centred on 2) by aggregated occupational types, labour force populations aged 16 to 65, 2003

	25th percentile		50th percentile		75th percentile	
B. Reading engagement at work						
Bermuda						
Knowledge expert	1.6	(0.1)	2.3	(0.1)	3.8	(0.3)
Managers	1.8	(0.1)	2.2	(0.1)	3.0	(0.3)
Information high-skill	1.7	(0.1)	2.4	(0.1)	3.0	(0.3)
Information low-skill	1.4	(0.1)	1.9	(0.0)	2.5	(0.1)
Services low-skill	0.7	(0.1)	1.5	(0.1)	2.1	(0.1)
Goods	0.8	(0.1)	1.5	(0.1)	2.5	(0.1)
Canada						
Knowledge expert	2.1	(0.1)	2.5	(0.1)	3.8	(0.2)
Managers	1.8	(0.0)	2.4	(0.1)	3.8	(0.3)
Information high-skill	1.9	(0.0)	2.4	(0.0)	3.0	(0.0)
Information low-skill	1.4	(0.0)	1.9	(0.0)	2.5	(0.0)
Services low-skill	0.8	(0.1)	1.4	(0.1)	2.0	(0.1)
Goods	1.0	(0.1)	1.7	(0.1)	2.7	(0.1)
Italy						
Knowledge expert	1.6	(0.1)	2.2	(0.1)	2.9	(0.1)
Managers	1.1	(0.2)	1.8	(0.1)	2.8	(0.4)
Information high-skill	1.2	(0.1)	1.9	(0.1)	2.6	(0.1)
Information low-skill	1.2	(0.0)	1.8	(0.1)	2.5	(0.2)
Services low-skill	0.3	(0.1)	1.0	(0.1)	1.7	(0.1)
Goods	0.3	(0.1)	0.9	(0.1)	1.6	(0.1)
Norway						
Knowledge expert	2.0	(0.1)	2.4	(0.1)	3.0	(0.1)
Managers	1.9	(0.1)	2.3	(0.1)	2.8	(0.1)
Information high-skill	1.8	(0.0)	2.2	(0.0)	2.7	(0.1)
Information low-skill	1.6	(0.1)	2.0	(0.1)	2.5	(0.1)
Services low-skill	1.2	(0.1)	1.6	(0.1)	2.2	(0.1)
Goods	1.2	(0.1)	1.7	(0.1)	2.2	(0.1)
Switzerland						
Knowledge expert	2.0	(0.1)	2.5	(0.1)	3.0	(0.2)
Managers	1.9	(0.1)	2.4	(0.1)	2.8	(0.0)
Information high-skill	1.7	(0.0)	2.2	(0.1)	2.7	(0.1)
Information low-skill	1.4	(0.1)	2.0	(0.1)	2.4	(0.1)
Services low-skill	1.0	(0.1)	1.6	(0.1)	2.2	(0.1)
Goods	1.2	(0.1)	1.7	(0.1)	2.3	(0.1)
United States						
Knowledge expert	2.1	(0.1)	2.5	(0.0)	3.0	(0.2)
Managers	1.9	(0.1)	2.5	(0.1)	3.8	(0.3)
Information high-skill	1.8	(0.1)	2.4	(0.1)	3.0	(0.1)
Information low-skill	1.5	(0.1)	2.0	(0.1)	2.5	(0.1)
Services low-skill	0.9	(0.1)	1.4	(0.0)	2.2	(0.0)
Goods	1.0	(0.1)	1.7	(0.1)	2.7	(0.1)

Source: Adult Literacy and Life Skills Survey, 2003.

TABLE 6.5

Index scores of reading, writing and numeracy engagement at work on a standardized scale (centred on 2) by aggregated occupational types, labour force populations aged 16 to 65, 2003

	25th percentile		50th percentile		75th percentile	
C. Numeracy engagement at work						
Bermuda						
Knowledge expert	2.1	(0.1)	2.6	(0.1)	3.0	(0.0)
Managers	2.1	(0.1)	2.6	(0.1)	3.1	(0.2)
Information high-skill	1.9	(0.1)	2.5	(0.1)	3.0	(0.1)
Information low-skill	1.6	(0.1)	2.3	(0.1)	2.8	(0.1)
Services low-skill	0.6	(0.3)	1.6	(0.1)	2.2	(0.1)
Goods	1.3	(0.1)	2.1	(0.1)	2.7	(0.1)
Canada						
Knowledge expert	2.0	(0.0)	2.5	(0.0)	3.0	(0.1)
Managers	2.1	(0.1)	2.6	(0.1)	3.1	(0.0)
Information high-skill	1.8	(0.1)	2.4	(0.0)	2.9	(0.1)
Information low-skill	1.4	(0.0)	2.1	(0.0)	2.7	(0.0)
Services low-skill	0.7	(0.1)	1.5	(0.1)	2.2	(0.1)
Goods	0.9	(0.1)	1.8	(0.1)	2.5	(0.0)
Italy						
Knowledge expert	1.4	(0.1)	2.0	(0.1)	2.7	(0.1)
Managers	1.6	(0.1)	2.1	(0.1)	2.8	(0.1)
Information high-skill	1.0	(0.2)	1.8	(0.1)	2.5	(0.1)
Information low-skill	1.3	(0.1)	1.9	(0.0)	2.5	(0.1)
Services low-skill	-0.3	(0.0)	1.1	(0.2)	1.9	(0.1)
Goods	-0.3	(0.0)	0.8	(0.1)	1.6	(0.1)
Norway						
Knowledge expert	1.8	(0.1)	2.3	(0.1)	2.6	(0.0)
Managers	2.1	(0.0)	2.5	(0.0)	2.8	(0.1)
Information high-skill	1.8	(0.0)	2.2	(0.0)	2.5	(0.0)
Information low-skill	1.6	(0.1)	2.0	(0.0)	2.5	(0.1)
Services low-skill	1.1	(0.1)	1.6	(0.1)	2.1	(0.1)
Goods	1.4	(0.1)	2.0	(0.1)	2.5	(0.0)
Switzerland						
Knowledge expert	2.1	(0.1)	2.5	(0.0)	3.0	(0.1)
Managers	2.3	(0.1)	2.8	(0.0)	3.1	(0.2)
Information high-skill	1.8	(0.1)	2.4	(0.0)	2.8	(0.1)
Information low-skill	1.8	(0.1)	2.3	(0.1)	2.7	(0.1)
Services low-skill	0.8	(0.1)	1.7	(0.1)	2.4	(0.1)
Goods	1.4	(0.1)	2.0	(0.1)	2.5	(0.1)
United States						
Knowledge expert	2.0	(0.1)	2.6	(0.1)	3.1	(0.0)
Managers	2.4	(0.1)	3.0	(0.1)	3.7	(0.1)
Information high-skill	1.9	(0.1)	2.5	(0.1)	3.0	(0.1)
Information low-skill	1.6	(0.1)	2.3	(0.1)	3.0	(0.1)
Services low-skill	0.9	(0.1)	1.9	(0.1)	2.5	(0.0)
Goods	1.1	(0.1)	1.9	(0.1)	2.6	(0.1)

Source: Adult Literacy and Life Skills Survey, 2003.

TABLE 6.6

Per cent of labour force populations aged 16 to 65 whose skills match or mismatch their level of practice engagement at work, 2003

	Match				Mismatch			
	Low-skill and low-engagement		Medium- to high- skill and high-engagement		Low-skill and high-engagement (skills deficit)		Medium- to high- skill and low-engagement (skills surplus)	
A. Prose literacy skills and writing engagement at work								
Bermuda	25.9	(1.2)	39.3	(1.1)	11.8	(0.9)	22.9	(1.3)
Canada	24.1	(0.7)	37.4	(0.9)	14.2	(0.6)	24.2	(0.8)
Italy	42.3	(1.5)	16.5	(1.2)	34.1	(1.4)	7.2	(0.6)
Norway	17.0	(0.9)	40.0	(0.9)	14.0	(0.9)	29.0	(1.0)
Switzerland	27.5	(1.9)	32.1	(1.7)	19.7	(1.1)	20.7	(1.9)
United States	28.1	(1.2)	31.5	(1.3)	20.2	(1.2)	20.2	(0.8)
B. Document literacy skills and reading engagement at work								
Bermuda	26.9	(1.4)	35.0	(1.4)	16.1	(1.3)	21.9	(1.3)
Canada	20.8	(0.7)	37.5	(1.0)	14.7	(0.8)	27.0	(0.7)
Italy	40.3	(1.5)	18.3	(1.6)	31.8	(1.4)	9.7	(0.8)
Norway	17.2	(0.9)	42.0	(1.2)	11.2	(0.7)	29.6	(1.3)
Switzerland	24.6	(1.3)	33.4	(1.4)	18.2	(1.3)	23.8	(1.3)
United States	26.1	(1.1)	32.8	(1.3)	19.0	(1.1)	22.1	(1.0)
C. Numeracy skills and numeracy engagement at work								
Bermuda	33.8	(1.6)	30.9	(1.1)	20.1	(1.0)	15.1	(1.3)
Canada	28.4	(0.6)	34.1	(0.8)	17.5	(0.7)	19.9	(0.7)
Italy	42.3	(1.6)	17.7	(1.3)	32.7	(1.5)	7.3	(0.6)
Norway	22.6	(1.0)	39.8	(1.2)	14.0	(0.9)	23.6	(1.2)
Switzerland	21.9	(1.3)	39.3	(1.3)	12.9	(1.2)	25.9	(1.0)
United States	32.2	(1.1)	28.8	(1.1)	22.2	(1.3)	16.8	(1.1)
D. Problem solving skills[1] and combined reading, writing and numeracy engagement at work								
Bermuda	38.7	(1.4)	21.1	(1.1)	28.8	(1.3)	11.3	(1.3)
Canada	36.1	(1.0)	21.9	(1.0)	28.1	(1.0)	13.9	(0.9)
Italy	45.5	(1.2)	8.3	(1.4)	41.6	(1.8)	4.6	(0.8)
Norway	32.6	(1.0)	24.5	(1.4)	25.4	(1.4)	17.5	(1.0)
Switzerland[2]	34.7	(1.4)	20.9	(1.1)	29.1	(1.2)	15.3	(1.3)

1. United States did not field the problem solving skills domain.
2. The problem solving skills scores for Switzerland apply to the German and French speaking communities only since they did not field the problem solving skills domain in the Italian speaking community.

Source: Adult Literacy and Life Skills Survey, 2003.

Chapter 7

Skills and Economic Outcomes

7

Summary

This chapter examines economic outcomes associated with differences in observed skills. First, the rewards to literacy, numeracy and problem solving skills on labour markets are studied with a structural model that specifies the joint determination of personal earnings, education and cognitive skills. Second, the likelihood of receiving social assistance transfers for individuals at different skill levels is estimated. This latter analysis adjusts for education, age, gender and household income levels. Similarly, findings on the likelihood of earning investment income for respondents at different skill levels are presented.

Table of Contents

Skills and Economic Outcomes

7

7.1 Overview and highlights

This chapter examines economic outcomes associated with differences in observed skills. First, the rewards to literacy, numeracy and problem solving skills on labour markets are studied with a structural model that specifies the joint determination of personal earnings, education and cognitive skills. Second, the likelihood of receiving social assistance transfers for individuals at different skill levels is estimated. This latter analysis adjusts for education, age, gender and household income levels. Similarly, findings on the likelihood of earning investment income for respondents at different skill levels are presented.

Key findings of these analyses are:

- Skills have a large effect on earnings in the majority of countries. The extent to which economic rewards are attributable to either skill or education is mixed and varies by country.
- In Bermuda and Italy, the returns to skill overshadow the effect of education. After accounting for individual skills, wage returns to education are either zero or negative. This suggests that adults with additional years of schooling who do not display a commensurate level of skill are not rewarded for their additional schooling on the labour market.
- In Canada and the United States, the labour market appears to separately reward both the skills measured in ALL and additional schooling.
- In Norway, the findings indicate that both education and skill are valued, but with a higher relative return accruing to the latter. In fact, the labour market returns to numeracy overshadow the return to education. Hence if well-educated adults lack in numeracy skill then they derive no benefit from any additional years of schooling.
- Results suggest that the labour market in Switzerland does not reward prose, document, numeracy or problem solving skills separately from

years of schooling. Skills are only rewarded in so far as adults who have completed additional years of schooling also have higher skill proficiencies.

- Despite the strong associations between skill and economic outcomes reported above, there are significant proportions of workers who have medium to high levels of skill but who nevertheless occupy low-paying jobs. Naturally the opposite is also true. There are low to medium skilled workers who are nevertheless well paid.
- Low-skilled respondents are more likely than high skilled respondents to receive social transfers in half of the countries surveyed. This is the case in Canada, Norway and the United States, even after adjusting for education as well as age, gender and household income. This relationship is not significant in Bermuda, Italy and Switzerland.
- Not surprisingly, since medium to high skilled adults tend to be paid higher wages, they also have more opportunity to accumulate capital. Hence they are more likely than low skilled workers to have investment income on top of their wage earnings. This is the case in Bermuda, Canada, Switzerland and the United States. In Italy, however, this relationship is not significant once the effect of education and household income have been taken into account.

7.2 Earnings returns to skills and education

According to neo-classical economic theory, individuals who contribute more to the final value of production are expected to earn more. Furthermore, the theory of human capital suggests that the relative contribution of individuals depends on the knowledge, skills and other attributes embodied within them (Schultz, 1961; Becker, 1964; Blaug, 1976). Education plays an important role by imparting skills and also by providing easy to observe information about skills on the labour market (Stigler, 1961; Arrow, 1973; Spence, 1973). Thus education and skills are expected to influence the distribution of economic rewards. Previous research indeed supports the notion that skills are rewarded on the labour market (Rivera-Batiz, 1992; Murnane, Willet and Levy, 1995; OECD and HRDC, 1997; Osberg, 2000; Green and Riddell, 2001; Murnane, *et al.*, 2001). This section examines the extent to which the skills measured in ALL are rewarded by labour markets.

Figure 7.1 compares the labour market returns attributable to skill with those accruing to schooling. Results are obtained in a multivariate model that specifies the joint determination of earnings, education and skills (see Box 7A). Because prose and document literacy, numeracy and problem solving skills are highly correlated, four models, each focusing on a particular skills domain, are estimated. Each adjusts for years of schooling and several other factors such as age, experience, community size, language status and gender. The findings confirm labour markets are unique in the sense that they reward schooling and skills differently.

When interpreting the results it is important to note that the potential effects of education on the development of skills measured in ALL are fully taken into account. Each additional year of schooling is estimated to raise an individual's ranking in the distribution of skills by a substantial amount. Thus for the purposes of this analysis, it is useful to attribute any remaining effects of education on earnings to other unobserved skills not measured in ALL, such as communication skills, leadership or entrepreneurial skills, as well as attitudinal factors.

In Bermuda and Italy, the returns to skill overshadow those accruing to education. This suggests that skills are highly valued on the labour market and that education is rewarded only in so far as it is associated with these skills. For example, every increase of 10 percentiles in the ranking of the distribution of prose, document, numeracy or problem solving skills is associated with between 15 to 55 per cent higher weekly earnings, depending on the skill domain considered. Returns to education that are not statistically different from zero or are negative imply that if additional years of schooling are not associated with higher skill proficiencies, then those extra years of schooling are not rewarded on the labour market.

In Canada, Norway and the United States, there is evidence that the labour market directly rewards both the observed skills in ALL and other unobserved skills associated with schooling. The results for Canada are consistent with previously reported findings that use data from IALS (see Green and Riddell, 2001). Skills of the type measured in ALL are rewarded separately from schooling, ranging from about seven to 11 per cent for every increase of 10 percentiles in the ranking of distributions, depending on the skill domain. Also, each additional year of schooling is on average associated with about five per cent higher weekly earnings even after adjusting for directly observed skills. This suggests that the Canadian labour market rewards schooling above and beyond its effect on the development of cognitive skills. The results are similar in the United States with returns ranging from six to nine per cent.

Returns to skills in Norway range from eight to 15 per cent, depending on the domain. The returns to skill are also larger relative to the return to years of schooling. This is especially the case for numeracy skills. This suggests that in the Norwegian context, additional years of schooling are only rewarded if they are also associated with higher numeracy skills.

Finally, results suggest that the labour market in Switzerland does not reward prose, document, numeracy or problem solving skills separately from education. Skills are only rewarded when adults have also completed an expected corresponding number of years of schooling. Accordingly, those in high paying jobs have more years of schooling on average, but skills of the type measured in ALL are more evenly distributed among high and low paying jobs compared to other countries.

Findings reported in Figure 7.2 suggest that skills and education alone do not fully explain who benefits from high wages – occupation also plays an important role in the wage determination process. High-skill occupations such as experts, managers, and high-skill information jobs are on average well-paying jobs in all countries. These are also jobs that require higher engagement in reading, writing and numeracy tasks (see Figure 6.5). Thus the expectation is that literacy and numeracy skills are rewarded systematically, but it is shown in Chapter 6 that there is a degree of possible "mismatch" between the literacy and numeracy skills of individuals and the extent to which workers are required to engage in reading, writing and numeracy tasks at work.

FIGURE 7.1

Returns to skills and education

Per cent increase in weekly earnings per increase of 10-percentiles on the prose, document, numeracy and problem solving scales, and per increase of additional year of schooling, adjusted three stage least squares model[1], labour force populations aged 16 to 65, 2003

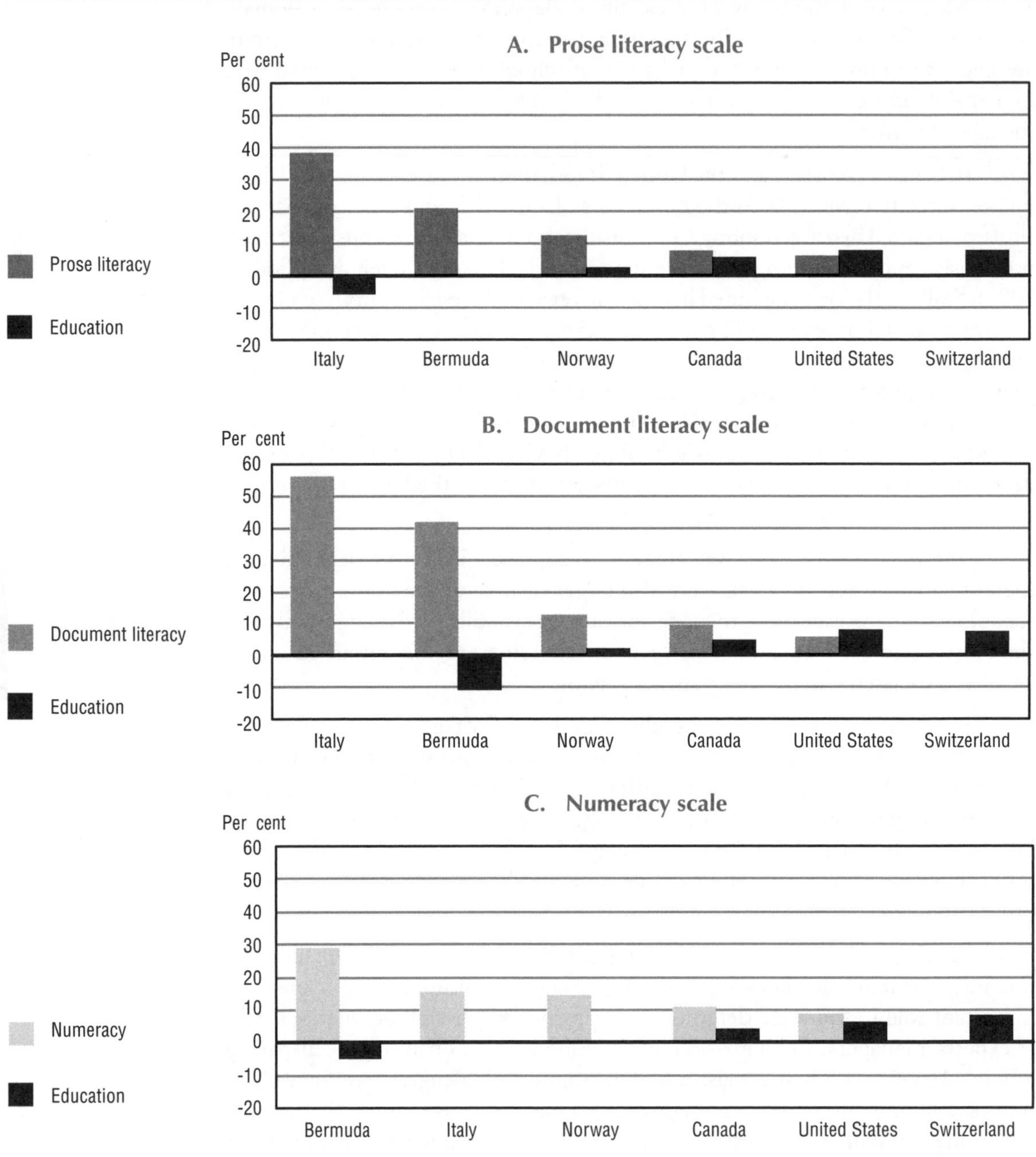

A. Countries are ranked by the effect of prose literacy.

B. Countries are ranked by the effect of document literacy.

C. Countries are ranked by the effect of numeracy.

Source: Adult Literacy and Life Skills Survey, 2003.

FIGURE 7.1 (concluded)

Returns to skills and education

Per cent increase in weekly earnings per increase of 10-percentiles on the prose, document, numeracy and problem solving scales, and per increase of additional year of schooling, adjusted three stage least squares model[1], labour force populations aged 16 to 65, 2003

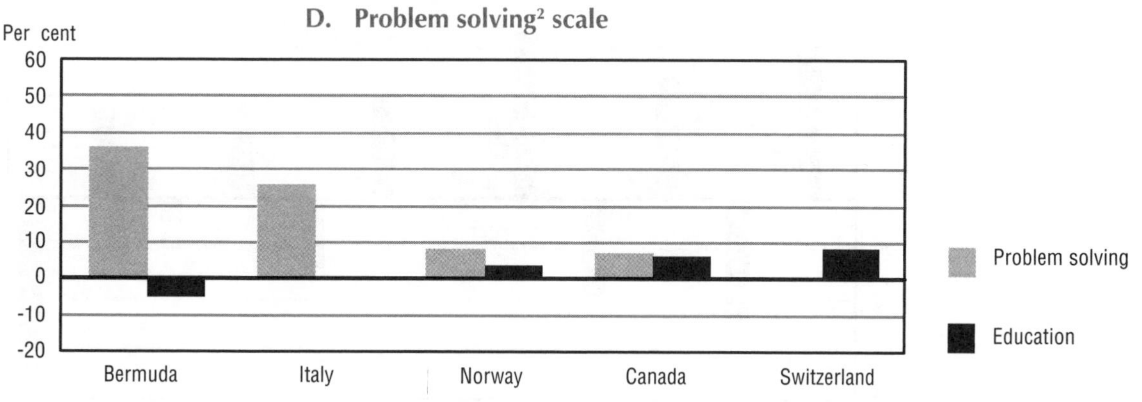

D. Countries are ranked by the effect of problem solving.

1. See Box 7A.
2. Switzerland (Italian) and the United States did not field the problem solving skills domain.

Source: Adult Literacy and Life Skills Survey, 2003.

Earnings premiums reported in Figure 7.2 are calculated as the percentage difference of expected weekly earnings for each occupational type relative to "goods related" or manufacturing type occupations. Experts and managers earn the most in all countries, with premiums on the order of 36 to 68 per cent. High-skill information jobs earn an average premium of 13 to 33 per cent, while low-skill information jobs earn less than manufacturing type jobs in Canada, Italy, Switzerland and the United States. In Bermuda and Norway, low-skill information jobs earn more on average than "goods related" occupations. In all countries, low-skills service occupations earn less on average than manufacturing employment. This ranges from as low as 69 per cent in Canada to eight per cent in Norway.

FIGURE 7.2

Earnings premiums associated with occupational types

Per cent difference of expected weekly earnings for each occupational type relative to "goods related" occupations, labour force populations aged 16 to 65, 2003

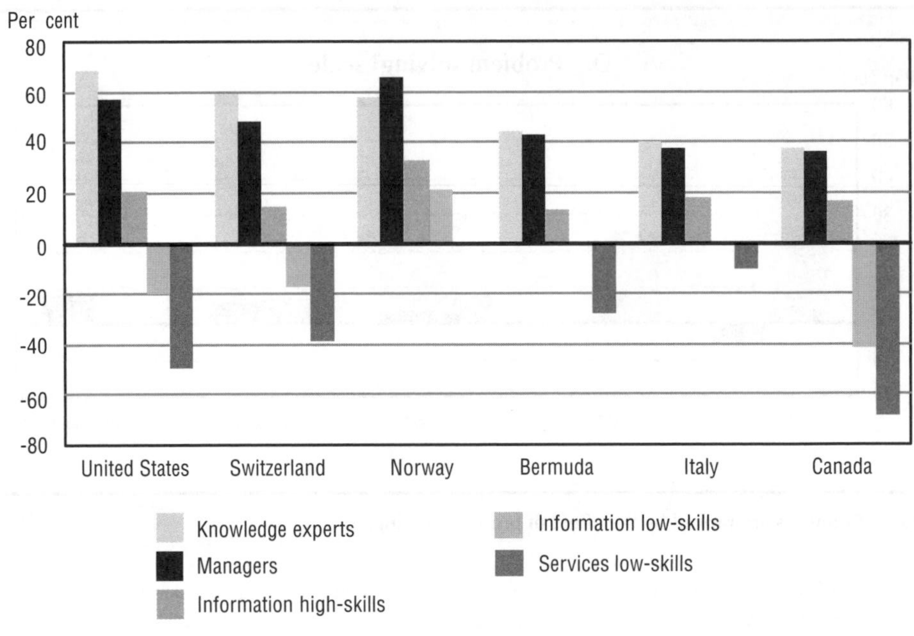

Countries are ranked by the earnings premium associated with expert occupations.

1. Difference estimates that are not statistically different from "goods related" occupations at conventional levels of significance are set to zero in the figure.

Source: Adult Literacy and Life Skills Survey, 2003.

Box 7A

Estimating the rates of return to skill

The rates of return to skill are estimated using a structural model. The estimation method is three stage least squares. This allows for the possible correlation between some of the explanatory variables and unobserved factors, which would otherwise lead to bias, to be taken into account. The model is based on Green and Riddell (2001). Both education and observed skill are specified as endogenous variables in the first equation, which is essentially an extension of Mincer's (1974) human capital model, and includes experience and some other factors commonly adjusted for in a model predicting earnings. The full model is based on the assumption that education affects skill proficiencies, and in turn, both skills and education influence weekly earnings.

Other control variables in the analysis are potential work experience, gender, community size, parents' education and non-native language. The instrumental variable used for education is the respondent's age when the highest level of schooling was completed, which is thought to affect directly educational attainment but not directly earnings. Non-native language is the instrumental variable adjusting variance in skill proficiencies.

7.3 Skills, social assistance and investment income

Skills yield potential economic returns to both individuals and societies beyond employment and earnings. Previous research suggests that there is an association between more education and reduced dependence on social transfers during prime working years (Kiefer, 1985; An, Haveman, and Wolfe, 1993). The findings presented in Figure 7.3 suggest that skills are a part of the explanation. Adults who score at Levels 1 and 2 on the numeracy scale are more likely to obtain social assistance payments from the state. This is the case in Canada, Norway and the United States, even after adjusting for education as well as age, gender and household income. The results are rather similar for the other skills domains measured. In Bermuda, Italy and Switzerland, the relationship is not significant when education and household income are taken into account.

Many adults have difficulties to earn sufficient income because they do not have the literacy and numeracy skills needed to cope with modern working life. For example, numeracy was shown to be associated with employability in Chapter 5. Other previous research shows that low skills are a common barrier to employment among recipients of social assistance, and that individuals who fail to obtain remedial education have lower odds of succeeding in the labour market (Heinrich, 1998; Danziger et al., 1999).

FIGURE 7.3

Likelihood of low-skilled adults collecting social assistance payments

Adjusted and unadjusted odds ratios[1] showing the likelihood of low-skilled adults (Levels 1 and 2) collecting social assistance payments, numeracy scale, populations aged 16 to 65, 2003

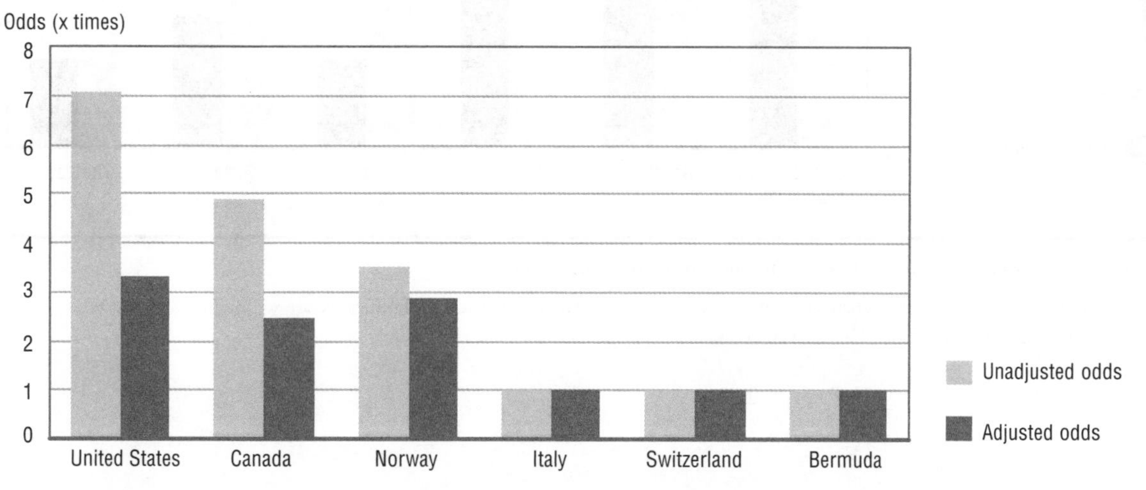

Countries are ranked according to the difference in the unadjusted odds.

1. Odds estimates that are not statistically different from one at conventional levels of significance are set to one in the figure.

Source: Adult Literacy and Life Skills Survey, 2003.

Figure 7.4 shows the relationship between skills and the likelihood of earning income from interest, dividends, capital gains or other investment income such as net rental income. Previous research provides some evidence that more schooling is associated with higher savings rates (Solomon 1975). But even after adjusting for levels of education and income, the findings show that in Bermuda, Canada, Switzerland and the United States, medium to high skilled adults (Levels 3 and 4/5) are more likely to earn investment income. In Italy, there is a relationship but not above and beyond the effect of education and household income on wealth. This suggests that in most countries, numeracy skills are a prerequisite to individuals realizing investment income.

FIGURE 7.4

Likelihood of medium to high-skilled adults earning investment income

Adjusted and unadjusted odds ratios[1] showing the likelihood of medium to high-skilled adults (Levels 3 and 4/5) earning investment income, numeracy scale, populations aged 16 to 65, 2003

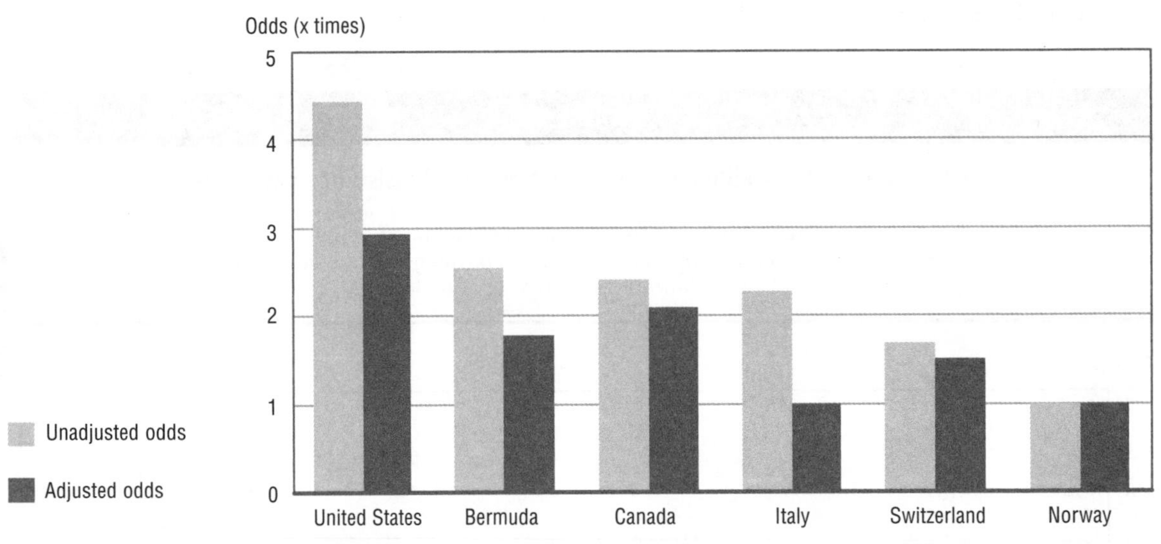

Countries are ranked according to the difference in the unadjusted odds.

1. Odds estimates that are not statistically different from one at conventional levels of significance are set to one in the figure.

Source: Adult Literacy and Life Skills Survey, 2003.

References

An, C.B., Haveman, R.H., and Wolfe, B.L. (1993), "Teen Out-of-Wedlock Births and Welfare Receipt: The Role of Childhood Events and Economic Circumstances", *Review of Economics and Statistics*, Vol. 75(2), pp. 195–208.

Arrow, K.J. (1973), "Higher Education as a Filter", *Journal of Public Economics*, Vol. 2, pp. 193-216.

Becker, G.S. (1964), *Human Capital: A Theoretical and Empirical Analysis with Special References to Education* (Editions revised in 1975 and 1993), University of Chicago Press, Chicago.

Blaug, M. (1976), "The Empirical Status of Human Capital Theory: A slightly jaundiced survey", *Journal of Economic Literature*, Vol. 14(3), pp. 827-855.

Danziger, S., Corcoran, M., Danziger, S. Heflin, C., Kalil, A., Levine, J., Rosen, D., Seefeldt, K., Siefert, K. and Tolman, R. (1999), "Barriers to the Employment of Welfare Recipients", Discussion Paper no. 1193-99, Institute for Research on Poverty, University of Michigan.

Green, D.A. and Riddell, W.C. (2001), *Literacy, Numeracy and Labour Market Outcomes in Canada,* Statistics Canada and Human Resources Development Canada, Ottawa and Hull.

Heinrich, C.J. (1998), "Aiding Welfare-to-Work Transitions: Lessons from JTPA on the Cost-Effectiveness of Education and Training Services", Working Paper 98-12, Joint Center for Poverty Research, Northwestern University/University of Chicago.

Kiefer, N. (1985), "Evidence on the Role of Education in Labor Turnover", *Journal of Human Resources,* Vol. 20(3), pp. 445–452.

Mincer, J. (1974), *Schooling, Experience, and Earnings,* Columbia University Press, New York.

Murnane, R.J., Willet, J.B. and Levy, F. (1995), "The Growing Importance of Cognitive Skills in Wage Determination", *Review of Economics and Statistics*, Vol. 77(2), pp. 251-266.

Murnane, R. J., Willet, J. B., Braatz, M. J. and Duhaldeborde, Y. (2001), "Do Different Dimensions of Male High School Students' Skills Predict Labour Market Success a Decade Later? Evidence from the NLSY", *Economics of Education Review*, Vol. 20, pp. 311-320.

OECD and HRDC (1997), *Literacy Skills for the Knowledge Society: Further Results from the International Adult Literacy Survey,* Paris and Hull.

Osberg, L. (2000), *Schooling, Literacy and Individual Earnings,* Statistics Canada and Human Resources Development Canada, Ottawa and Hull.

Rivera-Batiz, F.L. (1992), "Quantitative Literacy and the Likelihood of Employment Among Young Adults in the United States", *Journal of Human Resources*, Vol. 27, pp. 313-328.

Solomon, L.C. (1975), "The Relation between Schooling and Savings Behavior: An Example of the Indirect Effects of Education", in F.T. Juster (ed.), *Education, Income, and Human Behavior*, McGraw-Hill, New York, pp. 253-293.

Schultz, T.W. (1961), "Investment in Human Capital", *American Economic Review*, Vol. 51(1), pp. 1-17.

Spence, A.M. (1973), "Job Market Signalling", *Quarterly Journal of Economics*, Vol. 87(3), pp. 355-374.

Stigler, G. (1961), "The Economics of Information", *Journal of Political Economy*, Vol. 69, pp. 213-225.

Contributors

Richard Desjardins, *Statistics Canada*
Patrick Werquin, *OECD*
Lauren Dong, *Statistics Canada*

Annex 7

Data Values for the Figures

TABLE 7.1

Three stage least squares estimates of the effect of observed skills (percentile scale) on weekly log-earnings, prose, document, numeracy and problem solving scales, labour force populations aged 16 to 65, 2003

	Prose literacy		Document literacy		Numeracy		Problem solving[1]	
Bermuda								
Observed skills (percentiles)	0.18***	(0.05)	0.37***	(0.06)	0.25***	(0.05)	0.29***	(0.07)
Years of schooling	0.01	(0.02)	-0.07	(0.03)	-0.02	(0.02)	-0.01	(0.02)
Years of experience	0.04***	(0.00)	0.04***	(0.01)	0.04***	(0.00)	0.03***	(0.01)
Years of experience-squared	0.00***	(0.00)	0.00***	(0.00)	0.00***	(0.00)	0.00***	(0.00)
Male	0.39***	(0.04)	0.26***	(0.04)	0.16***	(0.05)	0.41***	(0.04)
Urban resident	4.98***	(0.10)	5.16***	(0.12)	5.25***	(0.12)	4.71***	(0.12)
Canada								
Observed skills (percentiles)	0.09***	(0.01)	0.11***	(0.01)	0.13***	(0.01)	0.08***	(0.01)
Years of schooling	0.06***	(0.00)	0.05***	(0.00)	0.04***	(0.01)	0.07***	(0.00)
Years of experience	0.06***	(0.00)	0.06***	(0.00)	0.06***	(0.00)	0.06***	(0.00)
Years of experience-squared	0.00***	(0.00)	0.00***	(0.00)	0.00***	(0.00)	0.00***	(0.00)
Male	0.42***	(0.02)	0.37***	(0.01)	0.30***	(0.02)	0.39***	(0.01)
Urban resident	0.04	(0.02)	0.04	(0.02)	0.02	(0.02)	0.03	(0.02)
Italy								
Observed skills (percentiles)	0.35***	(0.09)	0.40***	(0.19)	-0.06	(0.10)	0.38***	(0.10)
Years of schooling	-0.03	(0.02)	-0.05***	(0.04)	0.07***	(0.03)	-0.03	(0.02)
Years of experience	0.01	(0.01)	0.01***	(0.01)	0.02***	(0.01)	0.00	(0.01)
Years of experience-squared	0.00	(0.00)	0.00***	(0.00)	0.00**	(0.00)	0.00**	(0.00)
Male	0.37***	(0.05)	0.21***	(0.05)	0.24***	(0.03)	0.34***	(0.05)
Urban resident	0.00	(0.04)	0.00***	(0.06)	0.07***	(0.04)	-0.05	(0.05)
Norway								
Observed skills (percentiles)	0.05	(0.08)	0.08	(0.08)	0.05	(0.07)	0.00	(0.07)
Years of schooling	0.06 ***	(0.02)	0.05 ***	(0.02)	0.06 **	(0.02)	0.07 ***	(0.02)
Years of experience	0.07 ***	(0.01)	0.07 ***	(0.01)	0.07 ***	(0.01)	0.07 ***	(0.01)
Years of experience-squared	0.00 ***	(0.00)	0.00 ***	(0.00)	0.00 ***	(0.00)	0.00 ***	(0.00)
Male	0.34 ***	(0.04)	0.29 ***	(0.07)	0.28 ***	(0.08)	0.34 ***	(0.04)
Urban resident	0.30 ***	(0.05)	0.30 ***	(0.05)	0.31 ***	(0.05)	0.32 ***	(0.05)

TABLE 7.1 (concluded)

Three stage least squares estimates of the effect of observed skills (percentile scale) on weekly log-earnings, prose, document, numeracy and problem solving scales, labour force populations aged 16 to 65, 2003

	Prose literacy		Document literacy		Numeracy		Problem solving[1]	
Switzerland								
Observed skills (percentiles)	0.03	(0.03)	0.04*	(0.02)	0.02	(0.02)	0.03	(0.03)
Years of schooling	0.07***	(0.01)	0.07***	(0.01)	0.08***	(0.01)	0.08***	(0.01)
Years of experience	0.04***	(0.00)	0.04***	(0.00)	0.04***	(0.00)	0.04***	(0.00)
Years of experience-squared	0.00***	(0.00)	0.00***	(0.00)	0.00***	(0.00)	0.00***	(0.00)
Male	0.72***	(0.03)	0.69***	(0.03)	0.69***	(0.03)	0.72***	(0.03)
Urban resident	0.18***	(0.03)	0.18***	(0.03)	0.18***	(0.03)	0.18***	(0.03)
United States								
Observed skills (percentiles)	0.05*	(0.03)	0.06	(0.03)	0.08**	(0.04)	...	...
Years of schooling	0.09***	(0.02)	0.09***	(0.02)	0.07***	(0.02)	...	...
Years of experience	0.06***	(0.01)	0.06***	(0.01)	0.06***	(0.01)	...	...
Years of experience-squared	0.00***	(0.00)	0.00***	(0.00)	0.00***	(0.00)	...	...
Male	0.50***	(0.04)	0.47***	(0.04)	0.42***	(0.05)	...	...
Urban resident	0.15***	(0.05)	0.15***	(0.05)	0.15***	(0.06)	...	...

* $p<0.10$, statistically significant at the 10 per cent level.

** $p<0.05$, statistically significant at the 5 per cent level.

*** $p<0.01$, statistically significant at the 1 per cent level.

... Not applicable.

1. Switzerland (Italian) and the United States did not field the problem solving skills domain.

Note: The results reported in the table are from the first equation of the three equation system. The estimates for the other two equations are available upon request.

Source: Adult Literacy and Life Skills Survey, 2003.

TABLE 7.2

Per cent difference of expected weekly earnings for each occupational type relative to "goods related" occupations, labour force populations aged 16 to 65, 2003

Bermuda		
Experts	44.6***	(0.06)
Managers	43.0***	(0.07)
Information high-skills	13.2 *	(0.07)
Information low-skills	4.3	(0.06)
Services low-skills	-27.8***	(0.07)
Canada		
Experts	37.1***	(0.04)
Managers	36.0***	(0.04)
Information high-skills	16.4***	(0.04)
Information low-skills	-41.3***	(0.03)
Services low-skills	-68.6***	(0.04)
Italy		
Experts	40.0***	(0.07)
Managers	37.2***	(0.08)
Information high-skills	18.1***	(0.04)
Information low-skills	-2.6	(0.04)
Services low-skills	-10.2 *	(0.06)
Norway		
Experts	57.9***	(0.08)
Managers	65.5***	(0.10)
Information high-skills	32.7***	(0.07)
Information low-skills	21.1***	(0.08)
Services low-skills	-7.9	(0.08)
Switzerland		
Experts	59.2***	(0.10)
Managers	48.2***	(0.08)
Information high-skills	14.4 *	(0.09)
Information low-skills	-17.6 *	(0.09)
Services low-skills	-39.0***	(0.11)
United States		
Experts	68.3***	(0.07)
Managers	57.1***	(0.07)
Information high-skills	20.9***	(0.08)
Information low-skills	-19.9***	(0.06)
Services low-skills	-49.8***	(0.07)

* p<0.10, statistically significant at the 10 per cent level.

** p<0.05, statistically significant at the 5 per cent level.

*** p<0.01, statistically significant at the 1 per cent level.

Note: Values in brackets are standard errors for the per cent estimates divided by 100.

Source: Adult Literacy and Life Skills Survey, 2003.

TABLE 7.3

Adjusted and unadjusted odds ratios showing the likelihood of low skilled adults (Levels 1 and 2) collecting social assistance payments, numeracy scale, populations aged 16 to 65, 2003

	Adjusted odds[1]		Unadjusted odds	
Bermuda	1.00	(1.0)	2.11	(1.0)
Canada	2.45***	(0.2)	4.89***	(0.2)
Italy	2.13	(0.8)	3.49	(0.8)
Norway	2.86**	(0.4)	3.52***	(0.4)
Switzerland	1.92	(0.7)	2.61	(0.6)
United States	3.32**	(0.5)	7.06***	(0.4)

* p<0.10, statistically significant at the 10 per cent level.

** p<0.05, statistically significant at the 5 per cent level.

*** p<0.01, statistically significant at the 1 per cent level.

1. Odds are adjusted for gender, age, educational attainment and total personal income.

Note: Standard errors are of the logarithm of the odds ratios.

Source: Adult Literacy and Life Skills Survey, 2003.

TABLE 7.4

Adjusted and unadjusted odds ratios showing the likelihood of medium to high skilled adults (Levels 3 and 4/5) earning investment income, numeracy scale, populations aged 16 to 65, 2003

	Adjusted odds[1]		Unadjusted odds	
Bermuda	1.77***	(0.18)	2.54***	(0.12)
Canada	2.10***	(0.13)	2.42***	(0.10)
Italy	1.36	(0.28)	2.28***	(0.26)
Norway	0.98	(0.20)	1.32	(0.17)
Switzerland	1.52**	(0.15)	1.68***	(0.09)
United States	2.93***	(0.19)	4.44***	(0.15)

* p<0.10, statistically significant at the 10 per cent level.

** p<0.05, statistically significant at the 5 per cent level.

*** p<0.01, statistically significant at the 1 per cent level.

1. Odds are adjusted for gender, age, educational attainment and total personal income.

Note: Standard errors are of the logarithm of the odds ratios.

Source: Adult Literacy and Life Skills Survey, 2003.

Chapter 8

Skills and Information and Communications Technologies

Summary

This chapter explores the relationship between skills and Information and Communications Technology (ICT) use and familiarity. The ALL survey collected information on the use of, and familiarity with ICTs, at the individual level, including a series of self-assessment questions on ICT use, perceptions of experience, and degree of comfort with ICTs. First, access rates to computers and the Internet are considered. Second, the relationship between ICT use and literacy skills is studied. This is important because it demonstrates the fundamental relationship between ICT use and other skill sets. Third, the determinants of ICT use are examined, including income, age, gender, educational attainment and occupation. Finally, outcomes associated with the use of ICTs in combination with literacy skills are explored.

Table of Contents

Skills and Information and Communications Technologies

8.1 Overview and highlights

This chapter explores the relationship between skills and Information and Communications Technology (ICT) use and familiarity. The ALL survey collected information on the use of, and familiarity with ICTs, at the individual level, including a series of self-assessment questions on ICT use, perceptions of experience, and degree of comfort with ICTs. First, access rates to computers and the Internet are considered. Second, the relationship between ICT use and literacy skills is studied. This is important because it demonstrates the fundamental relationship between ICT use and other skill sets. Third, the determinants of ICT use are examined, including income, age, gender, educational attainment and occupation. Finally, outcomes associated with the use of ICTs in combination with literacy skills are explored.

8

The main findings presented in this chapter are summarized below:

- Patterns of Internet and computer access confirm the existence of "digital divides" both within and between nations. Apart from Italy, differences in ICT use and access between countries are not large. Home computer access rates are about 80 per cent and home Internet access rates approximately 70 per cent for the majority of countries surveyed.
- Within countries, however, there are large divides in access and use of ICTs. Among other factors, income differentials stand out in predicting access to, and use of ICTs. Home computer and Internet access vary significantly by income and the largest drop in access rates typically occurs between the third and second income quartiles.
- Many factors including age, gender, level of education, type of occupation and level of literacy proficiency are associated with adults' use and familiarity of computers and the Internet. These factors help to predict whether a respondent is a "high-intensity" computer user.
- Age exerts a strong influence on computer use, showing a significant decline after age 45.

- Clear gender differences in computer and Internet use exist in the European countries but not in North America.
- Respondents with less than upper secondary education use computers significantly less often for task-oriented purposes. This effect is most pronounced in Bermuda and Italy.
- Those without access to ICTs also tend to have lower literacy levels than the rest of the population. Non-users tend to have significantly lower literacy skills than computer users.
- The proportion of adults in different literacy and computer use profiles varies substantially by country. In half of the countries, respondents with both low literacy (Levels 1 and 2) and "low-intensity" computer use represent the largest group. The group of respondents with both medium to high literacy (Levels 3 and 4/5) and "high-intensity" computer use is small in all countries.
- As prose, document, numeracy and problem solving levels increase, adults' perceived usefulness and attitude toward computers, Internet use, and use of computers for various tasks also increase. In most countries, respondents with medium to high literacy have between two and three times the odds of being a high-intensity computer user.
- Finally, literacy and computer use profiles are strongly related to the likelihood that respondents have high earnings. In most countries, adults who have medium to high literacy skills (Levels 3 and 4/5) and are high-intensity computer users have about three to six times the odds of being in the top quartile of personal income compared to respondents who have low literacy and are low-intensity computer users.

8.2 Connectivity and income as a key determinant

The widespread diffusion and use of ICTs, including the personal computer and the Internet, is a major source of change on many fronts. In parallel with the profound economic and social transformations underway, people have learned to develop new and rapidly changing skill sets to use ICTs effectively. This has brought to the fore the notion that ICT skills are necessary to function in today's world. Differences in the penetration and use of various ICTs, both within and between countries, have been well documented in recent years. Studies of the digital divide (e.g., U.S. Department of Commerce, 1995; 1998, 1999, 2000, 2002; OECD, 2001; Sciadas, 2002, 2003) have also identified and analyzed many factors that influence connectivity and use of ICTs, whether at the household or individual level. While income is usually a key determinant, many other factors are found to exert an influence. These include education, age, gender, area of residence (urban vs rural) and even family composition.

Results presented in Figure 8.1 confirm previous findings on the digital divide. Apart from Italy, differences in ICT use and access between countries are not large. Estimates show that computer access ranges from a high of over 80 per cent in Switzerland to just over 40 per cent in Italy. Closely related to this pattern is Internet access, where nearly three-quarters of individuals in Switzerland compared to less than one-third of individuals in Italy live in a home with Internet access.

FIGURE 8.1

Home computer and internet access at home

Per cent of adults aged 16 to 65 who report having access to a computer and the internet at home, 2003

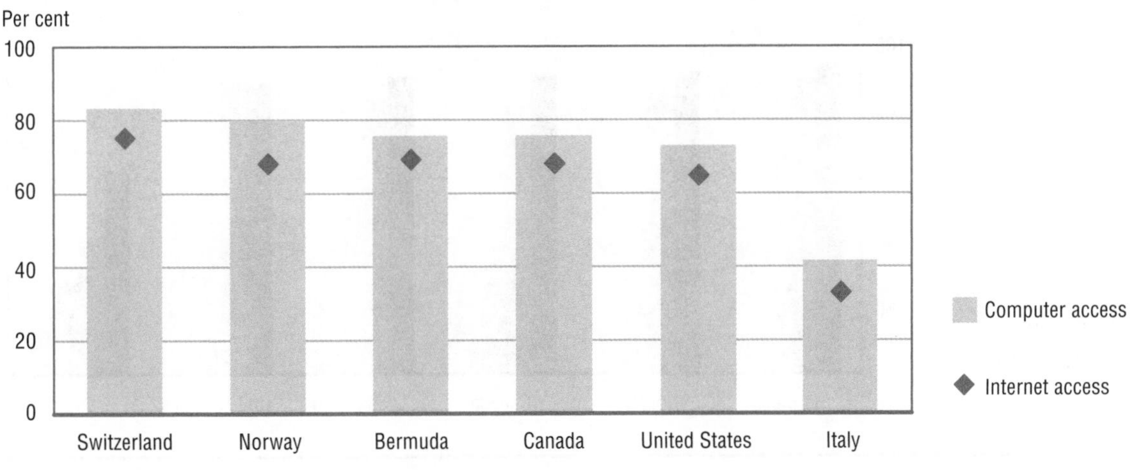

Countries are ranked by the per cent who have access to computers at home.

Source: Adult Literacy and Life Skills Survey, 2003.

Confirming previous findings, Figure 8.2 shows the strong correlation between income and ICT use and access. Income is a key factor shaping the digital divide. It determines whether households can afford to purchase computers and access to the Internet as well as other ICTs. Use and access of computers and the Internet by income quartile varies substantially by country. These results have potentially serious consequences because individuals living in low-income households may face computer-related learning disadvantages (Felstead, Duncan and Green, 2002).

There exists little difference between the highest and second income quartiles. It is between the second, third, and lowest quartiles that differences become evident. Italy lags the other countries in terms of computer and Internet access for each quartile. In fact, computer and Internet access for users in the top income quartile living in Italy approximates the access rates of the lower quartiles of other countries. In this respect Italy is not only lagging behind the other countries, but it is subject to a greater divide within the nation in terms of computer and Internet access.

FIGURE 8.2

Home computer access by income quartiles

Per cent of adults aged 16 to 65 who report having access to a computer at home, by household income quartiles, 2003

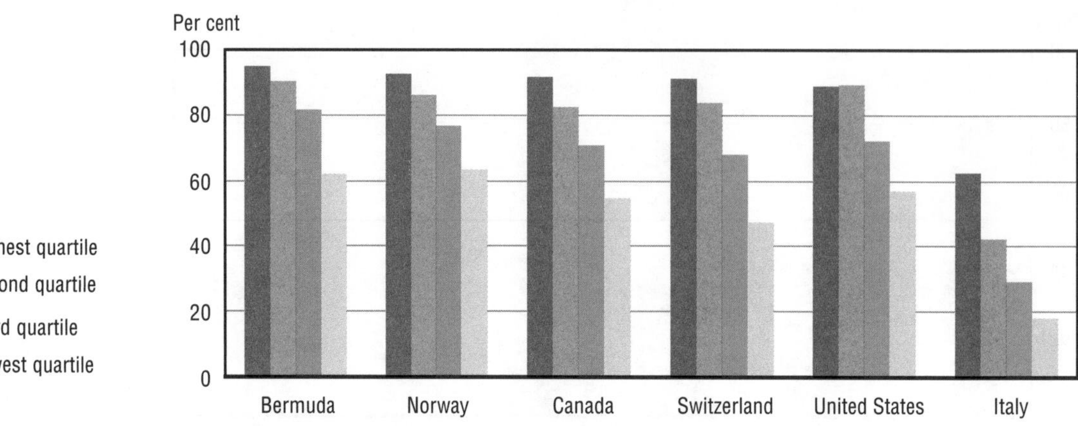

Countries are ranked by the rate of access among those in the highest income quartile.

Source: Adult Literacy and Life Skills Survey, 2003.

8.3 ICTs and literacy skills

A key question that emerged from the IALS is the extent to which foundation skills relate to other skills such as ICT skills, which are thought to be important for workplace productivity and labour market success (OECD and Statistics Canada, 2000; McAuley and Lowe, 1999). In practice, ICT use is linked to literacy skills in a number of ways. Some studies suggest that literacy skills are essential to the development of ICT literacy (e.g., Massé, Roy and Gingras, 1998). While ICT skills may depend on technological proficiency to a certain extent, it also requires cognitive skills, such as those underlying literacy, numeracy and problem solving, which are critical for using ICTs effectively (International ICT Literacy Panel, 2002). Most ICT content, notably the Internet, remains text-based (Stewart, 2000), and the format and content of web pages often demand skills similar in nature to those assessed by the document literacy domain in ALL, namely unstructured and non-continuous texts such as tables and documents. In general, literacy is becoming increasingly important as more information is transmitted and shared through ICTs than ever before (Leu Jr., 2000).

A comparison of computer users and non-users reveals a literacy gap in all countries. Figure 8.3 shows that users consistently score higher on average by approximately 50 or more points. Thus, non-users face not only a digital divide, but also a literacy gap. Separately, among 15-year-old students, findings show a positive relationship between access to home computers and reading skills (Bussière and Gluszynski, 2004).

Three broad indices of ICT use and familiarity are used for further analysis. These assess the respondent's perceived usefulness and attitude towards computers, the diversity and intensity of their Internet use, and their use of computers for specific task-oriented purposes (see Box 8A). Figure 8.4 displays the average index scores by country. Bermuda emerges as a leader in all three measures, but it is closely followed by Canada, Norway, Switzerland and the United States. Scores are substantially lower in Italy, particularly for diversity and intensity of Internet use, and use of computers for task-oriented purposes. In Switzerland, scores for the perceived usefulness of computers, and diversity and intensity of Internet use, are lower than most other countries, but together with Bermuda it is one of the leading countries for use of computers for task-oriented purposes.

FIGURE 8.3

Skills of computer users and non-users

Mean scores on the prose literacy scale ranging from 0 to 500 points, by whether respondents are computer users or non-users, populations aged 16 to 65, 2003

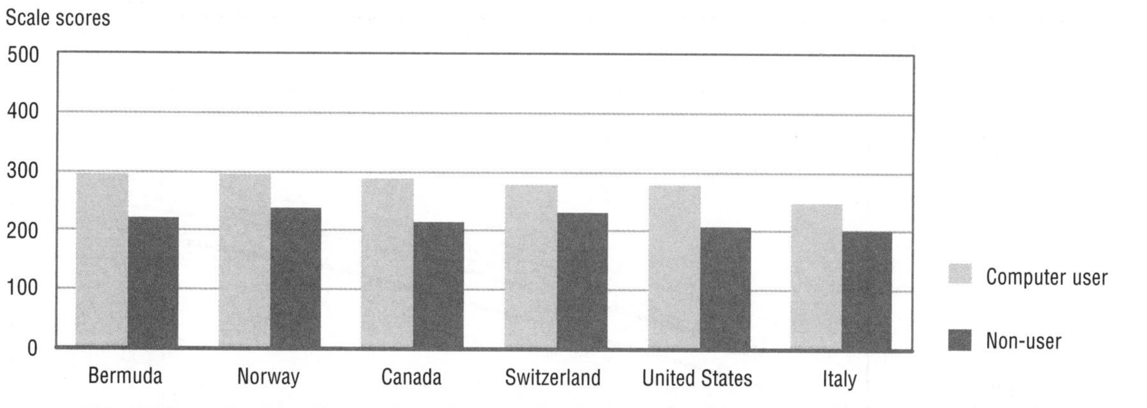

Countries are ranked by the scores of computer users.

Source: Adult Literacy and Life Skills Survey, 2003.

FIGURE 8.4

Index scores of ICT use and familiarity

Mean index scores on three scales of ICT use and familiarity, perceived usefulness and attitude towards computers, diversity and intensity of Internet use, and use of computers of for specific task-oriented purposes, populations aged 16 to 65, 2003

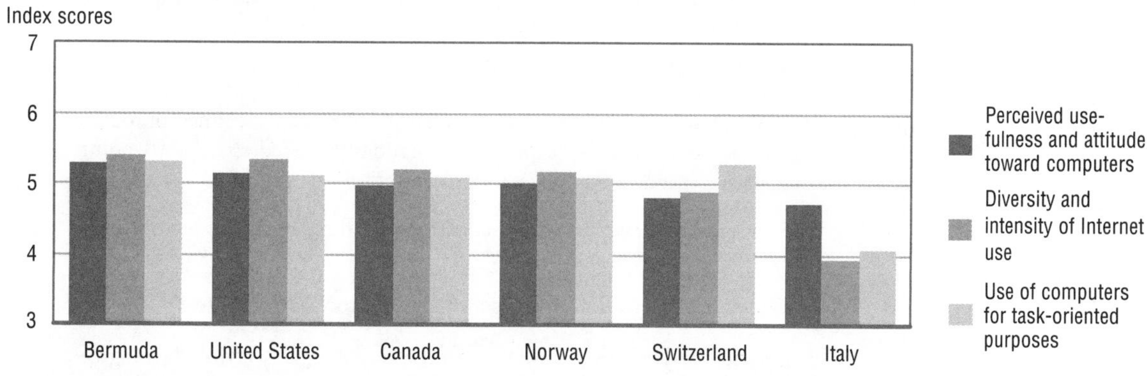

Countries are ranked by the sum of the mean scores on the three scales.

Source: Adult Literacy and Life Skills Survey, 2003.

Results displayed in Figure 8.5 demonstrate that prose literacy increases with the use of computers for task-oriented purposes. The findings are similar for the other two indices and for other skills measured in ALL. Moreover, the patterns are similar for all countries in the survey, without exceptions. These results are consistent with another study that suggests that adults with higher literacy and numeracy skills also perform better on an assessment of ICT skills (see DfES, 2003).

FIGURE 8.5

Use of computers for task-oriented purposes by literacy skills

Mean index scores on a scale measuring the intensity of use of computers for specific task-oriented purposes, by prose literacy levels, populations aged 16 to 65, 2003

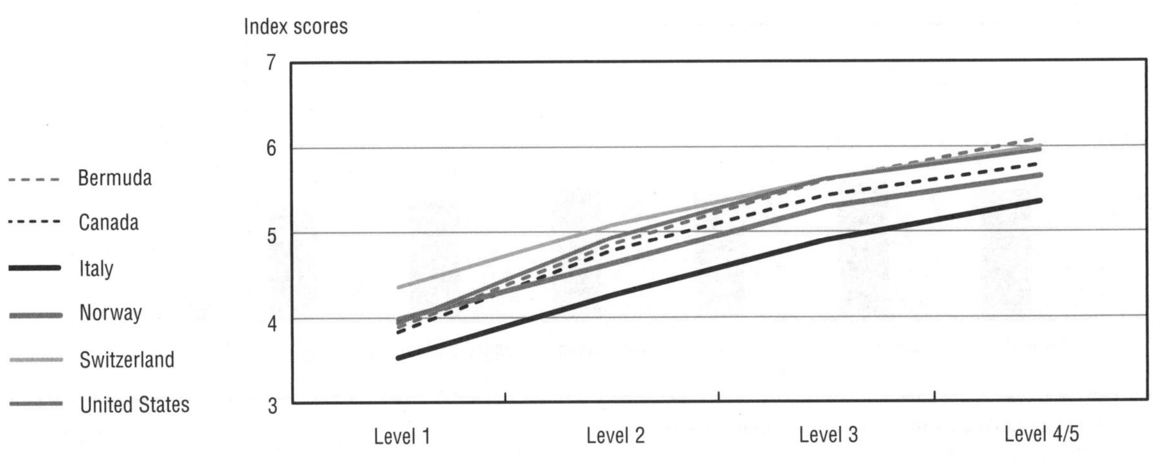

Source: Adult Literacy and Life Skills Survey, 2003.

Box 8A

Indices of ICT use and familiarity

Three indices of ICT use and familiarity were derived from several observed variables that were collected in the ALL survey. ICT related variables were examined using Exploratory Factor Analysis with principal components specified as the method. Confirmatory Factor Analysis was then used to validate three models that were hypothesized on the basis of the exploratory results and an interpretation of the observed variables. Index scores were derived according to the specified models using a Rasch scaling approach. Scores for each index are expressed as standardized scores on a 10-point scale, with a mean of 5 and a standard deviation of 1.5.

The underlying variables used to construct the three measures are outlined below:

1. Index of perceived usefulness and attitude toward computers

Please tell me whether you strongly agree, agree, disagree, or strongly disagree with each of the following statements:

- Computers have made it possible for me to get more done in less time

- Computers have made it easier for me to get useful information
- Computers have helped me to learn new skills other than computer skills
- Computers have helped me to communicate with people
- Computers have helped me reach my occupational (career) goals

2. Index of diversity and intensity of Internet use

In a typical month, how often did you use the Internet for the following purposes? (Daily, a few times a week, a few times a month, never)

- Electronic mail (email)
- Participate in chat groups or other on-line discussions
- Shopping (including browsing for products or services but not necessarily buying)
- Banking
- Formal education or training (part of a formal learning activity such as a course or a program of studies)
- Obtain or save music
- Read about news and current events
- Search for employment opportunities
- Search for health related information
- Search for weather related information
- Search for government information
- Playing games with others
- General browsing
- Other purposes; specify
- In a typical month, how many hours did you use a computer at home?

3. Index of using computers for task-oriented purposes

In a typical month, how often did you use a computer for the following purposes? (Daily, a few times a week, a few times a month, never).

- Writing or editing text
- Accounts, spreadsheets or statistical analysis
- Creating graphics, designs, pictures or presentations
- Programming or writing computer code
- Keeping a schedule or calendar
- Reading information on a CD-ROM or DVD
- In a typical month, how many hours did you use a computer at home?

8.4 ICT use and familiarity by key demographic characteristics

The strong relationship between income and ICT use and access was established above. This section examines other factors that are associated with using computers for task-oriented purposes (see Box 8A). In particular, these factors include age, gender, educational attainment and occupation.

Some are concerned that older workers have fewer ICT skills and that this may result in a deterioration of their position in the labour force (OECD, 2004). A 'generation gap' with respect to exposure to computers and other ICTs may explain a reduced opportunity to learn ICT skills. Younger adults are more likely to grow up with a computer in the home than those who are older than 25 (DfES, 2003). As a result, there are fears of a growing mismatch between the skills of older workers and the demand for ICT skills. Further, a lack of skills may cause a slowdown in the introduction of ICTs in the jobs filled by older workers, hurting a company's productivity growth and competitiveness (OECD, 2004). However, to date there is no firm evidence of such a competitive disadvantage.

Results presented in Figure 8.6 suggest that there is a strong relationship between age and the intensity of using computers for task-oriented purposes. Moreover, the patterns are similar across countries. Older adults use computers for task-oriented purposes less intensively than younger adults. Many of the tasks used to construct the index are associated with computer use at work, such as writing or editing text, managing accounts or spreadsheets, programming, creating presentations or keeping a schedule or calendar. The largest difference in intensity of use is between the ages of 46 to 55 and 56 to 65, suggesting that older workers and retired persons are not performing these tasks regularly. While not reported here, the ICT-age relationship is even stronger with respect to the diversity and intensity of Internet use. In contrast, the index measuring the perceived usefulness and attitudes toward computers does not decrease uniformly with increasing age.

Many studies have found gender differences in patterns of computer use. For example, in Canada, one study found that with the exception of word processing, men were more likely than women to use computers for a range of common tasks (Marshall, 2001). Men have also been found to perform slightly higher than women on a practical performance assessment of ICT skills, and also to have higher awareness of ICTs (DfES, 2003). The fact that men were more likely to be frequent users of computers is suggested as a reason for much of the difference in performance (DfES, 2003). Access to ICTs is found to be lowest among unemployed women (Commission of the European Communities, 2002).

FIGURE 8.6

Use of computers for task-oriented purposes by age groups

Mean index scores on a scale measuring the intensity of use of computers for specific task-oriented purposes, by age groups, populations aged 16 to 65, 2003

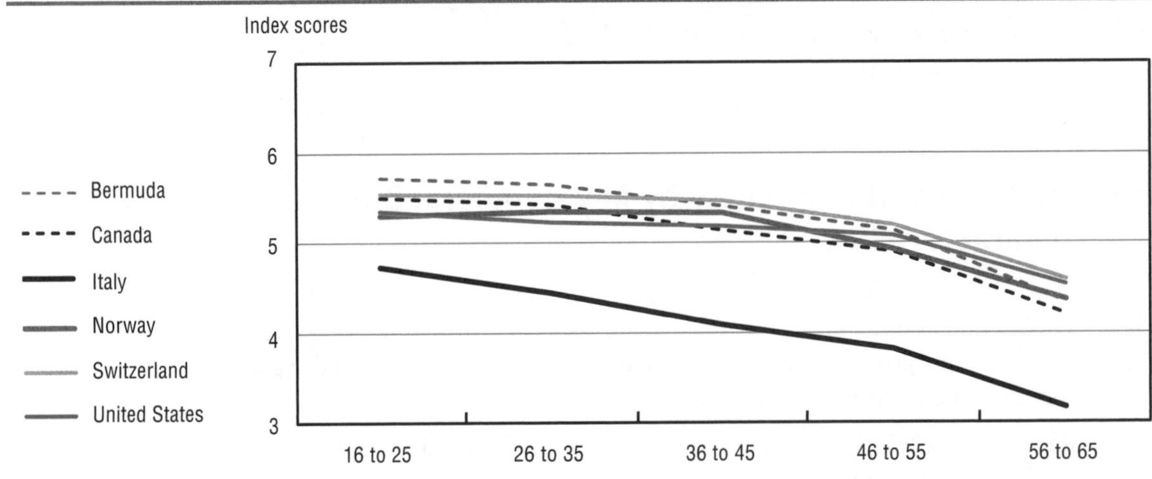

Source: Adult Literacy and Life Skills Survey, 2003.

Figure 8.7 shows that differences in using computers for task-oriented purposes by gender are more pronounced in Italy, Norway and Switzerland. The results are similar for the other two measures of ICT use and familiarity. In these countries, men tend to be more familiar with and use ICTs more intensively than women. In contrast, gender differences are much smaller in Bermuda, Canada and the United States. In fact, in Bermuda, women score higher than men on all three ICT measures.

Although there appears to be a relationship between gender and ICT use, gender alone does not tell the entire story. There is ample evidence that gender differences in ICT usage are higher during the early stages of the introduction of new ICTs but decline over time. Therefore, gender differences must be analyzed in conjunction with the actual penetration of ICTs, as well as the fact that significant inter-dependencies exist with age. For example, while a Canadian study found that the gender difference increases with age, it was non-existent among 15 to 19 year olds (Silver, 2001).

FIGURE 8.7

Use of computers for task-oriented purposes by gender

Mean index scores on a scale measuring the intensity of use of computers for specific task-oriented purposes, by gender, populations aged 16 to 65, 2003

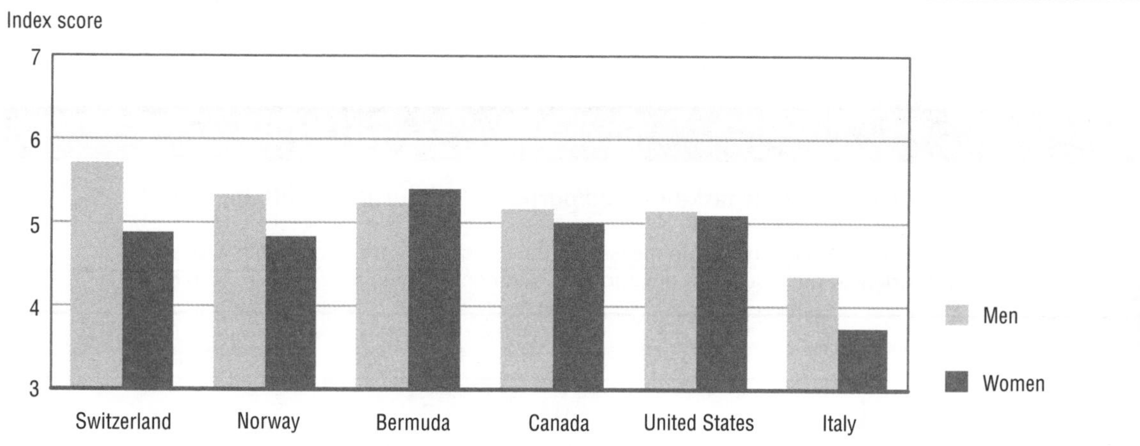

Countries are ranked by mean index scores for men.

Source: Adult Literacy and Life Skills Survey, 2003.

While an individual may master certain skills — for example, the ability to produce tables and graphs using spreadsheet software — one characteristic of ICT skills is that they are often the product of a process of continuous learning (HRDC, 2002; Bertelsmann Foundation and AOL Time Warner Foundation, 2002; Committee on Information Technology Literacy, 1999; Ginsburg and Elmore, 1998). Because the learning process is continuous, learners often incorporate several methods to learn necessary computer skills, both formal and informal, and seldom rely on only one method of learning. Formal methods include courses sponsored by an employer, while less formal methods may include help from colleagues or family, the use of manuals and books, observing others, or self-teaching through trial-and-error, for example (Dryburgh, 2002; Felstead *et al.*, 2002). Skill requirements change because of the particularly rapid introduction of new ICTs (e.g., software upgrades, new supporting hardware or interface technologies). The ability to learn and keep up with application-specific knowledge while also developing and maintaining a growing set of foundation skills therefore becomes essential to one's level of participation in a digital world.

The role of formal education in building a workforce equipped with ICT skills is currently debated. While training at schools, colleges and universities may be an effective means to reach the future workforce, the rapid pace of technological change necessitates lifelong learning rather than one-time instruction. Nonetheless, education can be an important means to develop at least basic ICT skills. The relatively recent introduction of ICTs in schools may mean that as time goes by, higher proportions of people are likely to become ICT users (OECD, 2004). One study found that those with more formal education have higher proficiency in ICT skills. But because more educated people also tend to work with computers more intensively, it is difficult to determine whether education or employment has the biggest impact on ICT skills (DfES, 2003). While beyond the scope of this study, more effort is needed in future to measure ICT skills directly and gain insight into their development.

Differences in ICT use and familiarity between levels of education are largest in Bermuda and Italy and slightly smaller in Canada, Norway, Switzerland and the United States. Figure 8.8 displays the intensity of computer use by levels of educational attainment. The pattern is similar for the intensity and diversity of Internet use, but those with less education still perceive computers to be useful, even if they do not use them as much.

FIGURE 8.8

Use of computers for task-oriented purposes by educational attainment

Mean index scores on a scale measuring the intensity of use of computers for specific task-oriented purposes, by educational attainment, populations aged 16 to 65, 2003

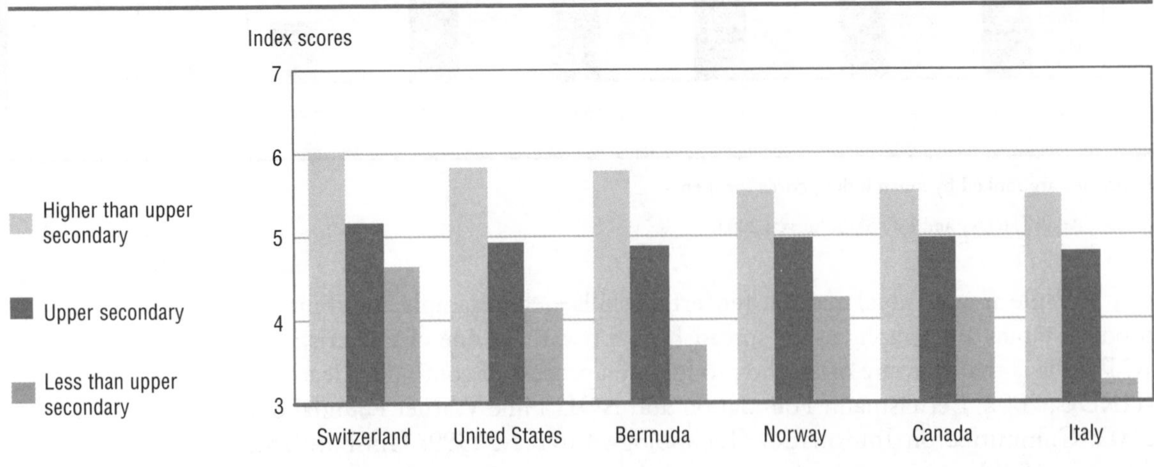

Countries are ranked by mean index scores for respondents with higher than upper secondary education.

Source: Adult Literacy and Life Skills Survey, 2003.

ICT skills have become necessary for a broad range of activities in many workplaces (OECD, 2002). While the introduction of ICTs has affected the workplace at many levels, the distribution of ICT-related tasks is not necessarily even. Certain types of workers, in particular "knowledge" and "information" workers, have become an important part of the knowledge economy. The intensity of ICT use can be expected to vary both by industrial sector and by type of occupation.

'Expert' knowledge workers (e.g., scientists, computing and other professionals) and managers tend to use ICTs more intensively and be more familiar with them than those in other types of occupations. But the pervasive nature of ICTs in the workplace is demonstrated by the fact that 'low-skill' information workers (e.g., office and customer service clerks) are just as likely to use ICTs as 'high-skill' information workers (e.g., professionals, teachers and most technicians). Figure 8.9 shows that managers and information workers use computers for task-oriented purposes at about the same level of intensity. The only types of jobs with substantially lower ICT use and familiarity are low-skill services and goods-related manufacturing type jobs, but even for low-skill service jobs, ICT use is becoming an important phenomenon.

FIGURE 8.9

Use of computers for task-oriented purposes by type of occupation

Mean index scores on a scale measuring the intensity of use of computers for specific task-oriented purposes, by type of occupations, populations aged 16 to 65, 2003

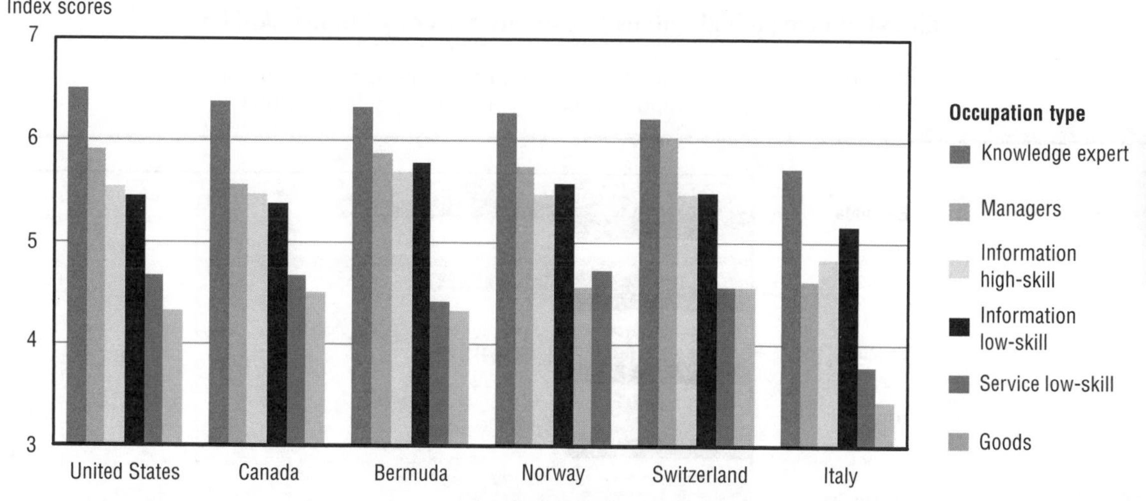

Countries are ranked by mean index score for knowledge expert occupations.

Source: Adult Literacy and Life Skills Survey, 2003.

The following analysis considers all the above factors including age, gender, education, occupation and literacy skill in a multivariate framework. Logistic regression analysis is used to study the factors affecting the intensity of computer use for task-oriented purposes (see Box 3A — Using odds ratios). In particular, the influence of literacy on the likelihood of being a high-intensity computer user for task-oriented purposes is presented in Figure 8.10.

The results vary substantially by country. Gender, for example, exerts a particularly strong influence in some countries. While controlling for other factors, men in Italy, Norway and Switzerland are also more likely to be high-intensity computer users for task-oriented purposes. In contrast, gender differences with respect to ICTs are smaller in North America and in Italy. In fact, in Bermuda there is no difference between men and women in the odds of being a high-intensity computer user.

Education exerts a significant influence on computer use. In the United States and Italy, adults with more than upper secondary education have more than two times the odds of being high-intensity computer users compared to those with less education. In the remaining countries, the odds are approximately twice as high for adults with post-secondary attainment. The results also confirm that those with high levels of household income are more likely to be intense computer users. In most countries, respondents whose income falls in the top income quartile have approximately two times the odds of being high-intensity computer users.

Finally, literacy skills are also an important factor. Figure 8.10 shows that as literacy skill levels increase, the odds of being a high-intensity computer user also increase. In Switzerland and the United States, adults scoring at Level 4/5 have nearly twice the odds of being a high-intensity user compared to respondents with low literacy (Levels 1 and 2). Comparable estimates range from two to over three times for Italy, Canada, Norway and Bermuda.

FIGURE 8.10

Likelihood of being a high-intensity computer user by literacy skill levels

Adjusted odds ratios showing the likelihood of adults aged 16 to 65 of being high-intensity computer users, by prose literacy levels, 2003

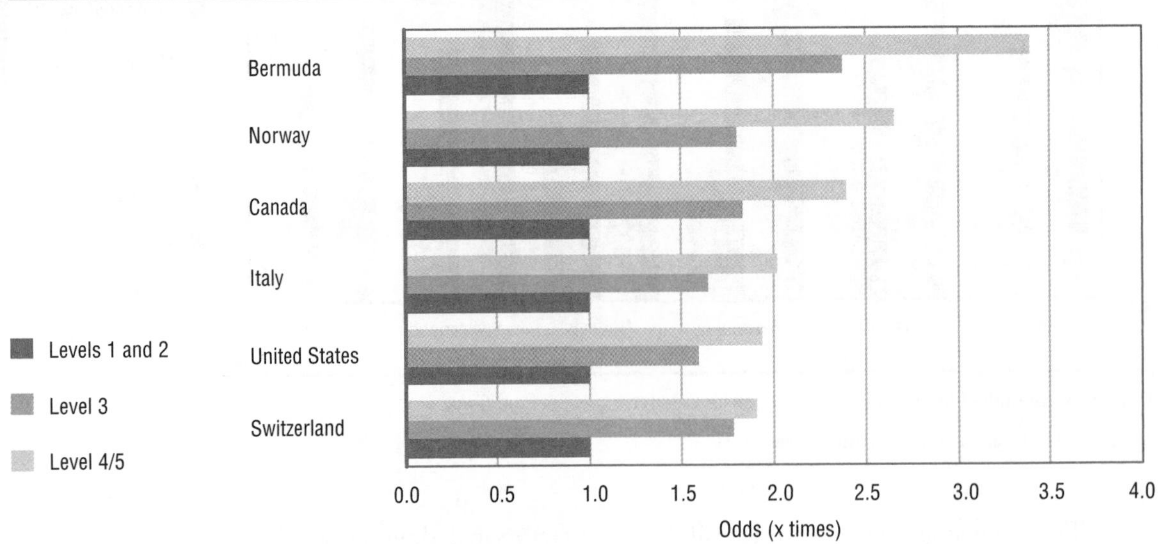

Countries are ranked by the odds of those who score at Level 4/5.

Source: Adult Literacy and Life Skills Survey, 2003.

8.5 ICT use and outcomes

This section considers the possible outcomes associated with ICT use. In particular, the combined effect of literacy skills and different levels of ICT use on personal income are studied. Logistic regression analysis is used to estimate the odds of being a high-income earner, while controlling for various socio-economic characteristics, including different combinations of literacy skill and computer use profiles (see Box 8B).

Box 8B

Measuring combined literacy skill and computer use profiles

The logistic regression in this section models the effects of various socio-economic characteristics, as well as combined literacy skill and computer use profiles, on personal income. The combined profiles consist of four groups as follows:

Profile	Literacy level	Use of computers for task-oriented purposes
Group 1	Low (Levels 1 and 2)	Low-intensity (< top quartile of computer users)
Group 2	Medium/high (Levels 3 and 4/5)	Low-intensity (< top quartile of computer users)
Group 3	Low (Levels 1 and 2)	High-intensity (top quartile of computer users)
Group 4	Medium/high (Levels 3 and 4/5)	High-intensity (top quartile of computer users)

Figure 8.11 displays the distribution of different literacy and computer use profiles by country. In Italy, Switzerland and the United States, adults with a combined profile of low literacy and low intensity computer use is the largest group. In Italy this group is particularly large, reaching over 60 per cent of all adults aged 16 to 65. Conversely, in Bermuda, Canada and Norway, the largest group consists of users with medium to high literacy skills (Levels 3 and 4/5) and low intensity computer use. For all countries except Italy, adults with medium to high literacy skills and high intensity computer use represent the third largest group. The smallest group is composed of individuals with high computer use but low literacy skills.

Results of the logistic regression analysis are presented in Figure 8.12. The findings suggest that combined literacy skill and computer use profiles are strongly associated with personal income. Apart from Italy, respondents who have medium to high literacy skills and are high-intensity computer users have about three to six times the odds of being in the top quartile of personal income compared to respondents with low literacy levels and low computer use. In Italy the same group has almost twice the likelihood of being a top earner. Thus a good foundation of literacy skills combined with a high use of ICTs is associated with high income. Further research is necessary to shed more light on the economic and social outcomes associated with ICT use and literacy skills.

FIGURE 8.11

Combined literacy and computer use profiles

Per cent of adults aged 16 to 65 in each combined literacy and computer use profile[1], 2003

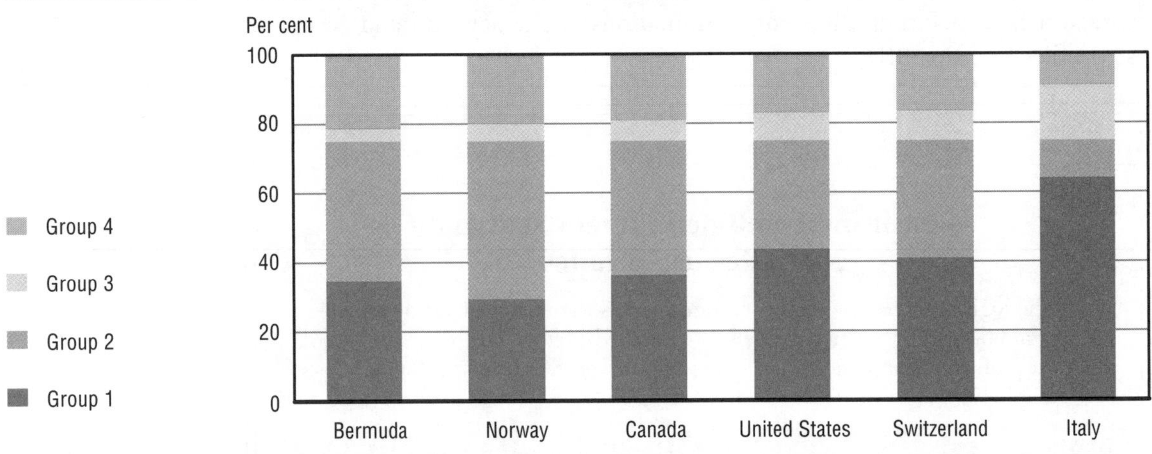

Countries are ranked by the per cent in Group 4.

1. See Box 8B.

Source: Adult Literacy and Life Skills Survey, 2003.

FIGURE 8.12

Likelihood of being a top income quartile earner by combined skill and user profiles

Adjusted odds ratios[1] showing the likelihood of adults aged 16 to 65 of being a top income quartile earning, by combined literacy and computer user profiles[2], 2003

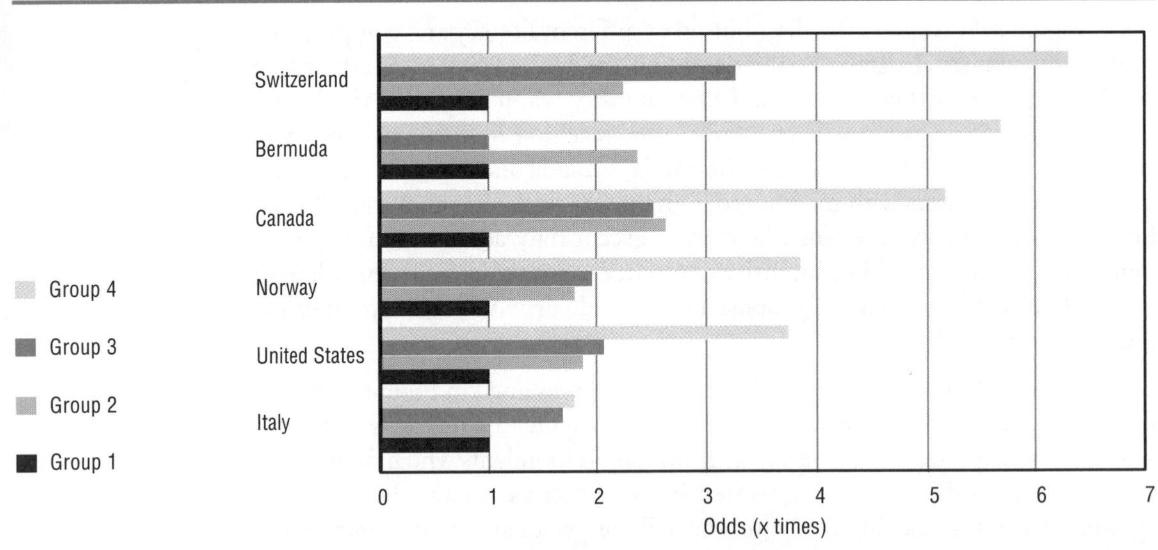

Countries are ranked by the odds of those in Group 4.

1. Odds estimates that are not statistically different from one at conventional levels of significance are reported as one in the figure. For the actual estimate and its corresponding significance, see Table 8.12 in the annex to this chapter.
2. See Box 8B.

Source: Adult Literacy and Life Skills Survey, 2003.

References

Bertelsmann Foundation and AOL Time Warner Foundation (2002), "21st Century Literacy in a Convergent Media World", White paper, 21st Century Literacy Summit, Berlin, March 7-8.

Bussière, P. and Gluszynski, T. (2004), *The Impact of Computer Use on Reading Achievement of 15-year-olds,* Human Resources and Skills Development Canada, Hull.

Commission of the European Communities (2002), "Information Society Jobs - quality for change", Commission Staff Working Paper, Employment and Social Dimension of the Information Society (ESDIS) working group, Brussels.

Committee on Information Technology Literacy (1999), *Being Fluent with Information Technology*, Computer Science and Telecommunications Board, Commission on Physical Sciences, Mathematics, and Applications, National Academy Press, Washington, D.C.

DfES (2003), *The Skills for Life Survey: A National Needs and Impact Survey of Literacy, Numeracy and ICT Skills,* Department for Education and Skills, United Kingdom.

Dryburgh, H. (2002), "Learning Computer Skills", *Canadian Social Trends*, Cat. No. 11-008, Statistics Canada, Spring 2002.

Felstead, A., Duncan, G. and Green, F. (2002), *Work Skills in Britain 1986-2001,* January 2002.

Ginsburg, L. and Elmore, J. (1998), *Technology in the Workplace: Issues of Workers' Skills,* National Center on Adult Literacy, University of Pennsylvania, Pennsylvania.

HRDC (2002), *Knowledge Matters: Skills and Learning for Canadians,* Human Resources Development Canada, Hull.

International ICT Literacy Panel (2002), *Digital Transformation: A framework for ICT literacy*, Educational Testing Service, Princeton, NJ.

Leu Jr., D. (2000), *Literacy and Technology: Deictic consequences for literacy education in an information age*, Syracuse University.

Marshall, K. (2001), "Working with Computers", *Perspectives on Labour and Income*, Cat. No. 75-001-XIE, Statistics Canada, May 2001.

Massé, P., Roy, R. and Gingras, Y. (1998), *The Changing Skill Structure of Employment in Canada,* Human Resources and Development Canada, Hull.

McAuley, J. and Lowe, G. (1999), "International Life Skills Survey Computer Literacy Assessment Framework", Draft document, October 26, 1999.

OECD (2001), *Understanding the Digital Divide,* Paris.

OECD (2002), "ICT Skills and Employment", STI Working Paper, Paris, July 17, 2002.

OECD (2004), "ICT Skills and Employment", *Information Technology Outlook,* Paris.

OECD and Statistics Canada (2000), *Literacy in the Information Age: Final report of the International Adult Literacy Survey,* Paris and Ottawa.

Sciadas, G. (2002), "Unveiling the Digital Divide", *Connectedness Series,* No. 7, Statistics Canada, Cat. No. 56F0004MPE, Ottawa.

Sciadas, G. (2003), *Monitoring the Digital Divide...and Beyond,* National Research Council of Canada, Ottawa.

Silver, C. (2001), "Internet Use among Older Canadians", *Connectedness Series*, No. 4, Statistics Canada, Cat. No. 56F0004MPE, Ottawa.

Stewart, J. (2000), *The Digital Divide in the UK: A review of quantitative indicators and public policies*, Research Centre for Social Sciences, University of Edinburgh, Scotland.

U.S. Department of Commerce (1995), *Falling through the Net: A Survey of the 'Have-Nots' in Urban and Rural America,* Washington D.C.

U.S. Department of Commerce (1998), *Falling through the Net II: New Data on the Digital Divide,* Washington D.C.

U.S. Department of Commerce (1999), *Falling through the Net III: Defining the Digital Divide,* Washington D.C.

U.S. Department of Commerce (2000), *Falling through the Net IV: Toward Digital Inclusion,* Washington D.C.

U.S. Department of Commerce (2002), *A Nation Online: How Americans Are Expanding Their Use of the Internet,* Washington D.C.

Contributors

Ben Veenhof, *Statistics Canada*

Yvan Clermont, *Statistics Canada*

George Sciadas, *Statistics Canada*

Annex 8

Data Values for the Figures

TABLE 8.1

Per cent of adults aged 16 to 65 who report having access to a computer and the Internet at home, 2003

	Computer access		Internet access	
Bermuda	75.6	(1.0)	69.4	(1.1)
Canada	75.6	(0.6)	68.1	(0.6)
Italy	41.5	(0.8)	33.2	(0.9)
Norway	79.9	(0.7)	68.3	(0.8)
Switzerland	83.3	(0.7)	74.9	(1.2)
United States	72.8	(1.0)	64.9	(1.3)

Source: Adult Literacy and Life Skills Survey, 2003.

8

TABLE 8.2

Per cent of adults aged 16 to 65 who report having access to a computer at home, by household income quartiles, 2003

	Lowest quartile		Third quartile		Second quartile		Highest quartile	
Bermuda	57.0	(2.6)	72.2	(3.3)	89.6	(1.5)	88.9	(2.3)
Canada	54.6	(1.5)	70.9	(1.3)	82.5	(1.1)	91.8	(0.9)
Italy	18.2	(2.0)	29.2	(1.8)	42.5	(2.1)	62.5	(1.7)
Norway	63.6	(1.4)	76.8	(1.7)	86.2	(1.5)	92.9	(0.9)
Switzerland	62.0	(2.7)	81.9	(1.9)	90.2	(1.4)	94.9	(1.1)
United States	47.6	(2.1)	68.2	(1.8)	84.2	(1.1)	91.3	(1.4)

Source: Adult Literacy and Life Skills Survey, 2003.

TABLE 8.3

Mean scores on the prose literacy scale ranging from 0 to 500 points, by whether respondents are computer users or non-users, populations aged 16 to 65, 2003

	Computer users		Non-users	
Bermuda	296.9	(1.4)	221.9	(3.7)
Canada	289.1	(0.7)	214.1	(2.3)
Italy	249.3	(1.6)	202.2	(2.6)
Norway	294.1	(1.0)	238.5	(3.6)
Switzerland	279.7	(1.4)	231.5	(4.8)
United States	278.1	(1.3)	207.5	(3.5)

Source: Adult Literacy and Life Skills Survey, 2003.

TABLE 8.4

Mean index scores on three scales of ICT use and familiarity, perceived usefulness and attitude toward computers, diversity and intensity of Internet use, and use of computers for specific task-oriented purposes, populations aged 16 to 65, 2003

	Perceived usefulness and attitude toward computers		Diversity and intensity of Internet use		Use of computers for task-oriented purposes	
Bermuda	5.3	(0.0)	5.4	(0.0)	5.3	(0.0)
Canada	5.0	(0.0)	5.2	(0.0)	5.1	(0.0)
Italy	4.7	(0.1)	3.9	(0.0)	4.1	(0.0)
Norway	5.0	(0.0)	5.2	(0.0)	5.1	(0.0)
Switzerland	4.8	(0.0)	4.9	(0.0)	5.3	(0.0)
United States	5.1	(0.0)	5.4	(0.0)	5.1	(0.0)

Source: Adult Literacy and Life Skills Survey, 2003.

TABLE 8.5

Mean index scores on a scale measuring the intensity of use of computers for specific task-oriented purposes, by prose literacy levels, populations aged 16 to 65, 2003

	Prose literacy scale							
	Level 1		Level 2		Level 3		Level 4/5	
Bermuda	3.9	(0.1)	4.9	(0.1)	5.6	(0.1)	6.1	(0.1)
Canada	3.8	(0.1)	4.8	(0.0)	5.4	(0.0)	5.8	(0.1)
Italy	3.5	(0.0)	4.3	(0.1)	4.9	(0.1)	5.3	(0.2)
Norway	4.0	(0.2)	4.6	(0.1)	5.3	(0.0)	5.7	(0.0)
Switzerland	4.4	(0.1)	5.1	(0.1)	5.6	(0.0)	6.0	(0.1)
United States	3.9	(0.1)	4.9	(0.1)	5.6	(0.1)	6.0	(0.1)

Source: Adult Literacy and Life Skills Survey, 2003.

TABLE 8.6

Mean index scores on a scale measuring the intensity of use of computers for specific task-oriented purposes, by age groups, populations aged 16 to 65, 2003

	Age groups									
	16 to 25		26 to 35		36 to 45		46 to 55		56 to 65	
Bermuda	5.7	(0.1)	5.6	(0.1)	5.4	(0.1)	5.1	(0.1)	4.3	(0.1)
Canada	5.5	(0.0)	5.4	(0.0)	5.1	(0.0)	4.9	(0.0)	4.2	(0.1)
Italy	4.7	(0.1)	4.4	(0.1)	4.1	(0.1)	3.8	(0.0)	3.2	(0.0)
Norway	5.3	(0.1)	5.4	(0.0)	5.3	(0.1)	4.9	(0.1)	4.4	(0.1)
Switzerland	5.5	(0.1)	5.5	(0.1)	5.5	(0.0)	5.2	(0.0)	4.6	(0.1)
United States	5.4	(0.1)	5.2	(0.1)	5.2	(0.1)	5.1	(0.1)	4.5	(0.1)

Source: Adult Literacy and Life Skills Survey, 2003.

TABLE 8.7

Mean index scores on a scale measuring the intensity of use of computers for specific task-oriented purposes, by gender, populations aged 16 to 65, 2003

	Men		Women	
Bermuda	5.2	(0.1)	5.4	(0.0)
Canada	5.2	(0.0)	5.0	(0.0)
Italy	4.4	(0.0)	3.8	(0.0)
Norway	5.3	(0.0)	4.8	(0.0)
Switzerland	5.7	(0.0)	4.9	(0.0)
United States	5.2	(0.1)	5.1	(0.0)

Source: Adult Literacy and Life Skills Survey, 2003.

TABLE 8.8

Mean index scores on a scale measuring the intensity of use of computers for specific task-oriented purposes, by educational attainment, populations aged 16 to 65, 2003

	Less than upper secondary		Upper secondary		Higher than upper secondary	
Bermuda	3.7	(0.1)	4.9	(0.1)	5.8	(0.0)
Canada	4.3	(0.1)	5.0	(0.0)	5.5	(0.0)
Italy	3.3	(0.0)	4.8	(0.1)	5.5	(0.1)
Norway	4.3	(0.1)	5.0	(0.0)	5.5	(0.0)
Switzerland	4.6	(0.1)	5.2	(0.0)	6.0	(0.0)
United States	4.2	(0.1)	4.9	(0.0)	5.8	(0.0)

Source: Adult Literacy and Life Skills Survey, 2003.

TABLE 8.9

Mean index scores on a scale measuring the intensity of use of computers for specific task-oriented purposes, by type of occupation, populations aged 16 to 65, 2003

	Knowledge expert		Managers		Information high-skill		Information low-skill		Service low-skill		Goods	
Bermuda	6.3	(0.1)	5.9	(0.1)	5.7	(0.1)	5.8	(0.1)	4.4	(0.1)	4.3	(0.1)
Canada	6.4	(0.1)	5.6	(0.1)	5.5	(0.0)	5.4	(0.0)	4.7	(0.1)	4.5	(0.0)
Italy	5.7	(0.1)	4.6	(0.2)	4.8	(0.1)	5.2	(0.1)	3.8	(0.1)	3.4	(0.1)
Norway	6.3	(0.1)	5.7	(0.1)	5.5	(0.0)	5.6	(0.1)	4.6	(0.1)	4.7	(0.1)
Switzerland	6.2	(0.1)	6.0	(0.1)	5.5	(0.1)	5.5	(0.1)	4.6	(0.1)	4.6	(0.1)
United States	6.5	(0.1)	5.9	(0.1)	5.5	(0.1)	5.5	(0.1)	4.7	(0.1)	4.3	(0.1)

Source: Adult Literacy and Life Skills Survey, 2003.

TABLE 8.10

Adjusted odds ratio showing the likelihood of adults aged 16 to 65 of being high-intensity computer users, by prose literacy levels, 2003

	Levels 1 and 2	Level 3		Level 4/5	
Bermuda	1.00	2.38***	(0.26)	3.39***	(0.25)
Canada	1.00	1.83***	(0.12)	2.40***	(0.14)
Italy	1.00	1.64**	(0.19)	2.02**	(0.34)
Norway	1.00	1.80***	(0.19)	2.66***	(0.15)
Switzerland	1.00	1.78***	(0.19)	1.91**	(0.25)
United States	1.00	1.59***	(0.14)	1.94***	(0.15)

* p<0.10, statistically significant at the 10 per cent level.
** p<0.05, statistically significant at the 5 per cent level.
*** p<0.01, statistically significant at the 1 per cent level.

Notes: Standard errors are of the logarithm of the odds ratios.
Odds are adjusted for gender, age, educational attainment, labour force status and total household income.

Source: Adult Literacy and Life Skills Survey, 2003.

TABLE 8.11

Per cent of adults aged 16 to 65 in each combined literacy and computer use profile,[1] 2003

	Group 1		Group 2		Group 3		Group 4	
Bermuda	34.2	(1.2)	40.7	(1.3)	3.9	(0.6)	21.2	(1.0)
Canada	35.9	(0.7)	39.1	(0.7)	6.0	(0.4)	19.0	(0.5)
Italy	63.7	(1.1)	11.1	(0.7)	16.0	(0.5)	9.3	(0.6)
Norway	29.1	(1.0)	45.9	(1.0)	4.9	(0.6)	20.1	(0.6)
Switzerland	40.9	(1.7)	34.1	(1.5)	8.6	(0.9)	16.4	(0.9)
United States	43.4	(1.1)	31.6	(1.1)	8.1	(0.6)	17.0	(0.9)

1. See Box 8B.

Source: Adult Literacy and Life Skills Survey, 2003.

TABLE 8.12

Adjusted odds ratio showing the likelihood of adults aged 16 to 65 of being a top income quartile earning, by combined literacy and computer user profiles[1], 2003

	Group 1	Group 2		Group 3		Group 4	
Bermuda	1.00	2.38***	(0.25)	2.06	(0.42)	5.68***	(0.24)
Canada	1.00	2.63***	(0.08)	2.52***	(0.20)	5.18***	(0.10)
Italy	1.00	1.27	(0.22)	1.69***	(0.18)	1.80**	(0.26)
Norway	1.00	1.79***	(0.15)	1.95**	(0.29)	3.85***	(0.22)
Switzerland	1.00	2.25***	(0.16)	3.27***	(0.27)	6.30***	(0.27)
United States	1.00	1.86***	(0.17)	2.07***	(0.22)	3.75***	(0.17)

1. See Box 8B.

* p<0.10, statistically significant at the 10 per cent level.

** p<0.05, statistically significant at the 5 per cent level.

*** p<0.01, statistically significant at the 1 per cent level.

Notes: Standard errors are of the logarithm of the odds ratios.
Odds are adjusted for gender, age, educational attainment and labour force status.

Source: Adult Literacy and Life Skills Survey, 2003.

Chapter 9

Skills and Immigration

Summary

This chapter compares the skill profiles of immigrant and native-born adults for the countries participating in ALL. First, the significance of immigration in OECD countries is considered. Projections forecast declining population growth and for some countries a net decrease by 2050. Second, the knowledge and skills that immigrants contribute to host countries in terms of their educational attainment are examined. Third, the extent to which educational credentials translate into useable skills of the type measured in ALL for the host country is considered. In comparing the education credentials and observed skills of immigrants, it is apparent that there is an education-skills gap among immigrants. In light of this, the potential role of native versus foreign language status in explaining the education-skills gap is considered briefly. Finally, the chapter concludes by studying some of the labour market outcomes of immigrants.

Table of Contents

Skills and Immigration

9.1 Overview and highlights

This chapter compares the skill profiles of immigrant and native-born adults for the countries participating in ALL. First, the significance of immigration in OECD countries is considered. Projections forecast declining population growth and for some countries a net decrease by 2050. Second, the knowledge and skills that immigrants contribute to host countries in terms of their educational attainment are examined. Third, the extent to which educational credentials translate into useable skills of the type measured in ALL for the host country is considered. In comparing the education credentials and observed skills of immigrants, it is apparent that there is an education-skills gap among immigrants. In light of this, the potential role of native versus foreign language status in explaining the education-skills gap is considered briefly. Finally, the chapter concludes by studying some of the labour market outcomes of immigrants.

The highlights of the chapter are as follows:

- The continuing shift in immigration policies toward selecting those with higher skills is evident from the data. In all of the countries considered, recent immigrants appear more likely to have completed higher than upper secondary education.
- Education credentials, however, do not necessarily translate into functional levels of literacy, numeracy and problem solving skills in the official language(s) of the host country. It is apparent that in some countries there is an education-skills gap among immigrants. While the proportion of immigrants who complete higher than upper secondary education is relatively high, there are much fewer who score at Levels 3 and 4/5.
- The results confirm that knowledge of the official language (as measured by the mother tongue of the immigrant) is favourably associated with literacy performance in all countries studied.
- The pattern of skill composition of immigrants among countries is mixed.

- In Bermuda, recent and established immigrants are highly skilled, outperforming native-born adults in all skill domains.
- In Canada and the United States, the average proficiency of immigrants is significantly lower than their native-born counterparts. But recent immigrants tend to perform slightly better than established immigrants.
- Norway has a similar pattern to that observed in Canada and the United States except that recent immigrants have, on average, lower scores than established immigrants.
- In Switzerland, the distribution of skills among recent immigrants and native-born adults is similar. In contrast, the majority of established immigrants are low skilled with over 60 per cent scoring at Levels 1 and 2 on the prose scale.
- The patterns of labour market outcomes for immigrants by skill level among countries are mixed.
- In Switzerland, low skilled immigrants are particularly disadvantaged in terms of employment, even compared to low skilled native-born adults, whereas medium to high skilled immigrants do not face a comparable disadvantage.
- In Canada, both low and medium to high skilled immigrants are disadvantaged in terms of employment, even compared to low skilled native-born adults.
- In the United States, low skilled adults are more likely to be unemployed, regardless of whether adults have immigrated or are native-born.

9.2 The significance of immigration in OECD countries

Ageing populations, low birth rates and increased life expectancy are posing new challenges for policy makers in most OECD countries (OECD, 2003a). Natural population growth as measured by the difference between the birth and death rate is also expected to decline. Figure 9.1 portrays some projections of natural population growth in five OECD countries[1]. The trend is clear. Projections forecast declining population growth and are expected to be negative in Italy, Norway and Switzerland by 2050. Many are concerned that these trends will lead to slower economic growth in the long term and will put added strain on social security systems, including pension systems. Apart from encouraging older workers to remain longer in the work force, immigration is seen to provide a direct and immediate solution to this growing problem.

FIGURE 9.1

Natural population growth in OECD countries

The number of births minus number of deaths from 1950 to 1999 and projections to 2050

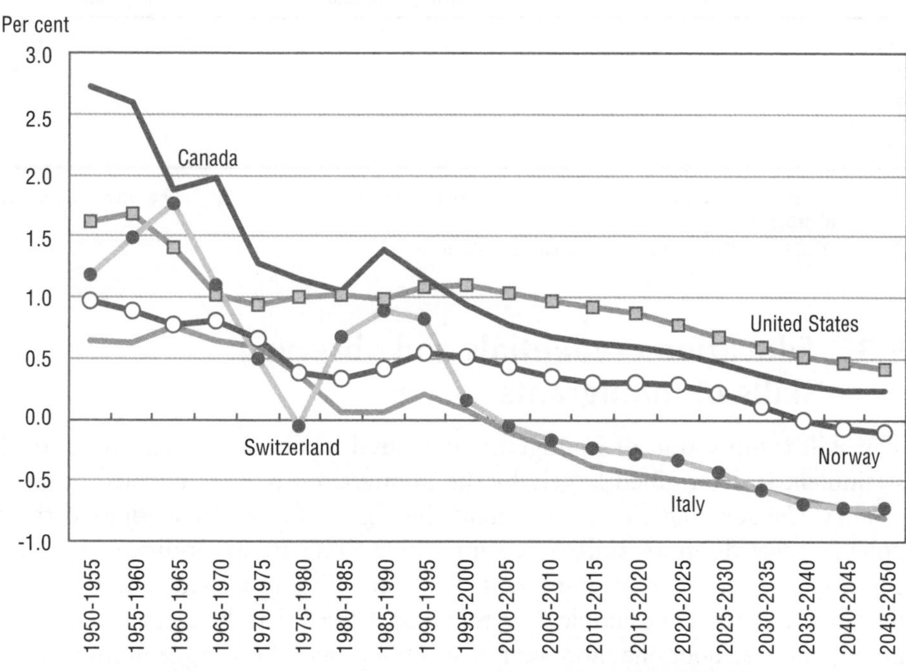

Note: The natural growth rate equals the birth rate minus the death rate.

Source: World Population Prospects: The 2004 Revision (population database), Population Division of the Department of Economic and Social Affairs of the United Nations Secretariat.

Indeed, there is a general upward trend in international migration in recent years that has partly addressed this problem (SOPEMI, 2002). In Canada, for example, nearly 60 per cent of population growth between 1991 and 2001 can be attributed to immigration (Statistics Canada, 2002). During the 1990s, more immigrants came to United States than in any decade in the nation's history. Both Canada and the United States have encouraged immigration for permanent settlement throughout the twentieth century. While some countries have embraced immigration as a solution, others are still setting their policies and have less experience. Many European countries have regulated immigration flows mainly for temporary migration (Bauer, Lofstrom and Zimmerman, 2000). Norway and Switzerland have used immigration for balancing the situation in the labour market. Figure 9.2 shows the proportion of immigrants for the OECD countries participating in the ALL survey. Canada and Switzerland have the highest proportions with nearly one in every five persons being foreign-born.

FIGURE 9.2

Per cent of foreign-born in population and in labour force for OECD countries participating in ALL, 2001

	Per cent of foreign-born in population	Per cent of foreign-born in labour force
Canada	18.4	19.9
Italy	2.4	3.8
Norway	4.1	4.9
Switzerland	19.7	18.1
United States	11.1	13.9

Note: The reference year for per cent of foreign-born in labour force in Italy is 2000. The reference year for all other data is 2001.

Source: OECD (2003b); Canada 2001 Census of Population.

9.3 Education credentials and observed skills of immigrants

The skill composition of immigrants measured in terms of their educational attainment is determined largely by the immigration policies pursued by each country. Canada, and to a lesser extent the United States, have adjusted their policies towards more skill-based migration. The trends indicate that the educational attainment of immigrants has been rising in Canada and falling in the United States. For example, Borjas (1993) showed that the average Canadian immigrant has about one more year of schooling than the average immigrant in the United States. Most countries now actively seek to attract skilled foreign workers with high credentials. In Norway, for example, high skilled workers or workers with specific skills readily receive immigration and work permits (SOPEMI, 1999). This section considers the education credentials of immigrants as well as their skill levels as measured by the ALL survey.

Figure 9.3 compares the highest levels of educational attainment of immigrants with those of the native-born population. A distinction is also made between recent and established immigrants. For the purposes of the analysis presented here, recent immigrants are those who have lived in the host country for five years or less, while established immigrants have lived there for more than five years.

A continuing shift in immigration policies toward selecting those with higher skills is evident from the data. In all countries, recent immigrants appear more likely to have completed higher than upper secondary education. Over 80 per cent of recent immigrants in Bermuda and nearly 65 per cent in Canada have attained higher than upper secondary education. The proportion of established immigrants with higher education exceeds those of the native population in all countries. A different pattern emerges at the lower end of the educational distribution. In Norway and the United States, there are more recent immigrants who have not attained upper secondary education when compared to the native-born population. Moreover, apart from Canada, the proportion of established immigrants with less than upper secondary education exceeds that of the native born population in all the countries. In summary, however, there is an overall tendency toward an increase in the educational attainment of recent immigrants. This is particularly noticeable in Bermuda, Canada and Switzerland.

FIGURE 9.3

Recent versus established immigrant status by educational attainment

Per cent of population aged 16 to 65 at each level of educational attainment, by recent vs established immigrant status, 2003

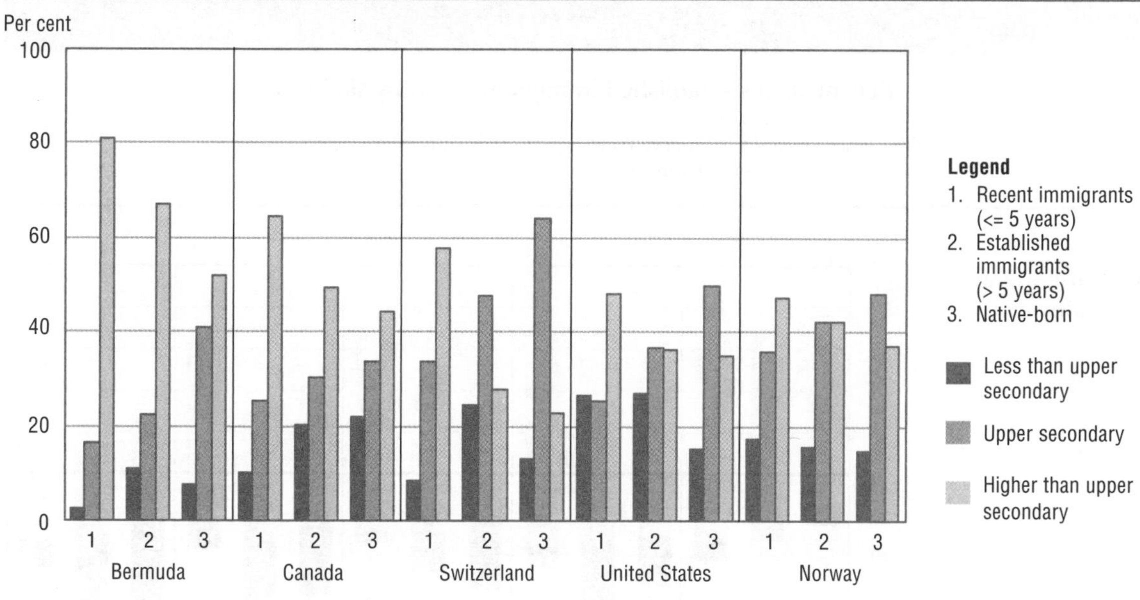

Countries are ranked by the per cent of recent immigrants with higher than upper secondary education.

Source: Adult Literacy and Life Skills Survey, 2003.

Education credentials do not necessarily translate into functional levels of literacy, numeracy and problem solving skills in the official language(s) of the host country. This is especially the case if the credentials were attained abroad in a language other than that used in the host country.

Figures 9.4a-d display the distributions of skill level by immigration status. In general, the patterns of skill composition among recent and established immigrant groups are mixed. In Bermuda, recent and established immigrants outperform native-born adults on all four domains. For example, only about 25 per cent of recent immigrants score at Levels 1 and 2 on the prose scale compared to 32 per cent of established immigrants and 42 per cent of native-born adults. This suggests that the majority of recent and established immigrants to Bermuda are highly skilled.

In Canada and the United States, the average proficiency of immigrants is significantly lower than their native-born counterparts. There are fewer immigrants compared to native-born adults who score at Levels 3 and 4/5. Both countries have large proportions (over 60 per cent) of immigrants at Levels 1 and 2. But there are appreciable differences in the literacy performance of recent and established immigrants. Recent immigrants tend to outperform established immigrants.

Norway has a similar pattern to that observed in Canada and the United States. However, in Norway, a higher proportion of recent immigrants perform at Levels 1 and 2 compared to established immigrants. In Switzerland, the distribution of skills among recent immigrants and native-born adults is similar, with nearly 50 per cent scoring at Levels 3 and 4/5. But the majority of established immigrants are low skilled with about 65 per cent scoring at Levels 1 and 2 on the prose scale.

FIGURE 9.4 A and B

Recent versus established immigrant status by skill level

Per cent of population aged 16 to 65 at each skill level, by recent vs established immigrant status, 2003

A. Prose literacy scale

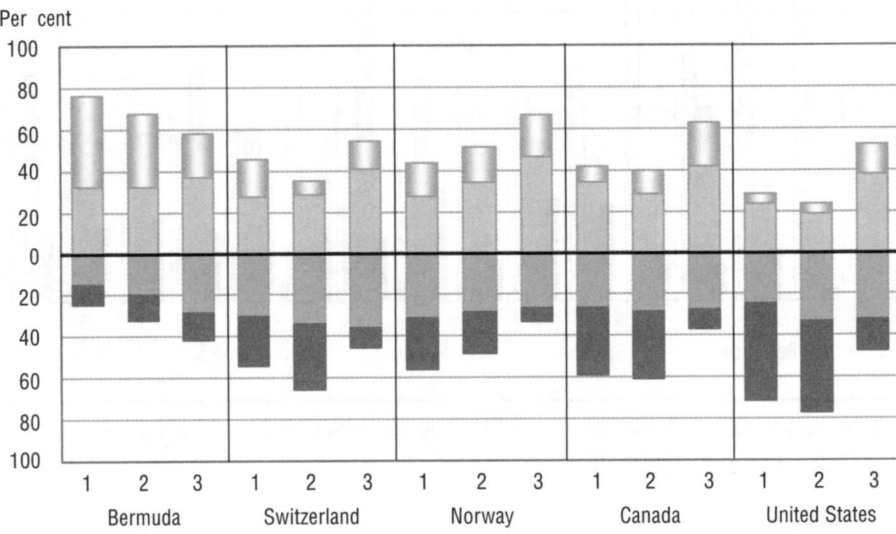

B. Document literacy scale

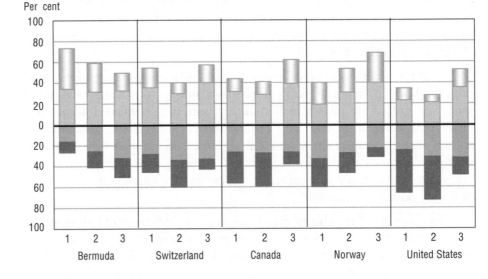

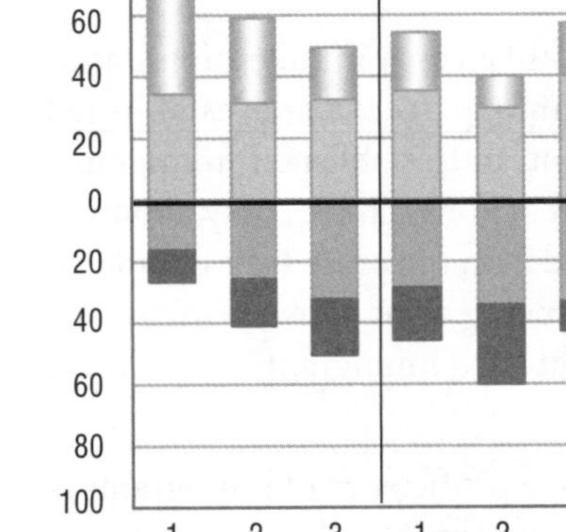

Legend
1. Recent immigrants (<= 5 years)
2. Established immigrants (> 5 years)
3. Native-born

Countries are ranked by the per cent of recent immigrants at Levels 3 and 4/5.

Source: Adult Literacy and Life Skills Survey, 2003.

FIGURE 9.4 C and D (concluded)

Recent versus established immigrant status by skill level

Per cent of population aged 16 to 65 at each skill level, by recent vs established immigrant status, 2003

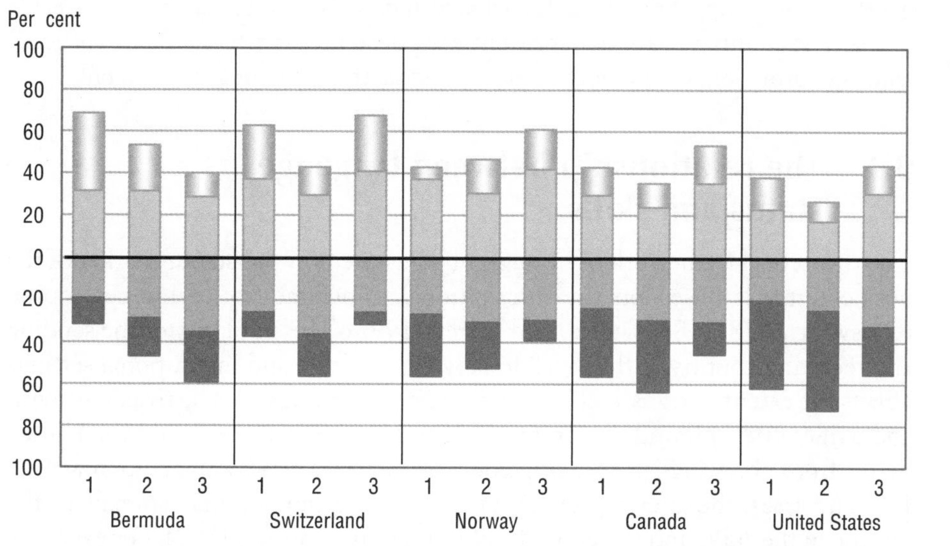

C. Numeracy scale

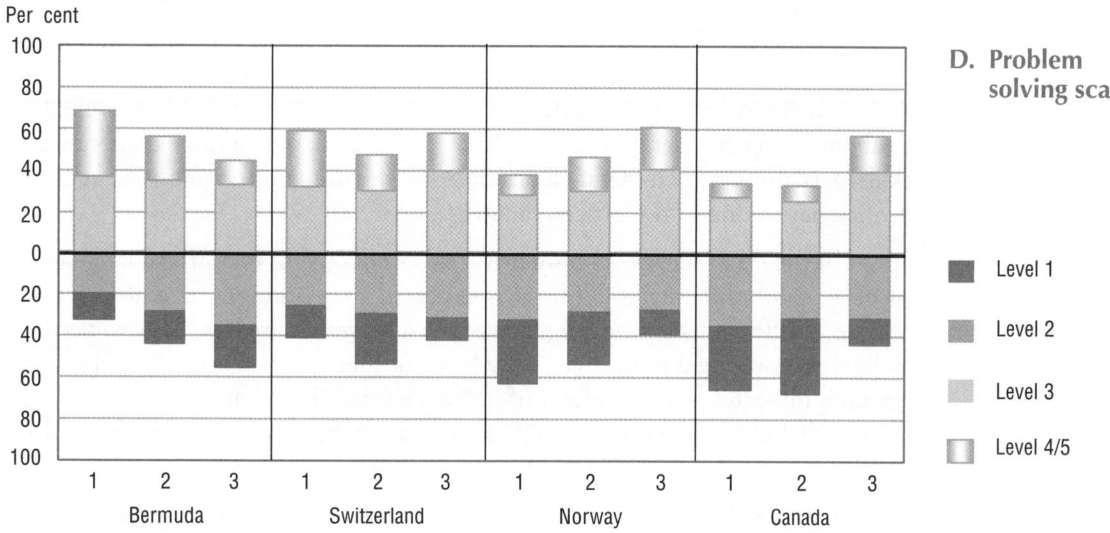

D. Problem solving scale

Legend
1. Recent immigrants (<= 5 years)
2. Established immigrants (> 5 years)
3. Native-born

Countries are ranked by the per cent of recent immigrants at Levels 3 and 4/5.

Source: Adult Literacy and Life Skills Survey, 2003.

When comparing the education credentials and skills of immigrants presented in Figures 9.3 and 9.4, it is apparent that in some countries there is an education-skills gap among immigrants. In Canada, for example, there are 65 per cent of recent immigrants who have completed higher than upper secondary education, but nevertheless only about 40 per cent attain Levels 3 and 4/5. The pattern is similar for Switzerland and the United States. This raises an important question regarding whether the knowledge and skills acquired abroad are useable in the host country and to what extent the portability is attenuated by (official) language proficiency. The next section explores this issue in greater detail.

9.4 The relationship between language status and skills

The theoretical framework of immigrant adjustment in the labour market of the host country is based on the international transferability of human capital (Chiswick, 1978, 1986; Duleep and Regets, 1997). The similarity of the sending and receiving country with regard to language, culture and institutional settings affects the extent of transferability and therefore earnings upon arrival. Chiswick and Miller (1992) found that immigrants who arrive in Canada and the United States from non-English speaking countries are at a disadvantage upon arrival. In many cases, the altering source-country mix of immigrants can explain the decline in the skills and the earnings of immigrants (Borjas, 1992). For example, in Canada, the proportion of immigrants who had no knowledge of either official language increased in the 1970s and 1980s, because of changes in the source-country mix (Beaujot, 2003). But more recently, the proportion of immigrants with some knowledge of Canada's official languages upon arrival has levelled off to about 66 per cent, and in June of 2002, Canada adopted a revised approach to skill-based immigration that includes among other things an emphasis on language proficiency in one of the official languages.

In the ALL survey, assessments were conducted in the official language(s) of participating countries. Thus it is expected that immigrants whose mother tongue is different than the language of the assessment are less likely to perform well when compared to immigrants whose mother tongue is the same. Previous research indicates that the effect of language status is a significant determinant of literacy skill proficiency, especially in countries with relatively large proportions of immigrants (Boudard, 2001; Desjardins, 2004).

Figure 9.5 compares the distribution of skill levels by language status. Three subgroups are considered for this analysis – immigrants whose mother tongue is different than the language of the test, immigrants whose mother tongue is same as the language of the test, and native-born adults. The results confirm that knowledge of the official language (as measured by the mother tongue of the immigrant) is favourably associated with literacy performance in all countries. There is a higher proportion of immigrants scoring at Levels 1 and 2 among those whose mother tongue is different than the language of the test. The data also reveal large differences between countries. For example, nearly 80 per cent of immigrants with a mother tongue different than the language of the test in Switzerland and the United States score at Level 1 and 2, but in Norway there are fewer than 60 per cent.[2]

In all countries, the distribution of skills is nearly the same among immigrants who have a mother tongue that is the same or very similar to the language of assessment and among native-born persons. In fact, in Bermuda and Norway, there are higher proportions of immigrants who have the same or similar mother tongue as the native-born adults who score at Level 4/5.

FIGURE 9.5

Native versus foreign language status of immigrants by skill level

Per cent of adults aged 16 to 65 at each literacy level on the prose scale, by whether their native tongue is same or different from the official language(s) of host country, 2003

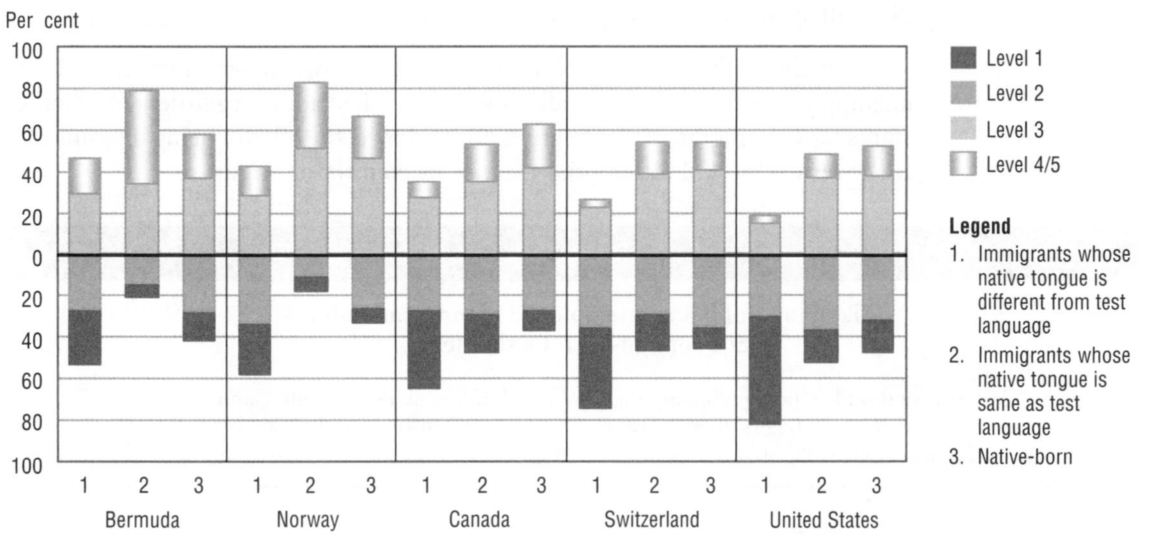

Countries are ranked by the per cent of immigrants whose native tongue is different from the language of test who score at Levels 3 and 4/5.

Source: Adult Literacy and Life Skills Survey, 2003.

9.5 Skills and labour market outcomes of immigrants

Country-of-origin differences and admission criteria have a strong influence on the labour market performance of immigrants. Nearly all countries have recently experienced a decline in the labour market performance of immigrants upon arrival. Bauer, Lofstrom and Zimmerman (2000) provide empirical evidence for 12 OECD countries including Canada and the United States. Although the relative earnings of immigrants are declining, they are declining less rapidly in the United States than in Canada. This section compares the labour market outcomes of immigrants by their skill levels. Previous research suggests that those with higher education credentials are more likely to find employment and earn more than those with low education credentials. But among immigrant populations an important question remains; that is, whether the knowledge and skills represented by educational credentials can be translated into useable human capital in the local labour market. For this reason, the analysis in this section controls for educational attainment, language status, age and gender, and therefore, focuses on observed skill proficiencies (on the prose scale).

Figure 9.6 displays the likelihood of unemployment among immigrants and native-born adults by skill level (see Box 3A – Using odds ratios). There are four groups for comparison purposes – low skilled immigrants, medium to high skilled immigrants, low skilled native-born adults and medium to high skilled native-born adults. All comparisons are with reference to the baseline group – medium to high skilled native-born adults. The first thing to note is that there is no uniform pattern across countries. This is not surprising since the immigration policies and their specific purposes do differ markedly across these countries.

In Switzerland, low skilled immigrants (Levels 1 and 2) are particularly disadvantaged in terms of employment, even compared to low skilled native-born adults. They are over two times more likely to be unemployed compared to native-born adults who score at Levels 3 and 4/5, whereas low skilled native-born adults have about the same chance of being unemployed than medium to high skilled native-born adults. In contrast, medium to high skilled immigrants are as likely to be unemployed as medium to high skilled native-born adults.

In the United States, a low skilled adult is two times more likely to be unemployed compared to a medium to high skilled adult, regardless of whether adults have immigrated or are native-born. Hence, the odds of being unemployed are governed by skill differential and not by country of origin.

FIGURE 9.6

Likelihood of being unemployed among native-born and foreign-born by skill level

Adjusted odds ratios[1] indicating the likelihood of low skilled (Levels 1 and 2) and medium to high skilled (Levels 3 and 4/5) foreign-born and native-born populations aged 16 to 65 of being unemployed, prose literacy scale, 2003

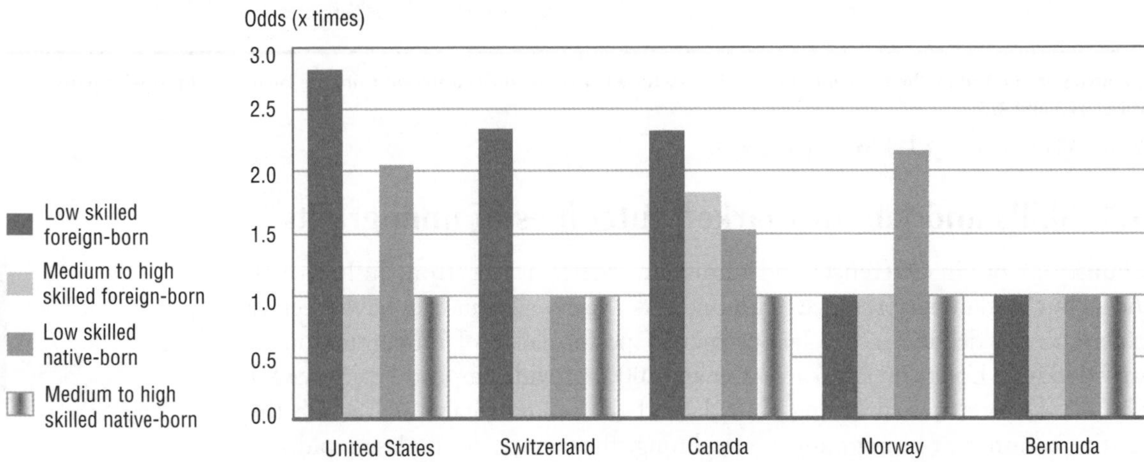

Countries are ranked by the odds ratios of foreign-born adults who score at Levels 1 and 2.

1. Odds estimates that are not statistically different from one at conventional levels of significance are reported as one in the figure. For the actual estimate and its corresponding significance, see Table 9.6 in the annex to this chapter.

Source: Adult Literacy and Life Skills Survey, 2003.

On the other hand, in Canada, there seems to be differential odds by skill level as well as country of origin. A low skilled immigrant is nearly 2.5 times more likely to be unemployed when compared to a medium to high skilled native-born worker. Similarly, medium to high skilled immigrants are two times more likely to be unemployed compared to medium to high skilled native-born adults, but low skilled native-born adults are only about 1.5 times more likely to be unemployed.

Are immigrants more likely to earn low incomes? Figure 9.7 shows the likelihood of earning in the lowest personal earnings quartile by skill level. Once again patterns differ across countries. There are no significant differences in the likelihood of earning in the lowest quartile by skill level or country of origin in Switzerland and the United States. It appears that the immigration policies in these countries are tightly connected to labour market outcomes. In terms of income, low skilled immigrants fair the worst in Bermuda and Norway, but in these countries low skilled native-born adults also have higher odds of earning in the lowest earnings quartile than medium to high skilled native-born adults.

FIGURE 9.7

Likelihood of earning low income among native-born and foreign-born by skill level

Adjusted odds ratios[1] indicating the likelihood of low skilled (Levels 1 and 2) and medium to high skilled (Levels 3 and 4/5) foreign-born and native-born populations aged 16 to 65 of being in the lowest personal earnings income quartile, prose literacy scale, 2003

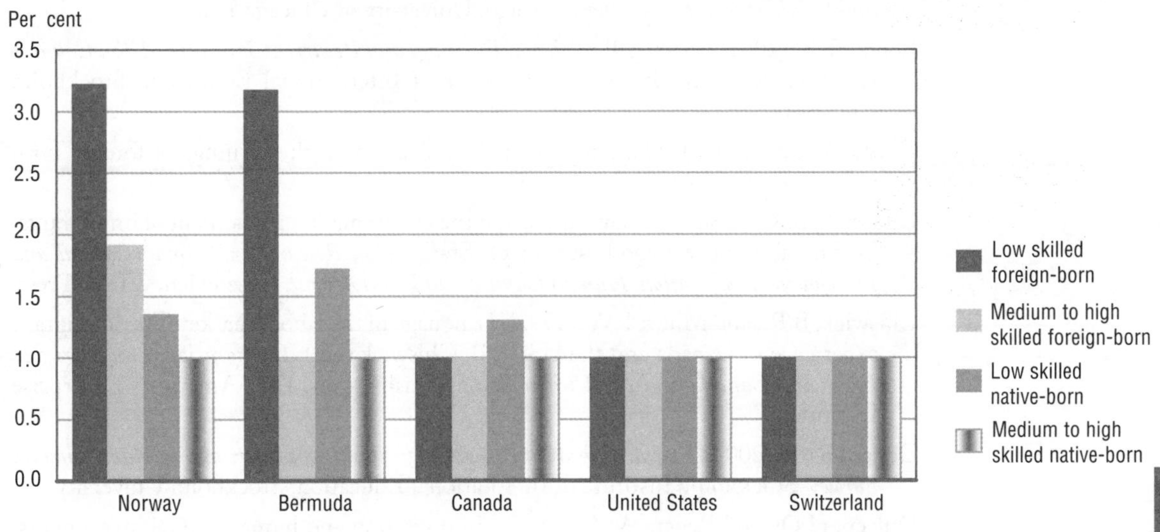

Countries are ranked by the odds ratios of foreign-born adults who score at Levels 1 and 2.

1. Odds estimates that are not statistically different from one at conventional levels of significance are reported as one in the figure. For the actual estimate and its corresponding significance, see Table 9.7 in the annex to this chapter.

Source: Adult Literacy and Life Skills Survey, 2003.

Endnotes

1. Note that while Italy included immigrants in the ALL survey, there were too few cases to be included in the remainder of this chapter.
2. For the purposes of this analysis, the Danish and Swedish languages are considered similar to the Norwegian language.

References

Bauer, T., Lofstrom, M., and Zimmermann, K.F. (2000). Immigration policy, assimilation of immigrants, and natives' sentiments towards immigrants: evidence from 12 OECD countries, *Swedish Economic Policy Review*, 7, 53-53.

Beaujot, R. (2003). Effect of immigration on demographic structure, in C.M. Beach, A.G. Green and J.G. Reitz, *Canadian Immigration Policy for the 21st Century*. Montreal: McGill-Queen's University Press.

Borjas, G.J. (1992). National origin and the skills of immigrants in the postwar period, in G.J. Borjas and R.B. Freeman (eds.), *Immigration and the Work Force: Economic Consequences for the United States and Source Areas*. Chicago: University of Chicago Press.

Borjas, G.J. (1993). Immigration policy, national origin, and immigration skills: A comparison of Canada and the United States, in D. Card and R.B. Freeman (eds.), *Small Differences that Matter*. Chicago: University of Chicago Press.

Boudard, E. (2001). *Literacy Proficiency, Earnings and Recurrent Training: A Ten Country Comparative Study*. Stockholm: Institute of International Education, Stockholm University.

Chiswick, B.R. (1978). The effect of americanization on the earnings of foreign-born men, *Journal of Political Economy*, 86.

Chiswick, B.R. (1986). Human capital and the labour market adjustment of immigrants: Testing alternative hypotheses, in O. Stark (ed.), *Research in Human Capital and Development: migration, Human Capital and Development*. Greenwich, CT: Jai Press.

Chiswick, B.R., and Miller, P.W. (1992). Language in the labour market: The immigrant experience in Canada and the US, in B. Chiswick (ed.), *Immigration, Language and Ethnicity: Canada and the United States*. Washington, DC: American Enterprise Institute.

Desjardins, R. (2004). *Learning for Well Being: Studies Using the International Adult Literacy Survey*. Stockholm: Institute of International Education, Stockholm University.

Duleep, H.O., and Regets, M.C. (1997). Immigration and human capital investments, *American Economic Review Papers and Proceedings*, 82.

OECD (2003a). *Ageing, Housing and Urban Development*. Paris: Author.

OECD (2003b). *Trends in International Migration*. Paris: Author.

SOPEMI (1999). *Trends in International Migration*. Paris: OECD.

SOPEMI (2002). *Trends in International Migration*. Paris: OECD.

Statistics Canada (2002). *Annual Demographic Statistics 2001*. Cat No. 91-213. Ottawa: Author.

Contributors

Lauren Dong, *Statistics Canada*

Urvashi Dhawan-Biswal, *Human Resources and Skills Development Canada*

Yvan Clermont, *Statistics Canada*

Annex 9

Data Values for the Figures

TABLE 9.1

The number of births minus number of deaths from 1950 to 1999 and projections to 2050

Period	Canada	Italy	Norway	Switzerland	United States
1950-1955	2.72	0.64	0.97	1.18	1.61
1955-1960	2.59	0.63	0.88	1.48	1.69
1960-1965	1.88	0.75	0.78	1.77	1.41
1965-1970	1.97	0.65	0.81	1.10	1.01
1970-1975	1.27	0.59	0.66	0.49	0.94
1975-1980	1.15	0.36	0.39	-0.06	1.00
1980-1985	1.05	0.06	0.33	0.67	1.02
1985-1990	1.39	0.05	0.42	0.89	0.98
1990-1995	1.16	0.20	0.55	0.82	1.08
1995-2000	0.94	0.08	0.51	0.15	1.09
2000-2005	0.77	-0.10	0.43	-0.05	1.03
2005-2010	0.67	-0.24	0.35	-0.17	0.97
2010-2015	0.63	-0.38	0.30	-0.24	0.92
2015-2020	0.60	-0.45	0.30	-0.28	0.87
2020-2025	0.54	-0.49	0.29	-0.33	0.78
2025-2030	0.47	-0.53	0.22	-0.43	0.68
2030-2035	0.36	-0.58	0.11	-0.57	0.59
2035-2040	0.28	-0.66	-0.01	-0.69	0.51
2040-2045	0.23	-0.73	-0.08	-0.73	0.46
2045-2050	0.23	-0.80	-0.10	-0.72	0.41

Source: World Population Prospects: The 2004 Revision (population database), Population Division of the Department of Economic and Social Affairs of the United Nations Secretariat

TABLE 9.2 For data values of TABLE 9.2 see FIGURE 9.2

TABLE 9.3

Per cent of populations aged 16 to 65 at each level of educational attainment, by recent vs established immigration status, 2003

	Less than upper secondary		Upper secondary		Higher than upper secondary	
Bermuda						
Recent immigrants (<= 5 years)	2.6	(1.2)	16.4	(2.8)	80.9	(2.7)
Established immigrants (> 5 years)	10.8	(1.3)	22.3	(2.5)	66.9	(2.4)
Native-born	7.4	(0.4)	40.9	(0.8)	51.7	(0.8)
Canada						
Recent immigrants (<= 5 years)	10.0	(2.0)	25.5	(3.5)	64.6	(3.9)
Established immigrants (> 5 years)	20.3	(1.1)	30.3	(1.5)	49.3	(1.3)
Native-born	21.8	(0.6)	33.8	(0.7)	44.4	(0.7)
Norway						
Recent immigrants (<= 5 years)	17.1	(8.2)	35.7	(11.4)	47.3	(10.3)
Established immigrants (> 5 years)	15.5	(3.0)	42.2	(3.1)	42.3	(3.2)
Native-born	14.7	(0.2)	48.2	(0.5)	37.1	(0.5)
Switzerland						
Recent immigrants (<= 5 years)	8.3	(4.4)	33.8	(9.7)	58.0	(9.7)
Established immigrants (> 5 years)	24.4	(2.1)	47.6	(1.7)	28.0	(0.9)
Native-born	13.2	(0.1)	64.2	(0.1)	22.7	(0.1)
United States						
Recent immigrants (<= 5 years)	26.7	(4.4)	25.3	(5.4)	48.0	(5.8)
Established immigrants (> 5 years)	26.8	(2.5)	36.9	(3.4)	36.3	(2.8)
Native-born	15.2	(0.3)	49.6	(1.0)	35.1	(0.9)

Source: Adult Literacy and Life Skills Survey, 2003.

TABLE 9.4 A

Per cent of populations aged 16 to 65 at each skill level, by recent vs established immigrant status, 2003

	Prose literacy scale							
	Level 1		Level 2		Level 3		Level 4/5	
Bermuda								
Recent immigrants (<= 5 years)	8.9	(2.2)	15.2	(3.4)	32.3	(4.7)	43.6	(4.3)
Established immigrants (> 5 years)	12.2	(2.2)	19.9	(2.8)	32.5	(2.5)	35.3	(2.5)
Native-born	13.2	(1.1)	28.7	(1.6)	37.0	(1.6)	21.1	(1.3)
Canada								
Recent immigrants (<= 5 years)	32.1	(4.0)	26.3	(4.1)	34.1	(5.6)	7.6	(1.6)
Established immigrants (> 5 years)	32.5	(1.5)	28.3	(1.6)	28.1	(1.6)	11.2	(0.9)
Native-born	9.9	(0.4)	27.0	(0.8)	41.2	(1.0)	21.8	(1.0)
Norway								
Recent immigrants (<= 5 years)	25.3	(11.4)	31.1	(11.9)	27.3	(11.2)	16.3	(7.3)
Established immigrants (> 5 years)	19.8	(3.1)	28.6	(3.6)	33.9	(3.8)	17.7	(3.8)
Native-born	7.0	(0.7)	26.1	(1.2)	46.2	(1.4)	20.7	(0.7)
Switzerland								
Recent immigrants (<= 5 years)	24.4	(11.0)	29.9	(13.1)	27.6	(6.1)	18.1	(6.8)
Established immigrants (> 5 years)	31.1	(3.2)	34.1	(2.9)	28.0	(3.7)	6.8	(1.9)
Native-born	10.1	(1.2)	35.5	(1.7)	40.2	(2.1)	14.3	(0.9)
United States								
Recent immigrants (<= 5 years)	47.0	(5.1)	24.4	(6.3)	23.6	(7.6)	4.9	(3.4)
Established immigrants (> 5 years)	44.0	(3.3)	32.9	(3.3)	18.2	(2.8)	4.9	(1.2)
Native-born	15.0	(0.9)	32.4	(1.1)	38.1	(1.3)	14.5	(1.1)

Source: Adult Literacy and Life Skills Survey, 2003.

TABLE 9.4 B

Per cent of population aged 16 to 65 at each skill level, by recent vs established immigrant status, 2003

	Document literacy scale							
	Level 1		Level 2		Level 3		Level 4/5	
Bermuda								
Recent immigrants (<= 5 years)	10.4	(3.1)	16.5	(3.4)	34.4	(3.4)	38.6	(3.5)
Established immigrants (> 5 years)	15.1	(2.2)	25.8	(2.8)	31.8	(3.5)	27.3	(3.0)
Native-born	18.1	(1.0)	32.5	(2.0)	32.6	(2.1)	16.7	(1.0)
Canada								
Recent immigrants (<= 5 years)	29.9	(4.1)	26.2	(3.9)	31.0	(4.7)	12.9	(2.9)
Established immigrants (> 5 years)	31.2	(1.2)	27.7	(1.6)	28.3	(1.6)	12.9	(1.1)
Native-born	11.5	(0.4)	26.8	(0.8)	39.2	(1.1)	22.5	(0.7)
Norway								
Recent immigrants (<= 5 years)	26.2	(11.6)	33.5	(14.2)	19.5	(9.2)	20.8	(7.8)
Established immigrants (> 5 years)	18.6	(4.0)	27.8	(5.0)	30.1	(4.4)	23.5	(3.9)
Native-born	8.2	(0.4)	23.2	(1.1)	40.4	(1.1)	28.2	(0.9)
Switzerland								
Recent immigrants (<= 5 years)	16.9	(7.8)	28.7	(11.5)	34.9	(10.4)	19.5	(6.1)
Established immigrants (> 5 years)	25.7	(2.7)	34.0	(2.9)	29.9	(4.0)	10.4	(3.4)
Native-born	9.6	(0.9)	33.3	(1.8)	39.6	(2.0)	17.5	(1.9)
United States								
Recent immigrants (<= 5 years)	40.4	(5.9)	24.9	(7.8)	23.3	(6.6)	11.4	(3.5)
Established immigrants (> 5 years)	41.0	(4.0)	31.1	(3.9)	20.7	(2.9)	7.2	(1.9)
Native-born	16.0	(1.0)	32.1	(1.5)	35.4	(1.3)	16.6	(1.0)

Source: Adult Literacy and Life Skills Survey, 2003.

TABLE 9.4 C

Per cent of population aged 16 to 65 at each skill level, by recent vs established immigrant status, 2003

	Numeracy scale							
	Level 1		Level 2		Level 3		Level 4/5	
Bermuda								
Recent immigrants (<= 5 years)	12.4	(3.6)	19.3	(3.1)	31.5	(3.8)	36.9	(3.2)
Established immigrants (> 5 years)	18.1	(2.2)	28.8	(3.3)	31.8	(2.5)	21.4	(1.6)
Native-born	23.8	(1.5)	35.7	(1.8)	29.2	(1.6)	11.3	(1.0)
Canada								
Recent immigrants (<= 5 years)	32.4	(4.7)	24.4	(3.5)	29.6	(4.6)	13.5	(4.6)
Established immigrants (> 5 years)	34.2	(1.7)	29.9	(1.8)	24.6	(1.7)	11.4	(1.2)
Native-born	15.6	(0.5)	30.6	(0.8)	35.6	(1.1)	18.3	(0.8)
Norway								
Recent immigrants (<= 5 years)	29.7	(12.8)	27.1	(19.0)	37.4	(15.3)	5.8	(4.9)
Established immigrants (> 5 years)	21.6	(4.4)	31.2	(5.2)	31.2	(5.6)	16.0	(2.6)
Native-born	9.8	(0.5)	29.5	(1.1)	42.1	(1.6)	18.6	(1.0)
Switzerland								
Recent immigrants (<= 5 years)	11.0	(6.8)	26.3	(13.1)	37.1	(18.0)	25.7	(9.9)
Established immigrants (> 5 years)	20.5	(2.0)	36.3	(3.8)	30.2	(3.2)	12.9	(3.1)
Native-born	5.6	(0.8)	26.3	(1.7)	41.1	(1.4)	27.1	(1.5)
United States								
Recent immigrants (<= 5 years)	41.5	(4.9)	20.5	(6.7)	23.5	(5.7)	14.5	(5.2)
Established immigrants (> 5 years)	47.2	(3.1)	25.4	(3.1)	17.8	(3.2)	9.6	(2.3)
Native-born	22.7	(0.8)	32.8	(1.1)	31.1	(1.2)	13.4	(1.2)

Source: Adult Literacy and Life Skills Survey, 2003.

TABLE 9.4 D

Per cent of population aged 16 to 65 at each skill level, by recent vs established immigrant status, 2003

	Problem solving[1] scale							
	Level 1		Level 2		Level 3		Level 4/5	
Bermuda								
Recent immigrants (<= 5 years)	12.0	(3.3)	19.7	(4.4)	37.3	(5.0)	31.0	(3.7)
Established immigrants (> 5 years)	15.5	(2.3)	28.4	(3.4)	34.5	(3.7)	21.6	(2.8)
Native-born	20.4	(1.4)	35.0	(2.1)	32.8	(2.1)	11.8	(1.2)
Canada								
Recent immigrants (<= 5 years)	30.9	(3.9)	35.1	(5.8)	27.0	(5.8)	6.9	(2.2)
Established immigrants (> 5 years)	36.0	(1.7)	31.2	(1.6)	25.7	(1.1)	7.1	(0.9)
Native-born	12.1	(0.6)	31.3	(0.6)	40.0	(1.0)	16.7	(1.1)
Norway								
Recent immigrants (<= 5 years)	30.2	(15.2)	32.1	(15.4)	28.0	(13.9)	9.7	(5.5)
Established immigrants (> 5 years)	24.9	(4.2)	28.4	(5.5)	30.5	(5.0)	16.3	(3.4)
Native-born	11.5	(1.0)	27.5	(1.2)	41.1	(1.3)	20.0	(1.0)
Switzerland								
Recent immigrants (<= 5 years)	15.2	(7.4)	25.5	(11.1)	32.0	(12.3)	27.3	(10.4)
Established immigrants (> 5 years)	23.8	(3.4)	29.1	(4.7)	30.2	(4.0)	16.9	(3.5)
Native-born	10.8	(1.2)	30.8	(2.2)	40.1	(1.7)	18.2	(1.4)

1. Switzerland (Italian) and United States did not field the problem solving skills domain.

Source: Adult Literacy and Life Skills Survey, 2003.

TABLE 9.5

Per cent of adults aged 16 to 65 at each literacy level on the prose scale, by whether their native tongue is same or different from the official language(s) of host country, 2003

	Level 1		Level 2		Level 3		Level 4/5	
Bermuda								
Immigrants whose native tongue is different from test language	25.7	(3.9)	27.6	(3.0)	29.6	(4.2)	17.2	(2.5)
Immigrants whose native tongue is same as test language	5.8	(1.4)	15.0	(2.2)	33.5	(2.6)	45.7	(2.8)
Native-born	13.2	(1.1)	28.7	(1.6)	37.0	(1.6)	21.1	(1.3)
Canada								
Immigrants whose native tongue is different from test language	37.4	(1.7)	27.5	(1.7)	27.2	(1.8)	7.9	(0.9)
Immigrants whose native tongue is same as test language	18.0	(2.8)	29.2	(3.0)	34.5	(2.6)	18.4	(2.1)
Native-born	9.9	(0.4)	27.0	(0.8)	41.2	(1.0)	21.8	(1.0)
Norway[1]								
Immigrants whose native tongue is different from test language	23.8	(3.7)	34.0	(4.1)	28.3	(4.8)	13.9	(4.2)
Immigrants whose native tongue is same as test language	6.5	(4.1)	10.8	(4.6)	51.5	(8.3)	31.2	(6.8)
Native-born	7.0	(0.7)	26.1	(1.2)	46.2	(1.4)	20.7	(0.7)
Switzerland								
Immigrants whose native tongue is different from test language	37.8	(3.6)	35.9	(3.4)	22.8	(3.2)	3.5	(1.1)
Immigrants whose native tongue is same as test language	16.6	(4.2)	29.5	(7.0)	38.3	(6.4)	15.7	(5.0)
Native-born	10.1	(1.2)	35.5	(1.7)	40.2	(2.1)	14.3	(0.9)
United States								
Immigrants whose native tongue is different from test language	51.4	(3.3)	30.0	(3.1)	15.3	(2.2)	3.4	(1.4)
Immigrants whose native tongue is same as test language	14.8	(6.0)	37.0	(8.5)	36.6	(9.4)	11.6	(4.6)
Native-born	15.0	(0.9)	32.4	(1.1)	38.1	(1.3)	14.5	(1.1)

1. For the purposes of this analysis, the Danish and Swedish languages are considered similar to the Norwegian language.

Source: Adult Literacy and Life Skills Survey, 2003.

TABLE 9.6

Adjusted odds ratios indicating the likelihood of low skilled (Levels 1 and 2) and medium to high skilled (Levels 3 and 4/5) foreign-born and native-born populations aged 16 to 65 of being unemployed, prose literacy scale, 2003

	Foreign-born				Native-born		
	Low skilled (Levels 1 and 2)		Medium to high skilled (Levels 3 and 4/5)		Low skilled (Levels 1 and 2)		Medium to high skilled (Levels 3 and 4/5)
Bermuda	2.51	(0.69)	1.26	(0.51)	1.41	(0.44)	1.00
Canada	2.32***	(0.23)	1.83**	(0.29)	1.52***	(0.15)	1.00
Norway	1.53	(0.66)	0.39	(0.76)	2.17**	(0.32)	1.00
Switzerland	2.34**	(0.32)	1.07	(0.60)	0.83	(0.40)	1.00
United States	2.82**	(0.45)	1.00	(0.43)	2.06***	(0.19)	1.00

* p<0.10, statistically significant at the 10 per cent level.

** p<0.05, statistically significant at the 5 per cent level.

*** p<0.01, statistically significant at the 1 per cent level.

Notes: Odds are adjusted for gender, age, educational attainment and language status.
Standard errors are of the logarithm of the odds ratios.

Source: Adult Literacy and Life Skills Survey, 2003.

TABLE 9.7

Adjusted odds ratios indicating the likelihood of low skilled (Levels 1 and 2) and medium to high skilled (Levels 3 and 4/5) foreign-born and native-born populations aged 16 to 65 of being in the lowest personal earnings income quartile, prose literacy scale, 2003

	Foreign-born				Native-born		
	Low skilled (Levels 1 and 2)		Medium to high skilled (Levels 3 and 4/5)		Low skilled (Levels 1 and 2)		Medium to high skilled (Levels 3 and 4/5)
Bermuda	3.17***	(0.28)	1.28	(0.32)	1.72**	(0.23)	1.00
Canada	1.25	(0.17)	1.08	(0.23)	1.30*	(0.13)	1.00
Norway	3.23***	(0.40)	1.92**	(0.30)	1.36*	(0.15)	1.00
Switzerland	0.69	(0.36)	0.98	(0.33)	1.02	(0.23)	1.00
United States	0.91	(0.34)	1.40	(0.41)	1.01	(0.14)	1.00

* p<0.10, statistically significant at the 10 per cent level.

** p<0.05, statistically significant at the 5 per cent level.

*** p<0.01, statistically significant at the 1 per cent level.

Notes: Odds ratios are adjusted for gender, age, educational attainment and language status.
Standard errors are of the logarithm of the odds ratios.

Source: Adult Literacy and Life Skills Survey, 2003.

Chapter 10

Skills, Parental Education and Literacy Practice in Daily Life

Summary

This chapter examines the relationship between the skills measured in ALL and family socio-economic background as well as literacy related practices in daily life. The analysis explores the extent to which observed differences in skills can be attributed to socio-economic inequalities. This is done for three cohorts of adults, namely youth aged 16 to 25, early middle aged adults 26 to 45 and late middle aged adults 46 to 65. The three age groups differ in the relationship between skills and socio-economic background. For example, the strength of the link between family background and skills among youth has changed in some countries over time between the IALS and ALL survey periods. The analysis further shows interesting variation in the impact of engaging in literacy practices at home and at work on inequality in skill.

10

Table of Contents

Skills, Parental Education and Literacy Practice in Daily Life

10.1 Overview and highlights

This chapter examines the relationship between the skills measured in ALL and family socio-economic background as well as literacy related practices in daily life. The analysis explores the extent to which observed differences in skills can be attributed to socio-economic inequalities. This is done for three cohorts of adults, namely youth aged 16 to 25, early middle aged adults 26 to 45 and late middle aged adults 46 to 65. The three age groups differ in the relationship between skills and socio-economic background. For example, the strength of the link between family background and skills among youth has changed in some countries over time between the IALS and ALL survey periods. The analysis further shows interesting variation in the impact of engaging in literacy practices at home and at work on inequality in skill.

The main results of the analysis undertaken in this chapter are:

- Family socio-economic background as measured by respondent's parents' level of education has a significant relationship with literacy scores in all countries. On average, adults whose parents have a high level of education score higher than adults whose parents have a low level of education. Moreover, the strength of this relationship varies substantially by country.
- A comparison of socio-economic gradients reveals that Norway has the least inequality in among youth from differing socio-economic backgrounds. In contrast, the United States exhibits the largest gap in skill levels by socio-economic background.
- Results suggest that the literacy scores of youth in Canada are on average lower in the ALL survey than in IALS. Moreover, the decline is predominantly among youth who are from lower socio-economic backgrounds, as gauged by parental education. In Norway and the United States, there is little change among the performance of youth between the two survey periods.

- After adjusting for parents' education, youth are on average performing lower than adults aged 26 to 45. Patterns of lower average youth performances in relation to parents' level of education are mixed. In Bermuda, Canada and the United States, youth performance is lower at nearly all levels of parental education. In Italy and Norway, it is lower for average to high levels of parental education, while performance among those whose parents' have low levels of education has improved compared to adults aged 26 to 45.
- The level of engagement in literacy activities at home has a significant impact on literacy scores. The magnitude of the association is similar across all age groups and is in the order of 16 to 20 points on the prose scale for the half of adults who engage in literacy activities the most. The relationship is similar for all age groups. There is an additional positive effect for engaging more in literacy practices at work of about 1 to 14 points, but the effect grows stronger with increasing age.

10.2 The relationship between parents' education and skills of youth

This section considers the impact of parental education upon the skill levels of young adults participating in the ALL study. Children are immersed in the language of their family from the moment they are born (DeCasper *et al.*, 1994; Werker and Tees, 2002; Kisilevsky *et al.*, 2003). Speech emerges naturally, with most children saying their first recognizable word at about 12 months, and thereafter there is rapid, exponential growth in their vocabulary (Huttenlocher *et al.*, 1991). But the pace of language development differs among children, and is related to their exposure to language in the home and the quality of their interactions with their parents (Hart and Risley, 1995). The importance of growing up in a nurturing and language-rich environment during the early years is supported further by studies of the effects of early childhood centres on children's linguistic, cognitive and social abilities (Ramey and Ramey, 1998).

When children reach school-age, they continue to develop their literacy skills both at school and at home. Several large-scale studies of school effectiveness have shown that the school a child attends affects the rate of literacy development (Hill and Crevola, 1999; Scheerens, 1992; Willms, 2001). While curriculum, the quality of classroom teaching and other factors relating to the atmosphere of the school and classroom affect student literacy, results from the Programme for International Student Assessment (PISA) suggest that the family environment also plays an important role during this period (Willms, 2004). Parents' background and their involvement in their child's schooling, exert strong long-term effects on life career outcomes (Epstein and Dauber, 1991; Ho and Willms, 1996; Stevenson and Baker, 1987; Tuijnman, 1989).

The ALL survey collected data to examine the persistence of this observed relationship among young adults. Figure 10.1 displays, for young persons aged 16 to 25, the relationship between literacy scores and parents' education measured in years. Each line was drawn to encompass the range of parents' education within each country from the 5th to the 95th percentiles. The graphs also map the individual prose reading literacy scores and corresponding parents' levels of education (these are the small black dots above and below the gradient lines).

The lines are commonly referred to as "socio-economic gradients", and they are useful because they portray the relative level of proficiency in each country, and the extent of inequalities among people with differing family socio-economic backgrounds (see Box 10A). The primary indicator of family socio-economic background is the respondent's parents' level of education. The research literature supports the notion that adults whose parents have attained higher levels of education are advantaged, not least in terms of better access to wealth, prestige and power, but also in the formation of foundation skills (Desjardins, 2004a).

Socio-economic gradients are summarized by three components: their level, their slope, and the strength of the relationship (see Box 10A).

The levels of the gradients reflect the average prose literacy scores at each level of parental education. On average, Bermuda and Norway have the highest scores at all levels of parental education. This means that independent of the educational investments made by the previous generation these countries were more successful in forming literacy skills among younger generations than other countries. Bermuda and Norway are also among the countries with the lowest socio-economic inequality with respect to prose literacy and parental education, as indicated by their relatively flat gradients. This suggests that they have also been successful at forming literacy skills among those youth whose parents' have low levels of education.

The slope of the gradients indicates the extent to which parents' education has influenced the development of literacy skills in their children. A steep slope suggests that youth whose parents have relatively low levels of education tend to be low skilled (Levels 1 and 2), and conversely, youth whose parents have higher levels of education tend to be more skilled. Large differences indicate that access to good literacy instruction and engagement in practices related to skills formation is systematically related to socio-economic differences.

A comparison of slopes suggests that Norway is the most successful at reducing the skills disadvantages that are typically associated with low levels of parental education. On average, there is an approximate 13 point difference between the skills of Norwegians whose parents completed eight years of schooling compared to those who completed 12 years. In contrast, the United States, followed by Canada and Switzerland, has the steepest socio-economic gradient. In the former country, youth whose parents have completed 12 years of schooling score about 39 points higher than those whose parents completed eight years. This difference is about 24 points in Canada and Switzerland, and 22 in Bermuda and Italy.

Although there are disproportionately more youth from low socio-economic backgrounds who score at Levels 1 and 2, there are also many youth at all levels of parental education who display low levels of literacy. In Figure 10.1, this is indicated by the black dots that lie below Level 3. Conversely, in some countries there are many "resilient" youth scoring at Level 4/5 whose parents had relatively low levels of education. This is especially the case in Canada and Norway. But in Switzerland and the United States few youth scoring at Level 4/5 have parents with below average levels of education.

FIGURE 10.1

Socio-economic gradients of youth

Relationship between respondent's prose literacy scores and parents' education in years, populations aged 16 to 25, 2003

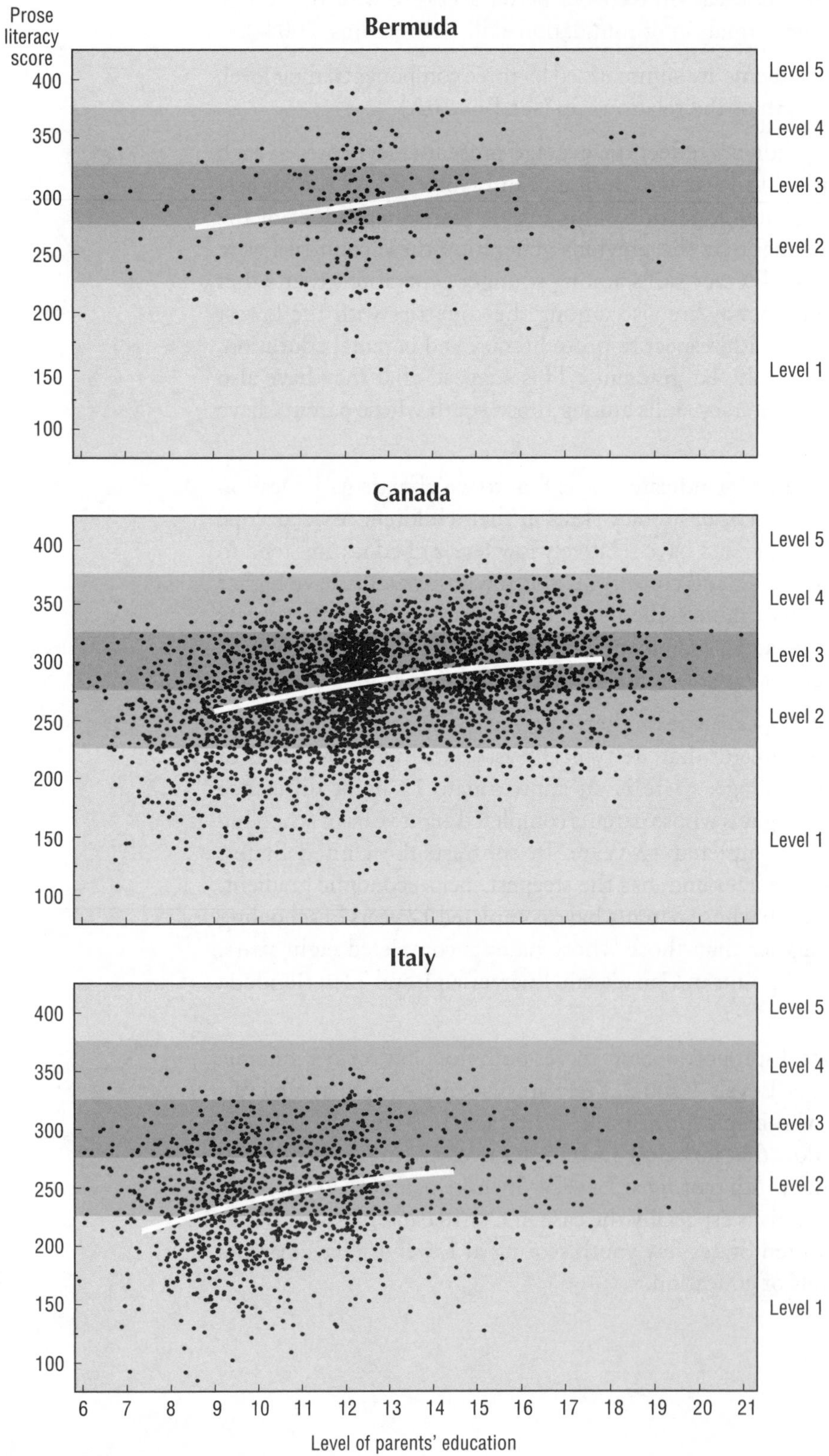

FIGURE 10.1 (concluded)

Socio-economic gradients of youth

Relationship between respondent's prose literacy scores and parents' education in years, populations aged 16 to 25, 2003

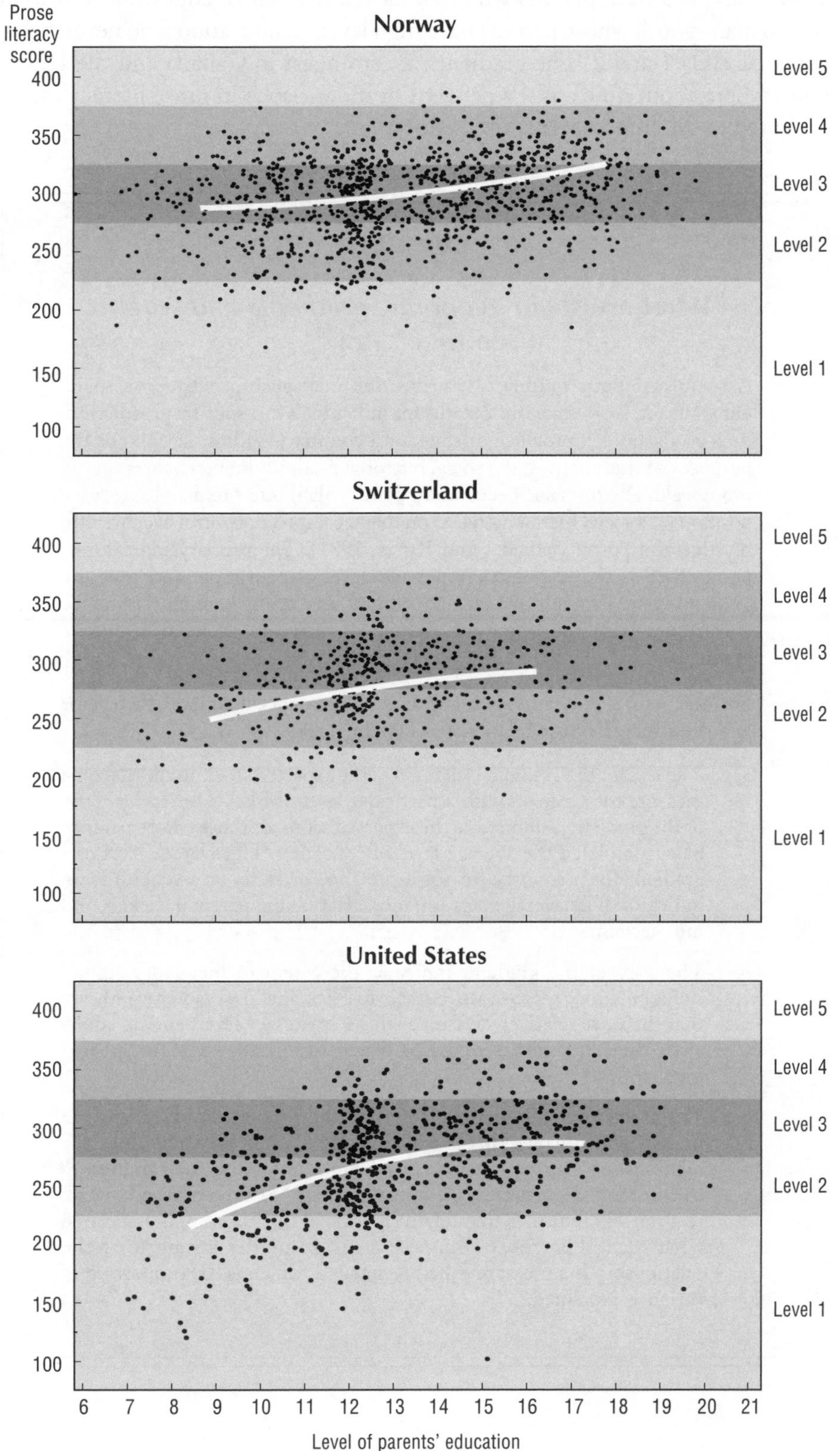

Finally, the strength of the gradient should be taken into account. This is indicated by the proportion of variance in literacy performance that is explained by differences in levels of parental education. The strength of this relationship varies substantially by country. It is the weakest in Bermuda and Italy, for example, with only about five and six per cent of the variation in literacy explained by differences in parents' levels of education. In Italy, many youth who score at Levels 3 and 4/5 have parents who also have low levels of education. But there are also many youth whose parents have high levels of education who nevertheless score at Levels 1 and 2. The gradients are strongest in Canada and the United States where about nine and 19 per cent of the variance in prose literacy can be attributed to differences in parental education.

Box 10A

What are *socio-economic gradients and what do they show*?

A socio-economic gradient describes the relationship between a social outcome and socio-economic status for individuals in a specific jurisdiction, such as a school, a province or state, or a country (Willms, 2002). For the purposes of this analysis, the social outcome is adults' literacy scores on the prose scale. The term socio-economic status (SES) refers to people's relative position on a social hierarchy, based on their access to, or control over, wealth, prestige and power (Mueller and Parcel, 1981). The primary indicator of family SES is the respondent's parents' level of education, and thus the gradients could be simply called "parental education gradients", but for consistency with the literature, they are referred to as socio-economic gradients.

Socio-economic gradients comprise three components: their level, their slope and the strength of the relationship (Willms, 2003):

a. The *level* of the gradient is defined as the expected score on the outcome measure for a person with a particular level of SES. The *average level* of the gradient is defined as the expected score for those whose parents' have completed the average level of education. The average level of a gradient for a country (or for a province or state, or a school) is an indicator of its average performance, after taking parental background into account.

b. The *slope* of the gradient indicates the extent of inequality among subpopulations that are attributable to SES. Shallow gradients indicate that there are relatively few inequalities in literacy levels among adults with differing levels of SES. Steep gradients indicate greater inequalities.

c. The *strength* of the gradient refers to the proportion of variance in literacy performance that is explained by SES. If the strength of the relationship is strong, then a considerable amount of the variation in the outcome measure is associated with SES, whereas a weak relationship indicates that relatively little of the variation is associated with SES. The most common measure of the strength of the relationship is a measure called R-squared, which is the proportion of variance explained.

The ALL and IALS prose and document literacy scales are identical. This allows one to examine whether changes in the relationship between the respondent's prose literacy scores and parents' education have occurred. Note that the IALS data for Canada and the United States were collected in 1994. Data for Norway was gathered in 1998. Figure 10.2 shows the gradients for youth aged 16 to 25 in IALS alongside the comparable results obtained using ALL data. The results suggest that in Canada, the levels of literacy scores for youth have declined during the intervening nine year period. This decline is predominantly among youth who are from lower socio-economic backgrounds. In Norway and the United States the gradients are fairly similar, indicating relatively small changes over the five and nine year periods, respectively.

FIGURE 10.2

Changes in socio-economic gradients of youth from IALS to ALL

Relationship between respondent's prose literacy scores and parents' education in years, populations aged 16 to 25, IALS 1994/1998 and ALL 2003

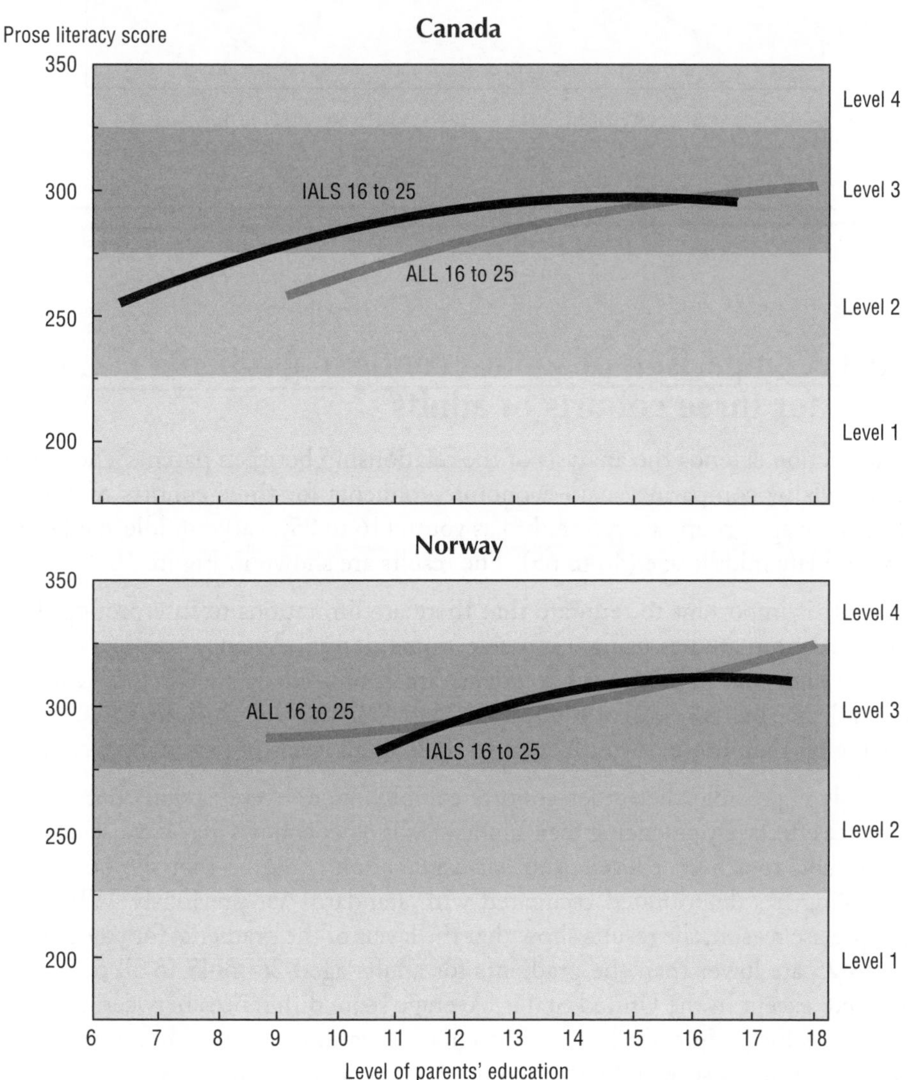

FIGURE 10.2 (concluded)

Changes in socio-economic gradients of youth from IALS to ALL

Relationship between respondent's prose literacy scores and parents' education in years, populations aged 16 to 25, IALS 1994/1998 and ALL 2003

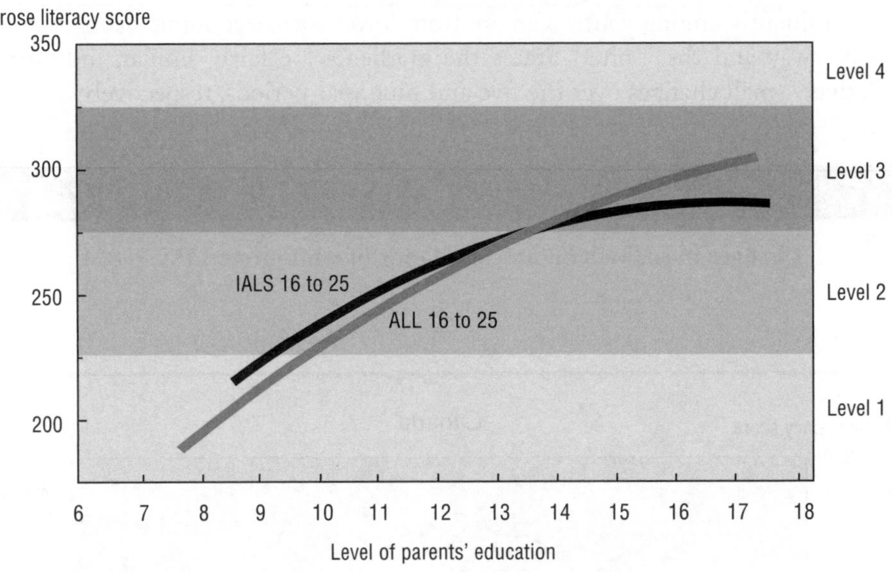

10.3 Comparison of socio-economic gradients for three cohorts of adults

This section extends the analysis of the relationship between parents' education and skills by comparing socio-economic gradients for three cohorts of adults. The three age groups are referred to as youth (16 to 25), early middle age (26 to 45) and late middle age (46 to 65). The results are shown in Figure 10.3.

It is important to reiterate that there are limitations to interpreting data obtained from studies using a cross-sectional design. Ageing, practice, cohort, period and quality of education effects are confounded (see Chapter 2). For example, the literacy skills of adults aged 26 to 45 in the United States and Canada are higher than those of youth aged 16 to 25 at all levels of parental education.

It is possible that older cohorts exhibit higher average skills because of practice effects. By practicing their literacy skills older cohorts may have developed their skills to a higher level. Another explanation could be that the quality of schooling has deteriorated compared with standards set previously. Whatever the precise reason, the results show that the levels of the gradients for youth aged 16 to 25 are lower than the gradients for adults aged 26 to 45 in all countries studied[1] except in the United States. Average score differences between the two cohorts, which adjust for levels of parental education, range from one point on the prose literacy scale in Switzerland to 12 points in Canada. It is interesting to compare these results with Figure 2.7 in Chapter 2, where the skills of youth aged 16 to 25 are slightly higher on average than the skills of adults aged 26 to 45, but this is without adjusting for parents' levels of education. This implies that the effect of parents' education is substantial.

Patterns of decline in average youth performance among countries are not uniform. In Bermuda, Canada and the United States, current youth performance is lower at nearly all levels of parental education. In Italy and Norway, current average youth performance is lower for average to high levels of parental education, while performance among those whose parents have low levels of education has improved compared to adults aged 26 to 45.

In contrast, the levels of gradients among adults aged 46 to 65 are uniformly lower in Norway and Switzerland at all levels of parental education. This suggests that educational reforms and a web of factors such as improved living standards, health care and nutrition, among others, have had a beneficial impact on all youth regardless of their socio-economic background. In Canada and the United States, however, the group aged 46 to 65 score, on average, somewhat higher once the variance associated with parental education has been removed.

Finally, the socio-economic gradients in Bermuda, Canada, Norway and Italy are steeper for adults aged 46 to 65 than for youth. This suggests that in these countries, there has been a reduction in socio-economic inequalities in recent years. The most marked reduction in observed inequality is in Bermuda and Italy. There is a significant gap of about 36 and 32 points in Bermuda and Italy, respectively, between the average literacy scores of adults whose parents had 12 years of schooling and those whose parents had only eight years of schooling. The comparable gap among the youth is slightly less – about 21 and 22 points – attributable mainly to shallower gradients.

FIGURE 10.3

Socio-economic gradients for three cohorts of adults

Relationship between respondent's prose literacy scores and parents' education in years, populations aged 16 to 25, 26 to 45 and 46 to 65, 2003

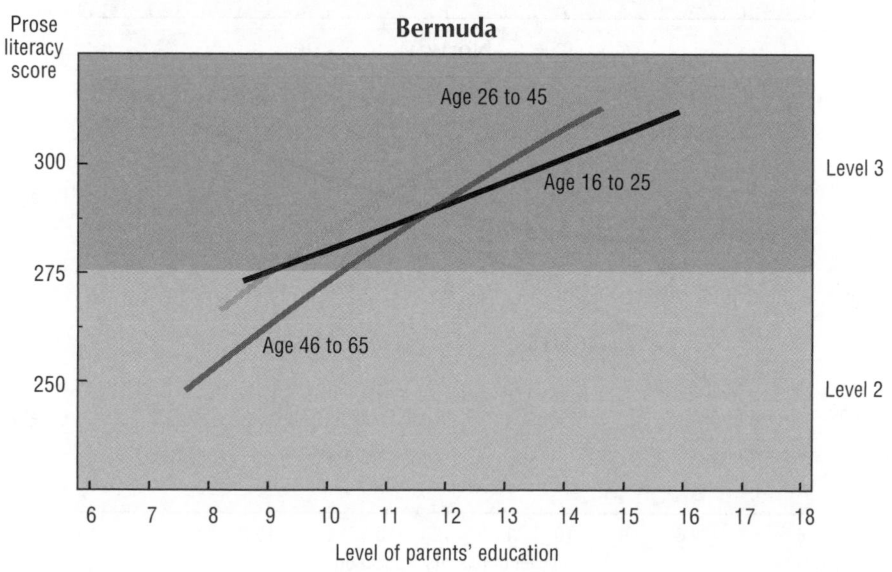

FIGURE 10.3 (continued)

Socio-economic gradients for three cohorts of adults

Relationship between respondent's prose literacy scores and parents' education in years, populations aged 16 to 25, 26 to 45 and 46 to 65, 2003

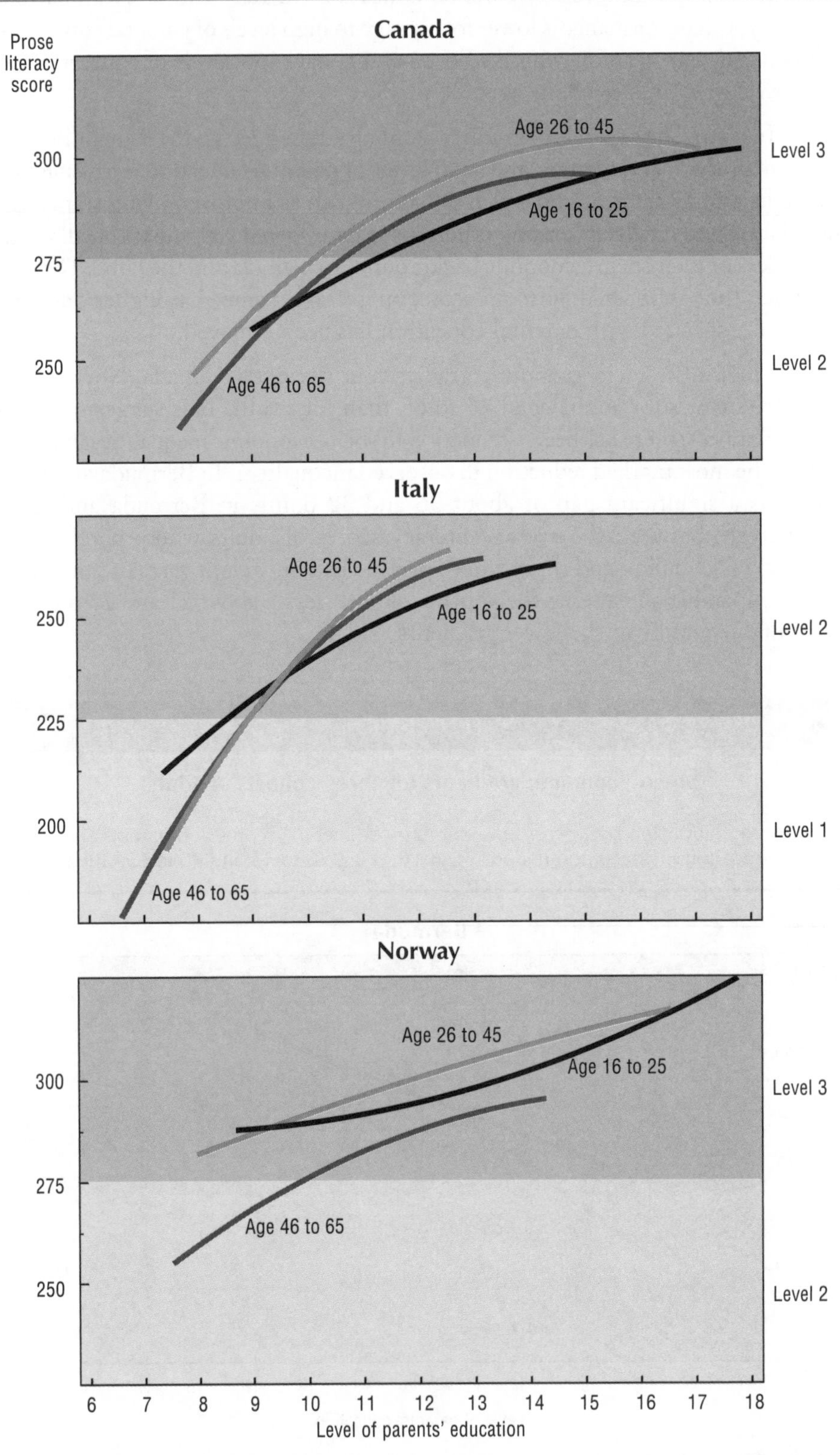

FIGURE 10.3 (concluded)

Socio-economic gradients for three cohorts of adults

Relationship between respondent's prose literacy scores and parents' education in years, populations aged 16 to 25, 26 to 45 and 46 to 65, 2003

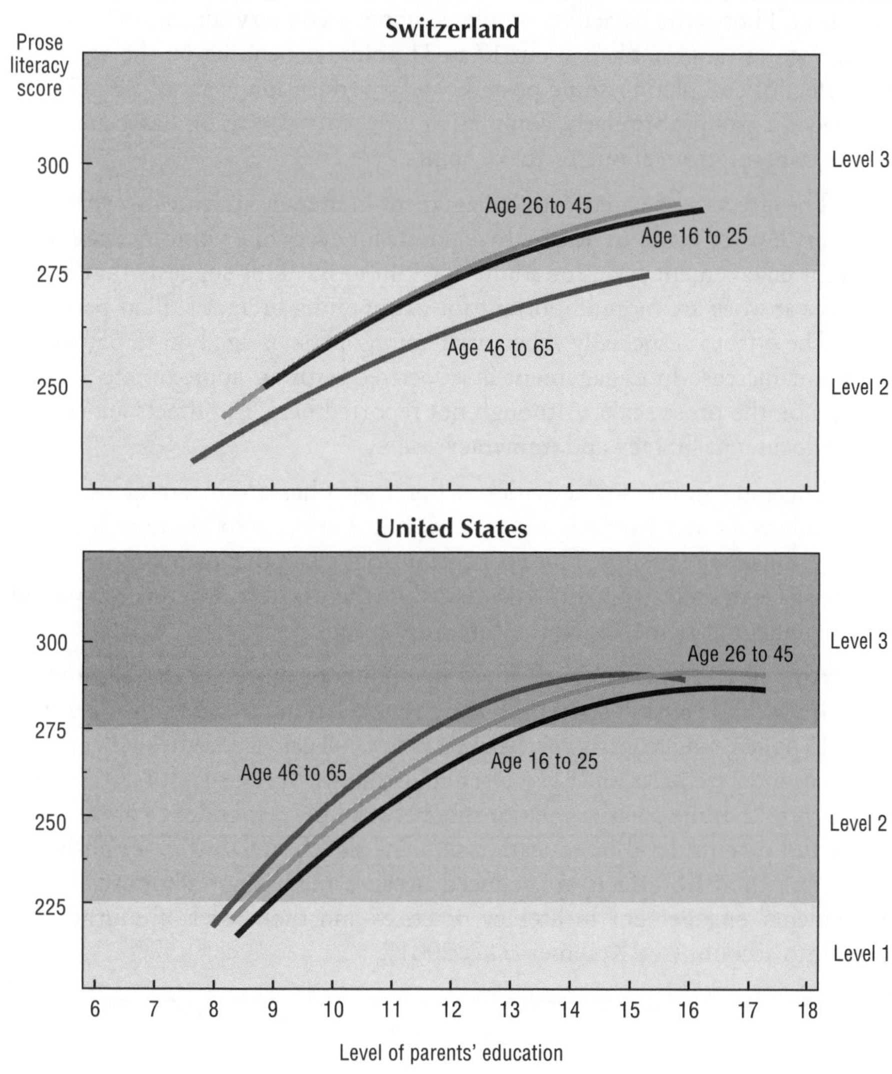

10.4 Engagement in literacy practices at home and in daily life

During and beyond schooling age, adult literacy continues to be affected by engagement in literacy activities at home and in daily life (Desjardins, 2004b). Moreover, after the transition period from school to work, a majority of adults are in the workforce and engage in literacy practices at work (see Chapter 6). This section considers the relationship between skills and engagement in literacy activities at home and at work.

To discern the potential impact of engagement, two 10-point scales of engagement in literacy activities at home and at work are constructed (see Box 10B). These measures are included in a multivariate analysis, which use pooled data for the six countries participating in ALL, and adjust for the respondent's level of education, parents' level of education, and the amount of time they spend watching television or videos each day (see Box 10C). The findings for prose literacy are summarized in Figure 10.4.

Not surprisingly, respondents' level of education has the strongest effect on literacy outcomes among the variables specified. The education effects are shown in relation to upper secondary graduates who are not pursuing post-secondary education. Those who have not completed upper secondary education have lower average scores ranging from about 17 to 31 points depending on the age group. The effect of completing some post-secondary education is about 20 points for all three age groups. Similarly, completing university education has a substantial impact, ranging from about 17 to 31 points.

The effects associated with engagement in literacy activities at work range from very low for youth to nearly three points for every one point increase on the 10-point engagement scale for adults aged 46 to 65. This suggests that literacy practices at work are more important for maintaining literacy skill as people get older. The effect is especially substantial among persons aged 46 to 65, where a five point increase in engagement is associated with an approximate 14 point increase on the prose scale. Although not reported here, the effects are stronger on the document literacy and numeracy scales.

Engaging in literacy activities at home also has a substantial effect. The magnitude is similar to engaging at work but it appears to be more important among younger age groups. This is likely due to the fact that comparatively fewer youth engage in literacy practices at work while there is little difference in patterns of engagement at home across the three age groups.

Among youth, watching TV for five hours or more per day significantly co-varies with lower skill scores. This negative relation to skill is on the order of about 13 points, which nearly corresponds to the skill gain associated with attaining upper secondary education. Even after adjusting for various factors,[2] the overall results show that the positive relationship between the respondent's prose literacy scores and parents' level of education remains significant. But in a multivariate framework the SES effects are reduced because mediating factors such as the respondents' engagement in literacy practices and their level of education are taken into account (see Kraemer *et al.*, 2001).

Box 10B

Measures of engagement at home and at work

Respondents were asked how often they read or use information from (a) letters, memos, or emails, (b) reports, articles, magazines or journals, and (c) manuals or reference books, including catalogues, (d) diagrams or schematics, (e) directions or instructions, and (f) bills, invoices, spreadsheets or budgets. They were also asked how often they write materials in each of these categories. The engagement in literacy activities at work scale is derived from responses to their frequency in reading or using information in the first three categories above, and writing material in the first two categories. The second scale, engagement in literacy activities at home, is based on respondents' reports of how often they read or used information from newspapers, magazines or books. Both scales were constructed such that one point represents 10 percentile points for the pooled sample. For example, a person scoring at 4.3 would be at the 43rd percentile, while a person at 7.6 would be at the 76th percentile. The median score is 5.0 points.

References

DeCasper, A.J., LeCanuet, J.P., Busnel, M.C., Granier-Deferre, C. and Maugeais, R. (1994), "Fetal Reactions to Recurrent Maternal Speech", *Infant Behavior and Development*, Vol. 17, pp. 159-164.

Desjardins, R. (2004a), "Determinants of Literacy Proficiency: A lifelong-lifewide learning perspective", *International Journal of Educational Research*, Vol. 39(3), pp. 205-245.

Desjardins, R. (2004b), "Learning for Well Being: Studies Using the International Adult Literacy Survey", Ph.D Thesis, Institute of International Education, Stockholm.

Epstein, J.L. and Dauber, S.L. (1991), "School Programs and Teacher Practices of Parent Involvement in Inner-City Elementary and Middle Schools", *Elementary School Journal*, Vol. 91, pp. 291-305.

Hart, B. and Risley, T.R. (1995), *Meaningful Differences in the Everyday Experience of Young American Children*, P.H. Brookes, Baltimore.

Hill, P.W. and Crevola, C.A. (1999), "Key Features of a Whole-school, Design Approach to Literacy Teaching in Schools", *Australian Journal of Learning Disabilities*, Vol. 4(3), pp. 5-11.

Ho, E. and Willms, J.D. (1996), "The Effects of Parental Involvement on Eighth Grade Achievement", *Sociology of Education*, Vol. 69, pp. 126-141.

Huttenlocher, J., Haight, W., Bryk, A., Seltzer, M. and Lyons, T. (1991), "Early Vocabulary Growth: Relation to language input and gender", *Developmental Psychology*, Vol. 27(2), pp. 236-248.

Kisilevsky, B.S., Hains, S.M., Lee, K., Xie, X., Huang, H., Ye, H.H., Zhang, K. and Wang, Z. (2003), "Effects of Experience on Fetal Voice Recognition", *Psychological Science*, Vol. 14(3), pp. 220-224.

Kraemer, H.C., Stice, E., Kazdin, A., Offord, D. and Kupfer, D. (2001), "How Do Risk Factors Work Together? Mediators, moderators, and independent, overlapping, and proxy risk factors", *American Journal of Psychiatry*, Vol. 158, pp. 848-856.

Ramey, C.T. and Ramey, S.L. (1998), "Early Intervention and Early Experience", *American Psychologist*, Vol. 53(2), pp. 109-120.

Scheerens, J. (1992), *Effective Schooling: Research, theory, and practice*, Cassell, London.

Stevenson, D.L. and Baker, D.P. (1987), "The Family-school Relation and the Child's Schools Performance", *Child Development*, Vol. 58, pp. 1348-1357.

Tuijnman, A.C. (1989), "Recurrent Education, Earnings and Well-being: A 45-year longitudinal study of a cohort of Swedish men", *Acta Universitatis Stockholmiensis,* Almqvist and Wiksell International, Stockholm.

Werker, J.F. and Tees, R.C. (2002), "Cross-language Speech Perception: Evidence for perceptual reorganization during the first year of life", *Infant Behavior and Development*, Vol. 25, pp. 121-133.

Willms, J.D. (2001), "Monitoring School Performance for "Standards-based Reform", *Evaluation and Research in Education*, Vol. 14(3 and 4), pp. 237-253.

Willms, J.D. (2003), *Ten Hypotheses about Socio-economic Gradients and Community Differences in Children's Developmental Outcomes*, Applied Research Branch of Human Resources Development Canada, Ottawa, Ontario.

Willms, J.D. (2004), "Considerations from an Education Perspective for the Proposed OECD Programme for International Assessment of Adult Competencies (PIACC)", Organisation for Economic Cooperation and Development, Paris.

Contributor

J. Douglas Willms, *University of New Brunswick*

Annex 10

Data Values for the Figures

TABLE 10.1

Relationship between respondent's prose literacy scores and parents' education in years, populations aged 16 to 25, 2003

	Gradient specifications for ALL 2003						
	Average level[1]		Slope[2]		Slope squared[3]		
	Estimate		Estimate		Estimate		Strength[4]
Bermuda	290.7 ***	(4.5)	5.3 **	(2.2)	0.05	(0.68)	0.05
Canada	279.9 ***	(2.7)	6.1 ***	(0.91)	-0.40	0.30)	0.09
Italy	253.2 ***	(3.6)	5.6 ***	(1.3)	-0.69	0.41)	0.06
Norway	294.7 ***	(2.7)	3.2 ***	(0.9)	0.36	0.28)	0.08
Switzerland	273.3 ***	(3.9)	6.1 ***	(1.4)	-0.51	(0.59)	0.07
United States	264.6 ***	(3.2)	9.8 ***	(1.1)	-1.07 ***	(0.32)	0.19

** $p<0.05$, statistically significant at the 5 per cent level.
*** $p<0.01$, statistically significant at the 1 per cent level.
1. The average level defines the expected score for those whose parents completed the average years of schooling in each country.
2. The slope defines the average effect on prose literacy associated with each additional year of parents' schooling.
3. The estimation model allows for the effect of parents' schooling on skill to be non-linear (i.e., quadratic).
4. The strength is measured by R-square, which is the variance explained.

Source: Adult Literacy and Life Skills Survey, 2003.

10

TABLE 10.2

Relationship between respondent's prose literacy scores and parents' education in years, populations aged 16 to 25, IALS 1994/1998

	Gradient specifications for IALS 1994/1998						
	Average level[1]		Slope[2]		Slope squared[3]		
	Estimate		Estimate		Estimate		Strength[4]
Canada	293.1 ***	(6.9)	3.2 *	(1.7)	-0.6	(0.6)	0.09
Norway	296.0 ***	(2.9)	7.8 ***	(1.5)	-1.0 ***	(0.3)	0.05
United States	260.3 ***	(5.0)	12.6 ***	(1.5)	-0.7	(0.5)	0.28

* p<0.10, statistically significant at the 10 per cent level.
*** p<0.01, statistically significant at the 1 per cent level.
1. The average level defines the expected score for those whose parents completed the average years of schooling in each country.
2. The slope defines the average effect on prose literacy associated with each additional year of parents' schooling.
3. The estimation model allows for the effect of parents' schooling on skill to be non-linear (i.e., quadratic).
4. The strength is measured by R-square, which is the variance explained.

Source: International Adult Literacy Survey, 1994-1998.

TABLE 10.3

Relationship between respondent's prose literacy scores and parents' education in years, populations aged 16 to 25, 26 to 45 and 46 to 65, 2003

	Average level[1]		Slope[2]		Slope squared[3]		
	Estimate		Estimate		Estimate		Strength[4]
A. Gradient specifications for ALL 2003 aged 16 to 25							
Bermuda	290.7 ***	(4.5)	5.3 **	(2.2)	0.1	(0.7)	0.05
Canada	279.9 ***	(2.7)	6.1 ***	(0.9)	-0.4	(0.3)	0.09
Italy	253.2 ***	(3.6)	5.6 ***	(1.3)	-0.7	(0.4)	0.06
Norway	294.7 ***	(2.7)	3.2 ***	(0.9)	0.4	(0.3)	0.08
Switzerland	273.3 ***	(3.9)	6.1 ***	(1.4)	-0.5	(0.6)	0.07
United States	264.6 ***	(3.2)	9.8 ***	(1.1)	-1.1 ***	(0.3)	0.19
B. Gradient specifications for ALL 2003 aged 26 to 45							
Bermuda	300.8 ***	(2.5)	7.3 ***	(1.0)	-0.5	(0.4)	0.09
Canada	291.7 ***	(1.4)	7.0 ***	(0.5)	-1.0 ***	(0.2)	0.11
Italy	263.2 ***	(3.9)	6.6 ***	(1.2)	-1.9 ***	(0.4)	0.05
Norway	300.8 ***	(1.4)	4.2 ***	(0.6)	-0.1	(0.2)	0.06
Switzerland	274.7 ***	(1.9)	6.4 ***	(0.9)	-0.5 *	(0.3)	0.11
United States	270.7 ***	(1.8)	9.6 ***	(0.6)	-1.1 ***	(0.3)	0.18
C. Gradient specifications for ALL 2003 aged 46 to 65							
Bermuda	291.6 ***	(3.4)	8.9 ***	(1.2)	-0.3	(0.5)	0.10
Canada	286.5 ***	(2.1)	6.8 ***	(0.7)	-1.2 ***	(0.3)	0.09
Italy	250.5 ***	(5.6)	7.9 ***	(1.6)	-2.5 ***	(0.8)	0.04
Norway	287.9 ***	(2.4)	4.6 ***	(0.7)	-0.6 *	(0.3)	0.05
Switzerland	262.2 ***	(1.6)	5.2 ***	(1.1)	-0.4	(0.4)	0.07
United States	276.1 ***	(2.9)	7.0 ***	(1.0)	-1.1 **	(0.4)	0.17

* p<0.10, statistically significant at the 10 per cent level.
** p<0.05, statistically significant at the 5 per cent level.
*** p<0.01, statistically significant at the 1 per cent level.
1. The average level defines the expected score for those whose parents' completed the average years of schooling in each country.
2. The slope defines the average effect on prose literacy associated with each additional year of parents' schooling.
3. The estimation model allows for the effect of parents' schooling on skill to be non-linear (i.e., quadratic).
4. The strength is measured by R-square, which is the variance explained.

Source: Adult Literacy and Life Skills Survey, 2003.

TABLE 10.4

Relationship between prose literacy scores and engagement in literacy practices at home and in daily life, adjusted for respondent's and parents' education, populations aged 16 to 25, 26 to 45 and 46 to 65, 2003

	Aged 16 to 25		Aged 26 to 45		Aged 46 to 65	
	Estimate		Estimate		Estimate	
Did not complete secondary school	-16.89 ***	(3.84)	-31.37 ***	(2.55)	-29.22 ***	(3.83)
Finished some college or university	23.27 ***	(4.69)	20.59 ***	(2.35)	19.11 ***	(3.11)
Graduated with university degree	31.19 ***	(5.11)	25.82 ***	(3.20)	17.38 ***	(3.56)
Engagement in literacy activities at work	0.12	(0.62)	1.71 ***	(0.47)	2.86 ***	(0.56)
Engagement in literacy activities at home	3.34 ***	(0.63)	3.10 ***	(0.52)	4.05 ***	(0.46)
Watches TV or video 2 to 5 hours per day	-3.01	(2.39)	3.00	(2.29)	3.37	(2.74)
Watches TV or video more than 5 hours per day	-12.76 ***	(3.87)	-4.61	(4.68)	-3.98	(3.53)
Level of parents' education	6.70 ***	(0.80)	3.90 ***	(0.40)	3.59 ***	(0.59)
Level of parents' education squared	-0.97 ***	(0.25)	-0.67 ***	(0.18)	-0.91 ***	(0.21)
R-Squared, explained variance	0.28		0.34		0.39	

*** $p<0.01$, statistically significant at the 1 per cent level.
Source: Adult Literacy and Life Skills Survey, 2003.

Chapter 11

Skills and Health

Summary

This chapter examines the relationship between skills measured in ALL and various aspects of individual health. Two latent class analyses are performed to identify groups of individuals sharing response tendencies to a set of 13 health-related background questions. The first analysis identifies four classes of individuals based upon questions related to general health status, as follows: excellent health, good health, fair health and poor health. The second analysis identifies four classes of individuals based upon questions related to their health status at work, as follows: no work-related limitations, physically limited at work, emotionally limited at work and physically and emotionally limited at work. These analyses are then used to explore the relationship between skills measured in ALL and health status.

Table of Contents

Skills and Health

11.1 Overview and highlights

This chapter examines the relationship between skills measured in ALL and various aspects of individual health. Two latent class analyses are performed to identify groups of individuals sharing response tendencies to a set of 13 health-related background questions. The first analysis identifies four classes of individuals based upon questions related to general health status, as follows: excellent health, good health, fair health and poor health. The second analysis identifies four classes of individuals based upon questions related to their health status at work, as follows: no work-related limitations, physically limited at work, emotionally limited at work and physically and emotionally limited at work. These analyses are then used to explore the relationship between skills measured in ALL and health status.

The results of these analyses are as follows:

- The findings indicate interesting similarities. First, the relative proportions of the four classes on both the general and work-related health status classifications are rather comparable across countries. Second, the pattern of average literacy and numeracy scores by health classes in surveyed countries is also similar.
- The respondents who answered health related questions in a way that led to their being classified as healthy not only represent the largest percentage of adults but are also the ones with noticeably higher average literacy and numeracy scores compared to the least healthy group of adults — those most likely to report experiencing emotional and physical adversities limiting their activities and capping their accomplishments.
- The analysis of general health status indicates that two identified classes of adults – comprising 20 and 52 per cent respectively – are very satisfied with their lives. Members of these groups tend to state that health does not impede their physical or social activities. The difference between the two groups lies in their assessment of their overall health. The smaller group of 20 per cent tends to evaluate

both their health and emotional status using the extreme positive categories, whereas the larger group reports their physical and mental well being in more moderate terms.

- Both the general and work-related health status analyses identified relatively small groups of adults who report that they are adversely affected by both physical and emotional problems. These groups have significantly lower average scores than the other groups on the literacy and numeracy scales.

While this chapter provides only a first look at the data from ALL relating to health status and literacy, it does support the growing recognition that skills and health status are related. It is not too surprising that as technology continues to evolve and becomes more integrated into all aspects of our lives, modern health care systems are increasingly being characterized by their complexity and sophistication (Bernhardt, Brownfield and Parker, 2005). This increase in complexity and sophistication comes at a time when some believe that individuals are expected to assume more responsibility for the management of their health and well being, thereby placing an even greater emphasis on the importance of literacy and numeracy skills. If true, how will this emerging trend impact current disparities in health outcomes noted in recent research?

11.2 Skills and general health status

While health professionals have long known about the association between years of schooling and health outcomes, education itself was not the major consideration, but was instead viewed as a marker of socioeconomic status. Large-scale national and international surveys such as the National Adult Literacy Survey (NALS) and the International Adult Literacy Survey (IALS)[1] offered researchers and policy makers critical insight into literacy as a possible pathway linking education and health outcomes (Rudd, Kirsch and Yamamoto, 2004). A number of studies conducted over the past decade have focused on the relationships between literacy and health-related outcomes. In summarizing some of these studies, Weiss (2005) noted that having lower health knowledge is associated with lower health status, higher utilization of health services and not too surprisingly increased costs for health care. These and other data suggest that literacy may be a contributing factor to the wide disparities in health care that many adults in the United States and elsewhere receive.

A growing recognition of the importance of literacy as a potential pathway linking years of schooling and health outcomes has led to two recent publications; one titled *Understanding Health Literacy: Implications for Medicine and Public Health,* published in 2005 by the American Medical Association and the other *Health Literacy: A Prescription to End Confusion* published in 2004 by the Institute of Medicine of the National Academies. It also led the developers of the ALL survey to include a set of background questions focusing on general and work-related health issues. This section presents results of a Latent Class Analysis (LCA) that is used to classify individuals into groups or "latent classes" based on their patterns of responses to a set of background questions associated with general health and emotional well being (see Box 11A). Eight questions from the ALL questionnaire were used to create a general health status variable (see Annex 11B for questions). Figure 11.1 reports the probability that the individuals in each class responded in a particular way to each question. A high probability indicates a strong likelihood that the characteristic is present in that class while a low probability indicates a strong likelihood that the characteristic is absent. Box 11B summarizes the response tendencies associated with each class and points out key differences between them.

Box 11A

How does latent class analysis work?

In this chapter, literacy and numeracy scores are analyzed in relationship to several derived variables that distinguish among groups of participants based on their self-reported health status. Individuals are organized into groups or "classes" based on their patterns of responses to a set of background questions associated with either work or general health and emotional well being. More specifically, the health related questions from the ALL background questionnaire are analyzed using Latent Class Analysis (LCA) methods (Lazarsfeld and Henry, 1968; Patterson, Dayton and Graubard, 2002). LCA is a statistical tool for clustering subjects based on categorical variables. This analysis yields a probabilistic classification for each survey participant, where the classes are represented by different tendencies to respond in a certain way (more formally, each class is characterized by its conditional response probabilities) to a set of questions. The population profiles and group sizes reported in this chapter are expressed in percentages. The different classes are identified by predominant response profiles. The necessary number of latent classes to describe the different response tendencies found in the data is determined using statistical measures based on the likelihood of the data given models with different numbers of classes. For parsimony, the model with the smallest number of latent classes that can adequately describe the data is chosen.

Most of the questions relating to general health status offer a range of ordered response options. With regard to their satisfaction with life, adults were asked to respond on a 5-point ordinal scale that ranged from extremely unsatisfied to extremely satisfied. Similarly, they could respond that their overall health ranged from poor to excellent. With regard to their activities, they had a 3-point scale that ranged from no limitations, to a little, to a lot. Adults could respond on a 6-point ordinal scale with respect to three additional questions focusing on: how calm and peaceful they felt, whether they had a lot of energy and whether they felt blue or downhearted. Finally, they had a 5-point scale on which they could indicate the extent to which their health or emotional well being interfered with their social activities. This scale ranged from none to all of the time.

FIGURE 11.1

Classification of general health status

Response profiles of the four latent classes based on general health status, populations aged 16 to 65, 2003

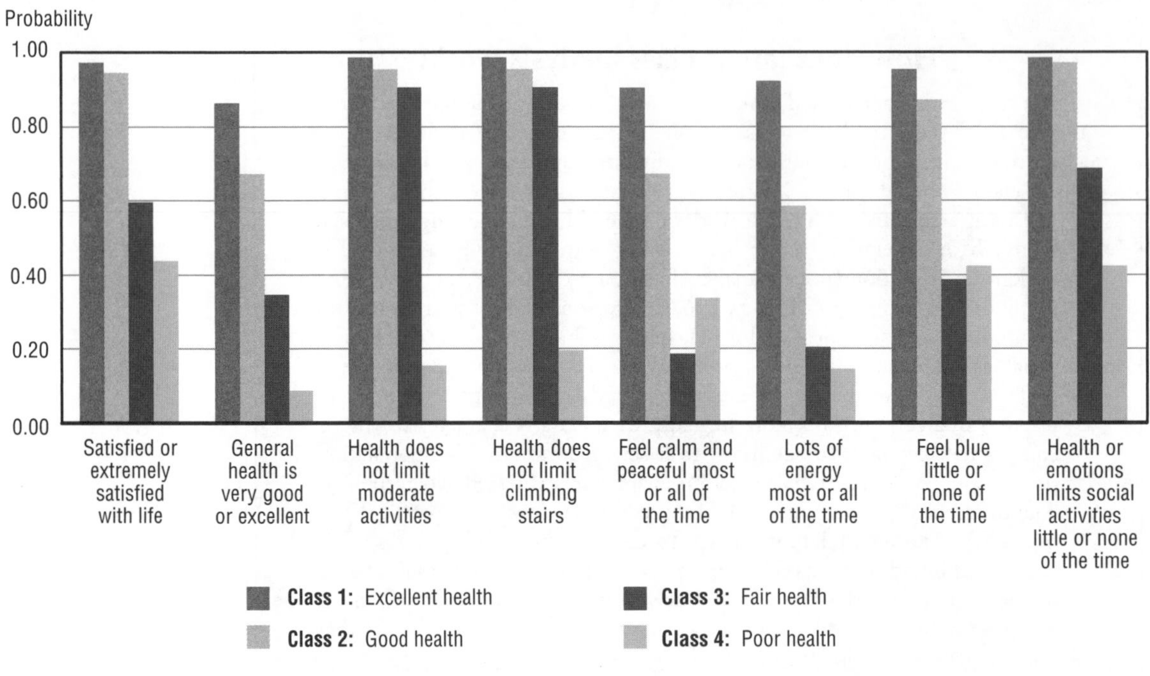

Source: Adult Literacy and Life Skills Survey, 2003.

Box 11B

Classifying adults' general health status

Eight questions from the ALL questionnaire (see Annex 11B) were combined into a general health status variable using the Latent Class Analysis method. The resulting four latent classes relating to general health status are interpreted as follows:

- Class 1 is labelled as a group with "excellent health". It represents about 20 per cent of the pooled sample. Adults in this group overwhelmingly report that they are satisfied with their life and that their general health is good or excellent. They are not limited in any of their activities by either physical or emotional issues. In addition, these adults report having a lot of energy and feeling calm and peaceful most or all of the time. As a result, they are also likely to report that they feel blue little or none of the time.

- Class 2 is labelled as a group with "good health". They represent 52 per cent of the pooled sample. Adults in this group are also very satisfied with their life and are not limited in their activities by either physical or emotional problems. What distinguishes them from Class 1 is that they are somewhat less likely to say that their overall health is very good or excellent and less likely to have lots of energy most or all the time.

- Class 3 is labelled as a group with "fair health". They comprise 20 per cent of the pooled sample. Unlike Class 1 or 2, this group is less likely to report being satisfied or extremely satisfied with their life and much less likely to say their health is very good or excellent. However, they are similar to adults in Classes 1 and 2 in that they are highly likely to report not being limited in their physical activities. Unlike adults in Classes 1 and 2, they have a much lower likelihood of reporting having a lot of energy or feeling calm and peaceful most or all of the time, and less likely to report their health does not limit their physical or social activities. They are also much less likely to report that they feel blue little or none of the time.

- Class 4 is labelled as a group with "poor health". It represents eight per cent of the pooled sample. These are the least healthy adults based on their responses to the eight general health questions. This group is much less likely to report being satisfied with life or that their health is good or excellent. They are also much more likely to report being limited in their physical or social activities by poor health. They seem to feel less energetic, less peaceful and more blue than adults in Classes 1 and 2 but they are more so than adults in Class 3.

How much does the distribution of general health status vary by country? Figure 11.2 shows the percentages by class for each participating ALL country or language group and for the total population, ranked with reference to the healthiest group. While the overall pattern is rather similar there are some interesting between-country variations. For example, while 20 per cent of all participating adults are in Class 1, the healthiest group, this percentage varies from a low of 10 per cent among French speaking Swiss adults to a high of 27 per cent among Italian speaking Swiss. Different language groups living in Switzerland account for both the highest and lowest percentages of adults classified as having the highest general health status. Note that the deviation in class sizes from the total sample is particularly large among the Swiss language-based samples, which are at the same time the smallest samples. Therefore, this variation within the Swiss population may be due in part to increased error variance associated with relatively small samples.

Countries also vary in terms of the proportion of adults who are in Class 2. The percentages range from a low of 42 per cent among Italian speaking Swiss to 62 per cent among German speaking Swiss. Corresponding figures for the other countries range from 45 to 54 per cent. Adults in Class 2 are similar to those in Class 1 in that they are likely to be very satisfied with their life and not limited in any of their activities by physical or emotional issues. Where they differ from adults in Class 1 is that they are somewhat less likely to report their health as *excellent* and they are also less likely to report that they have a lot of energy *all the time* or feel calm and peaceful *all the time*. Adults in Class 3 range from a low of 14 per cent among German speaking Swiss to a high of 30 per cent among French speaking Swiss. Among the least healthy adults (Class 4), the range was from four per cent among German speaking Swiss to 13 per cent among adults in the United States.

FIGURE 11.2

General health status by country

Per cent of adults in each of four general health status groups by country, populations aged 16 to 65, 2003

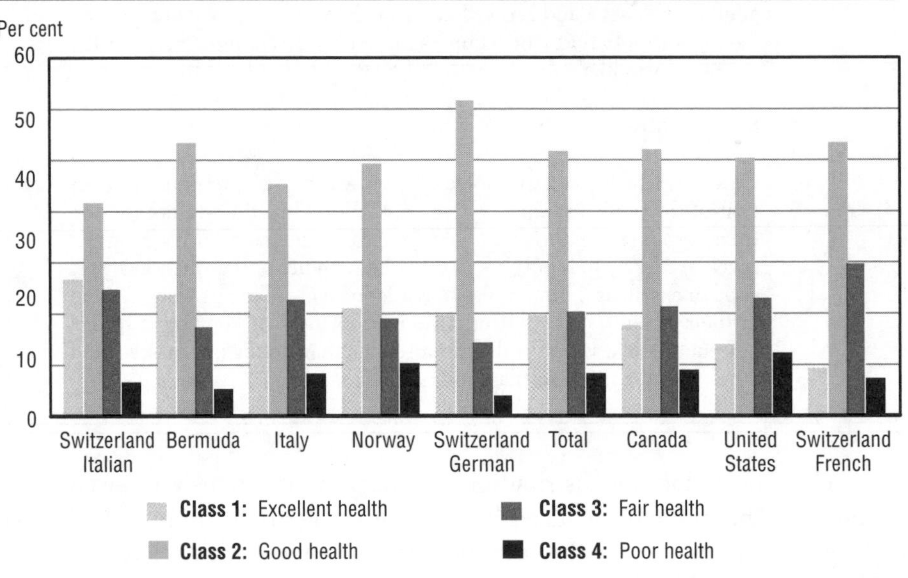

Countries are ranked by the per cent of adults in Class 1: Excellent health.

Source: Adult Literacy and Life Skills Survey, 2003.

Figure 11.3 shows the average literacy and numeracy scores for all respondents by their general health status and selected background characteristics. While there is variation in average literacy and numeracy scores among adults with various background characteristics, the pattern that emerges is quite similar in each of the countries. Adults who are classified as being among the most healthy have higher average literacy and numeracy scores while those who are classified as the least healthy (Class 4) have the lowest average proficiencies.

Interestingly, adults in Class 2 have somewhat higher average proficiencies than those in Class 1. As we noted, both groups are quite healthy and satisfied with their lives. The primary difference between these two classes lies in their assessment of their overall health; Class 1 tends to use the extreme values on the reporting scale in terms of their overall health whereas adults in Class 2 tend to use more modest values. It cannot be determined from these data whether these differences are real or reflect more subtle subjectivity in response styles. It is interesting to note, however, that adults in Class 1 (the smaller of the two groups) tend to be a bit over represented at the lower educational levels and tend to have more males. Nevertheless, this pattern of results holds across each of the selected background characteristics shown in Figure 11.3.

An interesting pattern emerges among age cohorts. As expected, average proficiencies begin to decrease in the group 36 to 45 years of age and continue to decline thereafter. The average decrease, however, is somewhat smaller between the two healthiest classes of adults (Class 1 and Class 2) when compared with the least healthy adults. For example, the average difference between the youngest and oldest cohort in Class 2 is 26 points on the prose scale, 31 points on the document scale and 22 points on the numeracy scale. Among adults in Class 4, the average difference between these two age cohorts is 30, 39 and 22 points, respectively. In addition, the average difference between the young adults in Class 2 and Class 4 is again somewhat smaller than between the oldest adults in Class 2 and Class 4. Among youth aged 16 to 25, the average difference across the three scales is 30, 30 and 38 points. Among adults 56 to 65, the average difference is 35, 38 and 37 points. These are significant differences in the sense that, on average, a 50 point gain is associated with an additional year of schooling in the IALS sample of 24 countries (Willms, 2003).

The distribution of health status by educational attainment is somewhat different from the pattern associated with age. The association is stronger for educational attainment. While average differences between adults in Class 2 and Class 4 range from 22 to 31 points depending on level of education and proficiency scale, the average difference between those with a primary or less education and those with more than upper secondary education is around 100 points, regardless of health status.

FIGURE 11.3

Skills and general health status by key demographic variables

Mean scores on the prose, document and numeracy scales ranging from 0 to 500 points by key demographic variables, populations aged 16 to 65, 2003

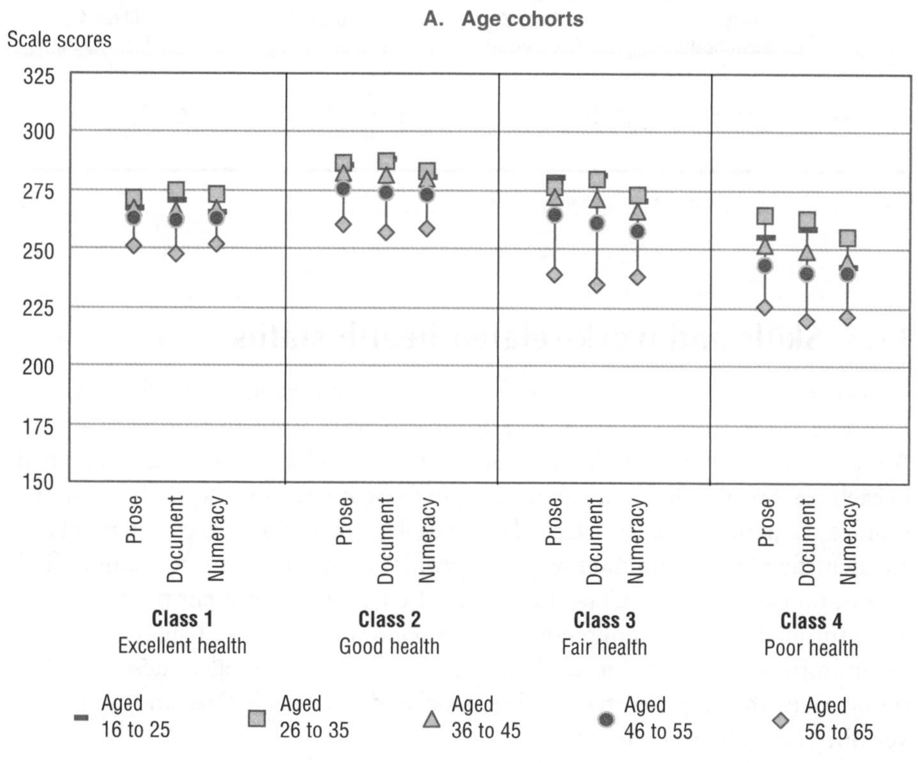

Source: Adult Literacy and Life Skills Survey, 2003.

FIGURE 11.3 (concluded)

Skills and general health status by key demographic variables

Mean scores on the prose, document and numeracy scales ranging from 0 to 500 points by key demographic variables, populations aged 16 to 65, 2003

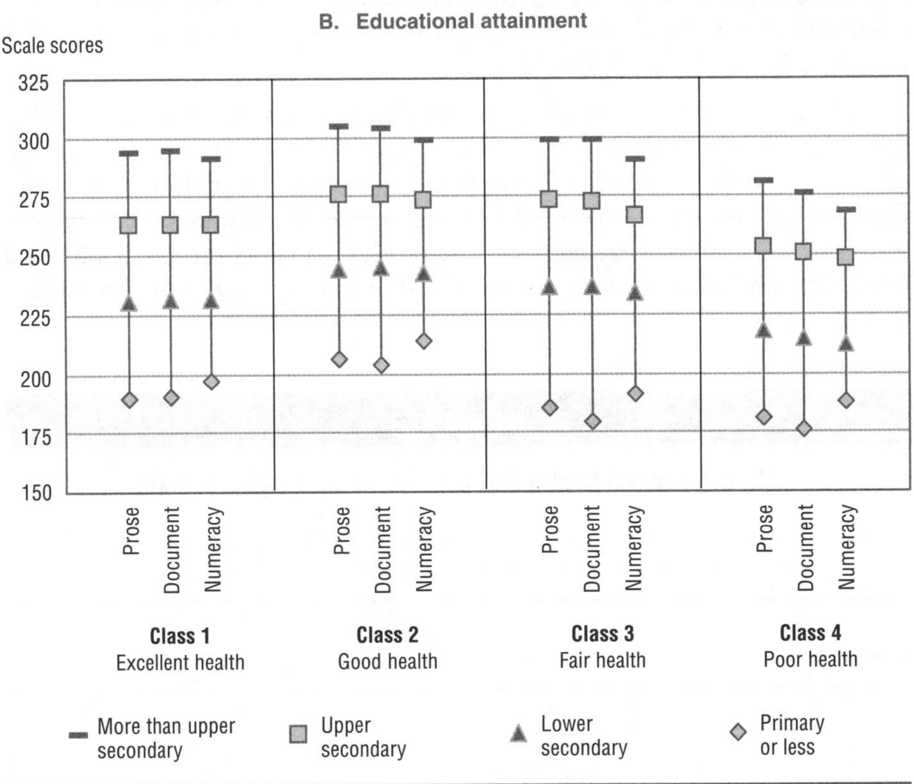

Source: Adult Literacy and Life Skills Survey, 2003.

11.3 Skills and work-related health status

A work-related health status variable was also created using latent class analysis. Five questions from the ALL questionnaire were used in this analysis (see Annex 11B for questions). Figure 11.4 reports the probability that the individuals in each class responded in a particular way to each question. Note that response profiles are an output of the latent class analysis, not an input. Accordingly, classes are identified by predominant response profiles found in the survey sample. This means, for example, that Class 4 was identified as being different from Classes 3 and 2 through the persistent tendency to respond with "yes" to all questions related to limitations at work due to *both* emotional and physical issues. Box 11C summarizes the response tendencies associated with each class and points out key differences between them.

FIGURE 11.4

Classification of work-related health status

Response profiles of the four latent classes based on work-related health status, populations aged 16 to 65, 2003

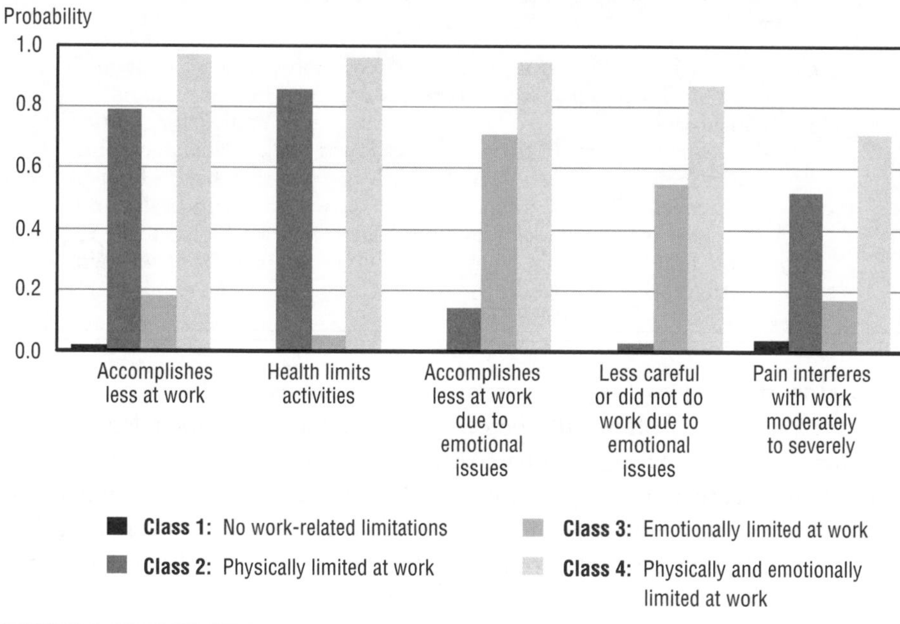

Source: Adult Literacy and Life Skills Survey, 2003.

Box 11C

Classifying adults' work related health status

Five questions from the ALL questionnaire (see Annex 11B) were combined to create a work-related health status variable using the Latent Class Analyses method. The resulting four latent classes relating to health status at work can be interpreted as follows:

- Class 1 is labelled as a group with "no work-related limitations". It represents the healthiest group of adults, accounting for 76 per cent of the pooled sample. Adults in this group overwhelmingly report that they are not limited in their activities or accomplishments at work by any physical or emotional issues. In addition, there is a low likelihood that individuals in this group report they suffer from any pain that interferes with their work.
- Class 2 is labelled as a group that reports being "physically limited at work". It represents about 12 per cent of the pooled sample. This group has a high likelihood of reporting that their health limits the work they are able to accomplish. However, they have a low likelihood of reporting any emotional issues that may detract from their work.

- Class 3 is labelled as a group that reports being "emotionally limited at work". It represents about nine per cent of the pooled sample. Unlike Class 2, this group is not characterized by limitations in either their activities or work-related accomplishments. However, they are reasonably likely to report limitations in activities due to emotional issues. Unlike adults in Class 2, they have a much lower likelihood of reporting moderate to severe pain related limitations with respect to work.
- Class 4 is labelled as a group that reports being "physically and emotionally limited at work". It represents about four per cent of the pooled sample. These are the least healthy adults participating in the ALL study in terms of their responses to the work-related questions. Adults in this latent class are highly likely to report that they are limited in their activities and accomplishments at work by both health and emotional issues. Unlike adults in Class 1 who are highly likely to report little or no pain, adults in this class are likely to report pain interferes with their work.

How much does the distribution of work-related health status vary by country? Figure 11.5 shows the percentages of adults by work-related health class for each participating country. Although the overall pattern is consistent across countries, there is some notable variation. For example, while 76 per cent of all participating adults are in Class 1, which predominantly report that they are not limited in their activities or accomplishments by any health or emotional issues, this varies from a low of 64 per cent among Italian speaking Swiss to a high of 85 per cent among German speaking Swiss.[2]

There is also variation among countries in terms of the percentages of adults who are likely to report their health limits their activities and accomplishments (Class 2). Here the percentages range from a low of seven per cent among Italian adults to 19 per cent in Norway. United States had about 14 per cent of their adults in this group. Adults in Canada had about 13 per cent of their adults in this group, as were Italian and French speaking Swiss adults. In comparison, only eight per cent of German speaking Swiss were likely to report that their health limits their activities (Class 2). Among adults who report that emotional issues impact their work and accomplishments (Class 3), the percentages range from a low of five per cent among German speaking Swiss to 15 per cent among Italian speaking Swiss. French speaking Swiss adults and those in the United States had 13 and 12 per cent respectively in Class 3. Among the least healthy adults in the sense that they were most likely to report health and emotional issues limited their activities and accomplishments at work (Class 4), the range was from two per cent in Bermuda to nine per cent among Italian speaking Swiss.

FIGURE 11.5

Work-related health status by country

Per cent of adults in each of four work-related health status groups by country, populations aged 16 to 65, 2003

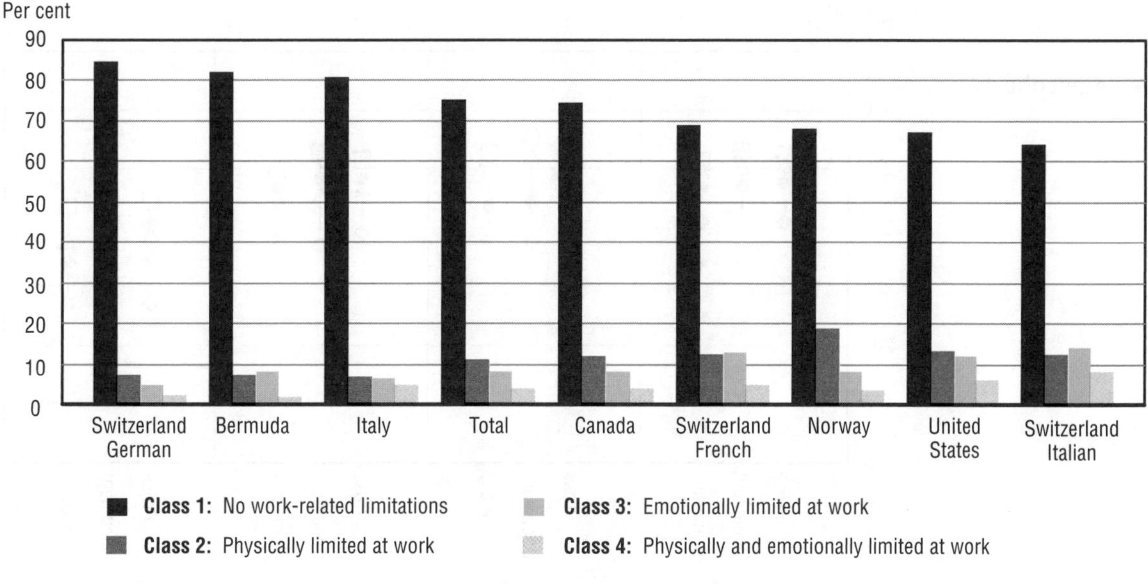

Countries are ranked by the per cent of adults in Class 1: No worked-related limitations

Source: Adult Literacy and Life Skills Survey, 2003.

Figure 11.6 shows the average literacy and numeracy scores for the total sample of adults participating in ALL by their work-related health status and selected background characteristics. The findings show substantial variation in literacy and numeracy scores among adults with various background characteristics. Adults who are classified as being the healthiest (Class 1) have the highest average literacy and numeracy scores while those who are classified as the least healthy (Class 4) have the lowest average proficiencies.

Among age cohorts the pattern is slightly different. As expected, average literacy and numeracy proficiencies begin to decrease as adults pass through the forties and into the fifties, sixties and beyond. The average difference between young and old age cohorts tends to be somewhat larger than the average difference between the most healthy (Class 1) and least healthy (Class 4) within each age cohort. With respect to their health status, the largest differences are among those adults who are classified as the least healthy (Class 4) and those in the other groups. There is little variation in skills among adults in Classes 1, 2 or 3.

The pattern found for age is similar to that observed for educational attainment. The average difference between adults with a primary or less education and those with more than upper secondary education is around 100 points. In addition, while there is little difference between adults in Classes 1, 2 or 3, there is a difference between these adults and those in Class 4, the least healthy, for every educational group.

FIGURE 11.6

Skills and work-related health status by key demographic variables

Mean scores on the prose, document and numeracy scales ranging from 0 to 500 points by key demographic variables, populations aged 16 to 65, 2003

A. Age cohorts

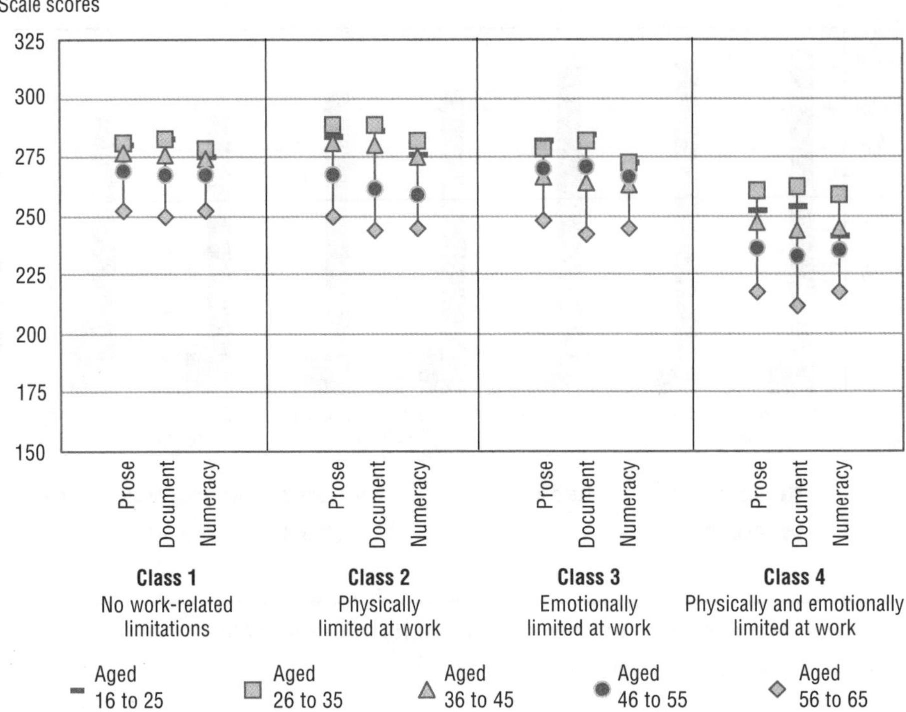

B. Educational attainment

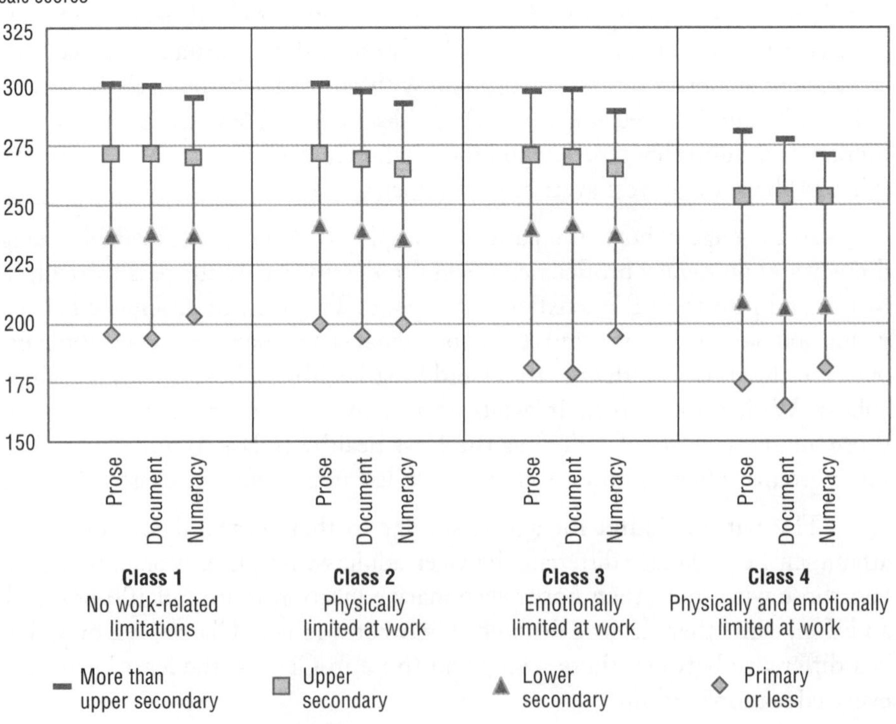

Source: Adult Literacy and Life Skills Survey, 2003.

References

Bernhardt, J.M., Brownfield, E.D. and Parker, R. (2005), "Understanding Health Literacy", in J.G. Schwartzberg, J.B. VanGeest and C.C. Wang (eds.), *Understanding Health Literacy: Implications for Medicine and Public Health,* American Medical Association, United States.

Institute of Medicine of the National Academies (2004), *Health Literacy: A Prescription to End Confusion,* The National Academies Press, Washington, DC.

Kirsch, I., Jungeblut, A., Jenkins, L. and Kolstad, A. (1993), *Adult Literacy in America: A First Look at the Results of the National Adult Literacy Survey,* US Department of Education, National Center for Education Statistics, Washington, DC.

Lazerfield, P.F. and Henry, N.W. (1968), *Latent Structure Analysis,* Houghton Miflin, Boston.

OECD and Statistics Canada (2000), *Literacy in the Information Age: Final Report of the International Adult Literacy Survey,* Paris and Ottawa.

Patterson, B., Dayton, C.M. and Graubard, B. (2002), "Latent Class Analysis of Complex Survey Data: application to dietary data", *Journal of the American Statistical Association*, Vol. 97, pp. 721-729.

Rudd, R., Kirsch, I. and Yamamoto, K. (2004), *Literacy and Health in America. A Policy Information Center Report,* Educational Testing Service, Princeton, NJ.

Schwartzberg, J.G., VanGeest, J.B. and Wang, C.C. (2005), *Understanding Health Literacy: Implications for Medicine and Public Health,* American Medical Association, United States.

Weiss, B.D. (2005), "Epidemiology of Low Health Literacy", in J.G. Schwartzberg, J.B. VanGeest and C.C. Wang (eds.), *Understanding Health Literacy: Implications for Medicine and Public Health,* American Medical Association, United States.

Willms, J.D. (2003), *Variation in Literacy Skill Among Canadian Provinces,* Statistics Canada, Ottawa.

Contributors

Irwin S. Kirsch, *Educational Testing Service*

Matthias von Davier, *Educational Testing Service*

Endnotes

1. For more information on NALS see Kirsch *et al.* (1993) and for more information on the IALS, see OECD and Statistics Canada (2000).
2. The amount of variation seen within a country like Switzerland may be due in part to error variance that results from estimating their latent classes based on relatively small samples.

Annex 11A

Data Values for the Figures

TABLE 11.1

Response profiles in the four latent classes based on general health status, populations aged 16 to 65, 2003

	Size of class	Satisfied or extremely satisfied with life	General health is very good or excellent	Health does not limit moderate activities	Health does not limit climbing stairs	Feel calm and peaceful most or all of the time	Lots of energy most or all of the time	Feel blue little or none of the time	Health or emotions limits social activities little or none of the time
					Probability				
Class 1									
Excellent health	19.6	0.97	0.86	0.98	0.98	0.90	0.92	0.95	0.98
Class 2									
Good health	51.6	0.94	0.67	0.95	0.95	0.67	0.58	0.87	0.97
Class 3									
Fair health	20.3	0.59	0.34	0.90	0.90	0.18	0.20	0.38	0.68
Class 4									
Poor health	8.4	0.43	0.08	0.15	0.19	0.33	0.14	0.42	0.42

Source: Adult Literacy and Life Skills Survey, 2003.

TABLE 11.2

Per cent of adults in each of four general health status groups by country, populations aged 16 to 65, 2003

	Class 1		Class 2		Class 3		Class 4	
Countries	Excellent health		Good health		Fair health		Poor health	
Bermuda	23.8	(1.0)	53.5	(1.0)	17.3	(0.8)	5.5	(0.6)
Canada	17.8	(0.6)	52.1	(0.8)	21.3	(0.6)	8.9	(0.4)
Italy	23.7	(1.0)	45.2	(1.4)	22.8	(1.0)	8.3	(0.4)
Norway	20.9	(0.7)	49.5	(0.9)	19.0	(0.5)	10.5	(0.5)
Switzerland (French)	9.5	(1.0)	53.3	(1.9)	29.7	(1.6)	7.4	(0.8)
Switzerland (German)	19.8	(1.3)	61.8	(1.6)	14.4	(0.8)	3.9	(0.9)
Switzerland (Italian)	26.7	(1.5)	41.8	(1.9)	24.6	(1.2)	6.8	(0.7)
United States	14.0	(0.6)	50.3	(1.1)	23.1	(0.8)	12.5	(0.7)
Total	19.6	(0.4)	51.6	(0.5)	20.3	(0.3)	8.4	(0.2)

Source: Adult Literacy and Life Skills Survey, 2003.

TABLE 11.3

Mean scores on the prose, document and numeracy scales ranging from 0 to 500 points by key demographic variables, populations aged 16 to 65, 2003

	Class 1: Excellent health						Class 2: Good health					
	Prose		Document		Numeracy		Prose		Document		Numeracy	
Total	264.7	(1.1)	265.2	(1.2)	264.7	(1.0)	279.8	(0.7)	279.6	(0.7)	276.6	(0.7)
Gender												
Male	262.1	(1.5)	266.4	(1.6)	269.3	(1.4)	277.6	(0.9)	282.4	(0.9)	283.8	(0.9)
Female	268.3	(1.4)	263.6	(1.6)	258.5	(1.6)	282.0	(0.8)	276.7	(0.9)	269.4	(0.9)
Age												
16 to 25	267.6	(2.2)	270.4	(2.3)	265.4	(2.3)	286.0	(1.4)	288.6	(1.5)	280.8	(1.9)
26 to 35	271.8	(2.4)	275.2	(2.1)	273.2	(1.7)	287.1	(1.6)	287.9	(1.3)	283.4	(1.6)
36 to 45	267.6	(2.5)	266.8	(2.4)	267.1	(2.4)	282.5	(1.1)	281.7	(1.1)	280.0	(1.1)
46 to 55	262.6	(2.3)	262.5	(2.4)	262.6	(2.4)	275.6	(1.6)	273.9	(1.9)	273.0	(1.9)
56 to 65	250.8	(2.1)	247.7	(2.5)	252.3	(1.6)	260.3	(1.5)	257.4	(1.8)	258.5	(1.7)
Education level												
More than upper secondary	293.5	(1.7)	294.5	(1.7)	291.7	(1.5)	305.1	(1.0)	304.3	(1.0)	298.7	(1.0)
Upper secondary	263.6	(1.8)	263.6	(2.1)	263.9	(1.8)	276.0	(1.0)	276.0	(1.0)	274.0	(1.1)
Lower secondary	230.6	(2.4)	231.3	(2.3)	231.6	(2.6)	244.1	(1.7)	245.3	(1.8)	242.9	(1.6)
Primary or less	189.6	(4.6)	190.2	(5.6)	196.8	(4.8)	206.2	(3.3)	204.2	(3.4)	214.0	(2.9)
Nativity												
Native	266.2	(1.2)	266.3	(1.4)	266.1	(1.0)	281.9	(0.6)	281.6	(0.7)	278.1	(0.7)
Non-native	257.5	(3.1)	260.1	(2.8)	258.3	(2.8)	278.1	(2.0)	277.9	(2.1)	274.6	(1.9)

	Class 3: Fair health						Class 4: Poor health					
	Prose		Document		Numeracy		Prose		Document		Numeracy	
Total	270.0	(1.2)	269.3	(1.2)	264.2	(1.3)	243.0	(1.8)	239.8	(1.7)	237.4	(1.6)
Gender												
Male	268.3	(1.7)	272.6	(1.6)	272.4	(1.6)	237.5	(2.6)	239.3	(3.0)	240.7	(2.8)
Female	271.3	(1.5)	266.8	(1.6)	257.7	(1.6)	246.5	(2.3)	240.1	(2.2)	235.3	(2.1)
Age												
16 to 25	280.6	(2.3)	281.9	(2.9)	271.1	(3.1)	255.6	(7.7)	258.9	(8.1)	242.8	(6.5)
26 to 35	276.9	(1.7)	279.7	(2.1)	273.1	(1.7)	264.8	(4.6)	263.0	(4.5)	255.6	(4.1)
36 to 45	272.7	(2.8)	271.2	(2.6)	266.8	(2.6)	251.8	(3.4)	249.7	(3.7)	245.5	(2.6)
46 to 55	265.1	(2.4)	261.5	(2.2)	258.0	(2.1)	243.5	(3.3)	240.0	(3.4)	240.1	(2.8)
56 to 65	239.4	(2.3)	235.2	(2.5)	238.5	(2.8)	225.3	(2.8)	219.4	(2.7)	221.2	(2.4)
Education level												
More than upper secondary	298.9	(1.5)	299.2	(1.6)	290.7	(1.9)	281.3	(2.9)	276.5	(2.9)	268.6	(2.8)
Upper secondary	273.8	(1.6)	272.5	(1.9)	266.6	(1.6)	253.9	(2.6)	251.3	(3.1)	248.5	(2.8)
Lower secondary	236.5	(2.4)	236.9	(2.1)	234.5	(2.6)	218.0	(3.4)	214.7	(3.7)	212.4	(3.4)
Primary or less	185.3	(3.2)	179.8	(3.4)	191.0	(3.7)	180.8	(4.6)	175.8	(5.2)	187.9	(4.3)
Nativity												
Native	270.8	(1.3)	269.4	(1.4)	264.3	(1.4)	245.3	(1.8)	241.7	(1.8)	238.6	(1.7)
Non-native	265.3	(3.3)	268.9	(2.9)	263.3	(2.8)	230.6	(5.5)	229.4	(4.8)	231.1	(4.0)

Note: See Box 11B in text for a description of Class 1 to Class 4 of health status.

Source: Adult Literacy and Life Skills Survey, 2003.

TABLE 11.4

Response profiles in the four latent classes based on work-related health status, populations aged 16 to 65, 2003

	Size of class	Accomp-lishes less at work	Health limits activities	Accomplishes less at work due to emo-tional issues	Less careful or didn't do work due to emo-tional issues	Pain interferes with work moderately to severely
	Per cent			Probability		
Class 1						
No work-related limitations	75.7	0.02	0.00	0.00	0.00	0.04
Class 2						
Physically limited at work	11.5	0.79	0.86	0.14	0.03	0.52
Class 3						
Emotionally limited at work	8.7	0.18	0.05	0.71	0.55	0.17
Class 4						
Physically and emotionally limited at work	4.1	0.97	0.96	0.95	0.87	0.71

Source: Adult Literacy and Life Skills Survey, 2003.

TABLE 11.5

Per cent of adults in each of four work-related health status groups by country, populations aged 16 to 65, 2003

	Class 1		Class 2		Class 3		Class 4	
Countries	No work-related limitations		Physically limited at work		Emotionally limited at work		Physically and emotionally limited at work	
Bermuda	82.2	(1.0)	7.5	(0.6)	8.4	(0.7)	2.0	(0.3)
Canada	74.8	(0.5)	12.5	(0.3)	8.4	(0.4)	4.3	(0.3)
Italy	81.2	(1.0)	7.2	(0.5)	6.7	(0.6)	4.9	(0.5)
Norway	68.4	(0.8)	19.0	(0.6)	8.6	(0.5)	3.9	(0.3)
Switzerland (French)	69.2	(2.2)	12.8	(1.3)	13.0	(1.3)	5.0	(0.8)
Switzerland (German)	84.8	(1.1)	7.6	(0.7)	5.2	(0.7)	2.4	(0.6)
Switzerland (Italian)	64.4	(1.2)	12.6	(1.1)	14.5	(1.0)	8.5	(1.1)
United States	67.6	(1.3)	13.7	(0.7)	12.4	(0.7)	6.4	(0.5)
Total	75.7	(0.5)	11.5	(0.2)	8.7	(0.2)	4.1	(0.2)

Source: Adult Literacy and Life Skills Survey, 2003.

TABLE 11.6

Mean scores on the prose, document and numeracy scales ranging from 0 to 500 points by key demographic variables, populations aged 16 to 65, 2003

	Class 1: No work-related limitations						Class 2: Physically limited at work					
	Prose		Document		Numeracy		Prose		Document		Numeracy	
Total	273.4	(0.7)	273.4	(0.6)	270.9	(0.6)	272.9	(1.3)	270.1	(1.3)	265.9	(1.6)
Gender												
Male	271.4	(0.9)	276.0	(0.9)	277.5	(0.8)	268.9	(2.1)	272.0	(2.2)	272.2	(2.3)
Female	275.6	(0.8)	270.6	(0.7)	263.7	(0.8)	276.0	(1.7)	268.7	(1.8)	260.8	(2.0)
Age												
16 to 25	280.1	(1.2)	282.4	(1.3)	275.1	(1.7)	283.6	(3.5)	286.4	(3.7)	276.1	(4.2)
26 to 35	280.9	(1.2)	282.6	(1.0)	278.9	(0.9)	289.0	(2.5)	288.8	(2.3)	282.0	(2.6)
36 to 45	276.9	(1.1)	276.2	(1.1)	274.2	(1.0)	281.4	(2.5)	279.9	(2.8)	274.8	(2.2)
46 to 55	269.2	(1.3)	267.8	(1.3)	267.1	(1.3)	267.8	(2.4)	261.8	(2.9)	259.1	(2.9)
56 to 65	252.3	(1.4)	249.6	(1.5)	251.9	(1.1)	249.8	(2.9)	243.8	(3.1)	244.6	(2.9)
Education level												
More than upper secondary	301.2	(0.8)	301.0	(0.9)	295.7	(0.8)	301.2	(1.9)	298.1	(1.9)	292.7	(2.0)
Upper secondary	272.2	(0.9)	272.0	(0.8)	270.2	(0.9)	272.3	(2.2)	269.7	(2.4)	265.2	(2.5)
Lower secondary	237.7	(1.4)	238.7	(1.5)	237.1	(1.4)	241.8	(2.7)	238.8	(3.3)	236.1	(3.4)
Primary or less	195.7	(2.0)	193.9	(2.3)	203.4	(2.6)	199.3	(5.9)	194.3	(5.8)	199.4	(5.5)
Nativity												
Native	275.1	(0.7)	274.8	(0.6)	272.0	(0.6)	274.3	(1.4)	271.2	(1.6)	266.7	(1.6)
Non-native	270.0	(1.6)	271.3	(1.7)	268.0	(1.4)	262.6	(3.6)	262.3	(4.0)	259.7	(3.5)

	Class 3: Emotionally limited at work						Class 4: Physically and emotionally limited at work					
	Prose		Document		Numeracy		Prose		Document		Numeracy	
Total	271.8	(1.7)	272.1	(1.3)	266.3	(1.5)	238.4	(2.7)	235.7	(3.0)	236.2	(2.5)
Gender												
Male	268.9	(2.6)	273.4	(2.3)	273.2	(2.3)	232.9	(3.8)	235.9	(4.8)	241.8	(3.5)
Female	274.1	(2.2)	271.2	(1.9)	260.9	(2.4)	241.5	(3.5)	235.7	(3.6)	233.1	(3.1)
Age												
16 to 25	281.9	(3.1)	284.1	(3.2)	272.3	(3.4)	252.5	(11.9)	254.1	(10.1)	241.5	(9.0)
26 to 35	278.9	(2.9)	281.9	(3.6)	272.6	(3.5)	260.8	(5.9)	262.8	(7.1)	259.3	(5.8)
36 to 45	266.3	(3.5)	264.0	(2.7)	262.9	(2.9)	246.8	(4.4)	244.2	(5.1)	244.5	(5.1)
46 to 55	269.9	(5.8)	271.2	(5.9)	266.5	(4.1)	236.3	(4.4)	232.9	(4.6)	235.4	(4.1)
56 to 65	248.0	(5.6)	242.2	(4.6)	245.0	(4.9)	217.7	(3.5)	212.1	(4.0)	217.4	(4.0)
Education level												
More than upper secondary	298.3	(3.0)	299.1	(3.1)	289.8	(2.6)	281.1	(4.2)	277.8	(3.5)	271.5	(3.8)
Upper secondary	271.1	(2.2)	270.4	(2.4)	265.1	(2.2)	253.6	(2.2)	253.2	(3.0)	253.2	(3.0)
Lower secondary	239.9	(4.1)	242.1	(4.1)	237.5	(3.0)	209.2	(3.5)	206.5	(3.8)	206.8	(3.5)
Primary or less	181.0	(13.5)	178.8	(14.9)	194.2	(7.3)	174.1	(6.1)	165.5	(6.6)	181.1	(6.4)
Nativity												
Native	273.8	(1.6)	274.0	(1.6)	267.6	(1.7)	239.4	(2.7)	235.8	(2.9)	236.3	(2.6)
Non-native	261.8	(5.5)	262.8	(4.8)	259.4	(3.9)	233.1	(6.3)	235.5	(8.0)	235.8	(6.7)

Note: See Box 11C in text for a description of Class 1 to Class 4 of work-related health status.

Source: Adult Literacy and Life Skills Survey, 2003.

Annex 11B

Work-Related and General Health Questions from ALL

G13A Because of your health, do you accomplish less at work…
G13B Health limits kind of work or activities …
G14A Accomplish less because of emotional problems
G14B Didn't do work or other activities as careful because of emotional…

Value	Label
1	Yes
2	No
8	Refused
9	Not stated

G15 How much did pain interfere with work?

Value	Label
1	Not at all
2	A little bit
3	Moderately
4	Quite a bit
5	Extremely
8	Refused
9	Not stated

G10 General feeling about your life?

Value	Label
1	Extremely satisfied
2	Satisfied
3	Neither satisfied nor dissatisfied
4	Unsatisfied
5	Extremely unsatisfied

Value Label

6 No opinion

8 Refused

9 Not stated

G11 In general, how is your health?

Value Label

1 Excellent

2 Very good

3 Good

4 Fair

5 Poor

8 Refused

9 Not stated

G12A Does your health limit moderate activities

G12B Does your health limit climbing stairs?

Value Label

1 Yes, limited a lot

2 Yes, limited a little

3 No, not at all limited

8 Refused

9 Not stated

G16A Feeling calm and peaceful?

G16B Did you have a lot of energy?

G16C Have felt downhearted and blue?

Value Label

1 All of the time

2 Most of the time

3 A good bit of the time

4 Some of the time

5 A little of the time

6 None of the time

8 Refused

9 Not stated

G17 Physical and emotional problems interfered with social activities?

Value Label

1 All of the time

2 Most of the time

3 Some of the time

4 A little of the time

5 None of the time

8 Refused

9 Not stated

Conclusion

Directions for further work

This report confirms many of the conclusions revealed through analysis of IALS data, including:

- Larges differences in skills exist both within and between countries.
- Most of the differences in the level and distribution of skill can be explained using the variables that are available from the study background questionnaire. These include social background, education and a range of variables that reflect how adults lead their lives.
- The differences in the level and distribution of skill are associated with large differences in outcomes in multiple life domains – work, education, home and the community.

This report also reveals a number of new insights including:

- Evidence of significant changes in the distribution of skill by skill level that differ by country and by age. Although changes in mean country performance are not substantial, the results show some improvement among the five per cent of adults with the lowest scores. There is also some evidence of skill loss in some population sub-group.
- Large differences within and between countries in the intensity of ICT use were observed. In some countries, respondents with medium to high literacy skills have between two and three times the odds of being high intensity computer user. This has implications for future wage inequality, given the strong relationship observed between literacy, high ICT use and income.
- General health status and health status at work both appear to be strongly related to literacy.

As mentioned at the outset, the ALL study also makes it possible to explore patterns of individual strength and weakness among the four skill domains assessed by the ALL. The fact that large numbers of adults in each country display weakness in multiple skill domains is a matter of serious concern. Figure C1 reveals, however, that the pattern of skill weakness varies considerably by country.

FIGURE C1

The depth of risk

Number of adults aged 16 to 65 at Levels 1 and 2 in prose literacy, document literacy and numeracy as a per cent of the total population at Level 1 and 2 in any domain by country, 2003

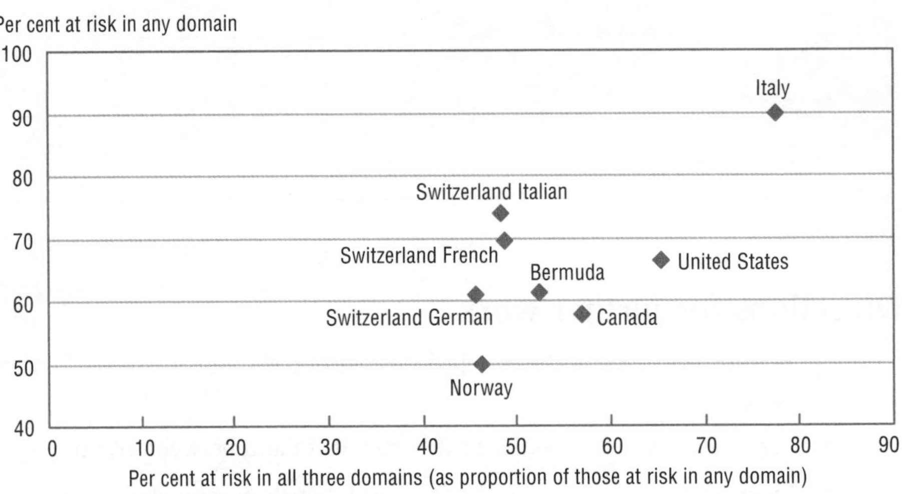

Source: Adult Literacy and Life Skills Survey, 2003.

Information on patterns of disadvantage provides useful input for the design of remedial education programs. Precisely what the policy prescription would be for each country will need to be the subject of focused national analysis, using the ALL data set. The purpose of this conclusion, therefore, is not to explore policy directions or options for countries to pursue. Rather the goal is to highlight priorities for further analysis of the ALL data and to identify missing data elements that must be addressed by future comparative surveys of adult skills.

Priorities for further analysis

As revealed in Figure C1 there are significant proportions of adults in all countries who display serious weaknesses in multiple skill domains. Thus, there is an urgent need to analyze the complementarity and substitutability of different skills clusters. It is not at all clear whether ad hoc part time workplace or informal approaches will yield the desired skill gains. There is a particular need to clarify this issue for vulnerable groups such as language minorities, immigrants and indigenous populations

The findings show that the high ICT use requires prior literacy and numeracy skill. ICT skills, in turn, amplify the productivity effects of capital and labour and hence drive inequality in wages. Thus any attempt to mitigate the digital divide must first address shortcomings in literacy and numeracy (Kirsch and Lennon, 2002). Thus more in-depth analysis is required to understand the link between the skills measured in ALL and industrial and occupational segmentation and productivity growth.

The countries surveyed here differ greatly in the investments they are making to support formal, non-formal and informal learning. These differences in strategy are often the result of unintended consequences of differing assumptions about the balance of skill demand and supply, in particular, the extent to which the initial education system can satisfy the skill requirements of labour markets. It has often been assumed that informal learning at work and in daily life can mitigate skill shortages. The ALL findings would seem to challenge this assumption but further analysis is required to understand the interaction between different modes of adult learning and especially the role of the workplace in skill formation.

The relationships between literacy, numeracy, health status, and various labour market outcomes are sufficiently strong to posit that investments in foundation skills would lead to improved levels of health, increased productivity, reduced social costs, and higher growth. Further analysis could attempt to identify separately the direct and indirect effects of literacy and numeracy on health.

Analyses of the IALS data have revealed much larger than expected effects of foundation skills on long-term macro-economic growth (Coulombe, Tremblay and Marchand, 2004). Yet there still remains considerable doubt about the relationship between literacy and numeracy and higher order skills, and how skill hierarchies precipitate growth. A large challenge for further analysis is therefore to undertake macro-economic growth modelling while disentangling the direct and mediated effects of different types of skill.

This report has presented the first analysis of change in skill profiles over time for the countries that collected data at two time intervals. The results point to significant skill loss in several countries. Given the high costs and returns accruing to skill development, the top priority for further work is to study the determinants of skill gain and loss.

Priorities for future adult skill assessments

Three priorities flow naturally from the findings presented above. First, there is a need to directly assess the ICT skills of workers to better understand their impact on productivity growth and individual outcomes. Second, the link between skill and health calls for a focused assessment of health literacy demands, corresponding skills, and direct observations on health indicators. Third, understanding the dynamic of skill gain and loss depends critically on a survey design that samples workers from within firms and segmented labour markets.

The *Definition and Selection of Key Competencies* (DeSeCo) programme of work (Rychen and Salganik, 2001, 2003) identifies key competencies that are essential for the personal and social development of people in modern, complex societies. Supported and endorsed by the OECD and Member states, DeSeCo provides a conceptual frame of reference to guide future adult skill assessments. It defines three skill categories: interacting in socially heterogeneous groups; acting autonomously; and using tools interactively. The ALL survey has made progress towards measuring the latter type of skill and related values and beliefs. It remains a priority for future surveys to enrich the DeSeCo conceptual framework as well as to develop more operational assessment frameworks and associated measurement instruments. The assessment of the ability to relate well to others, to co-operate, and to manage and resolve conflicts, and to act autonomously, is particularly relevant to future assessments of adult skills in pluralistic societies.

References

Coulombe, S., Tremblay, G.F. and Marchand, S. (2004), *Literacy Scores, Human Capital, and Growth across Fourteen OECD Countries,* Statistics Canada, Ottawa.

Rychen D.S. and Salganik L.H. (eds.) (2001), *Defining and Selecting Key Competencies,* Hogrefe and Huber Publishers, Göttingen.

Rychen D.S. and Salganik L.H. (eds.) (2003), *Key Competencies for a Successful Life and a Well-functioning Society,* Hogrefe and Huber Publishers, Göttingen.

Kirsch, I and Lennon, M, (2002), *Digital Transformation: A Framework for ICT Literacy. A Report of the International ICT Literacy Panel.* Educational Testing Service.

Contributors

T. Scott Murray, *Statistics Canada*

Albert Tuijnman, *European Investment Bank, Luxembourg*

Data Values for the Figures

TABLE C1

Number of adults aged 16 to 65 at Levels 1 and 2 in prose literacy, document literacy and numeracy as a per cent of the total population at Level 1 and 2 in any domain by country, 2003

	Number of domains in which individuals are at risk (Below Level 3)									
	0		1		2		3		At risk in all 3 domains as a percentage of those at risk in any domain	
Bermuda	38.8	(0.02)	16.0	(0.01)	13.1	(0.01)	32.1	(0.01)	52.5	(0.01)
Canada	42.1	(0.01)	14.5	(0.01)	10.5	(0.01)	32.9	(0.01)	56.8	(0.01)
Italy	10.3	(0.01)	8.5	(0.01)	11.7	(0.01)	69.5	(0.01)	77.4	(0.01)
Norway	50.2	(0.01)	16.0	(0.01)	10.8	(0.01)	23.1	(0.01)	46.3	(0.01)
Switzerland (French)	30.4	(0.02)	16.7	(0.02)	19.0	(0.02)	33.9	(0.02)	48.7	(0.02)
Switzerland (German)	39.1	(0.02)	15.8	(0.01)	17.3	(0.02)	27.8	(0.02)	45.6	(0.02)
Switzerland (Italian)	26.1	(0.02)	16.6	(0.01)	21.6	(0.02)	35.6	(0.01)	48.2	(0.01)
United States	33.7	(0.02)	12.3	(0.01)	10.7	(0.01)	43.3	(0.01)	65.4	(0.01)

Source: Adult Literacy and Life Skills Survey, 2003.

Annex A

A Construct-Centered approach to Understanding What was Measured in the Adult Literacy and Life Skills (ALL) Survey

A

Table of Contents

A Construct-Centered approach to Understanding What was Measured in the Adult Literacy and Life Skills (ALL) Survey

Overview

This annex offers a brief overview of the frameworks that were used to develop and interpret the scales used to measure prose and document literacy, numeracy, and problem solving in the Adult Literacy and Life Skills (ALL) survey. The importance of developing a framework is thought to be central in construct-based approaches to measurement. Among the things that should be included in any such framework are an agreed upon definition of what ought to be measured and the identification of characteristics that can be used in the construction and interpretation of tasks. In addition to describing these characteristics for each measure, this annex also includes sample items along with the identification of item features that are shown to contribute to item difficulty. Collectively this information provides a means for moving away from interpreting survey results in terms of discrete tasks or a single number and towards identifying levels of performance sufficiently generalized to have validity across assessments and groups.

Introduction

In 1992, the Organization for Economic Co-operation and Development (OECD) (OECD, 1992) concluded that low literacy levels were a serious threat to economic performance and social cohesion on an international level. But a broader understanding of literacy problems across industrialized nations – and consequent lessons for policy makers – was hindered due to a lack of comparable international data. Statistics Canada and Educational Testing Service (ETS) teamed up to build and deliver an international comparative study of literacy.

The International Adult Literacy Survey (IALS) was the first comparative survey of adults designed to profile and explore comparative literacy distributions among participating countries. In 2000, a final report was released (OECD and Statistics Canada, 2000) which included the results from three rounds of assessments involving some 23 country/language groups representing just over 50 per cent of the world's GDP. While IALS laid an important foundation for international comparative surveys of adults, there were also calls to expand what was being measured. There was a growing concern among governments and policy makers as to what additional competencies are relevant for an individual to participate fully and successfully in a modern society and for a society to meet the challenges of a rapidly changing world. One project aimed at addressing this issue was entitled *Definition and Selection of Key Competencies* (DeSeCo) and was carried out under the leadership of Switzerland. Its goal was to lay out, from a theoretical perspective, a set of key competencies that are believed to contribute to a successful life and a well-functioning society (Rychen and Salganik, 2003).

In response to these calls for broader measures, the ALL survey commissioned the development of frameworks to use as the basis for introducing new measures into the comparative assessments of adults. Those responsible for the development of ALL recognized that the design of any reliable and valid instrument should begin with a strong theoretical underpinning that is represented by a framework that characterizes current thinking in the field. According to Messick (1994) any framework that takes a construct-centered approach to assessment design should: begin with a general definition or statement of purpose – one that guides the rationale for the survey and what should be measured in terms of knowledge, skills or other attributes; identify various performances or behaviours that will reveal those constructs, and; identify task characteristics and indicate how these characteristics will be used in constructing the tasks that will elicit those behaviours.

This annex provides an overview of the frameworks used to develop tasks that measure prose and document literacy, numeracy, and problem solving in the ALL survey. In characterizing these frameworks this annex also provides a scheme for understanding the meaning of what has been measured in ALL and for interpreting levels along each of the scales. It borrows liberally from more detailed chapters that were developed in conjunction with the ALL survey (Murray, Clermont and Binkley, in press).

Scaling the literacy, numeracy and problem solving tasks in ALL

The results of the ALL survey are reported along four scales – two literacy scales (prose and document), a single numeracy scale, and a scale capturing problem solving – with each ranging from 0 to 500 points. One might imagine these tasks arranged along their respective scale in terms of their difficulty for adults and the level of proficiency needed to respond correctly to each task. The procedure used in ALL to model these continua of difficulty and ability is Item Response Theory (IRT). IRT is a mathematical model used for estimating the probability that a particular person will respond correctly to a given task from a specified pool of tasks (Murray, Kirsch and Jenkins, 1998).

The scale value assigned to each item results from how representative samples of adults in participating countries perform on each item and is based on the theory that someone at a given point on the scale is equally proficient in all tasks at that point on the scale. For the ALL survey, as for the IALS, proficiency was determined to mean that someone at a particular point on the proficiency scale would have an 80 per cent chance of answering items at that point correctly.

Just as adults within each participating country in ALL are sampled from the population of adults living in households, each task that was constructed and used in the assessment represents a type of task sampled from the domain or construct defined here. Hence, it is representative of a particular type of literacy, numeracy or problem solving task that is associated with adult contexts.

One obvious question that arises once one looks at the distributions of tasks along each of the described scales is, what distinguishes tasks at the lower end of each scale from those in the middle and upper ranges of the scale? Do tasks, that fall around the same place on each scale share some set of characteristics that result in their having similar levels of difficulty? Even a cursory review of the items reveals that tasks at the lower end of each scale differ from those at the higher end.

In an attempt to display this progression of complexity and difficulty, each proficiency scale was divided into levels. Both the literacy and numeracy scales used five levels where Level 1 represents the lowest level of proficiency and Level 5 the highest. These levels are defined as follows: Level 1 (0-225), Level 2 (226-275), Level 3 (276-325), Level 4 (326-375) and Level 5 (376-500). The scale for problem solving used four levels where Level 1 is the lowest level of proficiency and Level 4 the highest. These four levels are defined as follows: Level 1 (0-250), Level 2 (251–300), Level 3 (301–350), and Level 4 (351–500).

Since each level represents a progression of knowledge and skills, individuals within a particular level not only demonstrate the knowledge and skills associated with that level but the proficiencies associated with the lower levels as well. In practical terms, this means that individuals performing at 250 (the middle of Level 2 on one of the literacy or numeracy scales) are expected to be able to perform the average Level 1 and Level 2 task with a high degree of proficiency. A comparable point on the problem solving scale would be 275. In ALL, as in IALS, a high degree of proficiency is defined in terms of a response probability of 80 (RP80).[1] This means that individuals estimated to have a particular scale score are expected to perform tasks at that point on the scale correctly with an 80 per cent probability. It also means they will have a greater than 80 per cent chance of performing tasks that are lower on the scale. It does not mean, however, that individuals with given proficiencies can never succeed at tasks with higher difficulty values; they may do so some of the time. It does suggest that their probability of success is "relatively" low – i.e., the more difficult the task relative to their proficiency, the lower the likelihood of a correct response.

An analogy might help clarify this point. The relationship between task difficulty and individual proficiency is much like the high jump event in track and field, in which an athlete tries to jump over a bar that is placed at increasing heights. Each high jumper has a height at which he or she is proficient – that is, the jumper can clear the bar at that height with a high probability of success, and can clear the bar at lower heights almost every time. When the bar is higher than the athlete's level of proficiency, however, it is expected that the athlete will be unable to clear the bar consistently.

Measuring prose and document literacy in ALL

Defining prose and document literacy

The National Adult Literacy Survey (NALS), which was funded by the National Center for Education Statistics (NCES) as part of its overall assessment program in adult literacy, was the largest and most comprehensive study of adult literacy ever conducted in the United States (Kirsch, Jungeblut, Jenkins and Kolstad, 1993). Like all large-scale assessments funded by NCES, NALS was guided by a committee, which was comprised of a group of nationally recognized scholars, practitioners, and administrators who adopted the following definition of literacy:

> *"Literacy is using printed and written information to function in society, to achieve one's goals, and to develop one's knowledge and potential."*

This definition captures the initial work of the committee guiding the development of the assessment and provides the basis for creating other aspects of the framework to be discussed. It was also reviewed and adopted by the countries participating in the first round of IALS and was carried forward in ALL. This definition includes several assumptions made by panel members and, thus, it is important to consider various parts of this definition in turn.

Beginning with "*Literacy is…*", the term literacy is used in preference to "reading" because it is likely to convey more precisely to a non-expert audience what the survey is measuring. "Reading" is often understood as simply decoding, or reading aloud, whereas the intention of the adult surveys is to measure something broader and deeper. Researchers studying literacy within particular contexts noted that different cultures and groups may value different kinds of literacy practices (Sticht, 1975; Heath, 1980; Szwed, 1981). Heath, for example, found that uses for reading could be described in terms of instrumental, social interactional, news-related, memory supportive, substitutes for oral messages, provision of a permanent record, and personal confirmation. The fact that people read different materials for different purposes implies a range of proficiencies that may not be well captured by signing one's name, completing a certain number of years of schooling, or scoring at an 8th-grade level on a test of academic reading comprehension.

The phrase "… *using printed and written information*" draws attention to the fact that panel members view literacy not as a set of isolated skills associated with reading and writing, but more importantly as the application of those skills for specific purposes in specific contexts. When literacy is studied within varying contexts, diversity becomes its hallmark. First, people engage in literacy behaviours for a variety of uses or purposes (Sticht, 1978; Heath, 1980; Cook-Gumperz and Gumperz, 1981; Mikulecky, 1982). These uses vary across contexts (Heath, 1980; Venezky, 1983) and among people within the same context (Kirsch and Guthrie, 1984a). This variation in use leads to an interaction with a broad range of materials that have qualitatively different linguistic forms (Diehl, 1980; Jacob, 1982; Miller, 1982). In some cases, these different types of literacy tasks have been associated with different cognitive strategies or reading behaviours (Sticht, 1978, 1982; Crandall, 1981; Scribner and Cole, 1981; Kirsch and Guthrie, 1984b).

The phrase "… *to function in society, to achieve one's goals, and to develop one's knowledge and potential*" is meant to capture the full scope of situations in which literacy plays a role in the lives of adults, from private to public, from school to work, to lifelong learning and active citizenship. "To achieve one's goals and to develop one's knowledge and potential" points to the view that literacy enables the fulfillment of individual aspirations—those that are defined such as graduation or obtaining a job, and those less defined and less immediate which extend and enrich one's personal life. The phrase "to function in society" is meant to acknowledge that literacy provides individuals with a means of contributing to as well as benefiting from society. Literacy skills are generally recognized as important for nations to maintain or improve their standard of living and to compete in an increasingly global market place. Yet, they are equally as important for individual participation in technologically advancing societies with their formal institutions, complex legal systems, and large government programs.

Identifying task characteristics

The task characteristics represent variables that can be used in a variety of ways in developing an assessment and interpreting the results. Almond and Mislevy (1998) have identified five roles that variables can take on. They can be used to limit the scope of the assessment, characterize the features that should be used for constructing tasks, control the assembly of tasks into booklets or test forms, characterise examinees' performance on or responses to tasks, or help to characterise aspects of competencies or proficiencies. IALS focused on variables that can be used to help in the construction of tasks as well as in the characterization of performance along one or more proficiency scales.

Each task in the assessment represents a piece of evidence about a person's literacy (Mislevy, 2000). While the goal of the assessment will be to develop the best possible picture of an individual's skills and abilities, the test cannot include an infinite number of tasks nor can an infinite number of features of those tasks be manipulated. Therefore, decisions need to be made about which features should be part of the test development process. Three task characteristics were identified and used in the construction of tasks for the IALS. These characteristics include:

Adult contexts/content. Since adults do not read written or printed materials in a vacuum, but read within a particular context or for a particular purpose, materials for the literacy assessment are selected that represent a variety of contexts and contents. This is to help ensure that no one group of adults is either advantaged or disadvantaged due to the context or content included in the assessment. Six adult context/content categories have been identified as follows:

- Home and family: may include materials dealing with interpersonal relationships, personal finance, housing, and insurance.
- Health and safety: may include materials dealing with drugs and alcohol, disease prevention and treatment, safety and accident prevention, first aid, emergencies, and staying healthy.
- Community and citizenship: may include materials dealing with staying informed and community resources.
- Consumer economics: may include materials dealing with credit and banking, savings, advertising, making purchases, and maintaining personal possessions.

- Work: may include materials that deal in general with various occupations but not job specific texts, finding employment, finance, and being on the job.
- Leisure and recreation: may include materials involving travel, recreational activities, and restaurants.

Materials/texts. While no one would doubt that a literacy assessment should include a range of material, what is critical to the design and interpretation of the scores that are produced are the range and specific features of the text material which are included in constructing the tasks. A key distinction among texts that is at the heart of the IALS survey is their classification into continuous and non-continuous texts. Conventionally, continuous texts are formed of sentences organized into paragraphs. In these texts, organization occurs by paragraph setting, indentation, and the breakdown of text into a hierarchy signalled by headings that help the reader to recognize the organization of the text. The primary classification of continuous texts is by rhetorical purpose or text type. For IALS, these included: expository, descriptive, argumentative, and injunctive.

Non-continuous texts are organized differently than continuous texts and so allow the reader to employ different strategies for entering and extracting information from them. On the surface, these texts appear to have many different organizational patterns or formats, ranging from tables and schedules to charts and graphs, and from maps to forms. However, the organizational pattern for these types of texts, which Mosenthal and Kirsch (1998) refer to as documents, is said to have one of four basic structures: a simple list; a combined list; an intersected list; and a nested list. Together, these four types of documents make up what they have called matrix documents, or non-continuous texts with clearly defined rows and columns. They are also closely related to other non-continuous texts that these authors refer to as graphic, locative, and entry documents.

The distinction between continuous and non-continuous texts formed the basis for two of the three literacy scales used in IALS. Continuous texts were the basis for tasks that were placed along the prose scale while non-continuous texts formed the basis for tasks along the document scale. The quantitative scale included texts that were both continuous and non-continuous. The distinguishing characteristic for this scale was that respondents needed to identify and perform one or more arithmetic operations based on information contained in the texts. This scale was replaced in ALL with the numeracy scale, which is discussed in more detail later in this annex.

Processes/strategies. This task characteristic refers to the way in which examinees process text to respond correctly to a question or directive. It includes the processes used to relate information in the question (the given information) to the necessary information in the text (the new information) as well as the processes needed to either identify or construct the correct response from the information available. Three variables used to investigate tasks from national and international surveys will be summarized here. These are: type of match, type of information requested, and plausibility of distracting information.

Type of match

Four types of matching strategies were identified: locating, cycling, integrating, and generating. *Locating* tasks require examinees to match one or more features of information stated in the question to either identical or synonymous information provided in the text. *Cycling* tasks also require examinees to match one or more features of information, but unlike locating tasks, they require respondents to engage in a series of feature matches to satisfy conditions stated in the question.

Integrating tasks require examinees to pull together two or more pieces of information from the text according to some type of specified relation. For example, this relation might call for examinees to identify similarities (i.e., make a comparison), differences (i.e., contrast), degree (i.e., smaller or larger), or cause-and-effect relations. This information may be located within a single paragraph or it may appear in different paragraphs or sections of the text. In integrating information, examinees draw upon information categories provided in a question to locate the corresponding information in the text. They then relate the text information associated with these different categories based upon the relation term specified in the question. In some cases, however, examinees must *generate* these categories and/or relations before integrating the information stated in the text.

In addition to requiring examinees to apply one of these four strategies, the type of match between a question and the text is influenced by several other processing conditions which contribute to a task's overall difficulty. The first of these is the number of phrases that must be used in the search. Task difficulty increases with the amount of information in the question for which the examinee must search in the text. For instance, questions that consist of only one independent clause tend to be easier, on average, than those that contain several independent or dependent clauses. Difficulty also increases with the number of responses that examinees are asked to provide. Questions that request a single answer are easier than those that require three or more answers. Further, questions which specify the number of responses tend to be easier than those that do not. For example, a question which states, "List the 3 reasons..." would be easier than one which said, "List the reasons...". Tasks are also influenced by the degree to which examinees have to make inferences to match the given information in a question to corresponding information in the text, and to identify the requested information.

Type of information requested

This refers to the kinds of information that readers need to identify to answer a test question successfully. The more concrete the requested information, the easier the task is judged to be. In previous research based on large-scale assessments of adults' and children's literacy (Kirsch and Mosenthal, 1994; Kirsch, Jungeblut, and Mosenthal, 1998), the type of information variable was scored on a 5-point scale. A score of one represented information that was the most concrete and therefore the easiest to process, while a score of five represented information that was the most abstract and therefore the most difficult to process.

For instance, questions which asked examinees to identify a person, animal, or thing (i.e., imaginable nouns) were said to request highly concrete information and were assigned a value of one. Questions asking respondents to identify goals, conditions, or purposes were said to request more abstract types of information. Such tasks were judged to be more difficult and received a value of three. Questions that required examinees to identify an "equivalent" were judged to be the most abstract and were assigned a value of five. In such cases, the equivalent tended to be an unfamiliar term or phrase for which respondents had to infer a definition or interpretation from the text.

Plausibility of distractors

This concerns the extent to which information in the text shares one or more features with the information requested in the question but does not fully satisfy what has been requested. Tasks are judged to be easiest when no distractor information is present in the text. They tend to become more difficult as the number of distractors increases, as the distractors share more features with the correct response, and as the distractors appear in closer proximity to the correct response. For instance, tasks tend to be judged more difficult when one or more distractors meet some but not all of the conditions specified in the question and appear in a paragraph or section of text other than the one containing the correct answer. Tasks are judged to be most difficult when two or more distractors share most of the features with the correct response and appear in the same paragraph or node of information as the correct response.

Characterizing prose literacy tasks

There are 55 tasks ordered along the 500-point prose literacy scale representing 19 IALS prose literacy tasks and 36 new prose literacy tasks designed and developed for the ALL survey. These tasks range in difficulty value from 169 to 439. One of the easiest tasks (receiving a difficulty value of 188 and falling in Level 1) directs the reader to look at a medicine label to determine the "maximum number of days you should take this medicine." In terms of our process variables, type of match was scored as easy because the reader was required to locate a single piece of information that was literally stated in the medicine label. The label contained only one reference to number of days and this information was located under the label dosage. Type of information was scored as easy because it asked for a number of days and plausibility of distractor was judged to be easy because there is no other reference to days in the medicine label.

MEDCO ASPIRIN 500

INDICATIONS: Headaches, muscle pains, rheumatic pains, toothaches, earaches. RELIEVES COMMON COLD SYMPTOMS.

DOSAGE: ORAL. 1 or 2 tablets every 6 hours, preferably accompanied by food, for not longer than 7 days. Store in a cool, dry place.

CAUTION: Do not use for gastritis or peptic ulcer. Do not use if taking anticoagulant drugs. Do not use for serious liver illness or bronchial asthma. If taken in large doses and for an extended period, may cause harm to kidneys. Before using this medication for chicken pox or influenza in children, consult with a doctor about Reyes Syndrome, a rare but serious illness. During lactation and pregnancy, consult with a doctor before using this product, especially in the last trimester of pregnancy. If symptoms persist, or in case of an accidental overdose, consult a doctor. Keep out of reach of children.

INGREDIENTS: Each tablet contains
500 mg acetylsalicicylic acid.
Excipient c.b.p. 1 tablet.
Reg. No. 88246

Made in Canada by STERLING PRODUCTS, INC.
1600 Industrial Blvd., Montreal, Quebec H9J 3P1

Reprinted by permission

A second prose literacy task directs the reader to look at an article about impatiens. This task falls in the middle of Level 2 and has a difficulty value of 254. It asks the reader to identify "what the smooth leaf surfaces and the stems suggest about the plant." Again, the task directed the reader to locate information contained in the text so it was scored easy for type of information. The last sentence in the second paragraph under the heading *Appearance* states: "The smooth leaf surfaces and the stems indicate a great need of water." Type of information was scored as being moderate because it directs the reader to identify a condition. Plausibility of distractor was scored as being moderate also because the same paragraph contained a sentence which serves to distract a number of readers. This sentence states, "... stems are branched and very juicy, which means, because of the tropical origin, that the plant is sensitive to cold."

PROPER FRAME FIT

RIDER MUST BE ABLE TO STRADDLE BICYCLE WITH AT LEAST 2 cm CLEARANCE ABOVE THE HORIZONTAL BAR WHEN STANDING.

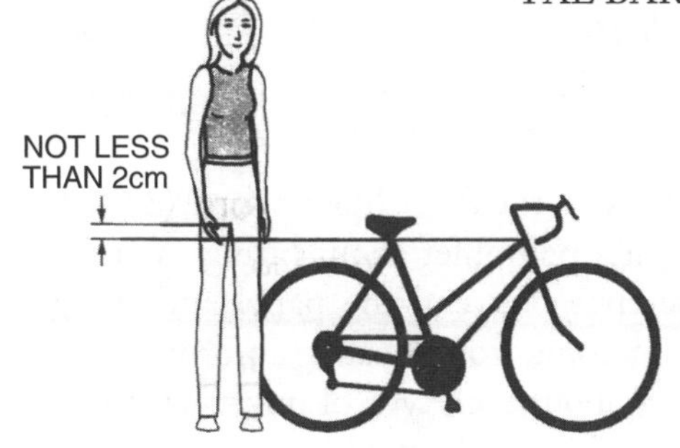

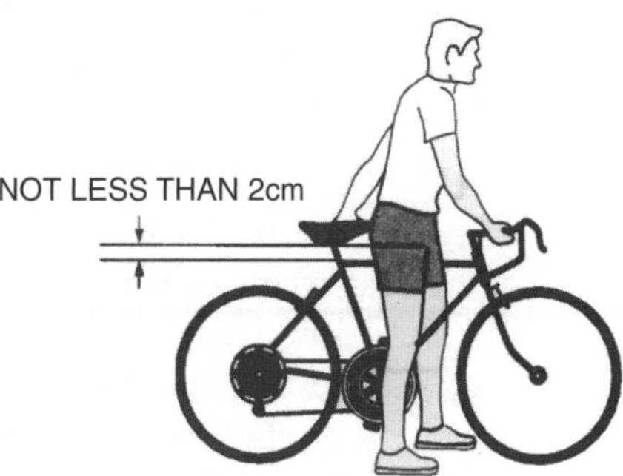

NOTE: Measurement for a female should be determined using a men's model as a basis.

PROPER SIZE OF BICYCLE

FRAME SIZE	LEG LENGTH OF RIDER
430mm	660mm-760mm
460mm	690mm-790mm
480mm	710mm-790mm
530mm	760mm-840mm
560mm	790mm-860mm
580mm	810mm-890mm
635mm	860mm-940mm

OWNER'S RESPONSIBILITY

1. **Bicycle Selection and Purchase:** Make sure this bicycle fits the intended rider. Bicycles come in a variety of sizes. Personal adjustment of seat and handlebars is necessary to assure maximum safety and comfort. Bicycles come with a wide variety of equipment and accessories... make sure the rider can operate them.
2. **Assembly:** Carefully follow all assembly instructions. Make sure that all nuts, bolts and screws are securely tightened.
3. **Fitting the Bicycle:** To ride safely and comfortably, the bicycle must fit the rider. Check the seat position, adjusting it up or down so that with the sole of rider's foot on the pedal in its lowest position the rider's knee is slightly bent. **Note:** Specific charts illustrated at left detail the proper method of deter-mining the correct frame size.

The manufacturer is not responsible for failure, injury, or damage caused by improper completion of assembly or improper maintenance after shipment.

Tasks which fall at higher levels along the scale present the reader with more varied demands in terms of the type of match that is required and in terms of the number and nature of distractors that are present in the text. One such task (with a difficulty value of 281 or the beginning of Level 3) refers the reader to a page from a bicycle's owner's manual to determine how to ensure the seat is in the proper position. Type of information was scored as moderate because the reader needed to identify and state two conditions that needed to be met in writing. In addition, they were not told how many features they needed to provide from among those stated. Type of information was also scored as moderate also because it involved identifying a condition and plausibility of distractor received a score indicating it was relatively easy.

A somewhat more difficult task (318), one near the top of Level 3, involves an article about cotton diapers and directs the reader to "list three reasons why the author prefers to use disposable rather than cotton diapers." This task is made more difficult because of several of our process variables. First, type of match was scored as difficult because the reader had to provide multiple responses, each of which required a text-based inference. Nowhere in the text does the author say, "I prefer cotton diapers because…". These inferences are made somewhat more difficult because the type of information being requested is a "reason" rather than something more concrete. This variable also was coded as difficult because of its abstractness. Finally, plausibility of distractor was scored as moderate because the text contains information that may serve to distract the reader.

An additional task falling in Level 4 on the Prose literacy scale (338) directs the reader to use the information from a pamphlet about hiring interviews to "write in your own words one difference between the panel and the group interview." Here the difficulty does not come from locating information in the text. Rather than merely locating a fact about each type of interview, the reader needs to integrate what they have read to infer a characteristic on which the two types of interviews differ. Experience from other surveys of this kind reveal that tasks in which readers are asked to contrast information are more difficult, on average, than tasks in which they are asked to find similarities. Thus, type of match was scored as complex and difficult. Type of information was scored as being difficult as well because it directs the reader to provide a difference. Differences tend to be more abstract in that they ask for the identification of distinctive or contrastive features related in this case to an interview process. Plausibility of distractor was judged as being easy because no distracting information was present in the text. Thus this variable was not seen as contributing to the overall difficulty of this task.

The Hiring Interview

Preinterview

Try to learn more about the business. What products does it manufacture or services does it provide? What methods or procedures does it use? This information can be found in trade directories, chamber of commerce or industrial directories, or at your local employment office.

Find out more about the position. Would you replace someone or is the position newly created? In which departments or shops would you work? Collective agreements describing various standardized positions and duties are available at most local employment offices. You can also contact the appropriate trade union.

The Interview

Ask questions about the position and the business. Answer clearly and accurately all questions put to you. Bring along a note pad as well as your work and training documents.

The Most Common Types of Interview

One-on-one: Self explanatory.

Panel: A number of people ask you questions and then compare notes on your application.

Group: After hearing a presentation with other applicants on the position and duties, you take part in a group discussion.

Postinterview

Note the key points discussed. Compare questions that caused you difficulty with those that allowed you to highlight your strong points. Such a review will help you prepare for future interviews. If you wish, you can talk about it with the placement officer or career counsellor at your local employment office.

The most difficult task on the prose literacy scale (377) falls in the lower range of Level 5 and required readers to look at an announcement from a personnel department and to "list two ways in which CIEM (an employee support initiative within a company) helps people who lose their jobs because of departmental reorganization." Type of match was scored difficult because the question contained multiple phrases that the reader needed to keep in mind when reading the text. In addition, readers had to provide multiple responses and make low text-based inferences. Type of information received a moderate score because readers were looking for a purpose or function and plausibility of distractor was scored as relatively difficult. This task is made somewhat more difficult because the announcement is organized around information that is different from what is being requested in the question. Thus while the correct information is listed under a single heading, this information is embedded under a list of headings describing CIEM's activities for employees looking for other work. Thus, this list of headings in the text serves as an excellent set of distractors for the reader who does not search for or locate the phrase in the question containing the conditional information – those who lose their jobs because of a departmental reorganization.

Characterizing document literacy tasks

There are 54 tasks ordered along the 500-point document literacy scale. These 54 tasks comprise 19 items from IALS and 35 new tasks developed for ALL. Together, these tasks range in difficulty value from 157 to 444. A Level 1 document literacy task with a difficulty value of 188 directs the reader to identify from a chart the percentage of teachers from Greece who are women. The chart shown here displays the percentage of teachers from various countries who are women. In terms of our process variables, type of match was judged to be easy because the reader was required to locate a single piece of information that was literally stated in the chart; type of information was judged to be relatively easy because it was an amount; and plausibility of distractor is also judged to be relatively easy because there are distractors for the requested information.

FEW DUTCH WOMEN AT THE BLACKBOARD

There is a low percentage of women teachers in the Netherlands compared to other countries. In most of the other countries, the majority of teachers are women. However, if we include the figures for inspectors and school principals, the proportion shrinks considerably and women are in a minority everywhere.

Percentage of women teachers (kindergarten, elementary, and secondary).

A second document task involving this same chart directs the reader to identify the country other than the Netherlands in which women teachers are in the minority. This item falls in the middle of Level 2 and received a difficulty value of 234. This task was made a bit more difficult than the first because rather than searching for a country and locating a percentage, the reader had to know that minority means less than 50 per cent. Then they had to cycle through to identify the countries in which the percentage of women teachers were less then 50 per cent. In addition, they had to remember the condition "other than the Netherlands"; otherwise they might have chosen it over the correct response. As a result, type of match was scored as moderately difficult; type of information as easy because the requested information is a country or place; and plausibility of distractor as relatively easy because there are distractors associated with the requested information.

A somewhat more difficult task, with a difficulty value of 295 and falling in the middle of Level 3 directs the reader to look at charts involving fireworks from the Netherlands and to write a brief description of the relationship between sales and injuries based on the information shown. Here the reader needs to look at and compare the information contained in the two charts and integrate this information making an inference regarding the relationship between the two sets of information. As a result, it was judged as being relatively difficult in terms of type of match. Type of information also was judged to be relatively difficult because the requested information is asking for a pattern or similarity in the data. Plausibility of distractor was scored moderately difficult primarily because both given and requested information is present in the task. For example, one of the things that may have contributed to the difficulty of this task is the fact that the sales graph goes from 1986 to 1992 while the injuries graph goes from 1983 to 1990. The reader needed to compare the information from the two charts for the comparable period time.

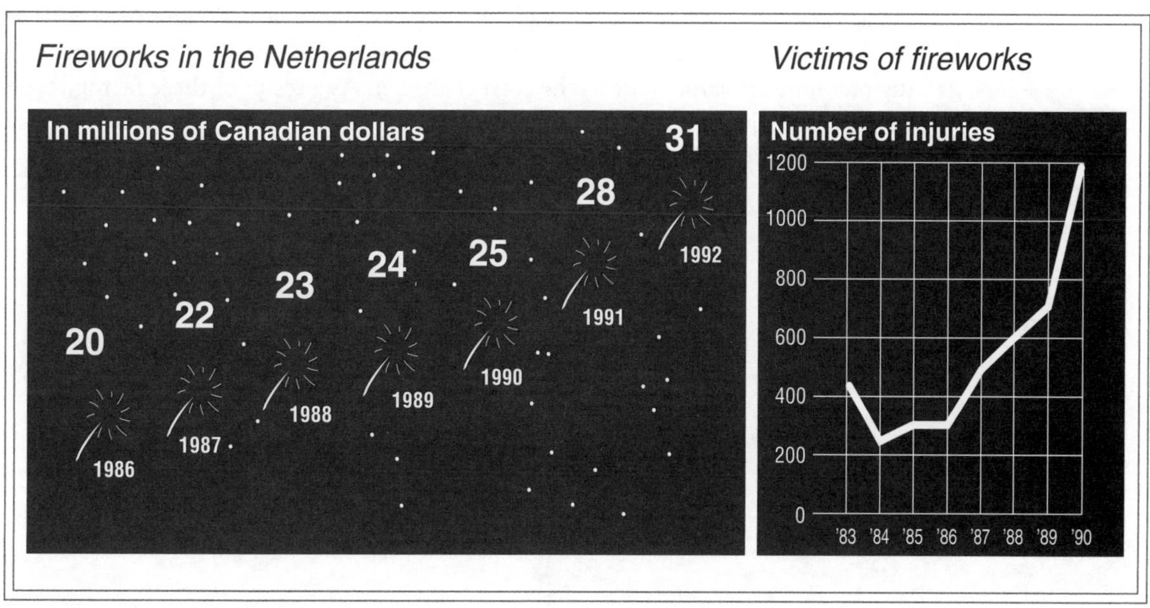

Another set of tasks covering a range of difficulty on the document scale involved a rather complicated document taken from a page in a consumer magazine rating clock radios. The easiest of the three tasks, receiving a difficulty value of 287 and falling in Level 3, asks the reader "which two features are not on any basic clock radio." In looking at the document, the reader has to cycle through the document, find the listing for basic clock radios, and then determine that a dash represents the absence of a feature. They then have to locate the two features indicated by the set of dashes. As a result, type of match was judged as being relatively difficult because it is a cycle requiring multiple responses with a condition or low text based inference. Type of information was scored as relatively easy because its features are an attribute of the clock radio and plausibility of distractor is relatively easy because there are some characteristics that are not associated with other clock radios.

A somewhat more difficult task associated with this document and falling in the lower end of Level 4 received a difficulty value of 327. It asks the reader "which full-featured clock radio is rated highest on performance." Here the reader must make a three-feature match (full-featured, performance, and highest) where one of the features requires them to process conditional information. It is possible, for example, that some readers were able to find the full-featured radios and the column listed under performance but selected the first radio listed assuming it was the one rated highest. In this case, they did not understand the conditional information which is a legend stating what the symbols mean. Others may have gone to the column labelled overall score and found the highest numerical number and chosen the radio associated with it. For this reason, plausibility of distractor was scored as moderately difficult. Type of information was judged as being easy because the requested information is a thing.

The most difficult task associated with this document, with a difficulty level of 408, and falling in Level 5 asks the reader to identify the average advertised price for the basic clock radio receiving the highest overall score. This task was made more difficult because the reader had to match four rather than three features; they also had to process conditional information and there was a highly plausible distractor in the same node as the correct answer. As a result of these factors, type of match was judged to be relatively difficult, type of information relatively easy and plausibility of distractor as having the highest level of difficulty.

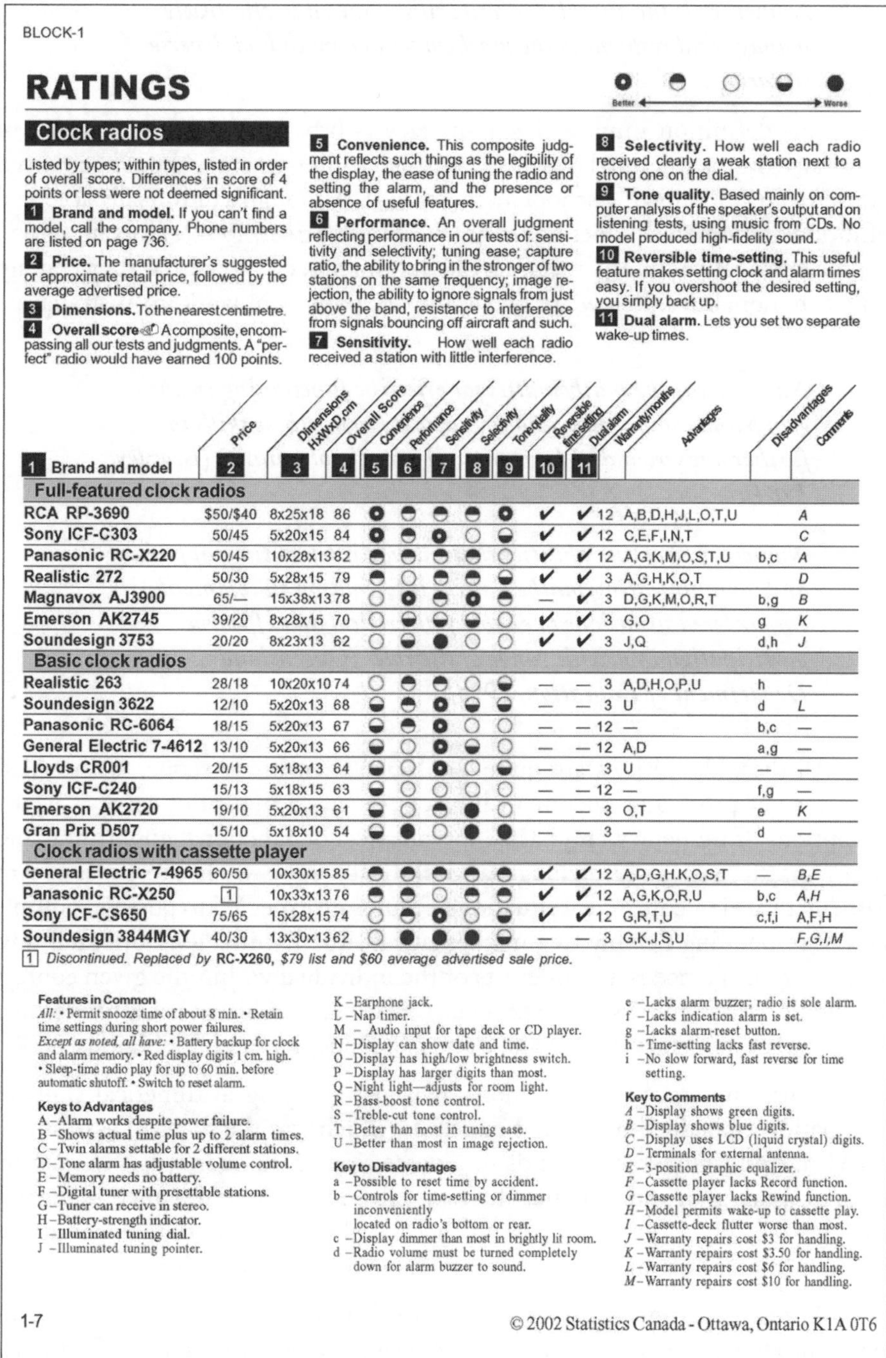

BLOCK-1

RATINGS

◉ ◓ ○ ◒ ●
Better ⟵⟶ Worse

Clock radios

Listed by types; within types, listed in order of overall score. Differences in score of 4 points or less were not deemed significant.

1 Brand and model. If you can't find a model, call the company. Phone numbers are listed on page 736.

2 Price. The manufacturer's suggested or approximate retail price, followed by the average advertised price.

3 Dimensions. To the nearest centimetre.

4 Overall score A composite, encompassing all our tests and judgments. A "perfect" radio would have earned 100 points.

5 Convenience. This composite judgment reflects such things as the legibility of the display, the ease of tuning the radio and setting the alarm, and the presence or absence of useful features.

6 Performance. An overall judgment reflecting performance in our tests of: sensitivity and selectivity; tuning ease; capture ratio, the ability to bring in the stronger of two stations on the same frequency; image rejection, the ability to ignore signals from just above the band, resistance to interference from signals bouncing off aircraft and such.

7 Sensitivity. How well each radio received a station with little interference.

8 Selectivity. How well each radio received clearly a weak station next to a strong one on the dial.

9 Tone quality. Based mainly on computer analysis of the speaker's output and on listening tests, using music from CDs. No model produced high-fidelity sound.

10 Reversible time-setting. This useful feature makes setting clock and alarm times easy. If you overshoot the desired setting, you simply back up.

11 Dual alarm. Lets you set two separate wake-up times.

1 Brand and model	2 Price	3 Dimensions HxWxD,cm	4 Overall Score	5 Convenience	6 Performance	7 Sensitivity	8 Selectivity	9 Tone quality	10 Reversible time setting	11 Dual alarm	Warranty, months	Advantages	Disadvantages	Comments
Full-featured clock radios														
RCA RP-3690	$50/$40	8x25x18	86	◉	◓	◓	◓	◉	✔	✔	12	A,B,D,H,J,L,O,T,U		*A*
Sony ICF-C303	50/45	5x20x15	84	◉	◓	◉	○	◒	✔	✔	12	C,E,F,I,N,T		*C*
Panasonic RC-X220	50/45	10x28x13	82	◓	◓	◓	◓	○	✔	✔	12	A,G,K,M,O,S,T,U	b,c	*A*
Realistic 272	50/30	5x28x15	79	◓	○	◓	◓	◒	✔	✔	3	A,G,H,K,O,T		*D*
Magnavox AJ3900	65/—	15x38x13	78	○	◉	◓	◉	◓	—	✔	3	D,G,K,M,O,R,T	b,g	*B*
Emerson AK2745	39/20	8x28x15	70	○	◒	◒	◒	○	✔	✔	3	G,O	g	*K*
Soundesign 3753	20/20	8x23x13	62	○	◒	●	○	○	✔	✔	3	J,Q	d,h	*J*
Basic clock radios														
Realistic 263	28/18	10x20x10	74	○	◓	◓	○	◒	—	—	3	A,D,H,O,P,U	h	—
Soundesign 3622	12/10	5x20x13	68	◒	◓	◉	◒	◒	—	—	3	U	d	*L*
Panasonic RC-6064	18/15	5x20x13	67	◒	◓	◉	○	○	—	—	12	—	b,c	—
General Electric 7-4612	13/10	5x20x13	66	◒	○	◉	◒	○	—	—	12	A,D	a,g	—
Lloyds CR001	20/15	5x18x13	64	◒	○	◉	○	◒	—	—	3	U	—	—
Sony ICF-C240	15/13	5x18x15	63	◒	○	○	○	○	—	—	12	—	f,g	—
Emerson AK2720	19/10	5x20x13	61	◒	○	◓	●	○	—	—	3	O,T	e	*K*
Gran Prix D507	15/10	5x18x10	54	◒	●	○	●	●	—	—	3	—	d	—
Clock radios with cassette player														
General Electric 7-4965	60/50	10x30x15	85	◓	◓	◓	◓	◓	✔	✔	12	A,D,G,H.K,O,S,T	—	*B,E*
Panasonic RC-X250	[1]	10x33x13	76	◓	◓	○	◓	◓	✔	✔	12	A,G,K,O,R,U	b,c	*A,H*
Sony ICF-CS650	75/65	15x28x15	74	○	◓	◉	○	◒	✔	✔	12	G,R,T,U	c,f,i	A,F,H
Soundesign 3844MGY	40/30	13x30x13	62	○	●	●	●	◒	—	—	3	G,K,J,S,U		*F,G,I,M*

[1] *Discontinued. Replaced by* **RC-X260**, *$79 list and $60 average advertised sale price.*

Features in Common

All: • Permit snooze time of about 8 min. • Retain time settings during short power failures.

Except as noted, all have: • Battery backup for clock and alarm memory. • Red display digits 1 cm. high. • Sleep-time radio play for up to 60 min. before automatic shutoff. • Switch to reset alarm.

Keys to Advantages

A – Alarm works despite power failure.
B – Shows actual time plus up to 2 alarm times.
C – Twin alarms settable for 2 different stations.
D – Tone alarm has adjustable volume control.
E – Memory needs no battery.
F – Digital tuner with presettable stations.
G – Tuner can receive in stereo.
H – Battery-strength indicator.
I – Illuminated tuning dial.
J – Illuminated tuning pointer.
K – Earphone jack.
L – Nap timer.
M – Audio input for tape deck or CD player.
N – Display can show date and time.
O – Display has high/low brightness switch.
P – Display has larger digits than most.
Q – Night light—adjusts for room light.
R – Bass-boost tone control.
S – Treble-cut tone control.
T – Better than most in tuning ease.
U – Better than most in image rejection.

Key to Disadvantages

a – Possible to reset time by accident.
b – Controls for time-setting or dimmer inconveniently located on radio's bottom or rear.
c – Display dimmer than most in brightly lit room.
d – Radio volume must be turned completely down for alarm buzzer to sound.
e – Lacks alarm buzzer; radio is sole alarm.
f – Lacks indication alarm is set.
g – Lacks alarm-reset button.
h – Time-setting lacks fast reverse.
i – No slow forward, fast reverse for time setting.

Key to Comments

A – Display shows green digits.
B – Display shows blue digits.
C – Display uses LCD (liquid crystal) digits.
D – Terminals for external antenna.
E – 3-position graphic equalizer.
F – Cassette player lacks Record function.
G – Cassette player lacks Rewind function.
H – Model permits wake-up to cassette play.
I – Cassette-deck flutter worse than most.
J – Warranty repairs cost $3 for handling.
K – Warranty repairs cost $3.50 for handling.
L – Warranty repairs cost $6 for handling.
M – Warranty repairs cost $10 for handling.

1-7

Measuring numeracy in ALL

Defining numeracy in ALL

The conception of numeracy developed for ALL is built upon recent research and work done in several countries on functional demands of different life contexts, on the nature of adults' mathematical and statistical knowledge and skills, and on how such skills are applied or used in different circumstances. In light of the general intention of the ALL survey to provide information about a diverse set of life skills, this framework defines numeracy as follows:

Numeracy is the knowledge and skills required to effectively manage and respond to the mathematical demands of diverse situations.

This definition implies that numeracy is broader than the construct of quantitative literacy defined by IALS[2]. Further, adult numeracy should be viewed as different from "knowing school mathematics". Although a universally accepted definition of "numeracy" does not exist (Baker and Street, 1994), an examination of some perspectives on the meaning of adult numeracy shows that they contain many commonalities. Below are two examples, both from work in Australia:

Numeracy is the mathematics for effective functioning in one's group and community, and the capacity to use these skills to further one's own development and of one's community (Beazley, 1984).

Numeracy involves abilities that include interpreting, applying and communicating mathematical information in commonly encountered situations to enable full, critical and effective participation in a wide range of life roles (Queensland Department of Education, 1994)

All these definitions are quite similar, in their broad scope, to the ALL definitions of prose and document literacy presented in a prior section. Many conceptions of numeracy emphasize the practical or functional application and use of mathematical knowledge and skills to cope with the presence of mathematical elements in real situations. Adults are expected to possess multiple ways of responding flexibly to a mathematical situation in a goal-oriented way, dependent on the needs and interests of the individual within the given context (i.e., home, community, workplace, etc...), as well as on his or her attitudes and beliefs toward numeracy (Gal, 2000; Coben, O'Donoghue and FitzSimons, 2000).

Thus, numeracy involves more than just applying arithmetical skills to information embedded in printed materials, which was the focus of assessment in IALS. Adult numeracy extends to a possession of number sense, estimation skills, measurement and statistical literacy. Given the extent to which numeracy pervades the modern world, it is not necessarily just commonly encountered situations that require numerate behaviour, but also *new* situations.

Another important element in defining numeracy is the role of communication processes. Numeracy not only incorporates the individual's abilities to use and apply mathematical skills efficiently and critically, but also requires the person to be able to interpret textual or symbolic messages as well as to communicate mathematical information and reasoning processes (Marr and Tout, 1997; Gal, 1997).

Definitions of numeracy explicitly state that numeracy not only refers to operating with numbers, as the word can suggest, especially to those familiar with conceptions of children's numeracy, but covers a wide range of mathematical skills and understandings. Further, in recent years there has been much discussion and debate about the relationship between mathematics and numeracy and about the concept of "critical" numeracy (Frankenstein, 1989; Steen, 2001). Johnston, for example, has argued that:

> *To be numerate is more than being able to manipulate numbers, or even being able to 'succeed' in school or university mathematics. Numeracy is a critical awareness which builds bridges between mathematics and the real-world, with all its diversity (Johnston, 1994).*

Many authors argue that a discussion of functional skills should also address supporting or enabling attitudes and beliefs. In the area of adults' mathematical skills, "at homeness" with numbers or "confidence" with mathematical skills is expected, as these affect how skills and knowledge are actually put into practice (Cockroft, 1982; Tobias, 1993).

The brief definition of numeracy developed for ALL and presented earlier above is complemented by a broader definition of *numerate behaviour* which was developed by the ALL Numeracy Team to serve as the basis for the development of numeracy items for ALL:

> *Numerate behaviour is observed when people manage a situation or solve a problem in a real context; it involves responding to information about mathematical ideas that may be represented in a range of ways; it requires the activation of a range of enabling knowledge, factors and processes.*

This conception of numerate behaviour implies that in order to assess people's numeracy, it is necessary to generate tasks and items which vary in terms of contexts, the responses called for, the nature of the mathematical information involved, and the representations of this information. These task characteristics are elaborated below. This conception is much broader than the definition of quantitative literacy used in IALS. Its key elements relate in a broad way to situation management and to a need for a range of responses (not only to responses that involve numbers). It refers to a wide range of skills and knowledge (not only to application of arithmetical knowledge and computational operations) and to the use of a wide range of situations that present respondents with mathematical information of different types (not only those involving *numbers* embedded in *printed* materials).

The item development process aimed to ensure that a certain proportion of the item pool would place a minimum reading burden on the respondents, i.e., that some of the stimuli would be text-free or almost so, allowing even respondents with limited mastery of the language of the test to comprehend the situation described. Other parts of the item pool included items requiring varying amounts of essential texts as dictated by the situation which the item aimed to represent.

As implied by the literature and ideas reviewed earlier, the nature of a person's responses to the mathematical and other demands of a situation will depend critically on the activation of various enabling knowledge bases (understanding of the context; knowledge and skills in the areas of mathematics, statistics and literacy), on reasoning processes and on their attitudes and beliefs with respect to numeracy. In addition, numerate behaviour requires the integration of mathematical knowledge and skills with broader literacy and problem solving skills along with the prior experiences and practices that each person brings to every situation. It is clear that numerate behaviour will involve an attempt to engage with a task and not delegate it to others or deal with it by intentionally ignoring its mathematical content.

Identifying task characteristics

Four key characteristics of numerate behaviour were used to develop and represent the numeracy tasks built for ALL – type of purpose/context, type of response, type of mathematical or statistical information, and type of representation of mathematical or statistical information. Each of these is described next.

Type of purpose/context. People try to manage or respond to a numeracy situation because they want to satisfy a purpose or reach a goal. Four types of purposes and goals are described below. To be sure, these are not mutually exclusive and may involve the same underlying mathematical themes.

Everyday life

The numeracy tasks that occur in everyday situations are often those that one faces in personal and family life, or revolve around hobbies, personal development, or interests. Representative tasks are handling money and budgets, comparison shopping, planning nutrition, personal time management, making decisions involving travel, planning trips, mathematics involved in hobbies like quilting or wood-working, playing games of chance, understanding sports scoring and statistics, reading maps and using measurements in home situations such as cooking or home repairs.

Work-related

At work, one is confronted with quantitative situations that often are more specialized than those seen in everyday life. In this context, people have to develop skills in managing situations that might be narrower in their application of mathematical themes. Representative tasks are completing purchase orders, totalling receipts, calculating change, managing schedules, using spreadsheets, organizing and packing different shaped goods, completing and interpreting control charts or quality graphs, making and recording measurements, reading blueprints, tracking expenditures, predicting costs and applying formulas.

Societal or community

Adults need to know about processes happening in the world around them, such as trends in crime, wages and employment, pollution, medical or environmental risks. They may have to take part in social or community events, or in political action. This requires that adults can read and interpret quantitative information presented in the media, including statistical messages and graphs. They may have to manage situations like organizing a fund-raiser, planning fiscal aspects of a community program, or interpreting the results of a study about risks of the latest health fad.

Further learning

Numeracy skills enable a person to participate in further study, whether for academic purposes or as part of vocational training. In either case, it is important to be able to know some of the more formal aspects of mathematics that involve symbols, rules, and formulas and to understand some of the conventions used to apply mathematical rules and principles.

Type of responses. In different types of real-life situations, people may have to respond in one or more of the following ways. (The first virtually always occurs;

others will depend on the interaction between situational demands and the goals, skills, dispositions, and prior learning of the person):

Identify or locate some mathematical information present in the task or situation confronting them that is relevant to their purpose or goal.

Act upon or react to the information in the situation. Bishop (1988), for example, proposed that there are six modes of mathematical actions that are common in all cultures: counting, locating, measuring, designing, playing and explaining. Other types of actions or reactions may occur, such as doing some calculations ("in the head" or with a calculator), ordering or sorting, estimating, measuring, or modeling (such as by using a formula).

Interpret the information embedded within the situation (and the results of any prior action) and comprehend what it means or implies. This can include making a judgment about how mathematical information or known facts actually apply to the situation or context. Contextual judgment may have to be used in deciding whether an answer makes sense or not in the given context, for example, that a result of "2.35 cars" is not a valid solution to how many cars are needed to transport a group. It can also incorporate a critical aspect, where a person questions the purpose of the task, the validity of the data or information presented, and the meaning and implications of the results, both for them as an individual and possibly for the wider community.

Communicate about the mathematical information given, or the results of one's actions or interpretations to someone else. This can be done orally or in writing (ranging from a simple number or word to a detailed explanation or analysis) and/or through drawing (a diagram, map, graph).

Type of mathematical or statistical information. Mathematical information can be classified in a number of ways and on different levels of abstraction. One approach is to refer to fundamental "big ideas" in the mathematical world. Steen (1990), for example, identified six broad categories pertaining to: quantity, dimension, pattern, shape, uncertainty, and change. Rutherford and Ahlgren (1990) described networks of related ideas: numbers, shapes, uncertainty, summarizing data, sampling and reasoning. Dossey (1997) categorized the mathematical behaviours of quantitative literacy as: data representation and interpretation, number and operation sense, measurement, variables and relations, geometric shapes and spatial visualization, and chance. The ALL Numeracy Team drew from these and other closely tied categorizations (e.g., National Council of Teachers of Mathematics, 2000) to arrive at a set of five fundamental ideas that characterize the mathematical demands facing adults in diverse situations at the beginning of the 21st century.

Quantity and number

Quantity is described by Fey (1990) as an outgrowth of people's need to quantify the world around us, using attributes such as: length, area and volume of rivers or land masses; temperature, humidity and pressure of our atmosphere; populations and growth rates of species; motions of tides; revenues or profits of companies, etc...

Number is fundamental to quantification and different types of number constrain quantification in various ways: whole numbers can serve as counters or estimators; fractions, decimals and per cents as expressions of greater precision, or as indications of parts-of-whole which are useful when comparing proportions.

Positive and negative numbers serve as directional indicators. In addition to quantification, numbers are used to put things in order and as identifiers (e.g., telephone numbers or zip codes). Facility with quantity, number, and operation on number requires a good "sense" for magnitude and the meaning of very large or very small numbers, and sometimes a sense for the relative magnitude of different proportions.

Money and time management, the ubiquitous mathematics that is part of every adult's life, depends on a good sense of number and quantity. Contextual judgment comes into play when deciding how precise one should be when conducting certain computations or affects the choice of which tool (calculator, mental math, a computer) to use. A low level numeracy task might be figuring out the cost of one can of soup, given the cost of four for $2.00; a task with a higher cognitive demand could involve "harder numbers" such as when figuring out the cost per kilo while buying 0.783 kg of cheese for 12,95 Euros.

Dimension and shape

Dimension includes "big ideas" related to one, two and three dimensions of "things". Understanding of dimensions is called for when encountering or generating spatial or numerical descriptions of objects, making projections, or working with lengths, perimeters, planes, surfaces, location, etc... Facility with each dimension requires a sense of "benchmark" measures, direct measurement, and estimations of measurements.

Shape is a category describing real or imaginary images and entities that can be visualized (e.g., houses and buildings, designs in art and craft, safety signs, packaging, knots, crystals, shadows and plants). Direction and location are fundamental qualities called upon when reading or sketching maps and diagrams. A basic numeracy task in this fundamental aspect could be shape identification whereas a more complex task might involve describing the change in the size or volume of an object when one dimension is changed, such as when choosing between different boxes for packaging certain objects.

Pattern, functions and relationships

It is frequently written that mathematics is the study of patterns and relationships. Pattern is seen as a wide-ranging concept that covers patterns encountered all around us, such as those in musical forms, nature, traffic patterns, etc... It is argued by Senechal (1990) that our ability to recognize, interpret and create patterns is the key to dealing with the world around us. The human capacity for identifying relationships and for thinking analytically underlies mathematical thinking. Algebra – beyond symbolic manipulation – provides a tool for representing relationships between amounts through the use of tables, graphs, symbols and words. The ability to generalize and to characterize functions, relationships between variables, is a crucial gateway to understanding even the most basic economic, political or social analyses. A relatively simple pattern-recognition task might require someone to describe the pattern in a sequence of given numbers or shapes, and in a functional context to understand the relationship between lists or variables (e.g., weight and volume of objects); having to develop a formula for an electronic spreadsheet would put a higher level of demand on the individual.

Data and chance

Data and chance encompass two related but separate topics. *Data* covers "big ideas" such as variability, sampling, error, or prediction, and related statistical topics such as data collection, data analysis, and common measures of center or spread, or the idea of a statistical inference. Modern society demands that adults are able to interpret (and at times even produce) frequency tables, basic charts and graphs, information about averages and medians, as well as identify questionable statistical claims (Gal, 2002).

Chance covers "big ideas" related to probability and relevant statistical concepts and tools. Few things in the world are 100 per cent certain; thus the ability to attach a number that represents the likelihood of an event (including risks or side-effects) is a valuable tool whether it has to do with the weather, the stock-market, or the decision to use a certain drug. In this category, a simple numeracy skill might be the interpretation of a simple pie chart or comprehension of a statement about an average; a more complex task would be to infer the likelihood of occurrence of an event based upon given information.

Change

This term describes the mathematics of how the world changes around us. Individual organisms grow, populations vary, prices fluctuate, objects traveling speed up and slow down. Change and rates of change help provide a narration of the world as time marches on. Additive, multiplicative or exponential patterns of change can characterize steady trends; periodic changes suggest cycles and irregular change patterns connect with chaos theory. Describing weight loss over time is a relatively simple task, while calculating compounded interest is a relatively complex task.

Type of representation of mathematical information. Mathematical information in an activity or a situation may be available or represented in many forms. It may appear as concrete objects to be counted (e.g., sheep, people, buildings, cars, etc…) or as pictures of such things. It may be conveyed through symbolic notation (e.g., numerals, letters, or operation signs). Sometimes, mathematical information will be conveyed by formulas, which are a model of relationships between entities or variables.

Further, mathematical information may be encoded in visual displays such as *diagrams* or *charts*; *graphs*, and *tables* may be used to display aggregate statistical or quantitative information. Similarly, *maps* of real entities (e.g., of a city or a project plan) may contain numerical data but also information that can be quantified or mathematized.

Finally, a person may have to extract mathematical information from various types of texts, either in prose or in documents with specific formats (such as in tax forms). Two different kinds of text may be encountered in functional numeracy tasks. The first involves mathematical information represented in textual form, i.e., with words or phrases that carry mathematical meaning. Examples are the use of number words (e.g., "five" instead of "5"), basic mathematical terms (e.g., fraction, multiplication, per cent, average, proportion), or more complex phrases (e.g., "crime rate cut by half") that require interpretation. The second involves cases where mathematical information is expressed in regular notations or symbols (e.g., numbers, plus or minus signs, symbols for units of measure, etc…), but is surrounded by text that despite its non-mathematical nature also has to be interpreted in order to provide additional information and context. An example is a bank deposit slip with some text and instructions in which numbers describing monetary amounts are embedded.

Characterizing numeracy tasks

A total of 40 numeracy tasks were selected and used in the ALL survey. These tasks range along the numeracy scale from 174 to 380 and their placement was determined by how well adults in participating countries responded to each task. Described below are sample tasks that reflect some of the conceptual facets of the numeracy construct and scale design principles described earlier, such as computations, spatial and proportional reasoning, measurement, and statistical knowledge.

As expected, the easiest task on the numeracy scale required adults to look at a photograph containing two cartons of coca cola bottles (174). They were directed to find the total number of bottles in the two full cases being shown. Part of what made this task easy is the fact that content was drawn from everyday life and objects of this kind would be relatively familiar to most people. Second, what adults were asked to do was apparent and explicit – this tasked used a photograph depicting concrete objects and required the processing of no text. A third contributing factor is that respondents could approach the task in a variety of ways that differ in sophistication, such as by multiplying rows and columns, but also by simple counting. This task requires that adults make a conjecture since the full set of bottles in the lower case is not visible, but as can be seen from the low difficulty level of the task, this feature did not present a problem for the vast majority of adults in all participating countries.

A second task that was also quite easy directed adults to look at a short text depicting the results of an election involving three candidates and determine the total number of votes cast. This task received a difficulty value of 192, falling in Level 1 on the numeracy scale. Again, respondents were asked to deal with a realistic type of situation where simple numerical information is displayed in a simple column format showing the name of each candidate and the number of votes that the candidate received. No other numerical information was present that can be a distractor. Finding the total number of votes cast in the election requires a single addition operation that is made explicit in the question by the use of the keyword "total", and the computation involves relatively small whole numbers.

A more complex numeracy task falling in the middle of Level 2 and receiving a difficulty value of 248 directs adults to look at a gas (petrol) gauge. This gauge has three lines or ticks on it with one showing an "F", one showing an "E" and the third in the middle between the two. A line on the gauge, representing the gauge's needle, shows a level that is roughly halfway between the middle tick and the tick indicating "F", suggesting that the tank is about three-quarters full. The directive states that the tank holds 48 gallons and asks the respondent to determine "how many gallons remain in the tank." This task is drawn from an everyday context and requires an adult to interpret a display that conveys quantitative information but carries virtually no text or numbers. No mathematical information is present other than what is given in the question.

What makes this task more difficult than the previous ones described above is the fact that adults must first estimate the level of gas remaining in the tank, by converting the placement of the needle to a fraction. Then they need to determine how many gallons this represents from the 48 gallon capacity stated in the question or directive. Thus, this task requires adults to apply multiple operations or procedures to arrive at a correct response, without specifying what the operations may be. Nonetheless, this task, like many everyday numeracy tasks, does not require an exact computation but allows an approximation that should fall within reasonable boundaries.

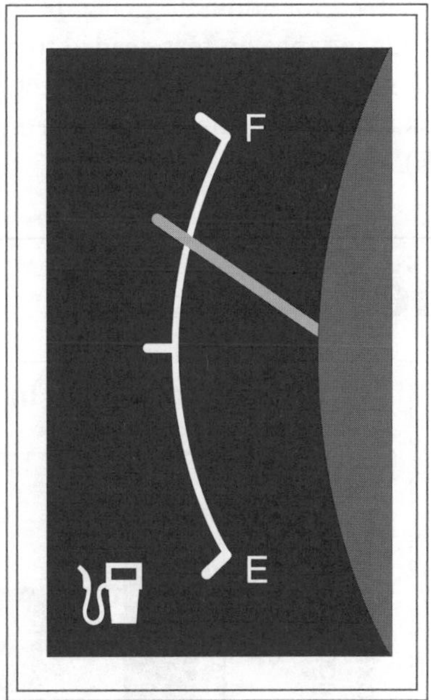

A somewhat more difficult numeracy task, falling at the top of Level 2 and receiving a difficulty value of 275, requires adults to look at a diagram of a container on which there are four markings or lines; respondents are asked to draw a line on the container indicating where one-third would be. The top line is marked "1" while the middle line is marked with "1/2". There are two other lines with no markings - one line midway between "1" and "1/2" and another midway between the line marked "1/2" and the bottom of the container. To respond correctly, adults need to mark a line on the container that is between the line marked "1/2" and the line below it indicating where one-quarter would be (although this line does not say "1/4" – this has to be inferred). Here the context may be less familiar to the respondent but again the visual image used is simple and realistic with virtually no text; the response expected does not involve writing a symbol or text, just drawing a line in a certain region on the drawing of the container. To answer this task correctly, adults need to have some working knowledge of fractions and a sense for proportions: they have to be familiar with the symbols for "1/2" and "1/3", know how to order fractions in terms of their relative size and be able to relate them to the existing markings on the container.

Some numeracy tasks were developed around a short newspaper article titled "Is breast milk safe?" which relates to environmental hazards and food safety. The article contained two brief text paragraphs describing a toxin, Dioxin, found in fish in the Baltic Sea plus a graph with bars indicating the levels of Dioxin found at three points in time, namely 1975, 1985, and 1995, in the breast milk of North European women. One question asked adults to describe how the amount of Dioxin changed from 1975 to 1995, i.e., provide a straightforward interpretation of data presented in a graph. Adults were not required to actually calculate the amount of change over each of the periods, just describe in their own words the change in the levels of Dioxin (e.g., decreased, increased, stayed the same).

This task received a difficulty value of 280, the lower end of Level 3. The graph clearly indicates that the amount of Dioxin decreased over each of the three time periods, yet some adults have difficulty coping with such a task, which is based on a stimulus with a structure that commonly appears in newspapers, i.e., brief text plus a graph. The increased difficulty level of this item may be attributable in part to the need for adults to generate their own description, to the moderate amount of dependence on text needed to comprehend the context to which the graph refers, or to the need to understand the direction of the decimal values on the vertical axis (which is common in reporting on concentrations of contaminating chemicals).

Is breast milk safe?

Since the 1970s, scientists have been worried about the amount of Dioxin, a toxin in fish caught in the Baltic sea. Dioxin tends to accumulate in breast milk and can harm newborn babies.

The diagram shows the amount of Dioxin in the breast milk of North European women, as found in studies done from 1975 to 1995.

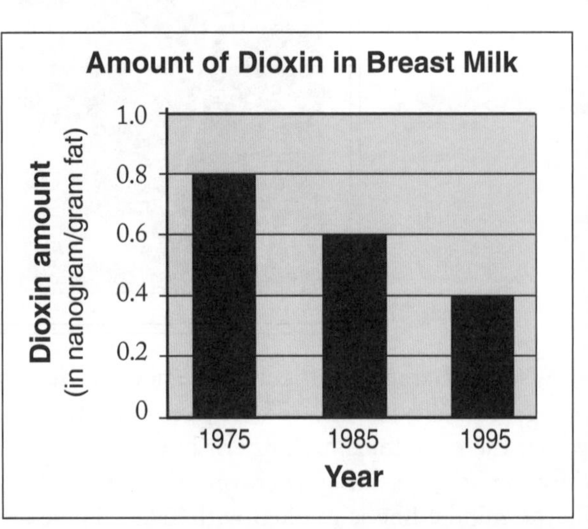

A second and more difficult task using this same stimulus directed adults to compare the per cent of change in Dioxin level from 1975 to 1985 to the per cent of change in Dioxin level from 1985 to 1995, determine which per cent of change is larger, and explain their answer. This task was considerably more difficult for adults in participating countries and received a difficulty value of 377 on the numeracy scale. Here the necessary information is embedded within the graph and requires a level of transformation and interpretation. To arrive at a correct response, adults have to look at the rate of change expressed in per cents, not just the absolute size of the change. Further, they have to work with per cents of entities smaller than one (i.e., the decimal values on the vertical axis) and realize that the base for the computation of per cent change shifts for each pair. It seems that the need to cope with such task features, use formal mathematical procedures, or deal with the abstract notion of rate of change, adds considerable difficulty to such tasks.

The most difficult numeracy task in this assessment, receiving a difficulty value of 380 (Level 5), presented adults with an advertisement claiming that it is possible for an investor to double an amount invested in seven years, based on a 10 per cent fixed interest rate each year. Adults were asked if it is possible to double $1000 invested at this rate after seven years and had to support their answer with their calculations. A range of responses was accepted as correct as long as a reasonable justification was provided, with relevant computations. Respondents were free to perform the calculation any way they wanted, but could also use a "financial hint" which accompanied the advertisement and presented a formula for estimating the worth of an investment after any number of years. Those who used the formula had to enter information stated in the text into variables in the formula (principal, interest rate and time period) and then perform the needed computations and compare the result to the expected amount if $1000 is doubled.

All respondents could use a hand-held calculator provided as part of the assessment. This task proved difficult because it involved per cents and the computation, whether with or without the formula, required the integration of several steps and several types of operations. Performing the computations without the formula required understanding of compound interest procedures. This task allowed adults to use a range of reasoning strategies, including informal or invented procedures. Yet, like the previous task involving the comparison of rates of change, it required the use of formal mathematical information and deeper understanding of non-routine computational procedures, all of which may not be familiar or accessible to many adults.

Measuring problem solving in ALL

Defining problem solving in ALL

Research on problem solving has a long tradition within both academic psychology and applied human resources research. A very general definition of problem solving that reflects how it is generally understood in the psychological literature (Hunt, 1994; Mayer, 1992; Mayer and Wittrock, 1996; Smith, 1991) is presented here:

> ***Problem solving is goal-directed thinking and action in situations for which no routine solution procedure is available.*** **The problem solver has a more or less well-defined goal, but does not immediately know how to reach it. The incongruence of goals and admissible operators constitutes a problem. The understanding of the problem situation and its step-by-step transformation, based on planning and reasoning, constitute the process of problem solving.**

One major challenge while developing a framework for problem solving that is to be used in a survey such as ALL is how best to adapt the psychological literature to the constraints imposed by a large-scale international comparative study. In order to do this, a decision was made to focus on an essential subset of problem solving – analytical problem solving. Our notion of analytical problem solving is not to be confused with the intuitive everyday use of the term or with the clinical-psychological concept in which problem solving is associated with the resolution of social and emotional conflicts. Nevertheless, social context is also relevant for our definition of analytical problem solving, for example when problems have to be approached interactively and resolved through co-operation. Motivational factors such as interest in the topic and task-orientation also influence the problem-solving process. However, the quality of problem solving is primarily determined by the comprehension of the problem situation, the thinking processes used to approach the problem, and the appropriateness of the solution.

The *problem* itself can be characterized by different aspects:

- The *context* can reflect different domains, which may be of a theoretical or a practical nature, related to academic situations or to the real world. Within these domains, problems can be more or less authentic.
- The *scope* of a problem can range from working on limited, concrete parts of a task to planning and executing complex actions or evaluating multiple sequences of actions.
- The problem can have a well-defined or an ill-defined goal, it can have transparent (explicitly named) or non-transparent constraints, and involve few independent elements or numerous interconnected ones. These features determine the *complexity* of the problem.

How familiar the context is to the target population, whether the problem involves concrete tasks or complex actions, how well the goal is defined, how transparent the constraints are, how many elements the problem solver has to take into account and how strongly they are interconnected – are all features that will determine the level of problem-solving competency required to solve a certain problem. The empirical difficulty, i.e., the probability of giving a correct solution, will depend on the relation between these problem features on the one hand, and the subjects' competency level on the other hand.

The *cognitive processes* that are activated in the course of problem solving are diverse and complex, and they are likely to be organized in a non-linear manner. Among these processes, the following five components may be identified:

1. Searching for information, and structuring and integrating it into a mental representation of the problem ("situational model").
2. Reasoning, based on the situational model.
3. Planning actions and other solution steps.
4. Executing and evaluating solution steps.
5. Continuous processing of external information and feedback.

Baxter and Glaser (1997) present a similar list of cognitive activities labelled "general components of competence in problem solving": problem representation, solution strategies, self-monitoring, and explanations. Analytical problem solving in everyday contexts, as measured by the ALL problem-solving instrument, focuses on the components 1 to 3 listed above (and to some extent 4).

One of the most important insights of recent research in cognitive psychology is that solving demanding problems requires at least some knowledge of the domain in question. The concept of a problem space through which a General Problem Solver moves by means of domain-independent search strategies (Newell and Simon, 1972) proved to be too simple to describe how problem situations are understood and the process of finding a solution. Efforts to identify a general, domain-independent competence for steering dynamic systems (operative intelligence) within the framework of complex problem-solving research were also unsuccessful; performance on such systems can only partially be transferred to other systems (Funke, 1991). However, research on grade 3 to grade 12 students showed that problem-solving skills clearly improve under well-tuned training conditions and that a substantial transfer across different problems can be achieved (Reeff et al. 1989, 1992, 1993; Regenwetter, 1992; Regenwetter and Müller, 1992; Stirner, 1993).

Problem solving is dependent on knowledge of concepts and facts (declarative knowledge) and knowledge of rules and strategies (procedural knowledge) in a given subject domain. Although it is evident from past research that declarative knowledge in the problem domain can substantially contribute to successful problem-solving strategies, procedural knowledge is crucial as well. The amount of relevant previous knowledge available could also account for the relation between intelligence and problem-solving performance, as shown in the work of Raaheim (1988) and Leutner (1999). People with no relevant previous knowledge at all are unable to explore the problem situation or plan a solution in a systematic manner and are forced to rely on trial and error instead. Those who are already very familiar with the task are able to deal with it as a matter of routine. General intellectual ability, as measured by reasoning tasks, plays no role in either of these cases. When problem solvers are moderately familiar with the task, analytical reasoning strategies can be successfully implemented.

The approach taken for the assessment of problem solving in ALL relies on the notion of (moderately) familiar tasks. Within a somewhat familiar context the problems to be solved are inexplicit enough so as not to be perceived as pure routine tasks. On the other hand, the domain-specific knowledge prerequisites are sufficiently limited as to make analytical reasoning techniques the main cognitive tool for solving the problems.

Identifying task characteristics

How can contextualized, real-life problems be defined and transformed into a set of assessment tasks? After reviewing the various approaches that have been taken in previous research to measure problem solving, a decision was made to use a project approach in ALL. The project approach has the potential to be a powerful means for assessing analytical problem solving skills in real world, everyday contexts for several reasons. Solving problems in project-like settings is important and relevant for adults in both their professional and their private life. In addition, the project approach has been successfully implemented in other large-scale assessments, and it can be realized as a paper-and-pencil-instrument, which is of crucial importance for contemporary large-scale surveys. Furthermore, the project approach uses different problem-solving stages as a dimension along which to generate the actual test items. Following Pólya (1945, 1980), the process of problem solving has been frequently described in terms of the following stages:

- Define the goal.
- Analyze the given situation and construct a mental representation.
- Devise a strategy and plan the steps to be taken.
- Execute the plan, including control and – if necessary – modification of the strategy.
- Evaluate the result.

The different action steps define the course of action for an "everyday" project. One or more tasks or items are generated to correspond to each of these action steps. Respondents are expected to work on individual tasks that have been identified as steps that need to be carried out as a part of their project (a sample project, for example, might involve "planning a reunion" or "renovating a clubhouse"). Embedding the individual tasks in a project is believed to yield a high degree of context authenticity. Although they are part of a comprehensive and coherent project, the individual tasks are designed so that they can be solved independently of one another and are expected to vary in complexity and overall difficulty for adults.

Since assessing problem solving skills in large-scale assessments is a relatively new endeavour, it might be helpful to provide a detailed account of the construction process. Table A1 provides an overview of the problem solving steps as they correspond to the action steps identified above. Different components and aspects of each of the problem solving steps are listed.

TABLE A1

Problem-solving steps and instantiations

Define the goals	• Set goals. • Recognize which goals are to be reached and specify the essential reasons for the decision. • Recognize which goals/wishes are contradictory and which are compatible. • Assign priorities to goals/wishes.
Analyze the situation	• Select, obtain and evaluate information. ⇒ What information is required, what is already available, what is still missing, and what is superfluous? ⇒ Where and how can you obtain the information? ⇒ How should you interpret the information? • Identify the people (e.g. with what knowledge and skills) who are to be involved in solving the problem. • Select the tools to be used. • Recognize conditions (e.g. time restrictions) that need to be taken into account.
Plan the solution	• Recognize which steps need to be taken. • Decide on the sequence of steps (e.g. items on the agenda). • Coordinate work and deadlines. • Make a comparative analysis of alternative plans (recognize which plan is suitable for reaching the goals). • Adapt the plan to changed conditions. • Opt for a plan.
Execute the plan	• Carry out the individual steps (e.g., write a letter, fill in a form, make calculations).
Evaluate the results	• Assess whether and to what extent the target has been reached. • Recognize mistakes. • Identify reasons for mistakes. • Assess consequences of mistakes.

The construction of a pool of assessment tasks that could be mapped back to these five action steps involved several phases of activities. First was the identification of appropriate projects that would be suitable for adults with varying educational backgrounds and relevant to the greatest number of people in the target group. Next, developers had to identify and sketch out the problem situation and the sequence of action steps that relate back to the model. Third, they had to develop a pool of items that were consistent with the action steps and that tapped into particular processes including the development of correct responses and appropriate distractors for multiple choice items and solution keys and scoring guides for open-ended tasks.

Characterizing problem solving tasks

ALL included a total of 4 projects involving 20 tasks in the assessment of problem solving. These resulted in 19 scorable items than ranged from 199 to 394 along the scale and, like the literacy and numeracy tasks, their placement was determined by the patterns of right and wrong responses among adults in participating countries. Rather than release one of the four projects that were used in ALL, we will characterize the hypothesized proficiency scale for analytical problem solving that was tested using pilot data and present an example from the pilot data that was not used in the main assessment[3]. Similar models have been described within the frameworks of other large-scale assessments of problem-solving competencies such as the project test for Hamburg/Germany (Ebach, Klieme and Hensgen, 2000) and the PISA 2003 assessment of cross-curricular problem solving (OECD, in press).

In ALL, four levels of problem-solving proficiency are postulated:

Level 1

At a very elementary level, concrete, limited tasks can be mastered by applying content-related, practical reasoning. At this level, people will use specific content-related schemata to solve problems.

Level 2

The second level requires at least rudimentary systematical reasoning. Problems at this level are characterized by well-defined, one-dimensional goals; they ask for the evaluation of certain alternatives with regard to transparent, explicitly stated constraints. At this level, people use concrete logical operations.

Level 3

At the third level of problem-solving proficiency, people will be able to use formal operations (e.g., ordering) to integrate multi-dimensional or ill-defined goals, and to cope with non-transparent or multiple dependent constraints.

Level 4

At the final and highest level of competency, people are capable of grasping a system of problem states and possible solutions as a whole. Thus, the consistency of certain criteria, the dependency among multiple sequences of actions and other "meta-features" of a problem situation may be considered systematically. Also, at this stage people are able to explain how and why they arrived at a certain solution. This level of problem-solving competency requires a kind of critical thinking and a certain amount of meta-cognition.

The following example illustrates a concrete realization of a project. For this purpose a project that is not included in the final ALL instrument is introduced and one typical problem-solving task is shown. The project is about "Planning a trip and a family reunion".

In the introductory part of the project, the respondent is given the following summary describing the scenario and overall problem:

> *"Imagine that you live in City A. Your relatives are scattered throughout the country and you would like to organize a family reunion. The reunion will last 1 day. You decide to meet in City B, which is centrally located and accessible to all. Since you and your relatives love hiking, you decide to plan a long hike in a state park close to City B. You have agreed to be responsible for most of the organization."*

The respondent is then given a list of steps he or she needs to work through, in this example the following list:

- *Set the date for the reunion*
- *Consider your relatives' suggestions for the hike*
- *Plan what needs to be done before booking your flight*
- *Answer your relative's questions about traveling by plane*
- *Book your flight*
- *Make sure your ticket is correct*
- *Plan the trip from City B to the airport*

The first task of this project "Set the date for the reunion" is a good example of a typical problem-solving task and is shown here as it would appear in a test booklet.

Example task: Set the date for the reunion

The family reunion should take place sometime in July.

You asked all your relatives to tell you which dates would be suitable. After talking to them, you made a list of your relatives' appointments during the month of July. Your own appointment calendar is lying in front of you. You realize that some of your relatives will have to arrive a day early in order to attend the family reunion and will also only be able to return home on the day after the meeting.

Please look at the list of your relatives' appointments and your own appointment calendar.

List of your relatives' appointments in July 1999

Henry	Karen	Peter	Janet	Anne	Frank
Vacation in City E beginning on July 26; Appointment on July 11	Every day of the week is okay except Thursdays and on July 16	Business appointments on July 2, July 13, and between July 27 and 29	Doesn't have any appointments	Unable to attend reunion on July 5, July 20, or July 24	Has to be away sometime during the 1st full week in July on business, but will find out the exact dates shortly before

Henry, Karen, and Peter could arrive on the same day as the reunion whereas Janet, Anne, and Frank can only arrive on the afternoon before and return home on the day after the reunion.

Example task (cont.)

Your appointment calendar for July 1999

July 1999

Thurs.	1	Meeting with David
Fri.	2	
Sat.	3	
Sun.	4	
Mon.	5	
Tue.	6	
Wed.	7	
Thurs.	8	
Fri.	9	
Sat.	10	*Hike in City C*
Sun.	11	
Mon.	12	
Tue.	13	
Wed.	14	
Thurs.	15	
Fri.	16	
Sat	17	
Sun.	18	
Mon.	19	
Tue.	20	
Wed.	21	
Thurs	22	
Fri.	23	
Sat.	24	
Sun.	25	
Mon.	26	
Tue.	27	
Wed.	28	Vacation
Thurs	29	Vacation
Fri.	30	Vacation
Sat.	31	

Question 1. Which of the following dates are possible for the family reunion?

Please select all possible dates.

- a July 4
- b July 7
- c July 14
- d July 18
- e July 25
- f July 29

This project illustrates nicely how the action steps logic is actually "translated" into a concrete thematic action flow. The underlying plot – planning a trip and a family reunion – constitutes a very typical everyday-type of action that presumably a large majority of people in different countries will be able to relate to. The action steps themselves and their sequence can deviate from the normative complete action model, as is the case here. The normative model is used as a guideline that is adapted to each specific context. In this case, for example, the task "Consider your relatives' suggestions for the hike" corresponds approximately to the action step "Analyze the situation", the task "Plan what needs to be done before booking your flight" corresponds to the action step "Plan the solution", and "Book your flight" is a typical example for the action step "Execute the plan".

The example task gives a first indication of item structures and formats. The tasks typically start off with a short introduction to the situation, followed by varying types and amounts of information that need to be worked through. In the example task, in order to set the date for the family reunion, the respondent needs to process, compare and integrate the information provided in the list of the relatives' appointments, including the addendum to this list, and their own appointment calendar. Here the information is mostly textual and in the form of tables. The answer format is a multiple-choice format with more than one correct response alternatives, although the number of correct response alternative is not specified.

Conclusion

This paper offers a brief overview of the frameworks that have been used for both developing the tasks used to measure prose and document literacy, numeracy and problem solving in ALL as well as for understanding the meaning of what is being reported with respect to the comparative literacy proficiencies of adults. The frameworks identify a set of variables that have been shown to influence successful performance on a broad array of tasks. Collectively, they provide a means for moving away from interpreting survey results in terms of discrete tasks or a single number, and towards identifying levels of performance sufficiently generalized to have validity across assessments and groups. As concern ceases to center on discrete behaviours or isolated observations and focuses more on providing meaningful interpretations of performance, a higher level of measurement is reached (Messick, 1989).

Endnotes

1. The 80 per cent criterion was drawn from the education literature on mastery learning to reflect a level of performance at which someone is judged to be proficient or competent. Some have argued that this is too high a standard and a response probability of 60 or even 50 per cent should be used. Lowering the criteria to 50 per cent would mean that an adult would be expected to perform tasks at a given level of proficiency with 50 per cent accuracy – hardly a standard we should accept as indicating someone is proficient at something. Would you visit a dentist that fixed the correct tooth 50 per cent of the time? How many employers would hire someone knowing they had a 50/50 chance of performing tasks correctly?
2. Quantitative literacy was defined in IALS as the knowledge and skills needed to apply arithmetic operations either alone or sequentially, using numbers embedded in printed materials.
3. This is the first time problem solving was used in an international survey of adult skills. It is expected that there will be subsequent rounds of ALL and at least some countries will want to measure problem solving using these materials. Therefore, it is important that these four projects be kept confidential for any future use.

References

Almond, R. G., and Mislevy, R. J. (1998). Graphical models and computerized adaptive testing. (TOEFL Tech. Rep. No. 14). Princeton, NJ: Educational Testing Service.

Baker, D., and Street, B. (1994). Literacy and numeracy: Concepts and definitions. In T. Husen and E. A. Postlethwaite (Eds.), Encyclopedia of education. New York: Pergamon Press.

Beazley, K. (1984). Education in Western Australia: Report of the Committee of Inquiry into Education in Western Australia. Education Department of Western Australia.

Coben, D., O'Donoghue, J., and FitzSimons, G. E. (Eds.)(2000). Perspectives on adults learning mathematics: Theory and practice. London: Kluwer Academic Publishers.

Cockcroft, W.H. (1982). Report of the Committee of Inquiry into the Teaching of Mathematics in Schools. London: HMSO.

Cook-Gumperz, J., and Gumperz, J. (1981). From oral to written culture: The transition to literacy. In M. Whitman (Ed.), Writing: The nature, development and teaching of written communication: Vol. 1. Hillsdale, NJ: Erlbaum.

Crandall, J. (1981, December). Functional literacy of clerical workers: Strategies for minimizing literacy demands and maximizing available information. Paper presented at the annual meeting of the American Association for Applied Linguistics, New York.

Diehl, W. (1980). Functional literacy as a variable construct: An examination of the attitudes, behaviours, and strategies related to occupational literacy. Unpublished doctoral dissertation, Indiana University.

Dossey, J.A. (1997). "Defining and measuring quantitative literacy". In L.A. Steen (Ed.), Why numbers count: Quantitative literacy for tomorrow's America. New York: College Entrance Examination Board.

Fey, James T. (1990). "Quantity" In L.A. Steen (Ed.) On the shoulders of giants: New approaches to numeracy. Washington, DC: National Academy Press.

Frankenstein, M. (1989). Relearning mathematics: A different third 'R' – Radical maths. London: Free Association Books.

Gal, I. (1997). Numeracy: Imperatives of a forgotten goal. In L.A. Steen (Ed.), Why numbers count: quantitative literacy for tomorrow's America (pp. 36-44). New York: The College Board.

Gal, I. (2000). The numeracy challenge. In I. Gal (Ed.), Adult numeracy development: Theory, research, practice (pp. 1-25). Cresskill, NJ: Hampton Press.

Gal, I. (2002). Adult Statistical literacy: Meanings, components, responsibilities. International Statistical Review, 70(1), 1-25.

Jacob, E. (1982). Literacy on the job: Final report of the ethnographic component of the industrial literacy project. Washington, DC: Center for Applied Linguistics.

Johnston, B. (1994, Summer). Critical numeracy? In Fine print, Vol. 16, No. 4.

Heath, S.B. (1980). The functions and uses of literacy. Journal of Communication, 30, 123–133.

Kirsch, I.S., and Guthrie, J.T. (1984a). Adult reading practices for work and leisure. Adult Education Quarterly, 34(4), 213–232.

Kirsch, I.S., and Guthrie, J. T. (1984b). Prose comprehension and text search as a function of reading volume. Reading Research Quarterly, 19, 331–342.

Kirsch, I. (2001). The International Adult Literacy Survey (IALS): Understanding What Was Measured (ETS Research Report RR-01-25). Princeton, NJ: Educational Testing Service.

Marr, B., and Tout, D. (1997). A numeracy curriculum: Australian Association of Mathematics Teachers (AAMT) conference proceedings. Melbourne: AAMT.

Messick, S. (1989). Validity. In R. Linn (Ed.), Educational measurement (3rd ed.). New York: Macmillan.

Messick, S. (1994). The interplay of evidence and consequences in the validation of performance assessments. Education Researcher, 32(2), 13-23.

Mikulecky, L. (1982). Job literacy: The relationship between school preparation and workplace actuality. Reading Research Quarterly, 17(3), 400–419.

Miller, P. (1982). Reading demands in a high-technology industry. Journal of Reading, 26(2), 109–115.

Mislevy, R.J. (September, 2000). Leverage points for improving educational assessment. Paper submitted to National Center for Research on Evaluation, Standards, and Student Testing (CRESST) as part of award #R305B60002 from the US Department of Education, Office of Educational Research and Improvement.

Mosenthal, P.B., and Kirsch, I.S. (1998). A new measure for assessing document complexity: The PMOSE/IKIRSCH document readability formula. Journal of Adolescent and Adult Literacy, 41(8), 638–657.

Murray, T.S., Clermont, Y. and Binkley, M. (Eds.) The Adult Literacy and Life Skills Survey: Aspects of Design, Development and Validation. Canada: Statistics Canada, in press.

Murray, T.S., Kirsch, I.S., and Jenkins, L. (1998). Adult Literacy in OECD Countries: Technical report on the First International Adult Literacy Survey. Washington, DC: National Center for Education Statistics.

National Council of Teachers of Mathematics. (2000). Principles and standards for school mathematics. Reston, VA: Author.

Organization for Economic Co-operation and Development. (1992). Adult illiteracy and economic performance. Paris, France: Author.

Rutherford, F.J and Ahlgren, A. (1990). Science for all Americans. New York: Oxford University Press.

Rychen, D.S. and Salganik, L.H. (Eds.) Key Competencies for a Successful Life and a Well-Functioning Society. Cambridge, MA: Hogrefe and Huber Publishers, 2003.

Senechal, Majorie (1990) "Shape" In L.A. Steen (Ed.) On the shoulders of giants: New approaches to numeracy. Washington, DC: National Academy Press.

Scribner, S., and Cole, M. (1981). The psychology of literacy. Cambridge, MA: Harvard University Press.

Steen, L.A. (Ed). (1990). On the shoulders of giants: New approaches to numeracy. Washington, DC: National Research Council.

Steen, L.A. (2001). Mathematics and democracy: the case for quantitative literacy. USA: National Council on Education and the Disciplines.

Sticht, T.G. (Ed.). (1975). Reading for working: A functional literacy anthology. Alexandria, VA: Human Resources Research Organization.

Sticht, T.G. (1978). Literacy and vocational competency (Occasional Paper 39, National Center for Research in Vocational Education). Columbus, OH: Ohio State University.

Sticht, T.G. (1982, January). Evaluation of the reading potential concept for marginally literate adults. (Final Report FR–ET50–82–2). Alexandria, VA: Human Resources Research Organization.

Szwed, J. (1981). The ethnography of literacy. In M. Whitman (Ed.), Writing: The nature, development, and teaching of written communication: Vol. 1. Hillsdale, NJ: Erlbaum.

Tobias, S. (1993). Overcoming math anxiety. New York: Norton.

Venezky, R.L. (1983). The origins of the present-day chasm between adult literacy needs and school literacy instruction. Visible Language, 16, 113–136.

Contributor

Irwin Kirsch, *Educational Testing Service*

Annex B

Adult Literacy and Life Skills Survey Survey Methodology

B

Table of Contents

Adult Literacy and Life Skills Survey Survey Methodology

Survey methodology

Each participating country was required to design and implement the Adult Literacy and Life Skills (ALL) survey according to the standards provided in the document '*Standards and Guidelines for the Design and Implementation of the Adult Literacy and Life Skills Survey*'. These ALL standards established the minimum survey design and implementation requirements for the following project areas:

1. Survey planning
2. Target population
3. Method of data collection
4.. Sample frame
5. Sample design
6. Sample selection
7. Literacy assessment design
8. Background questionnaire
9. Task booklets
10. Instrument requirements to facilitate data processing
11. Data collection
12. Respondent contact strategy
13. Response rate strategy
14. Interviewer hiring, training, supervision
15. Data capture
16. Coding
17. Scoring
18. All data file-format and editing
19. Weighting
20. Estimation
21. Confidentiality
22. Survey documentation
23. Pilot Survey

Assessment design

The participating countries, with the exception of the state of Nuevo Leon in Mexico, implemented an ALL assessment design. Nuevo Leon assessed literacy using the International Adult Literacy Survey (IALS) assessment instruments.

In both ALL and IALS a Balanced Incomplete Block (BIB) assessment design was used to measure the skill domains. The BIB design comprised a set of assessment tasks organized into smaller sets of tasks, or blocks. Each block contained assessment items from one of the skill domains and covers a wide range of difficulty, i.e., from easy to difficult. The blocks of items were organized into task booklets according to a BIB design. Individual respondents were not

B

required to take the entire set of tasks. Instead, each respondent was randomly administered one of the task booklets.

ALL assessment

The ALL psychometric assessment consisted of the domains Prose, Document, Numeracy, and Problem Solving. The assessment included four 30-minute blocks of Literacy items (i.e., Prose AND Document Literacy), two 30-minute blocks of Numeracy items, and two 30-minute blocks of Problem-Solving items.

A four-domain ALL assessment was implemented in Bermuda, Canada, Italy, Norway, and the French and German language regions of Switzerland. The United States and the Switzerland Italian language region carried out a three-domain ALL assessment that excluded the Problem Solving domain. In addition to the mentioned assessment domains, these participating countries assessed the use of information and communication technology via survey questions incorporated in the ALL Background Questionnaire.

The blocks of assessment items were organized into 28 task booklets in the case of the four-domain assessment and into 18 task booklets for the three domain assessment. The assessment blocks were distributed to the task booklets according to a BIB design whereby each task booklet contained two blocks of items. The task booklets were randomly distributed amongst the selected sample. In addition, the data collection activity was closely monitored in order to obtain approximately the same number of complete cases for each task booklet, except for two task booklets in the three-domain assessment containing only Numeracy items that required a larger number of complete cases.

IALS assessment

The state of Nuevo Leon, Mexico carried out an IALS assessment. The IALS assessment consisted of three literacy domains: Prose, Document, and Quantitative. In addition, the ALL Background Questionnaire was used in Nuevo Leon. The use of information and communication technology was assessed via survey questions incorporated in the ALL Background Questionnaire.

IALS employed seven task booklets with three blocks of items per booklet. The task booklets were randomly distributed amongst the selected sample. In addition, the data collection activity was monitored in order to obtain approximately the same number of complete cases for each task booklet.

Target population and sample frame

Each participating country designed a sample to be representative of its *civilian non-institutionalized persons 16 to 65 years old (inclusive).*

Countries were also at liberty to include adults over the age of 65 in the sample provided that a minimum suggested sample size requirement was satisfied for the 16 to 65 year age group. Canada opted to include in its target population adults over the age of 65. All remaining countries restricted the target population to the 16 to 65 age group.

Exclusions from the target population for practical operational reasons were acceptable provided a country's survey population did not differ from the target population by more than five percent, i.e. provided the total number of exclusions from the target population due to undercoverage was not more than five percent of the target population. All countries indicate that this five-percent requirement was satisfied.

Each country chose or developed a sample frame to cover the target population. The following table shows the sample frame and the target population exclusions for each country:

TABLE B1

Sample frame and target population exclusions

Country	Sample frame	Exclusions
Bermuda	Land Valuation List • an up-to-date listing of all housing units in Bermuda.	Persons residing in institutions, visitors to Bermuda (i.e., persons staying less than 6 months).
Canada	Census of Population and Housing database, reference date of May 15, 2001 • households enumerated by the Census long-form (20% sample)	Long-term institutional residents, members of the armed forces, individuals living on Indian Reserves, residents of sparsely populated regions.
Italy	Polling list – a list of individuals aged 18 and over that are resident in Italy and have civil rights	None
Norway	Norwegian Register of Education (2002 version)	Permanent residents in institutions, individuals for whom education level is unknown
Nuevo Leon, Mexico	Census of Population and Housing database, reference year 2000	Persons residing in institutions, members of the Mexican Navy
Switzerland	Register of private telephone numbers (September 2002)	Persons living in institutions, people living in very isolated areas, persons with no private telephone number
United States	Area Frame – 1,883 Primary Sampling Units covering all counties in the 50 states in the United States plus Washington, DC	Full-time military personnel, residents in institutionalized group quarters

Sample design

Each participating country was required to use a probability sample representative of the national population aged 16 to 65. Of course, the available sampling frames and resources varied from one country to another. Therefore, the particular probability sample design to be used was left to the discretion of each country. Each country's proposed sample design was reviewed by Statistics Canada to ensure that the sample design standards and guidelines were satisfied.

Each country's sample design is summarized below. The sample size and response rate for each country can be found in the section following this one.

Bermuda

A two-stage stratified probability design was employed. In stage one Bermuda's Land Valuation List of dwellings was stratified by parish, i.e., geographic region. Within each parish, a random sample of dwellings was selected with probability proportional to the number of parish dwellings. At stage two, one eligible respondent was selected using a Kish-type person selection grid.

Canada

A stratified multi-stage probability sample design was used to select the sample from the Census Frame. The sample was designed to yield separate samples for the two Canadian official languages, English and French. In addition, Canada increased the sample size in order to produce estimates for a number of population subgroups. Provincial ministries and other organizations sponsored supplementary samples to increase the base or to target specific subpopulations such as youth (ages 16 to 24 in Québec and 16 to 29 in British Columbia), adults aged 25 to 64 in Québec, linguistic minorities (English in Québec and French elsewhere), recent and established immigrants, urban aboriginals, and residents of the northern territories.

In each of Canada's ten provinces the Census Frame was further stratified into an urban stratum and a rural stratum. The urban stratum was restricted to urban centers of a particular size, as determined from the previous census. The remainder of the survey frame was delineated into primary sampling units (PSUs) by Statistics Canada's Generalised Area Delineation System (GArDS). The PSUs were created to contain a sufficient population in terms of the number of dwellings within a limited area of reasonable compactness. In addition, the Census Frame was ordered within each geographic region by highest level of education prior to sample selection, thus ensuring a representation across the range of educational backgrounds

Within the urban stratum, two stages of sampling were used. In the first stage, households were selected systematically with probability proportional to size. During the second stage, a simple random sample algorithm was used by the CAPI application to select an individual from the eligible household adults. Three stages were used to select the sample in the rural stratum. In the first stage, Primary Sampling Units were selected with probability proportional to population size. The second and third stages for the rural stratum repeated the same methodology employed in the two-stage selection for the urban stratum.

Italy

A stratified three-stage probability design was used to select a sample using municipal polling lists. Italy was stratified geographically into 22 regions. In general the sample was allocated proportionally to the 22 regions. However, the regions Piemonte, Veneto, Toscana, Campania, and Trento were oversampled to satisfy an objective to produce separate estimates in these five regions.

At the first stage, municipalities were the primary sampling units. Within each geographic region the municipalities were stratified, based on the municipality population size, into self-representing units and non-self-representing units. The self-representing units, i.e., the larger municipalities and metropolitan municipalities, were selected with certainty in the sample. In the non-self-representing stratum in each region, two municipalities were selected with a probability proportional to the target population size. In total, 256 municipalities were selected from the self-representing and non-self-representing strata.

The second stage of the sample design defined 'sex sub-lists' as the secondary sampling unit. The polling list for each selected municipality comprised a number of sub-lists that were stratified by gender, referred to as 'sex sub-lists'. The polling list included the household address of Italian residents aged 18 to 65. The same number of sex sub-lists was systematically selected for each gender. A total of

1,326 sex sub-lists (663 in the male stratum and 663 in the female stratum) were selected.

At the third stage of sample design, a sample of 18 to 65 year old individuals was systematically selected from the secondary sampling units. Subsequently, at the household contact phase, all 16 to 17 year olds living in the household of a selected 18 to 65 year old were included in the sample.

Norway

The sample was selected from the 2002 version of the Norwegian Register of Education using a two-stage probability sample design.

The design created 363 primary sampling units (PSUs) from the 435 municipalities in Norway. These PSUs were grouped into 109 geographical strata. Thirty-eight strata consisted of one PSU that was a municipality with a population of 25,000 or more. At the first stage of sample selection, each of these 38 PSUs was included with certainty in the sample. The remaining municipalities were allocated to 79 strata. The variables used for stratification of these municipalities were industrial structure, number of inhabitants, centrality, communication structures, commuting patterns, trade areas and (local) media coverage. One PSU was selected with probability proportional to size from each of these 79 strata.

The second stage of the sample design involved the selection of a sample of individuals from each sampled PSU. Each selected PSU was stratified by three education levels defined by the Education Register. The sample size for each selected PSU was determined by allocating the overall sample size to each selected PSU with probability proportional to the target population size. The PSU sample was then allocated with 30 percent from the low-education group, 40 percent from the medium-education group and 30 percent from the high-education group. Individuals for whom the education level (84,318 persons) was not on the Education Register were excluded from the sampling.

Nuevo Leon, Mexico

The sample design was a stratified probability design with two stages of sampling within each stratum.

The 51 municipalities in Nuevo Leon were grouped geographically into three strata: Stratum 1 – Census Metropolitan Area of Monterrey, consisting of 9 municipalities; Stratum 2 – the municipalities of Linares and Sabinas Hidalgo; Stratum 3 – the remaining 40 municipalities of Nuevo Leon. The initial sample was allocated to the three strata proportional to the number of dwellings in each stratum.

At the first stage of sample selection, in each stratum a simple random sample of households was selected. The second sampling stage consisted of selecting one person belonging to the target population from each selected household using a Kish-type person selection grid.

Switzerland

The sample design was a stratified probability design with two stages of sampling. Separate estimates were required for Switzerland's three language regions (i.e., German, French, Italian). Thus, the three language regions are the primary strata. Within the language regions, the population was further stratified into the metropolitan areas represented by the cantons of Geneva and Zurich and the rest of the language regions. At the first stage of sampling, in each stratum a systematic sample of households was drawn from a list of private telephone numbers. In the second stage, a single person belonging to the target population was selected from each household using a Kish-type person selection grid.

United States

A stratified multi-stage probability sample design was employed in the United States.

The first stage of sampling consisted of selecting a sample of 60 primary sampling units (PSUs) from a total Of 1,883 PSUs that were formed using a single county or a group of contiguous counties, depending on the population size and the area covered by a county or counties. The PSUs were stratified on the basis of the social and economic characteristics of the population, as reported in the 2000 Census. The following characteristics were used to stratify the PSUs: region of the country, whether or not the PSU is a Metropolitan Statistical Area (MSA), population size, percentage of African-American residents, percentage of Hispanic residents, and per capita income. The largest PSUs in terms of a population size cut-off were included in the sample with certainty. For the remaining PSUs, one PSU per stratum was selected with probability proportional to the population size.

At the second sampling stage, a total of 505 geographic segments were systematically selected with probability proportionate to population size from the sampled PSUs. Segments consist of area blocks (as defined by Census 2000) or combinations of two or more nearby blocks. They were formed to satisfy criteria based on population size and geographic proximity.

The third stage of sampling involved the listing of the dwellings in the selected segments, and the subsequent selection of a random sample of dwellings. An equal number of dwellings was selected from each sampled segment.

At the fourth and final stage of sampling, one eligible person was randomly selected within households with fewer than four eligible adults. In households with four or more eligible persons, two adults were randomly selected.

Sample size

A sample size of 5,400 completed cases in each official language was recommended for each country that was implementing the full ALL psychometric assessment (i.e., comprising the domains Prose and Document Literacy, Numeracy, and Problem-Solving). A sample size of 3,420 complete cases in each official language was recommended if the Problem Solving domain was excluded from the ALL assessment.

A sample size of 3,000 complete cases was recommended for the state of Nuevo Leon, Mexico, which assessed literacy skills with the psychometric task booklets of the International Adult Literacy Survey (IALS).

Table B2 shows the final number of respondents (complete cases) for each participating country's assessment language(s).

TABLE B2

Sample size by assessment language

Country	Assessment language	Assessment domains [1]	Number of respondents [2]
Bermuda	English	P, D, N, PS	2,696
Canada	English	P, D, N, PS	15,694
	French	P, D, N, PS	4,365
Italy	Italian	P, D, N, PS	6,853
Norway	Bokmal	P, D, N, PS	5,411
Nuevo Leon, Mexico	Spanish	P, D, Q	4,786
Switzerland	French	P, D, N, PS	1,765
	German	P, D, N, PS	1,892
	Italian	P, D, N	1,463
United States	English	P, D, N	3,420

1. P – Prose, D – Document, N – Numeracy, PS – Problem Solving, Q - Quantitative.
2. A respondent's data is considered complete for the purposes of the scaling of a country's psychometric assessment data provided that at least the Background Questionnaire variables for age, gender and education have been completed.

Data collection

The ALL survey design combined educational testing techniques with those of household survey research to measure literacy and provide the information necessary to make these measures meaningful. The respondents were first asked a series of questions to obtain background and demographic information on educational attainment, literacy practices at home and at work, labour force information, information communications technology uses, adult education participation and literacy self-assessment.

Once the background questionnaire had been completed, the interviewer presented a booklet containing six simple tasks (Core task). Respondents who passed the Core tasks were given a much larger variety of tasks, drawn from a pool of items grouped into blocks, each booklet contained 2 blocks which represented about 45 items. No time limit was imposed on respondents, and they were urged to try each item in their booklet. Respondents were given a maximum leeway to demonstrate their skill levels, even if their measured skills were minimal.

Data collection for the ALL project took place between the fall of 2003 and early spring 2004, depending on the country. Table B3 presents the collection periods for each participating country.

TABLE B3

Survey collection period

Country	Collection date
Bermuda	March through August 2003
Canada	March through September 2003
Italy	May 2003 through January 2004
Norway	January through November 2003
Nuevo Leon, Mexico	October 2002 through March 2003
Switzerland	January through November 2003
United States	January through June 2003

To ensure high quality data, the ALL Survey Administration Guidelines specified that each country should work with a reputable data collection agency or firm, preferably one with its own professional, experienced interviewers. The manner in which these interviewers were paid should encourage maximum response. The interviews were conducted in home in a neutral, non-pressured manner. Interviewer training and supervision was to be provided, emphasizing the selection of one person per household (if applicable), the selection of one of the 28 main task booklets (if applicable), the scoring of the core task booklet, and the assignment of status codes. Finally the interviewers' work was to have been supervised by using frequent quality checks at the beginning of data collection, fewer quality checks throughout collection and having help available to interviewers during the data collection period.

The ALL took several precautions against non-response bias, as specified in the ALL Administration Guidelines. Interviewers were specifically instructed to return several times to non-respondent households in order to obtain as many responses as possible. In addition, all countries were asked to ensure address information provided to interviewers was as complete as possible, in order to reduce potential household identification problems.

Countries were asked to complete a debriefing questionnaire after the Main study in order to demonstrate that the guidelines had been followed, as well as to identify any collection problems they had encountered. Table B4 presents information about interviews derived from this questionnaire.

TABLE B4

Interviewer information

Country	Number of languages	Number of interviewers	Average assignment size	Interviewer experience
Bermuda	1	105	40	No specific information provided.
Canada	2	317	62	Professional interviewers with at least 2 years experience.
Italy	1	150	45	Professional interviewers, most of which had at least 2 years experience.
Norway	1	320	30	Only a third of the interviewers had at least 2 years experience, the others were trained specifically for this survey.
Nuevo Leon, Mexico	1	209	29	Approximately 70% of interviewers had 2 years of experience.
Switzerland	3	110	60	No specific information provided.
United States	1	106	64	Professional interviewers approximately a quarter of which had no previous survey experience.

As a condition of their participation in the ALL study, countries were required to capture and process their files using procedures that ensured logical consistency and acceptable levels of data capture error. Specifically, countries were advised to conduct complete verification of the captured scores (i.e. enter each record twice) in order to minimize error rates. Because the process of accurately capturing the task scores is essential to high data quality, 100 per cent keystroke verification was required.

Each country was also responsible for coding industry, occupation, and education using standard coding schemes such as the International Standard Industrial Classification (ISIC), the International Standard Classification for Occupation (ISCO) and the International Standard Classification for Education (ISCED). Coding schemes were provided by Statistics Canada for all open-ended items, and countries were given specifics instructions about coding of such items.

In order to facilitate comparability in data analysis, each ALL country was required to map its national dataset into a highly structured, standardized record layout. In addition to specifying the position, format and length of each field, the international record layout included a description of each variable and indicated the categories and codes to be provided for that variable. Upon receiving a country's file, Statistics Canada performed a series of range checks to ensure compliance to the prescribed format, flow and consistency edits were also run on the file. When anomalies were detected, countries were notified of the problem and were asked to submit cleaned files.

Scoring of tasks

Persons charged with scoring in each country received intense training in scoring responses to the open-ended items using the ALL scoring manual. As well they were provided a tool for capturing closed format questions. To aid in maintaining scoring accuracy and comparability between countries, the ALL survey introduced the use of an electronic bulletin board, where countries could post their scoring questions and receive scoring decisions from the domain experts. This information could be seen by all countries who could then adjust their scoring.

To further ensure quality, countries were monitored as to the quality of their scoring in two ways.

First, within a country, at least 20 per cent of the tasks had to be re-scored. Guidelines for intra-country rescoring involved rescoring a larger portion of booklets at the beginning of the scoring process to identify and rectify as many scoring problems as possible. As a second phase, they were to select a smaller portion of the next third of the scoring booklets; the last phase was viewed as a quality monitoring measure, which involved rescoring a smaller portion of booklets regularly to the end of the re-scoring activities. The two sets of scores needed to match with at least 95 percent accuracy before the next step of processing could begin. In fact, most of the intra-country scoring reliabilities were above 95 per cent. Where errors occurred, a country was required to go back to the booklets and rescore all the questions with problems and all the tasks that belonged to a problem scorer.

Second, an international re-score was performed. Each country had 10 per cent of its sample re-scored by scorers in another country. For example, a sample of task booklets from the United States was re-scored by the persons who had scored Canadian English booklets, and vice-versa. The main goal of the re-score was to verify that no country scored consistently differently from another. Inter-country score reliabilities were calculated by Statistics Canada and the results were evaluated by the Educational Testing Service based in Princeton. Again, strict accuracy was demanded: a 90 per cent correspondence was required before the scores were deemed acceptable. Any problems detected had to be re-scored. Table B5 shows the high level of inter-country score agreement that was achieved.

TABLE B5

Scoring – per cent reliability by domain

Country pairing (rescoring country – original country)	Psychometric domain			
	Prose and document (%)	Numeracy (%)	Problem solving (%)	Total (%)
Canada English – Canada French	95	95	92	95
Canada French – Canada English	95	97	94	95
Norway – Canada	91	93	91	92
Canada – United States	94	97	...	95
United States – Canada	95	97	...	95
United States – Bermuda	91	94	...	90
Bermuda – United States	93	95	...	93
Canada French – Switzerland	95	98	97	96
Switzerland – Canada French	94	96	94	95
Switzerland – Italy	96	98	96	96
Italy – Switzerland	93	97	93	94
Canada – Bermuda	...	...	83	83
Canada – Nuevo Leon, Mexico	91	95 [1]	...	92

... Not applicable.

1. Quantitative literacy.

TABLE B6

Scoring operations summary

Country	Scoring start[1]	Number of scorers	Average scoring time per booklet
Bermuda	middle	5	20 min.
Canada	middle	18 [2]	13 min.
Italy	beginning	9	15 min.
Norway	middle	17	8 min.
Nuevo Leon, Mexico	middle	12	N.A.
Switzerland	beginning	11	22 min.
United States	beginning	7	12 min.

1. Indicates that the scoring started at the beginning, middle or end of collection.
2. Includes 15 scorers, 2 people to capture problem solving closed format questions and 1 person to capture scoring sheets.

Survey response and weighting

Each participating country in ALL used a multi-stage probability sample design with stratification and unequal probabilities of respondent selection. Furthermore, there is a need to compensate for the non-response that occurred at varying levels. Therefore, the estimation of population parameters and the associated standard errors is dependent on the survey weights.

All participating countries used the same general procedure for calculating the survey weights. However, each country developed the survey weights according to its particular probability sample design.

In general, two types of weights were calculated by each country, population weights that are required for the production of population estimates, and jackknife replicate weights that are used to derive the corresponding standard errors.

Population weights

For each respondent record the population weight was created by first calculating the theoretical or sample design weight. Then a base sample weight was derived by mathematically adjusting the theoretical weight for non-response. The base weight is the fundamental weight that can be used to produce population estimates. However, in order to ensure that the sample weights were consistent with a country's known population totals (i.e., benchmark totals) for key characteristics, the base sample weights were ratio-adjusted to the benchmark totals.

Table B7 provides the benchmark variables for each country and the source of the benchmark population counts.

Jackknife weights

It was recommended that 10 to 30 jackknife replicate weights be developed for use in determining the standard errors of the survey estimates.

Switzerland produced 15 jackknife replicate weights. The remaining countries produced 30 jackknife replicate weights.

TABLE B7

Benchmark variables by country

Country	Source of benchmark counts	Benchmark variables
Bermuda	Census 2000	Age, Gender, Education level
Canada	Census Demography Counts, June-2003	Province, Census geographic area (i.e., CMA/CA), Age, Gender
Italy	ISTAT Multipurpose Survey 2002	Region, Age, Gender, Education level, Employment status
Norway	Norwegian Register of Education (2002 version)	Age, Gender, Education level
Nuevo Leon, Mexico	Census of Population and Housing (2000)	Age, Gender, Education level
Switzerland	Swiss Labor Force Survey (SAKE)	Language region, Age, Gender, Education level, Immigrant status
United States	2003 Current Population Survey, March Supplement	Census region, Metropolitan Statistical Area (MSA) status, Age, Gender, Race/ethnicity, Immigrant status

The following table summarizes the sample sizes and response rates for each participating country.

TABLE B8

Sample size and response rate summary

Country	Population aged 16 to 65	Initial sample size (16 to 65)	Out-of-scope cases [1]	Number of respondents[2] (16 to 65)	Response rate [3] (16 to 65)
					%
Bermuda	43,274	4,049	745	2,696	82
Canada	21,960,683	35,270	4,721	20,059	66
Italy	38,765,513	16,727	971	6,853	44
Norway	2,945,838	9,719	16	5,411	56
Nuevo Leon, Mexico	2,382,454	6,000	36	4,786	80
Switzerland	1,161,735	18,282	5,310	5,120	40
United States	184,260,910	7,045	1,846	3,420	66

1. Out-of-scope cases are those that were coded as residents not eligible, unable to locate the dwelling, dwelling under construction, vacant or seasonal dwelling, or duplicate cases.
2. A respondent's data is considered complete for the purposes of the scaling of a country's psychometric assessment data provided that at least the Background Questionnaire variables for age, gender and education have been completed.
3. The response rate is calculated as number of respondents divided by the initial sample size minus the out-of-scope cases.

Contributors

Owen Power, *Statistics Canada*

Carrie Munroe, *Statistics Canada*

Annex C

Principal Participants in the Project

International Direction and Co-ordination

Mr. T. Scott Murray
International Study Director for ALL, Statistics Canada, Ottawa

Mr. Yvan Clermont
International Study Co-ordinator for ALL, Statistics Canada, Ottawa

Mr. Patrick Werquin
International Study Co-ordinator for ALL, OECD, Paris

International Scoring and Scaling

Mr. Irwin Kirsch
Educational Testing Service, Princeton

Mr. Kentaro Yamamoto
Educational Testing Service, Princeton

Ms. Minh-Wei Wang
Educational Testing Service, Princeton

Ms. Julie Eastland
Educational Testing Service, Princeton

National Study Managers

Bermuda — Mr. Crispin Boney
Statistics Department, Government of Bermuda, Hamilton

Canada — Mr. Jean Pignal
Statistics Canada, Ottawa

Italy — Ms. Vittoria Gallina
Istituto Nazionale per la Valutazione del Sistema dell'Istruzione, Frascati

National Study Managers

Norway	Mr. Egil Gabrielsen *Centre for Reading Research, Stavanger*
Nuevo Leon, (Mexico)	Mr. Edmundo Guajardo Garza *Ministerio de Educación, Monterrey*
Switzerland	Mr. Philippe Hertig *Office fédéral de la statistique, Neuchâtel*
	Mr. Philipp Notter *University of Zürich, Zürich*
United States	Ms. Mariann Lemke *National Center for Education Statistics, Washington*
	Mr. Eugene Owen *National Center for Education Statistics, Washington*

Domain Experts and Contributors

Prose and Document

Mr. Irwin Kirsch
Educational Testing Service, Princeton

Mr. Kentaro Yamamoto
Educational Testing Service, Princeton

Ms. Julie Eastland
Educational Testing Service, Princeton

Mr. Stan Jones
Atlantic Health Promotion Research Center, Yarmouth

Numeracy

Mr. Iddo Gal
University of Haifa, Haifa

Ms. Mieke van Groenestijn
Utrecht University of Professional Education, Utrecht

Ms. Myrna Manly
El Camino College, Palos Verdes

Ms. Mary Jane Schmitt
TERC, Cambridge

Mr. Dave Tout
Language Australia, Melbourne

Mr. Yvan Clermont
Statistics Canada, Ottawa

Mr. Stan Jones
Atlantic Health Promotion Research Center, Yarmouth

Domain Experts and Contributors

Problem Solving

Mr. Eckhard Klieme
German Institute for International Educational Research, Frankfurt

Mr. Jean-Paul Reeff
LIFE Research and Consult, Bonn

Ms. Anouk Zabal
LIFE Research and Consult, Bonn

Background Questionnaire

Ms. Lynn Barr-Telford
Statistics Canada, Ottawa

Mr. Stan Jones
Atlantic Health Promotion Research Center, Yarmouth

Mr. Trevor Williams
WESTAT, Rockville

Survey Team, Analysts and Production Team

Ms. Danielle Baum
Statistics Canada, Ottawa

Mr. Richard Desjardins
Statistics Canada, Ottawa

Ms. Sylvie Grenier
Statistics Canada, Ottawa

Mr. John Leung
Statistics Canada, Ottawa

Ms. Carrie Munroe
Statistics Canada, Ottawa

Mr. Owen Power
Statistics Canada, Ottawa

Authors

Mr. Yvan Clermont
Statistics Canada, Ottawa

Mr. Richard Desjardins (editor-in-chief)
Statistics Canada, Ottawa

Ms. Urvashi Dhawan-Biswal
Human Resources and Skills Development Canada, Ottawa

Ms. Lauren Dong
Statistics Canada, Ottawa

Mr. Irwin Kirsch
Educational Testing Service, Princeton

Ms. Carrie Munroe
Statistics Canada, Ottawa

Mr. T. Scott Murray (editor)
Statistics Canada, Ottawa

Mr. Owen Power
Statistics Canada, Ottawa

Ms. Isabelle Recotillet
Centre d'études et de recherches sur les qualifications, Marseilles

Mr. Kjell Rubenson
University of British Columbia, Vancouver

Mr. George Sciadas
Statistics Canada, Ottawa

Mr. Albert Tuijnman (editor)
European Investment Bank, Luxembourg

Mr. Ben Veenhof
Statistics Canada, Ottawa

Mr. Matthias Von Davier
Educational Testing Service, Princeton

Mr. Patrick Werquin
Organisation for Economic Co-operation and Development, Paris

Mr. J. Douglas Willms
University of New Brunswick, Fredericton

This report is dedicated to the memory of Peter B. Mosenthal (1947 - 2004)

OECD PUBLICATIONS, 2, rue André-Pascal, 75775 PARIS CEDEX 16
PRINTED IN FRANCE
(91 2005 03 1 P) ISBN 92-64-01038-6 – No. 54059 2005